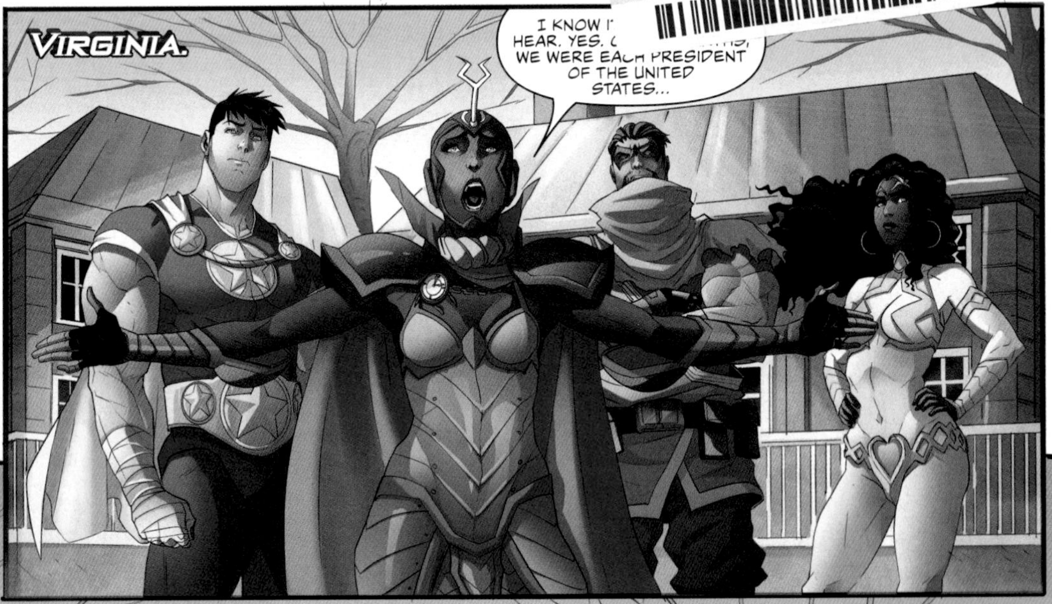
VIRGINIA.
I KNOW I
HEAR. YES.
WE WERE EACH PRESIDENT
OF THE UNITED
STATES...

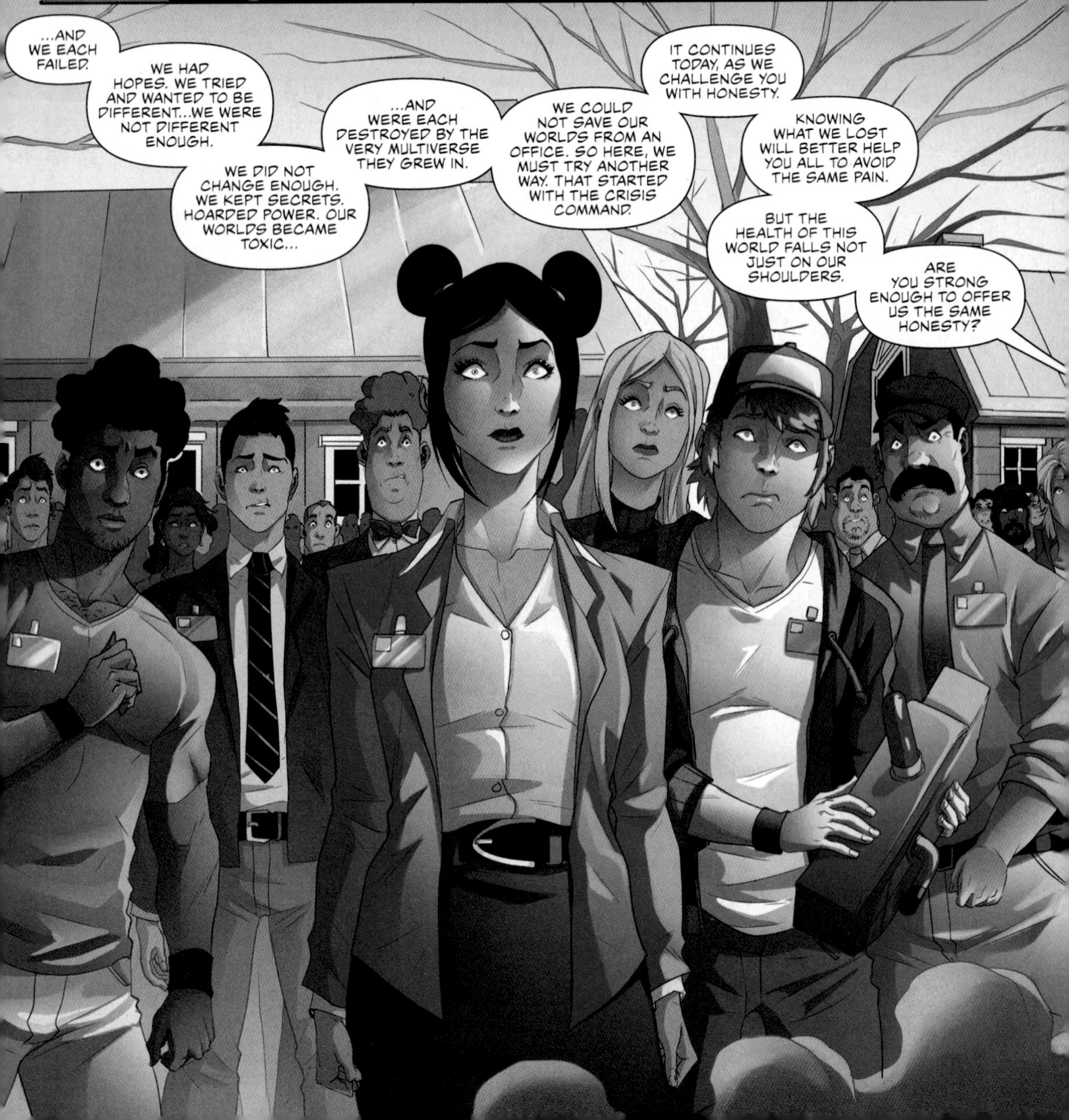
...AND WE EACH FAILED.
WE HAD HOPES. WE TRIED AND WANTED TO BE DIFFERENT...WE WERE NOT DIFFERENT ENOUGH.
WE DID NOT CHANGE ENOUGH. WE KEPT SECRETS. HOARDED POWER. OUR WORLDS BECAME TOXIC...
...AND WERE EACH DESTROYED BY THE VERY MULTIVERSE THEY GREW IN.
WE COULD NOT SAVE OUR WORLDS FROM AN OFFICE. SO HERE, WE MUST TRY ANOTHER WAY. THAT STARTED WITH THE CRISIS COMMAND.
IT CONTINUES TODAY, AS WE CHALLENGE YOU WITH HONESTY.
KNOWING WHAT WE LOST WILL BETTER HELP YOU ALL TO AVOID THE SAME PAIN.
BUT THE HEALTH OF THIS WORLD FALLS NOT JUST ON OUR SHOULDERS.
ARE YOU STRONG ENOUGH TO OFFER US THE SAME HONESTY?

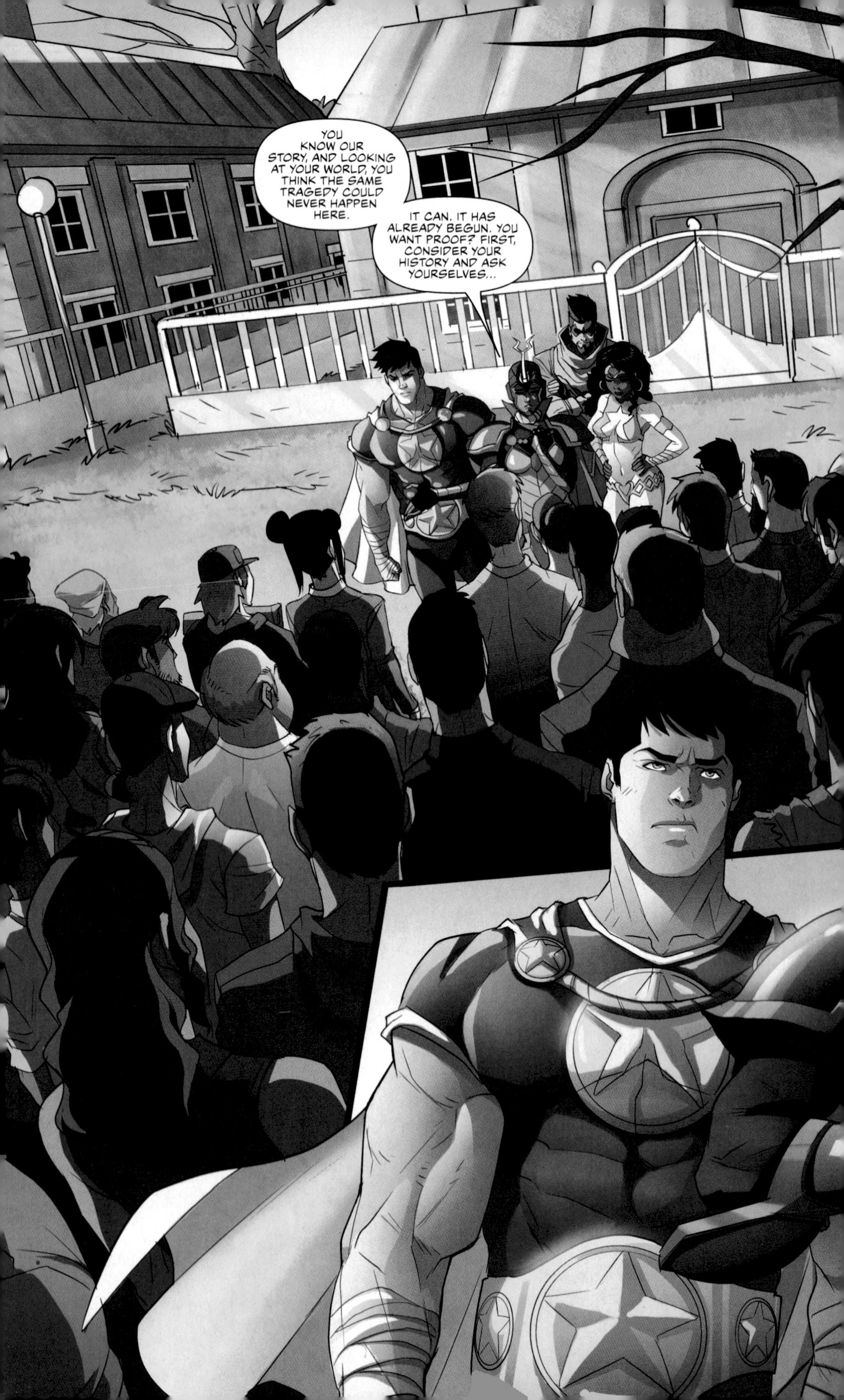
YOU KNOW OUR STORY, AND LOOKING AT YOUR WORLD, YOU THINK THE SAME TRAGEDY COULD NEVER HAPPEN HERE.
IT CAN. IT HAS ALREADY BEGUN. YOU WANT PROOF? FIRST, CONSIDER YOUR HISTORY AND ASK YOURSELVES...

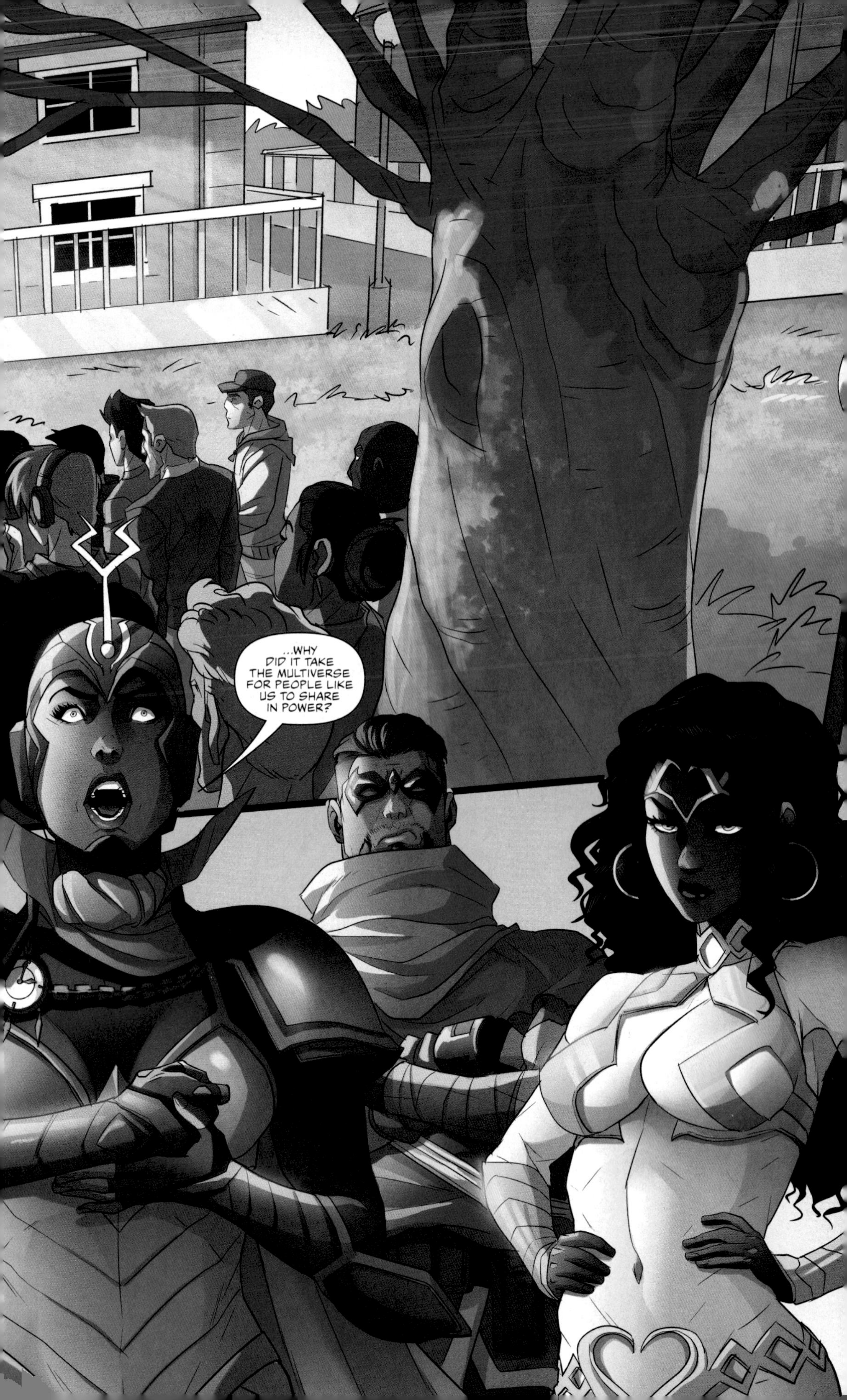
...WHY DID IT TAKE THE MULTIVERSE FOR PEOPLE LIKE US TO SHARE IN POWER?

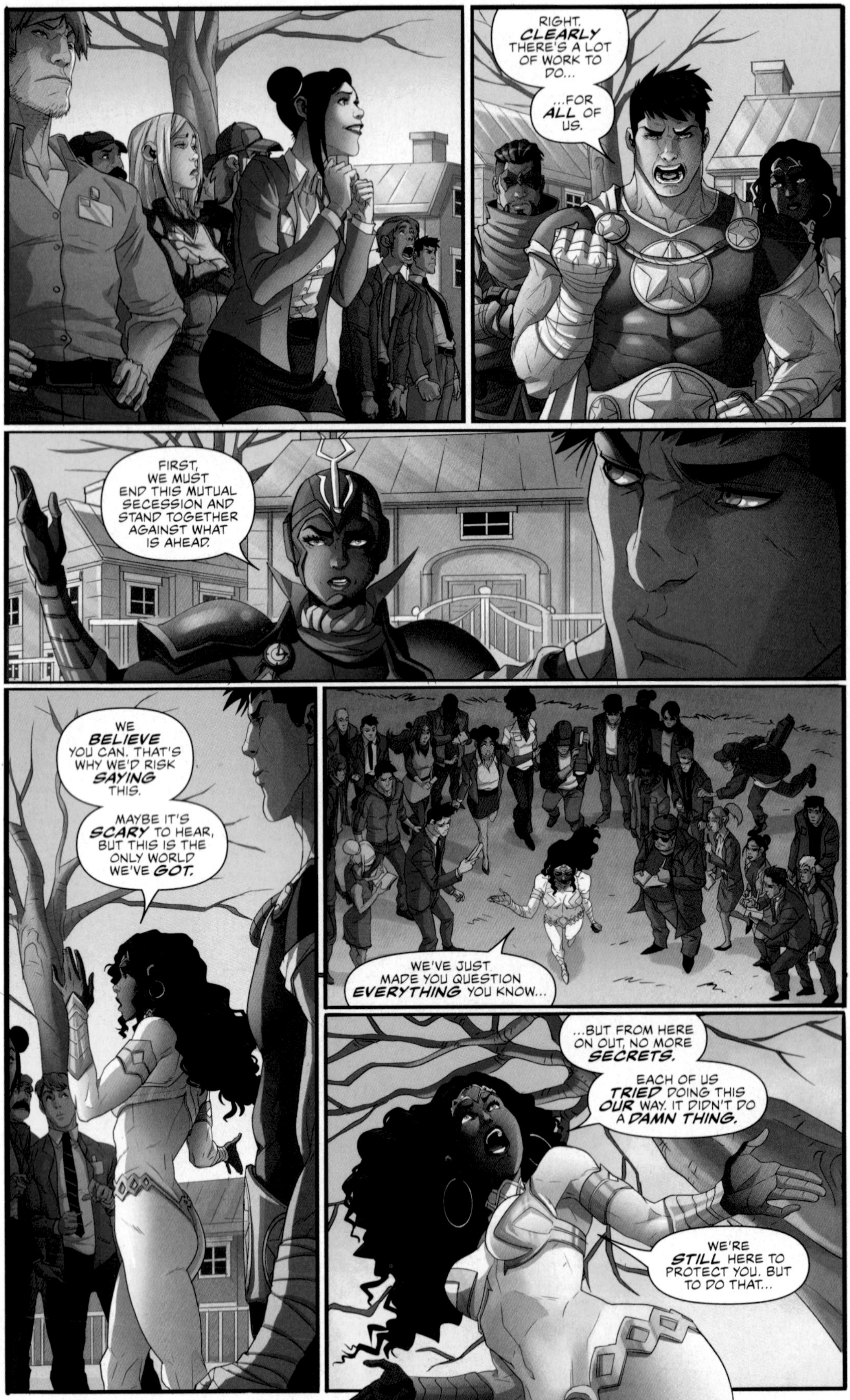
RIGHT. CLEARLY THERE'S A LOT OF WORK TO DO...
...FOR ALL OF US.
FIRST, WE MUST END THIS MUTUAL SECESSION AND STAND TOGETHER AGAINST WHAT IS AHEAD.
WE BELIEVE YOU CAN. THAT'S WHY WE'D RISK SAYING THIS.
MAYBE IT'S SCARY TO HEAR, BUT THIS IS THE ONLY WORLD WE'VE GOT.
WE'VE JUST MADE YOU QUESTION EVERYTHING YOU KNOW...
...BUT FROM HERE ON OUT, NO MORE SECRETS.
EACH OF US TRIED DOING THIS OUR WAY. IT DIDN'T DO A DAMN THING.
WE'RE STILL HERE TO PROTECT YOU. BUT TO DO THAT...

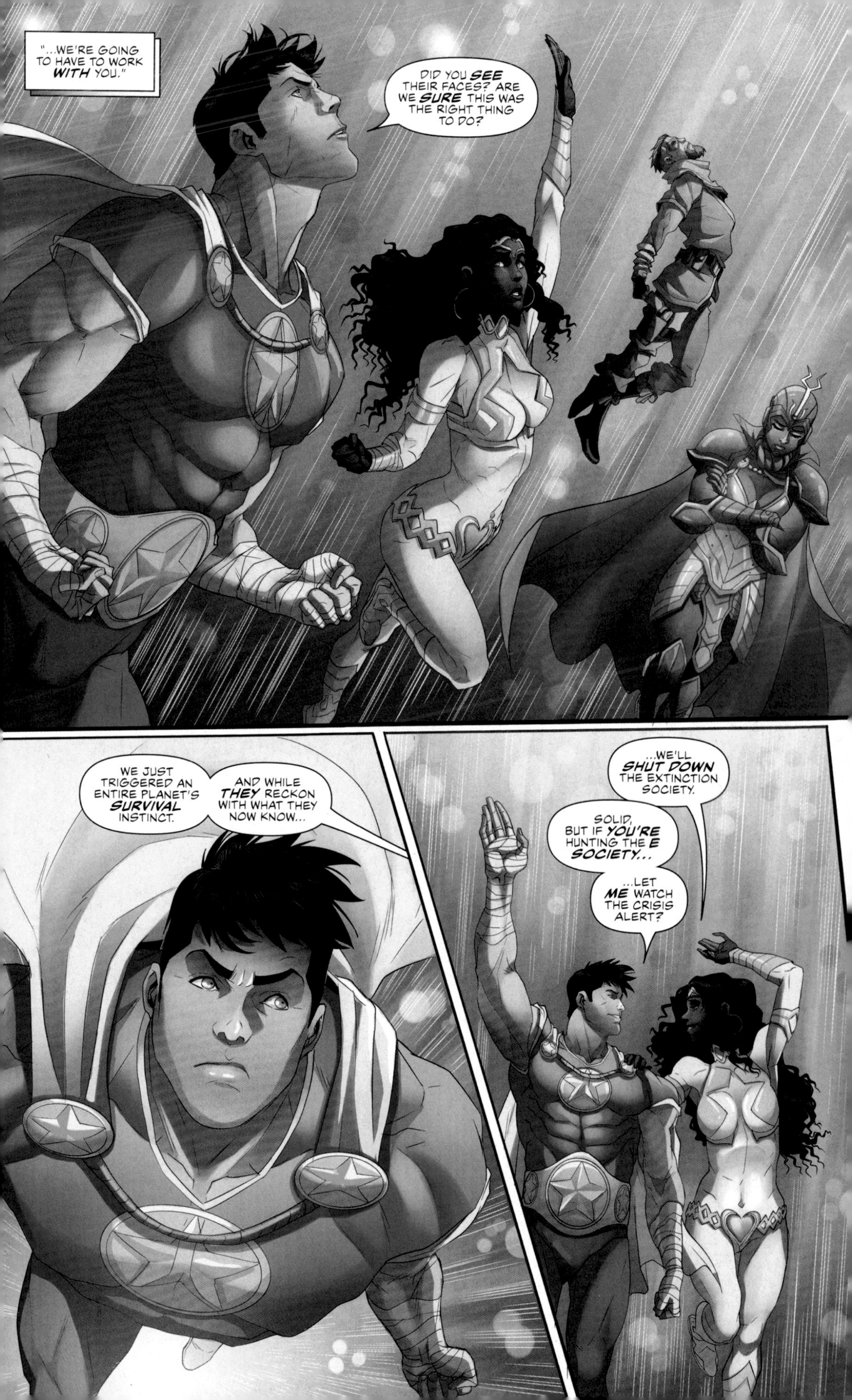
"...WE'RE GOING TO HAVE TO WORK WITH YOU."
DID YOU SEE THEIR FACES? ARE WE SURE THIS WAS THE RIGHT THING TO DO?
WE JUST TRIGGERED AN ENTIRE PLANET'S SURVIVAL INSTINCT.
AND WHILE THEY RECKON WITH WHAT THEY NOW KNOW...
...WE'LL SHUT DOWN THE EXTINCTION SOCIETY.
SOLID, BUT IF YOU'RE HUNTING THE E SOCIETY...
...LET ME WATCH THE CRISIS ALERT?

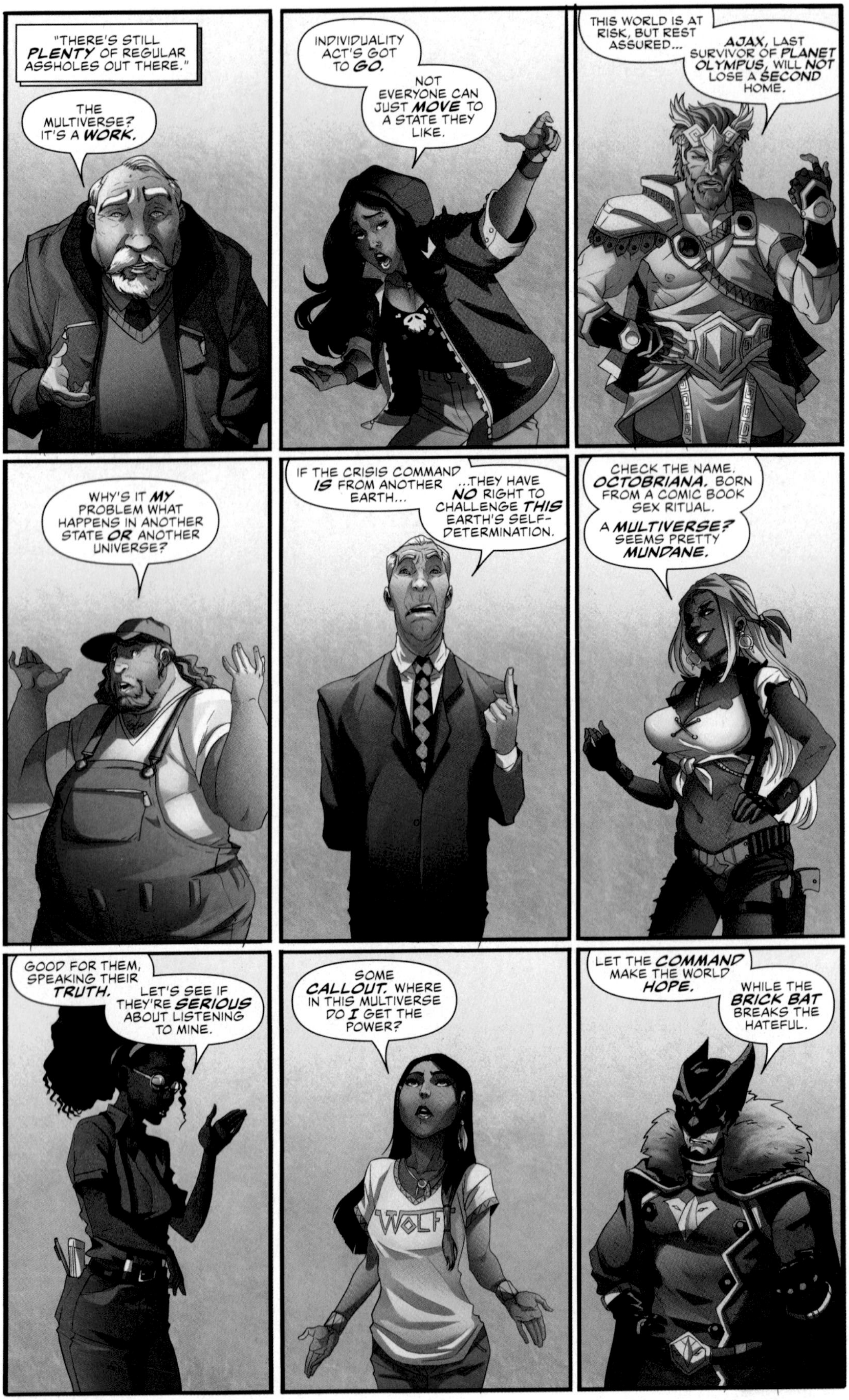
"THERE'S STILL PLENTY OF REGULAR ASSHOLES OUT THERE."
THE MULTIVERSE? IT'S A WORK.
INDIVIDUALITY ACT'S GOT TO GO.
NOT EVERYONE CAN JUST MOVE TO A STATE THEY LIKE.
THIS WORLD IS AT RISK, BUT REST ASSURED...
AJAX, LAST SURVIVOR OF PLANET OLYMPUS, WILL NOT LOSE A SECOND HOME.
WHY'S IT MY PROBLEM WHAT HAPPENS IN ANOTHER STATE OR ANOTHER UNIVERSE?
IF THE CRISIS COMMAND IS FROM ANOTHER EARTH...
...THEY HAVE NO RIGHT TO CHALLENGE THIS EARTH'S SELF-DETERMINATION.
CHECK THE NAME. OCTOBRIANA. BORN FROM A COMIC BOOK SEX RITUAL.
A MULTIVERSE? SEEMS PRETTY MUNDANE.
GOOD FOR THEM, SPEAKING THEIR TRUTH.
LET'S SEE IF THEY'RE SERIOUS ABOUT LISTENING TO MINE.
SOME CALLOUT. WHERE IN THIS MULTIVERSE DO I GET THE POWER?
WOLF
LET THE COMMAND MAKE THE WORLD HOPE.
WHILE THE BRICK BAT BREAKS THE HATEFUL.

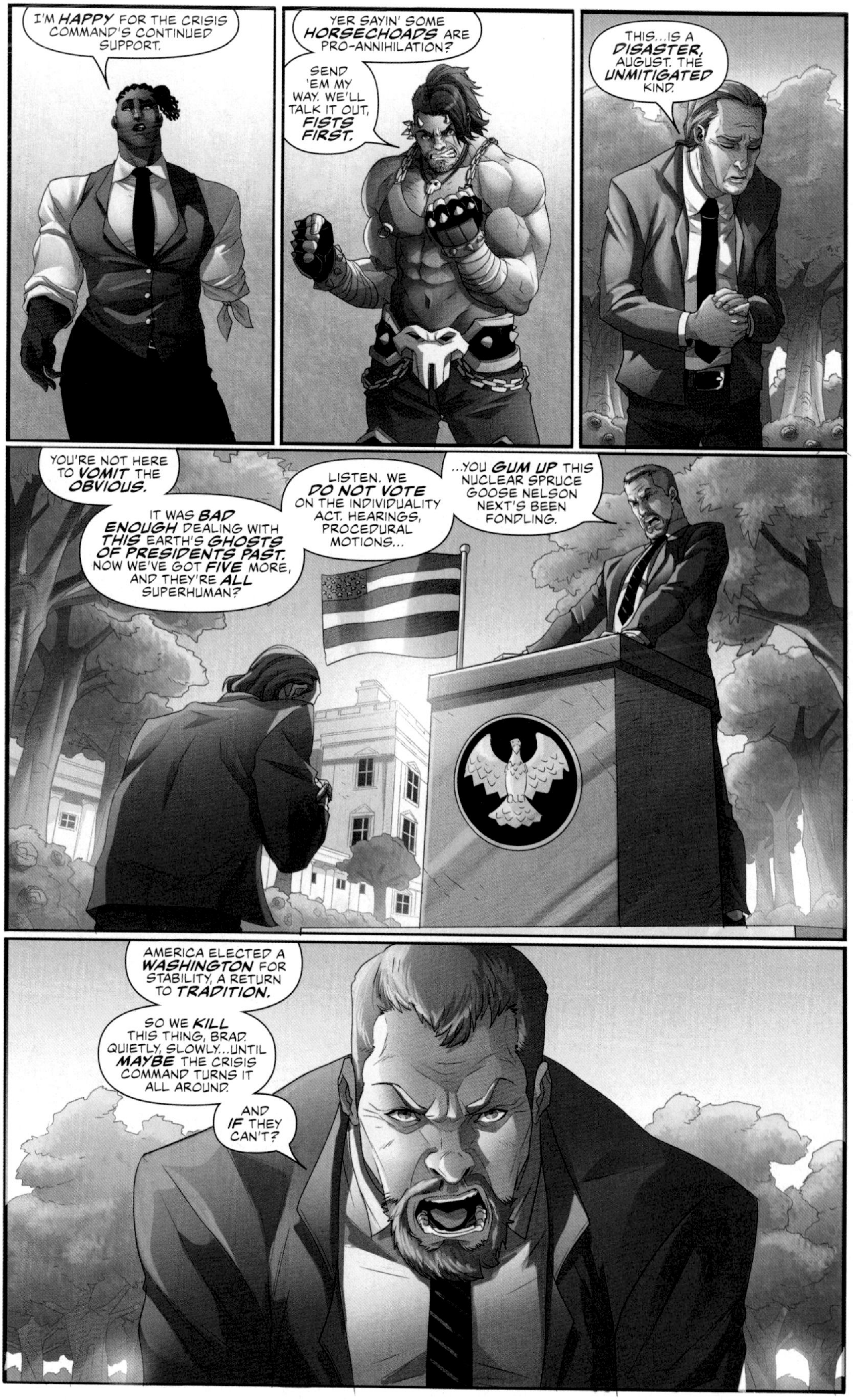

I'M HAPPY FOR THE CRISIS COMMAND'S CONTINUED SUPPORT.
YER SAYIN' SOME HORSECHOADS ARE PRO-ANNIHILATION?
SEND 'EM MY WAY. WE'LL TALK IT OUT, FISTS FIRST.
THIS...IS A DISASTER, AUGUST. THE UNMITIGATED KIND.
YOU'RE NOT HERE TO VOMIT THE OBVIOUS.
IT WAS BAD ENOUGH DEALING WITH THIS EARTH'S GHOSTS OF PRESIDENTS PAST. NOW WE'VE GOT FIVE MORE, AND THEY'RE ALL SUPERHUMAN?
LISTEN. WE DO NOT VOTE ON THE INDIVIDUALITY ACT. HEARINGS, PROCEDURAL MOTIONS...
...YOU GUM UP THIS NUCLEAR SPRUCE GOOSE NELSON NEXT'S BEEN FONDLING.
AMERICA ELECTED A WASHINGTON FOR STABILITY, A RETURN TO TRADITION.
SO WE KILL THIS THING, BRAD. QUIETLY, SLOWLY...UNTIL MAYBE THE CRISIS COMMAND TURNS IT ALL AROUND.
AND IF THEY CAN'T?

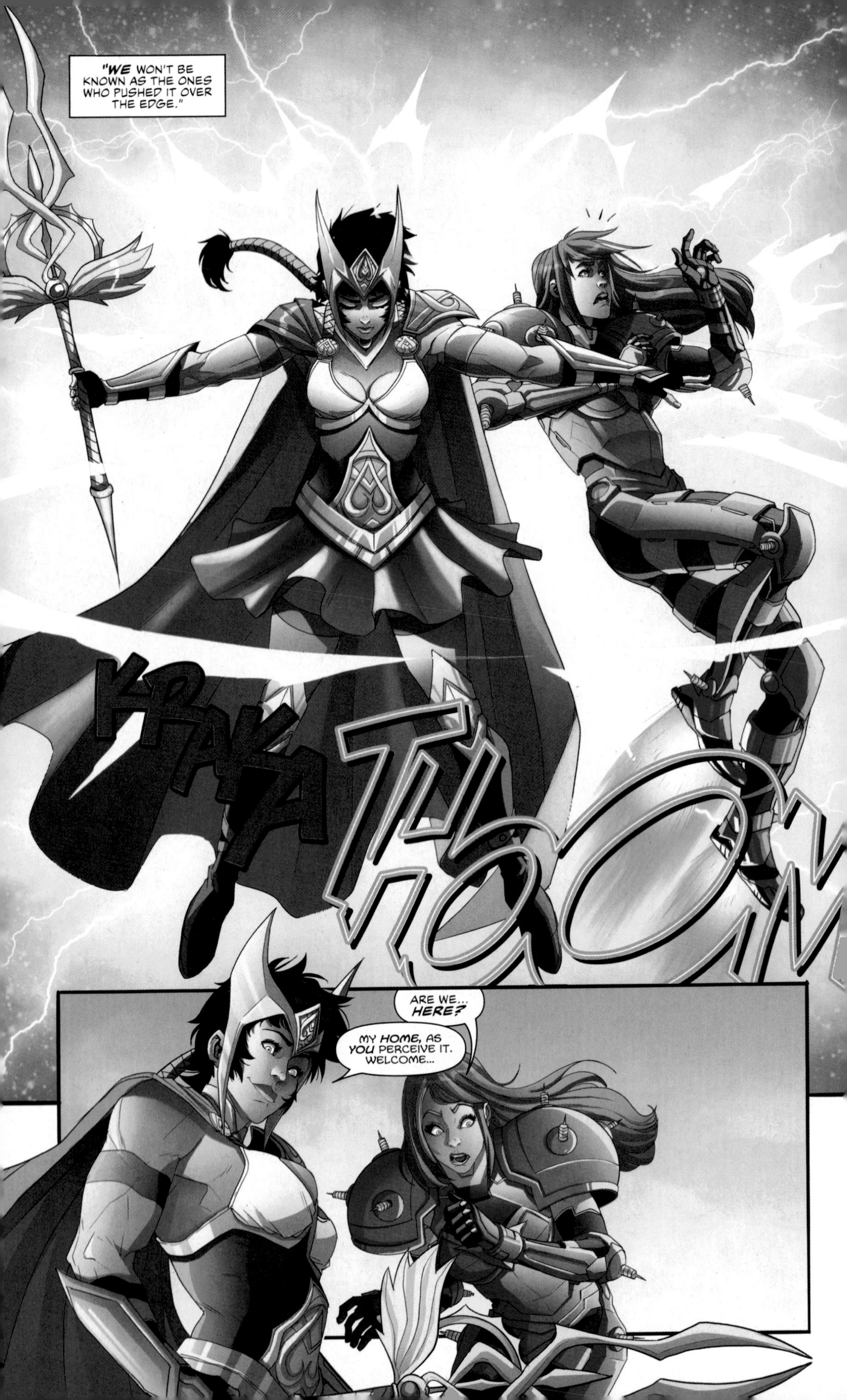
"WE WON'T BE KNOWN AS THE ONES WHO PUSHED IT OVER THE EDGE."
KRAKA
THOOM
ARE WE... HERE?
MY HOME, AS YOU PERCEIVE IT. WELCOME...

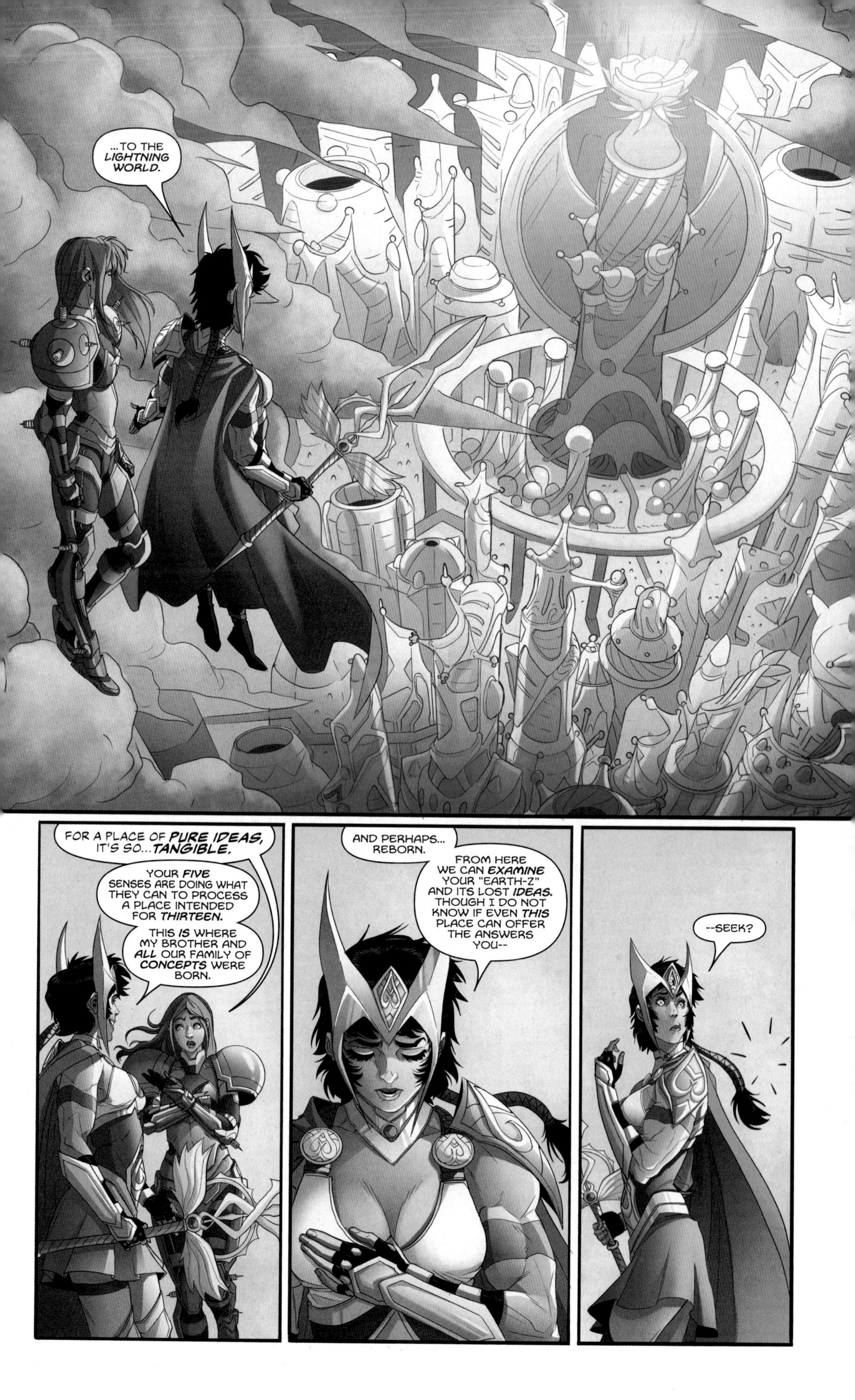
...TO THE LIGHTNING WORLD.
FOR A PLACE OF PURE IDEAS, IT'S SO...TANGIBLE.
YOUR FIVE SENSES ARE DOING WHAT THEY CAN TO PROCESS A PLACE INTENDED FOR THIRTEEN.
THIS IS WHERE MY BROTHER AND ALL OUR FAMILY OF CONCEPTS WERE BORN.
AND PERHAPS... REBORN.
FROM HERE WE CAN EXAMINE YOUR "EARTH-Z" AND ITS LOST IDEAS. THOUGH I DO NOT KNOW IF EVEN THIS PLACE CAN OFFER THE ANSWERS YOU--
--SEEK?

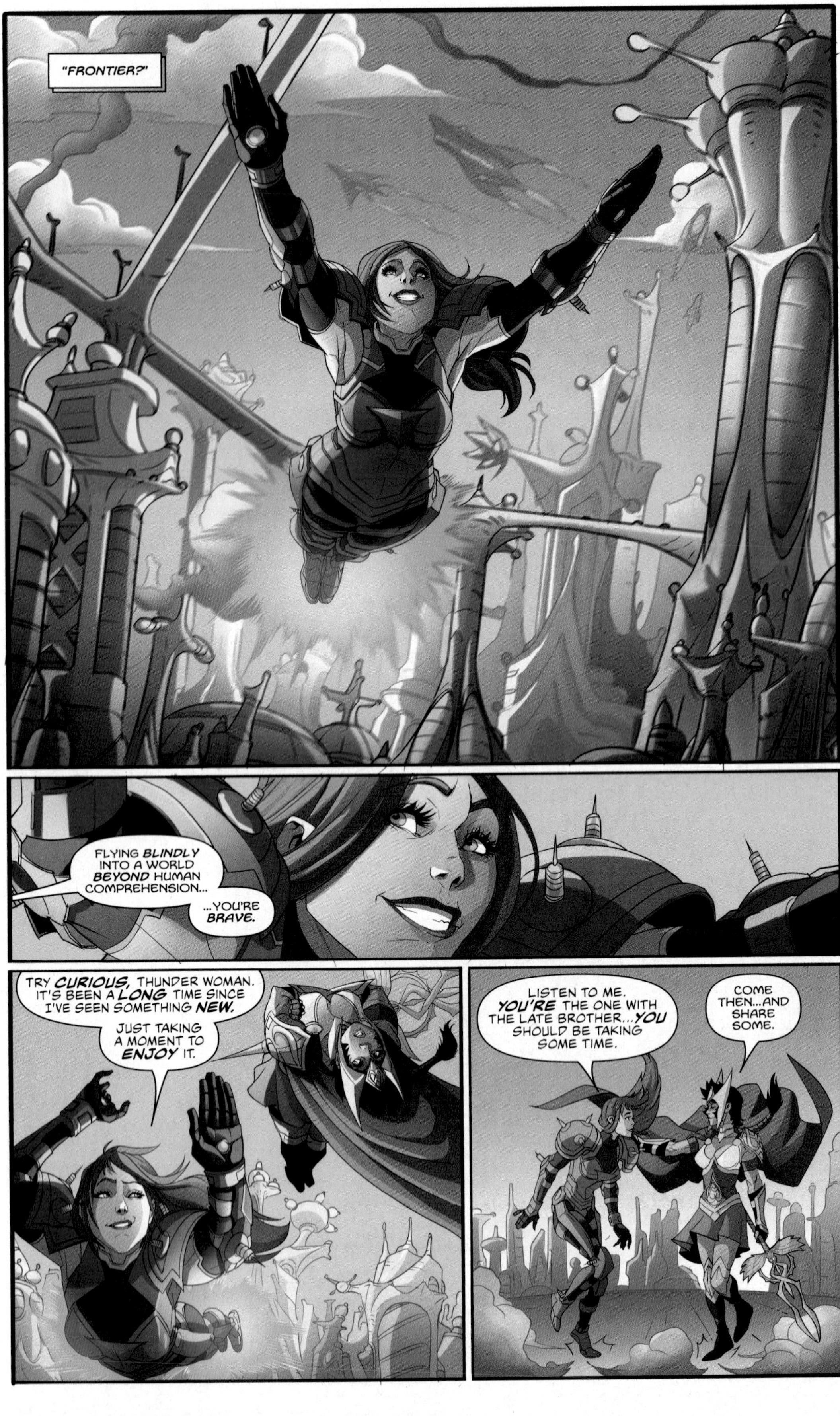
"FRONTIER?"
FLYING BLINDLY INTO A WORLD BEYOND HUMAN COMPREHENSION...
...YOU'RE BRAVE.
TRY CURIOUS, THUNDER WOMAN. IT'S BEEN A LONG TIME SINCE I'VE SEEN SOMETHING NEW.
JUST TAKING A MOMENT TO ENJOY IT.
LISTEN TO ME. YOU'RE THE ONE WITH THE LATE BROTHER...YOU SHOULD BE TAKING SOME TIME.
COME THEN...AND SHARE SOME.

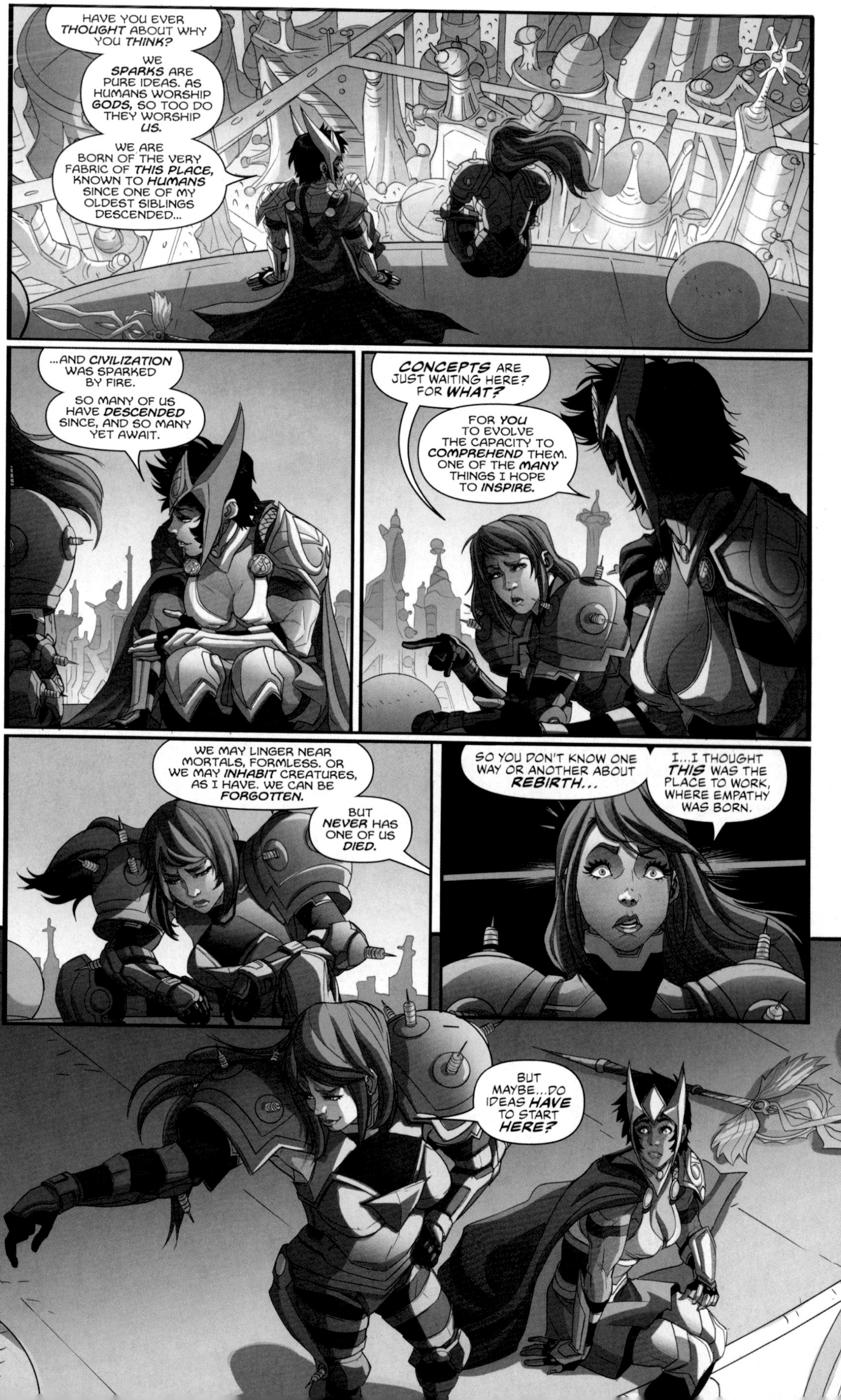
HAVE YOU EVER THOUGHT ABOUT WHY YOU THINK?
WE SPARKS ARE PURE IDEAS. AS HUMANS WORSHIP GODS, SO TOO DO THEY WORSHIP US.
WE ARE BORN OF THE VERY FABRIC OF THIS PLACE, KNOWN TO HUMANS SINCE ONE OF MY OLDEST SIBLINGS DESCENDED...
...AND CIVILIZATION WAS SPARKED BY FIRE.
SO MANY OF US HAVE DESCENDED SINCE, AND SO MANY YET AWAIT.
CONCEPTS ARE JUST WAITING HERE? FOR WHAT?
FOR YOU TO EVOLVE THE CAPACITY TO COMPREHEND THEM. ONE OF THE MANY THINGS I HOPE TO INSPIRE.
WE MAY LINGER NEAR MORTALS, FORMLESS. OR WE MAY INHABIT CREATURES, AS I HAVE. WE CAN BE FORGOTTEN.
BUT NEVER HAS ONE OF US DIED.
SO YOU DON'T KNOW ONE WAY OR ANOTHER ABOUT REBIRTH...
I...I THOUGHT THIS WAS THE PLACE TO WORK, WHERE EMPATHY WAS BORN.
BUT MAYBE...DO IDEAS HAVE TO START HERE?

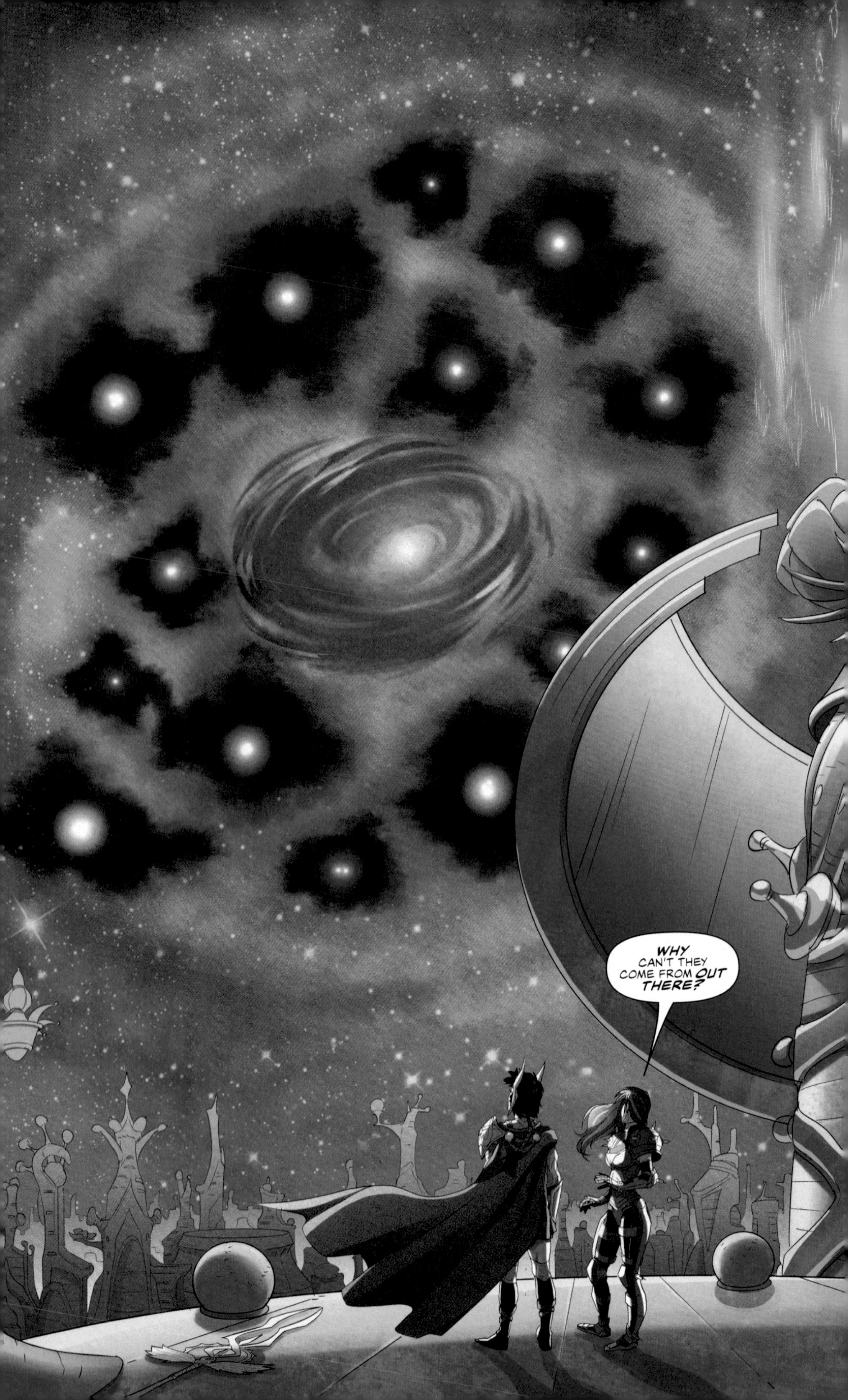
WHY CAN'T THEY COME FROM OUT THERE?

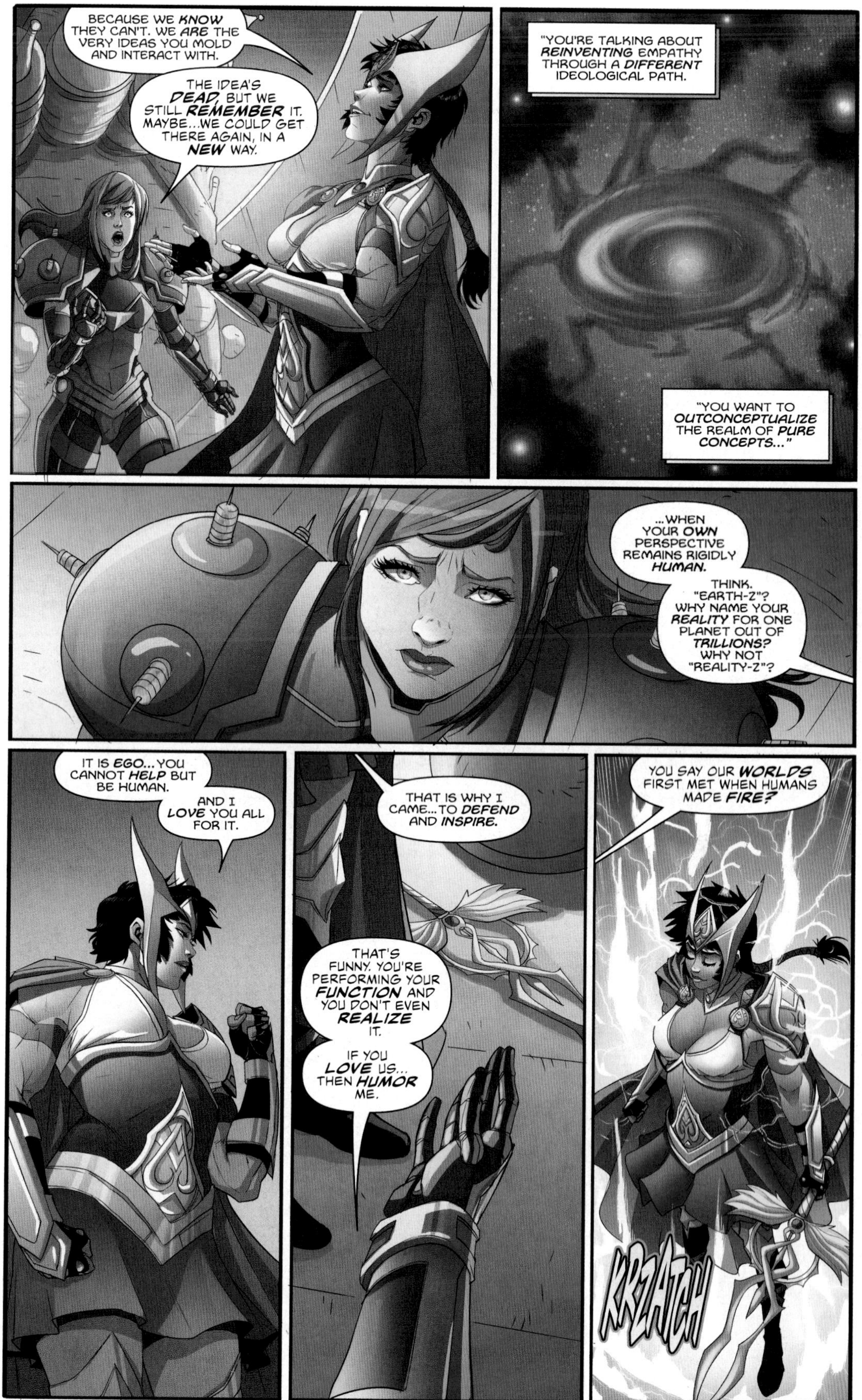

BECAUSE WE KNOW THEY CAN'T. WE ARE THE VERY IDEAS YOU MOLD AND INTERACT WITH.
THE IDEA'S DEAD, BUT WE STILL REMEMBER IT. MAYBE...WE COULD GET THERE AGAIN, IN A NEW WAY.
"YOU'RE TALKING ABOUT REINVENTING EMPATHY THROUGH A DIFFERENT IDEOLOGICAL PATH.
"YOU WANT TO OUTCONCEPTUALIZE THE REALM OF PURE CONCEPTS..."
...WHEN YOUR OWN PERSPECTIVE REMAINS RIGIDLY HUMAN.
THINK. "EARTH-Z"? WHY NAME YOUR REALITY FOR ONE PLANET OUT OF TRILLIONS? WHY NOT "REALITY-Z"?
IT IS EGO... YOU CANNOT HELP BUT BE HUMAN.
AND I LOVE YOU ALL FOR IT.
THAT IS WHY I CAME...TO DEFEND AND INSPIRE.
THAT'S FUNNY. YOU'RE PERFORMING YOUR FUNCTION AND YOU DON'T EVEN REALIZE IT.
IF YOU LOVE US... THEN HUMOR ME.
YOU SAY OUR WORLDS FIRST MET WHEN HUMANS MADE FIRE?
KRZATCH

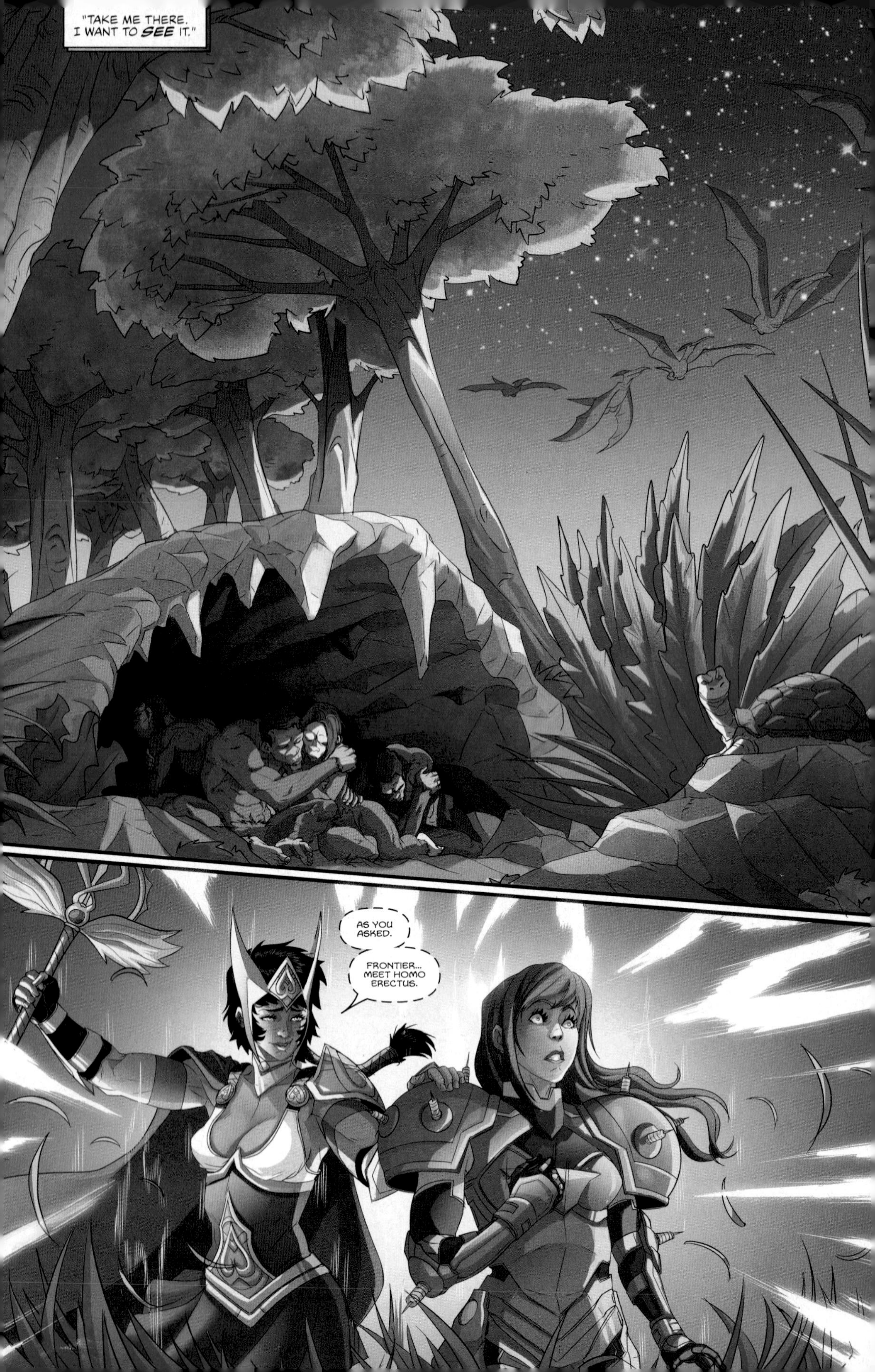
"TAKE ME THERE. I WANT TO SEE IT."
AS YOU ASKED.
FRONTIER... MEET HOMO ERECTUS.

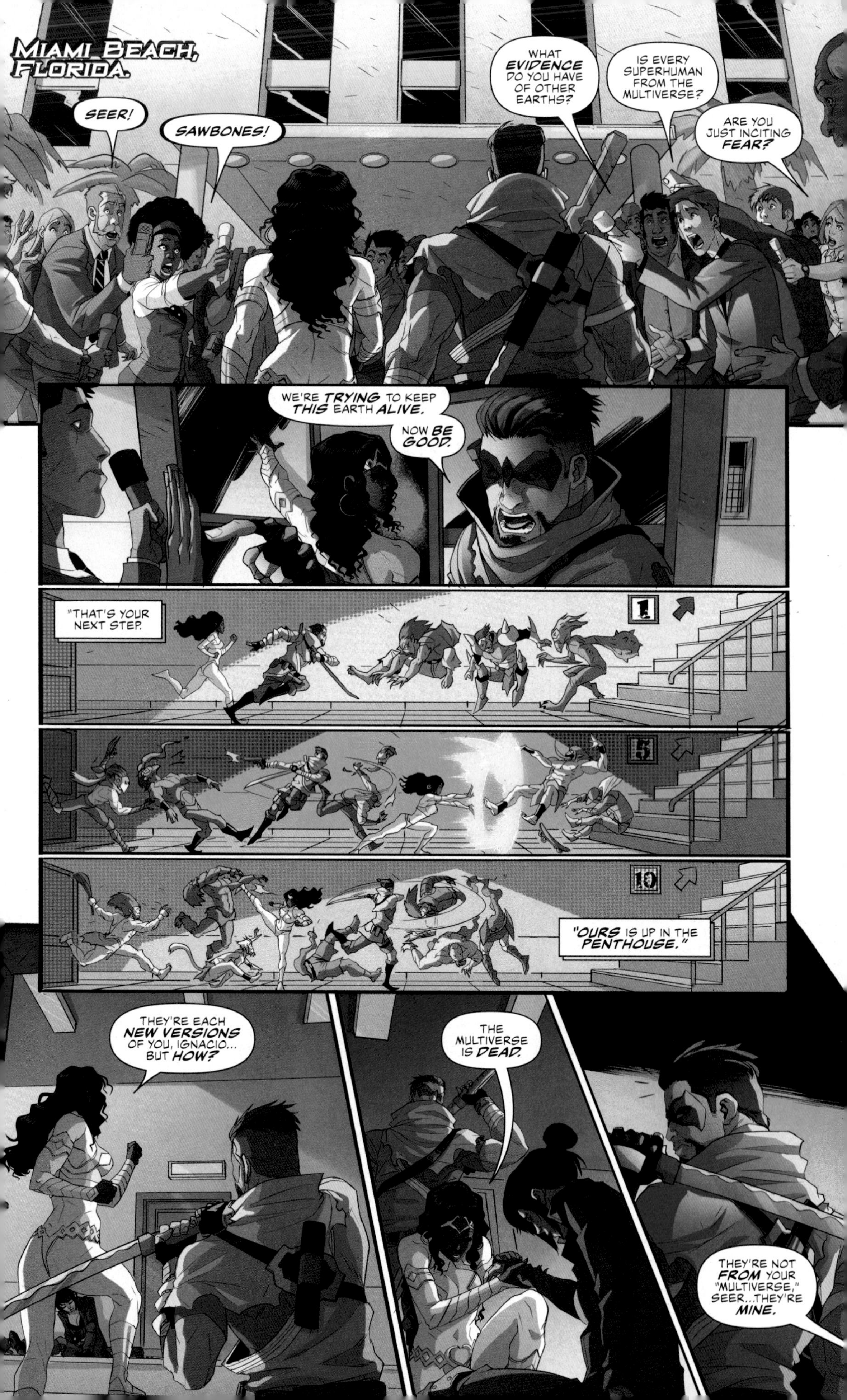
MIAMI BEACH, FLORIDA.
SEER!
SAWBONES!
WHAT EVIDENCE DO YOU HAVE OF OTHER EARTHS?
IS EVERY SUPERHUMAN FROM THE MULTIVERSE?
ARE YOU JUST INCITING FEAR?
WE'RE TRYING TO KEEP THIS EARTH ALIVE.
NOW BE GOOD.
"THAT'S YOUR NEXT STEP.
1
5
10
"OURS IS UP IN THE PENTHOUSE."
THEY'RE EACH NEW VERSIONS OF YOU, IGNACIO... BUT HOW?
THE MULTIVERSE IS DEAD.
THEY'RE NOT FROM YOUR "MULTIVERSE," SEER...THEY'RE MINE.

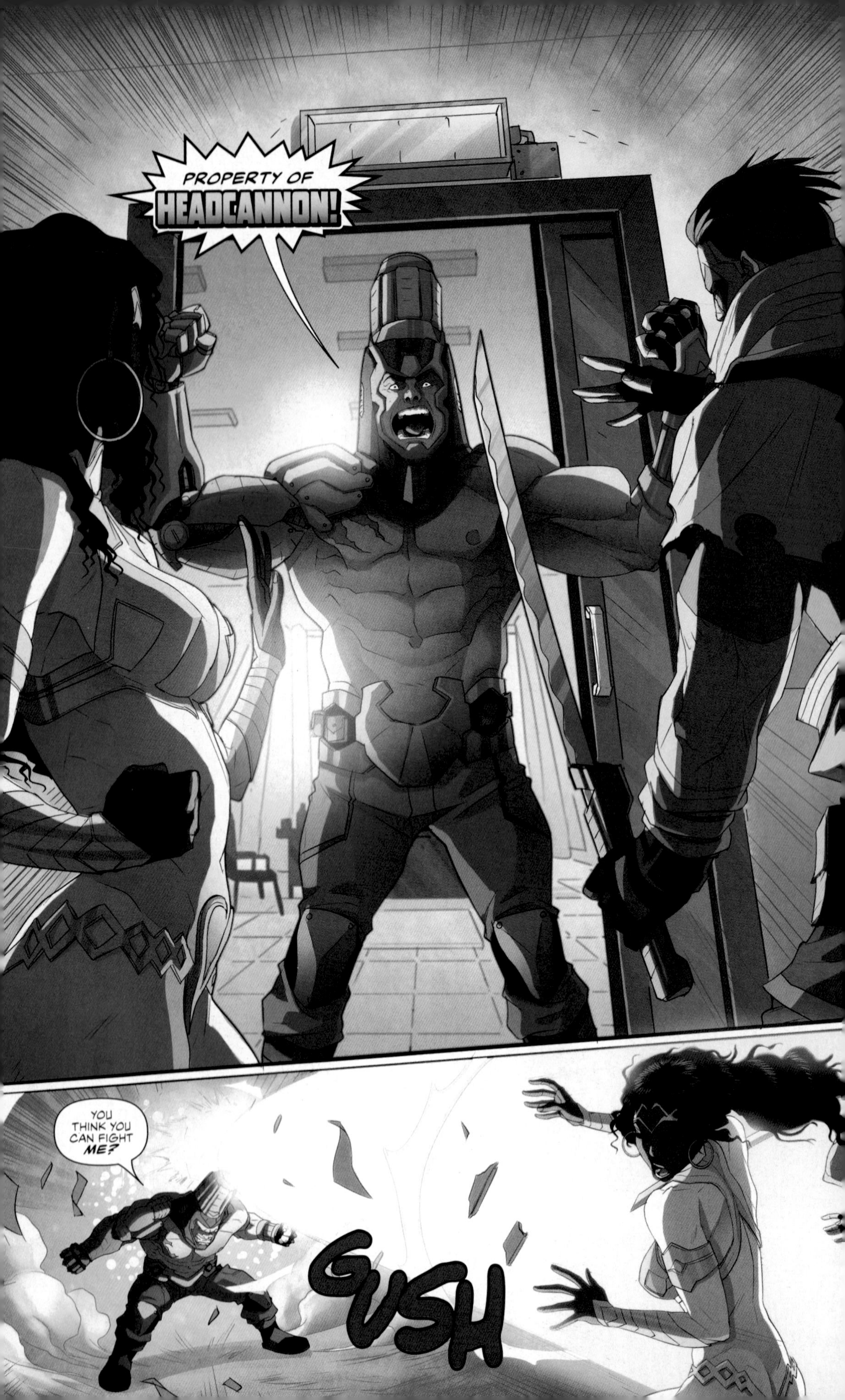
PROPERTY OF
HEADCANNON!
YOU THINK YOU CAN FIGHT ME?
GUSH

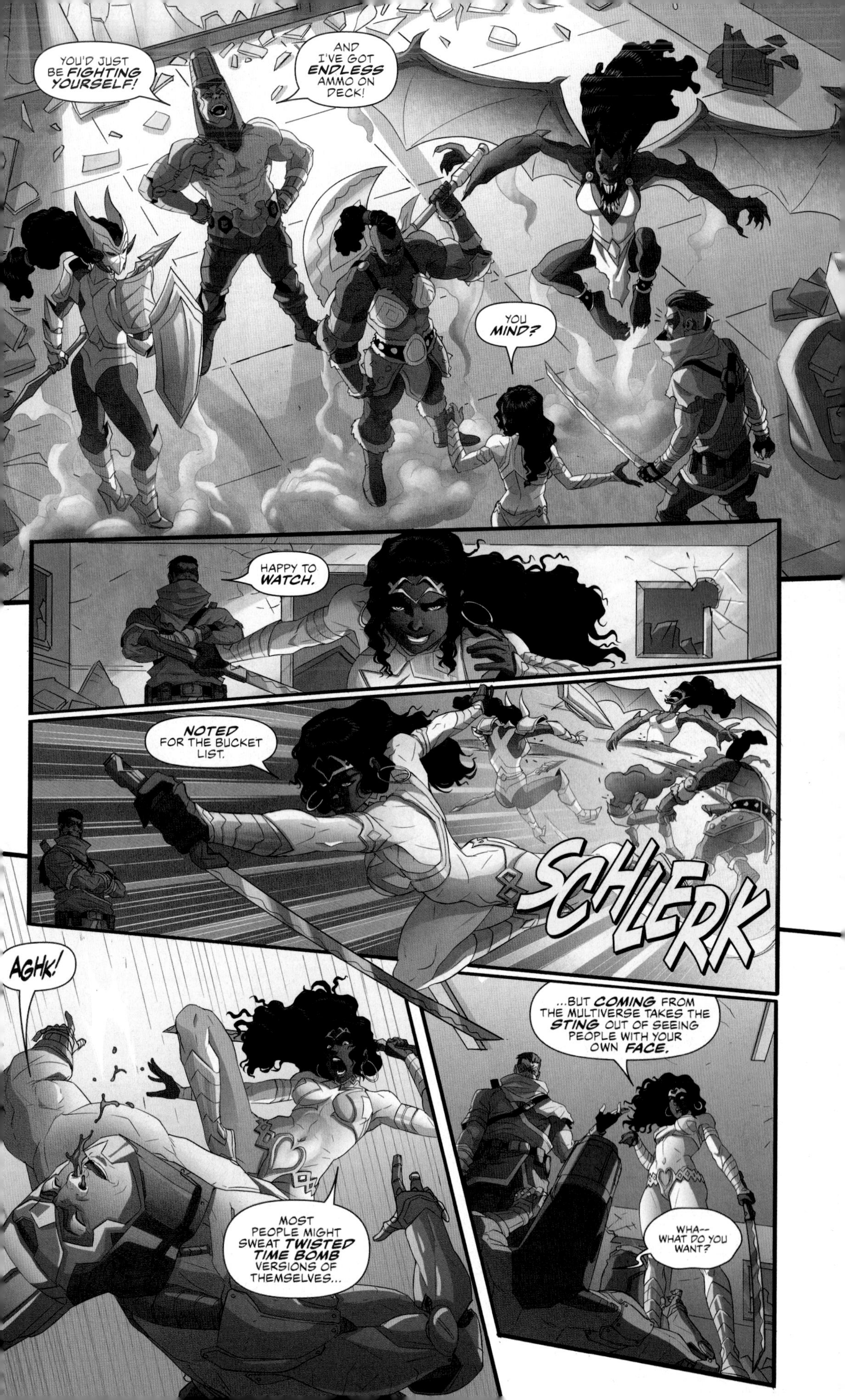
YOU'D JUST BE FIGHTING YOURSELF!
AND I'VE GOT ENDLESS AMMO ON DECK!
YOU MIND?
HAPPY TO WATCH.
NOTED FOR THE BUCKET LIST.
SCHLERK
AGHK!
MOST PEOPLE MIGHT SWEAT TWISTED TIME BOMB VERSIONS OF THEMSELVES...
...BUT COMING FROM THE MULTIVERSE TAKES THE STING OUT OF SEEING PEOPLE WITH YOUR OWN FACE.
WHA-- WHAT DO YOU WANT?

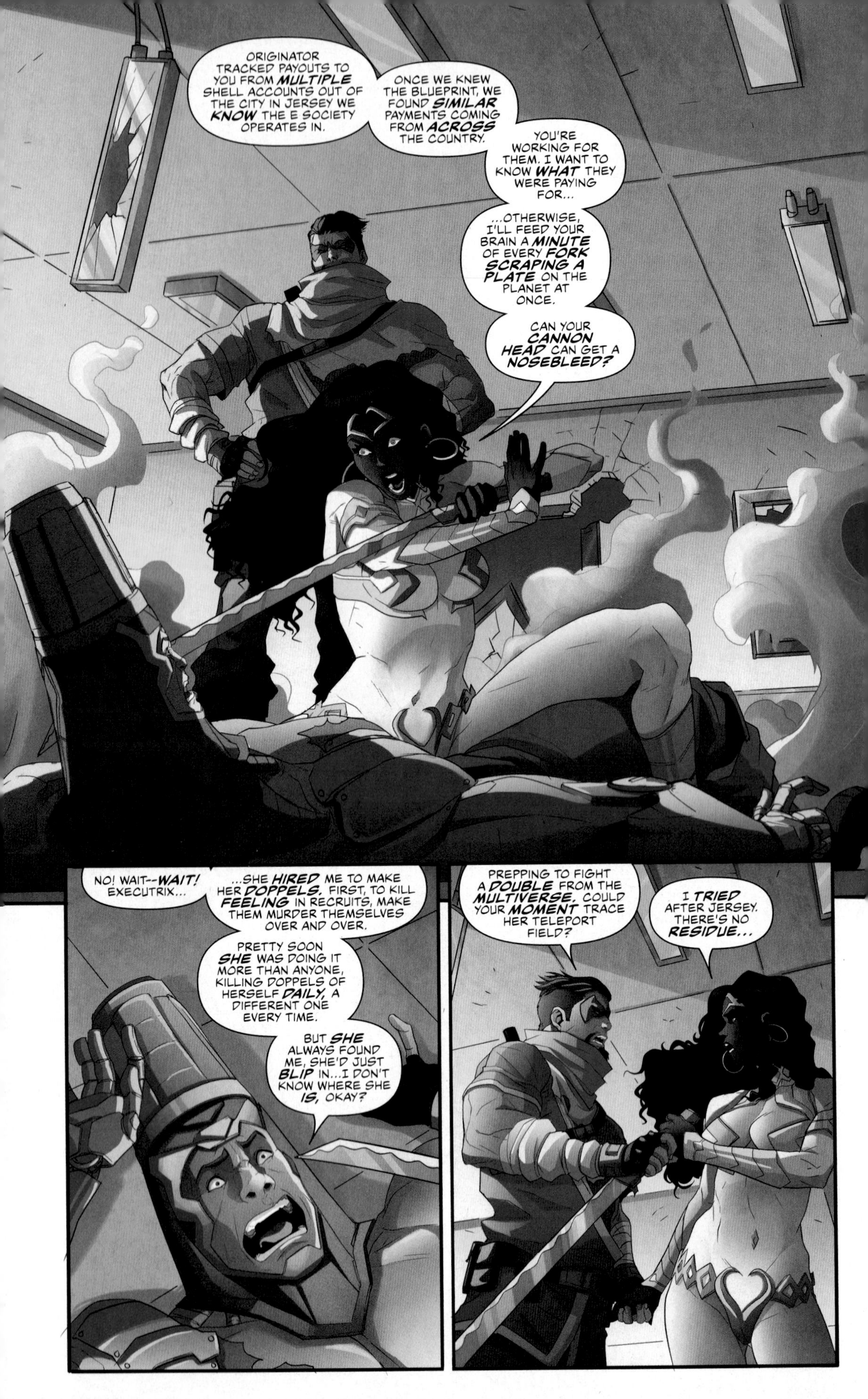
ORIGINATOR TRACKED PAYOUTS TO YOU FROM MULTIPLE SHELL ACCOUNTS OUT OF THE CITY IN JERSEY WE KNOW THE E SOCIETY OPERATES IN.
ONCE WE KNEW THE BLUEPRINT, WE FOUND SIMILAR PAYMENTS COMING FROM ACROSS THE COUNTRY.
YOU'RE WORKING FOR THEM. I WANT TO KNOW WHAT THEY WERE PAYING FOR...
...OTHERWISE, I'LL FEED YOUR BRAIN A MINUTE OF EVERY FORK SCRAPING A PLATE ON THE PLANET AT ONCE.
CAN YOUR CANNON HEAD CAN GET A NOSEBLEED?
NO! WAIT--WAIT! EXECUTRIX...
...SHE HIRED ME TO MAKE HER DOPPELS. FIRST, TO KILL FEELING IN RECRUITS, MAKE THEM MURDER THEMSELVES OVER AND OVER.
PRETTY SOON SHE WAS DOING IT MORE THAN ANYONE, KILLING DOPPELS OF HERSELF DAILY, A DIFFERENT ONE EVERY TIME.
BUT SHE ALWAYS FOUND ME, SHE'D JUST BLIP IN...I DON'T KNOW WHERE SHE IS, OKAY?
PREPPING TO FIGHT A DOUBLE FROM THE MULTIVERSE. COULD YOUR MOMENT TRACE HER TELEPORT FIELD?
I TRIED AFTER JERSEY. THERE'S NO RESIDUE...

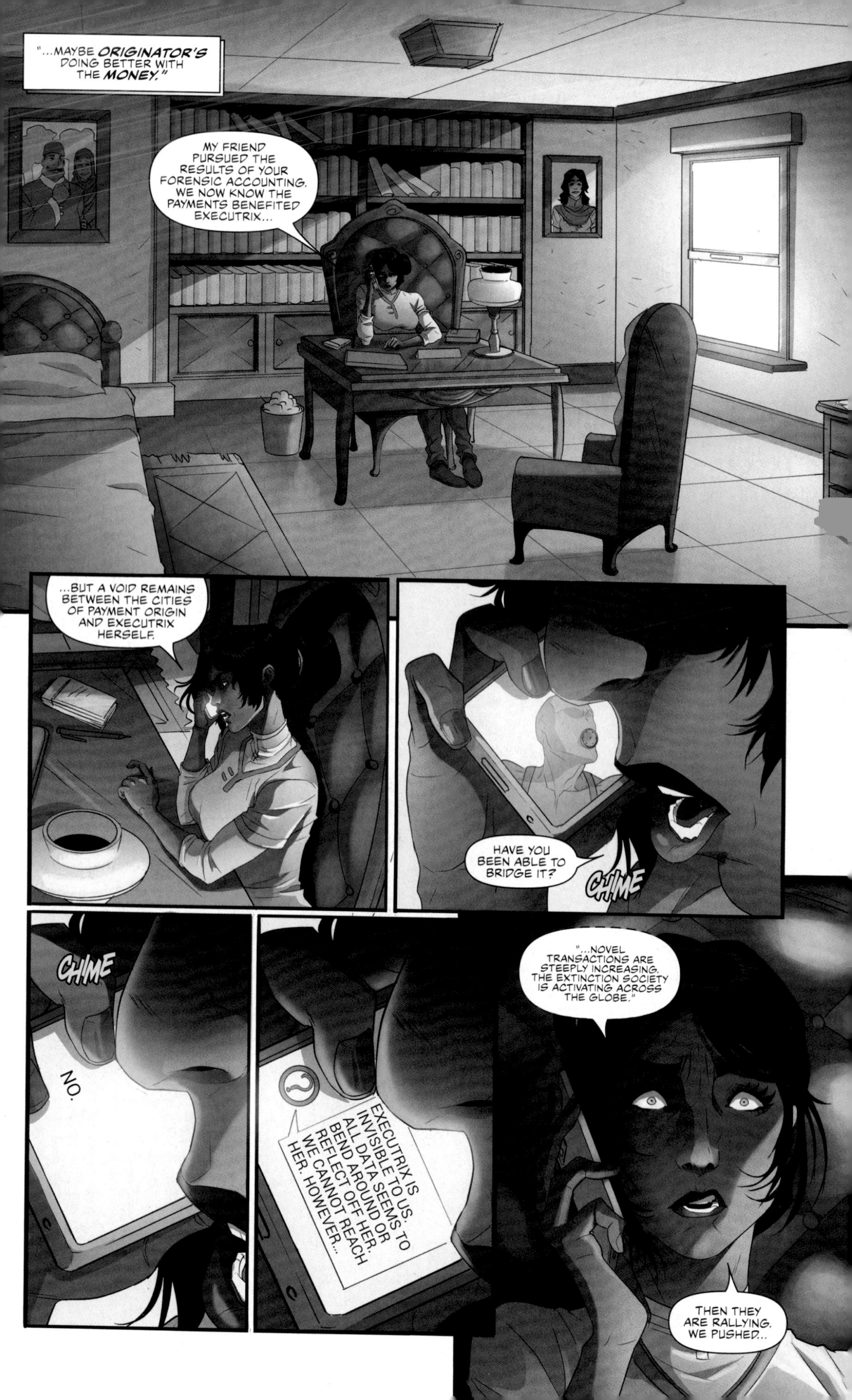
"...MAYBE ORIGINATOR'S DOING BETTER WITH THE MONEY."
MY FRIEND PURSUED THE RESULTS OF YOUR FORENSIC ACCOUNTING. WE NOW KNOW THE PAYMENTS BENEFITED EXECUTRIX...
...BUT A VOID REMAINS BETWEEN THE CITIES OF PAYMENT ORIGIN AND EXECUTRIX HERSELF.
HAVE YOU BEEN ABLE TO BRIDGE IT?
CHIME
CHIME
NO.
EXECUTRIX IS INVISIBLE TO US. ALL DATA SEEMS TO BEND AROUND OR REFLECT OFF HER. WE CANNOT REACH HER. HOWEVER...
"...NOVEL TRANSACTIONS ARE STEEPLY INCREASING. THE EXTINCTION SOCIETY IS ACTIVATING ACROSS THE GLOBE."
THEN THEY ARE RALLYING. WE PUSHED...

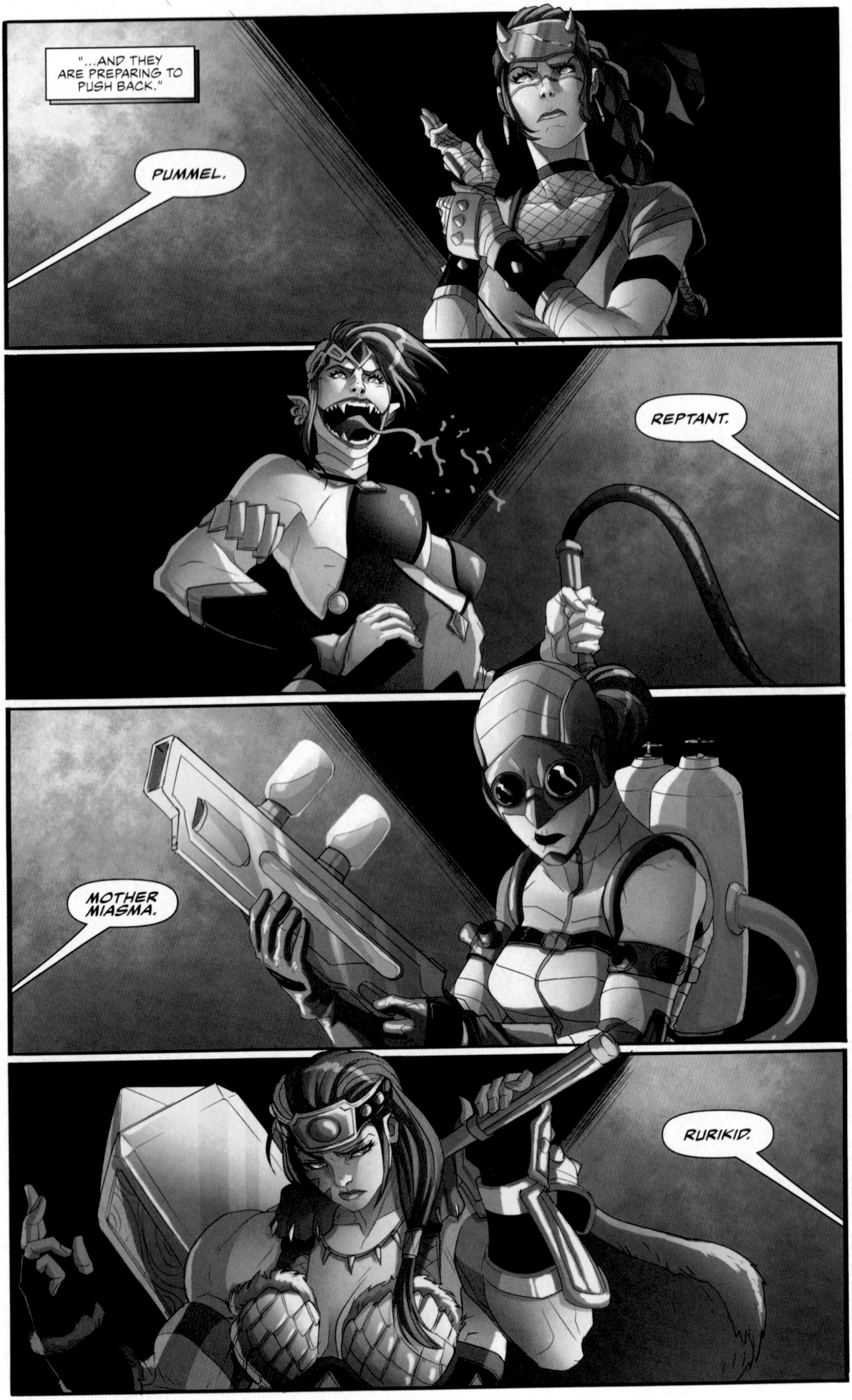
"...AND THEY ARE PREPARING TO PUSH BACK."
PUMMEL.
REPTANT.
MOTHER MIASMA.
RURIKID.

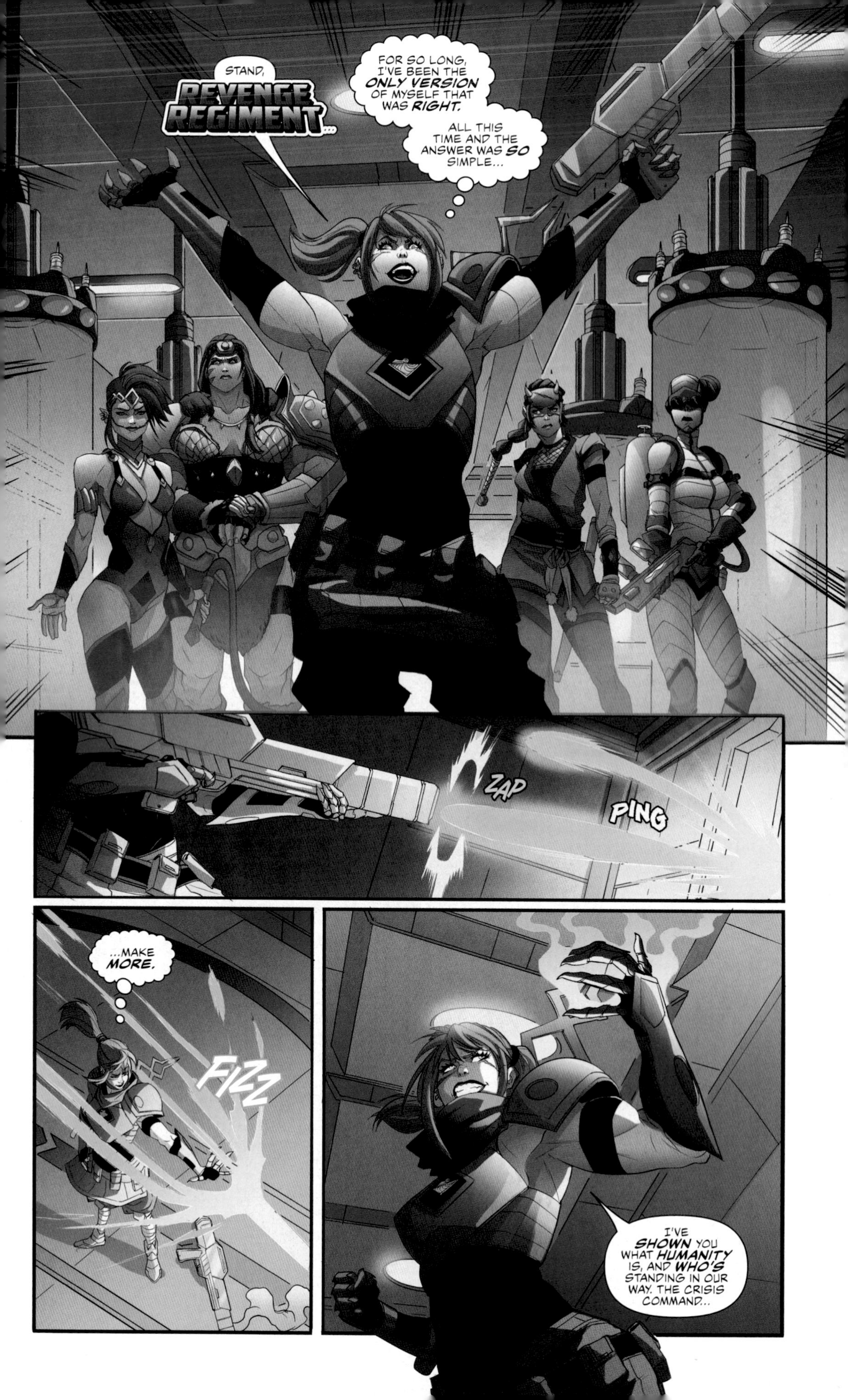

STAND, REVENGE REGIMENT...
FOR SO LONG, I'VE BEEN THE ONLY VERSION OF MYSELF THAT WAS RIGHT.
ALL THIS TIME AND THE ANSWER WAS SO SIMPLE...
ZAP
PING
...MAKE MORE.
FIZZ
I'VE SHOWN YOU WHAT HUMANITY IS, AND WHO'S STANDING IN OUR WAY. THE CRISIS COMMAND...

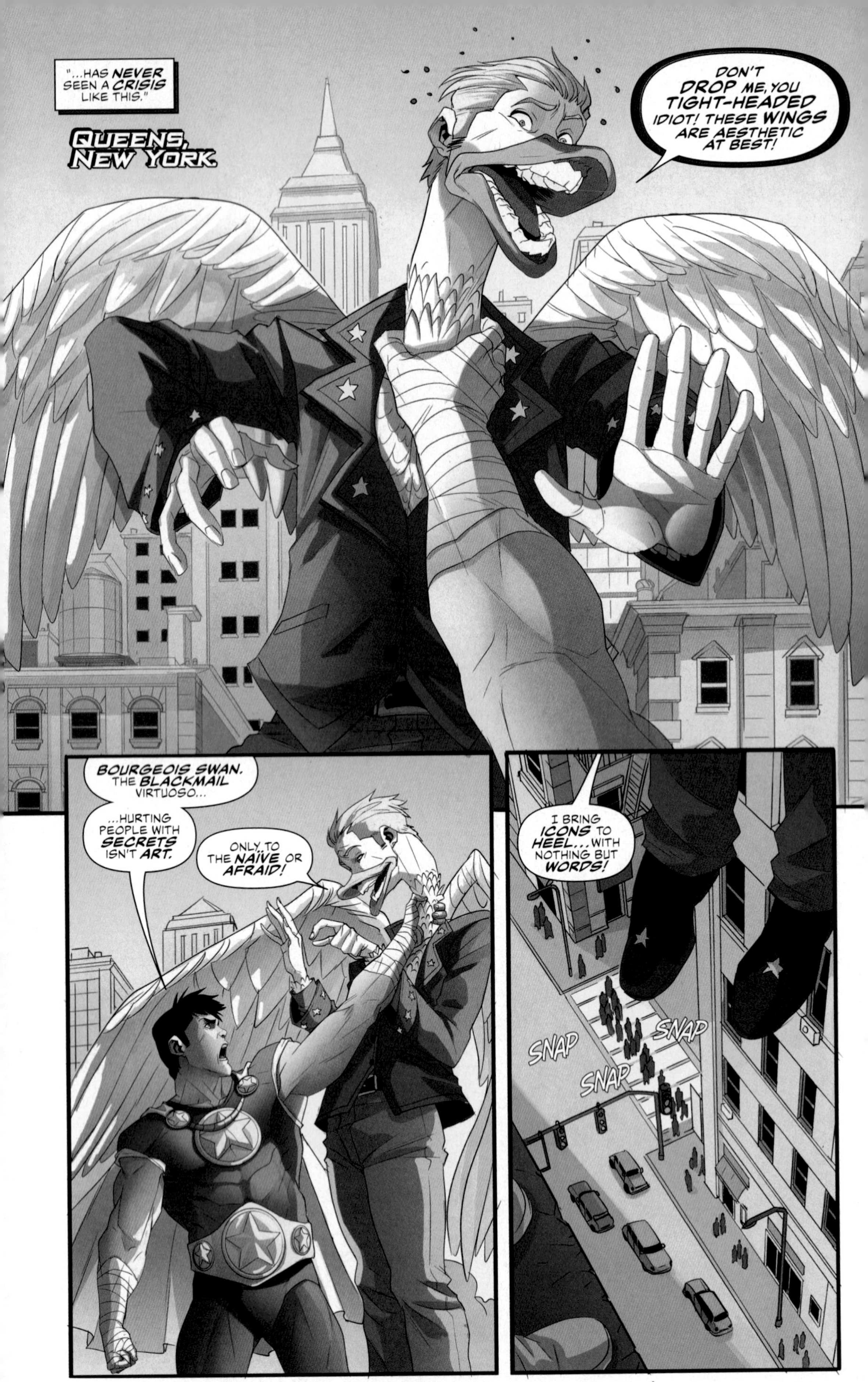
"...HAS NEVER SEEN A CRISIS LIKE THIS."
QUEENS, NEW YORK.
DON'T DROP ME, YOU TIGHT-HEADED IDIOT! THESE WINGS ARE AESTHETIC AT BEST!
BOURGEOIS SWAN. THE BLACKMAIL VIRTUOSO...
...HURTING PEOPLE WITH SECRETS ISN'T ART.
ONLY, TO THE NAÏVE OR AFRAID!
I BRING ICONS TO HEEL... WITH NOTHING BUT WORDS!
SNAP
SNAP
SNAP

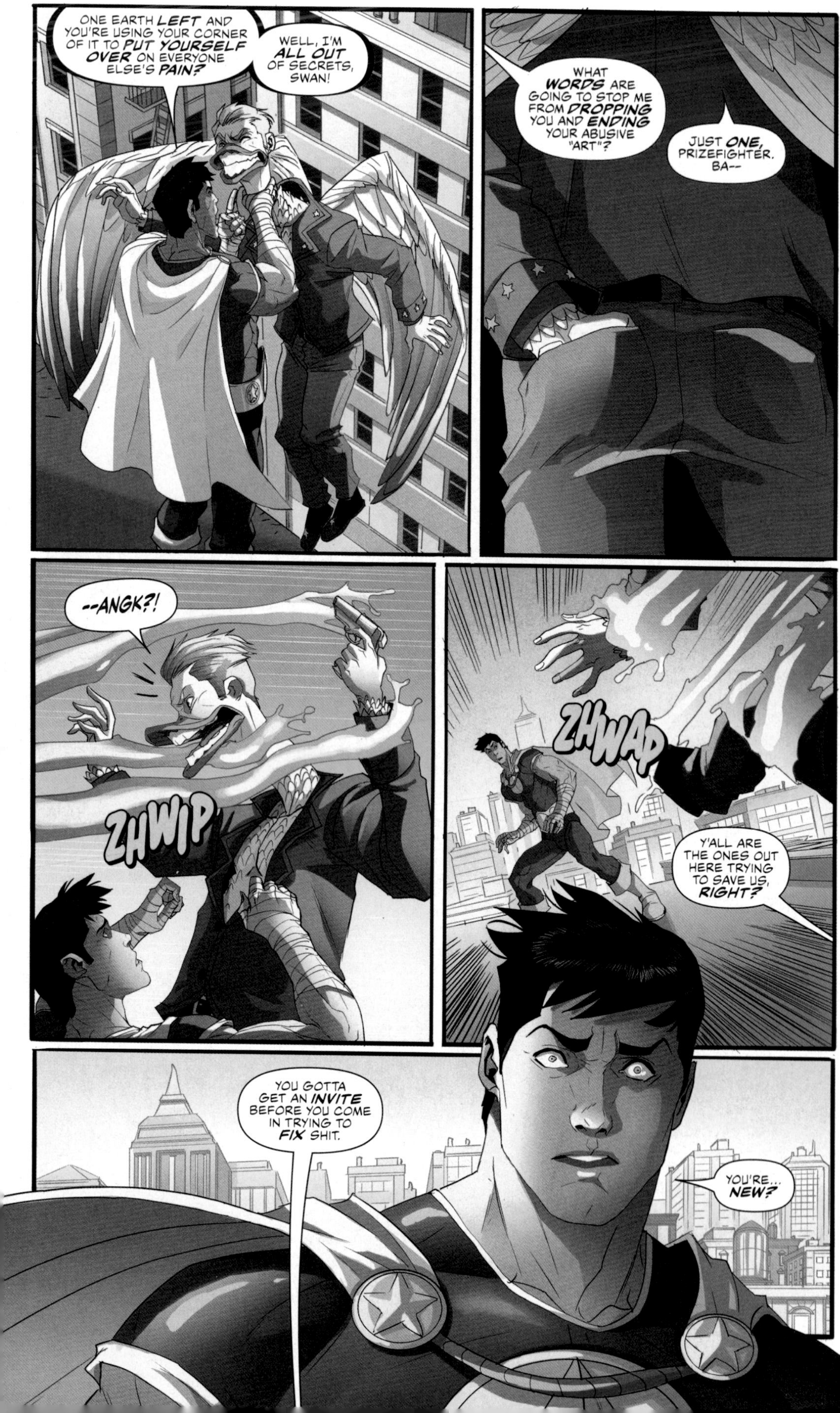
ONE EARTH LEFT AND YOU'RE USING YOUR CORNER OF IT TO PUT YOURSELF OVER ON EVERYONE ELSE'S PAIN?
WELL, I'M ALL OUT OF SECRETS, SWAN!
WHAT WORDS ARE GOING TO STOP ME FROM DROPPING YOU AND ENDING YOUR ABUSIVE "ART"?
JUST ONE, PRIZEFIGHTER. BA--
--ANGK?!
ZHWIP
ZHWAP
Y'ALL ARE THE ONES OUT HERE TRYING TO SAVE US, RIGHT?
YOU GOTTA GET AN INVITE BEFORE YOU COME IN TRYING TO FIX SHIT.
YOU'RE... NEW?

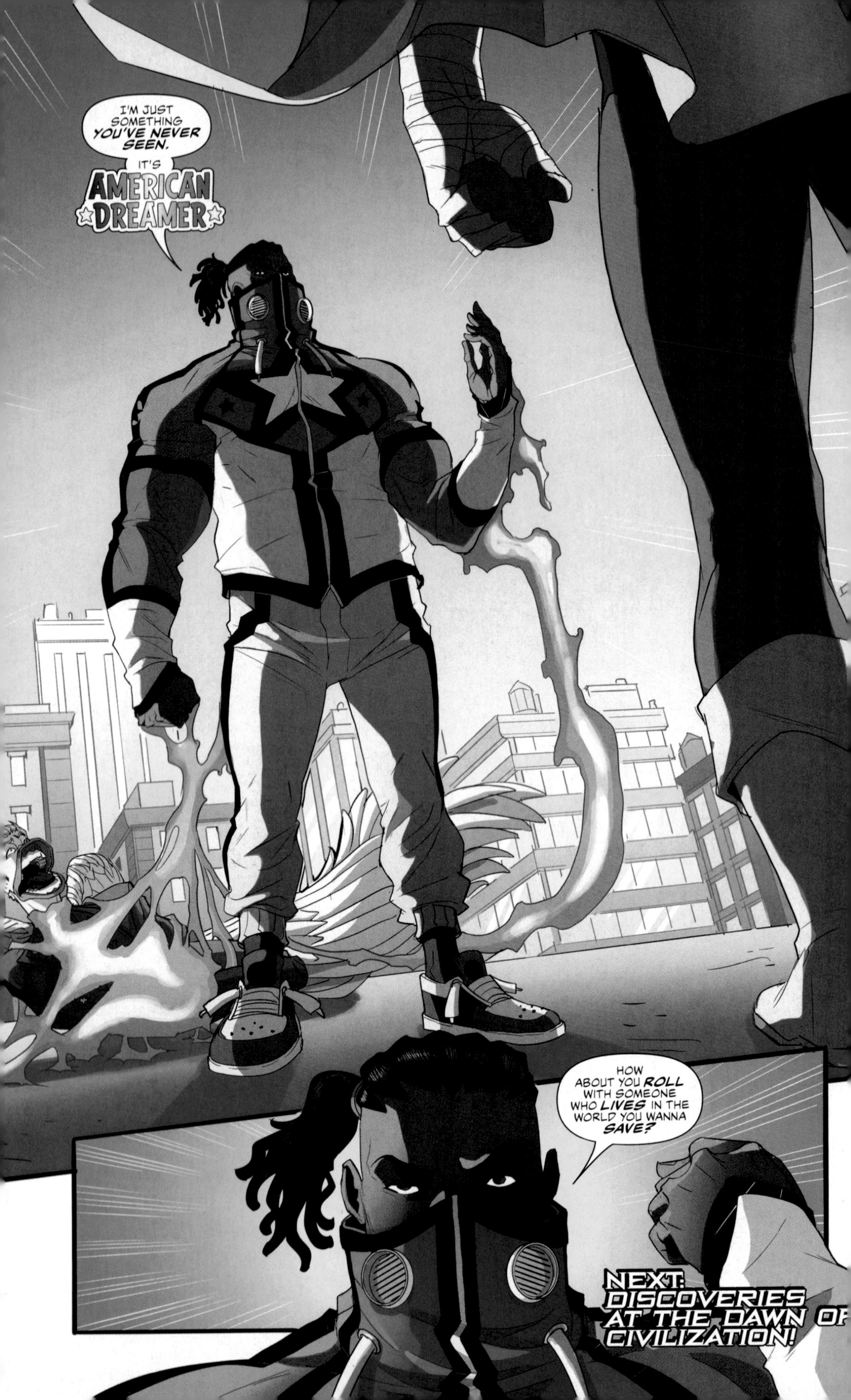
I'M JUST SOMETHING YOU'VE NEVER SEEN.
IT'S AMERICAN DREAMER
HOW ABOUT YOU ROLL WITH SOMEONE WHO LIVES IN THE WORLD YOU WANNA SAVE?
NEXT: DISCOVERIES AT THE DAWN OF CIVILIZATION!

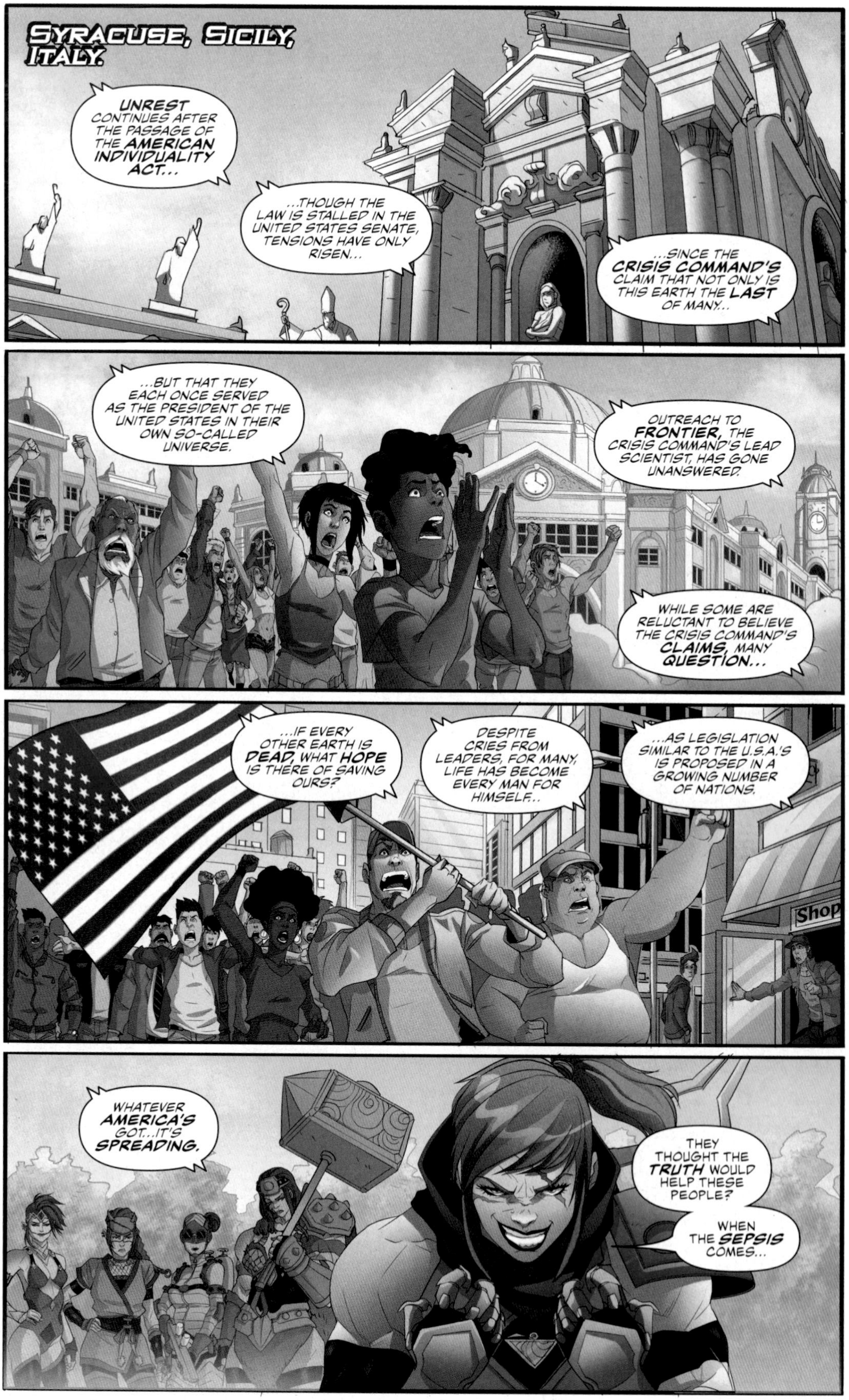
SYRACUSE, SICILY, ITALY.
UNREST CONTINUES AFTER THE PASSAGE OF THE AMERICAN INDIVIDUALITY ACT...
...THOUGH THE LAW IS STALLED IN THE UNITED STATES SENATE, TENSIONS HAVE ONLY RISEN...
...SINCE THE CRISIS COMMAND'S CLAIM THAT NOT ONLY IS THIS EARTH THE LAST OF MANY...
...BUT THAT THEY EACH ONCE SERVED AS THE PRESIDENT OF THE UNITED STATES IN THEIR OWN SO-CALLED UNIVERSE.
OUTREACH TO FRONTIER, THE CRISIS COMMAND'S LEAD SCIENTIST, HAS GONE UNANSWERED.
WHILE SOME ARE RELUCTANT TO BELIEVE THE CRISIS COMMAND'S CLAIMS, MANY QUESTION...
...IF EVERY OTHER EARTH IS DEAD, WHAT HOPE IS THERE OF SAVING OURS?
DESPITE CRIES FROM LEADERS, FOR MANY, LIFE HAS BECOME EVERY MAN FOR HIMSELF...
...AS LEGISLATION SIMILAR TO THE U.S.A.'S IS PROPOSED IN A GROWING NUMBER OF NATIONS.
Shop
WHATEVER AMERICA'S GOT...IT'S SPREADING.
THEY THOUGHT THE TRUTH WOULD HELP THESE PEOPLE?
WHEN THE SEPSIS COMES...

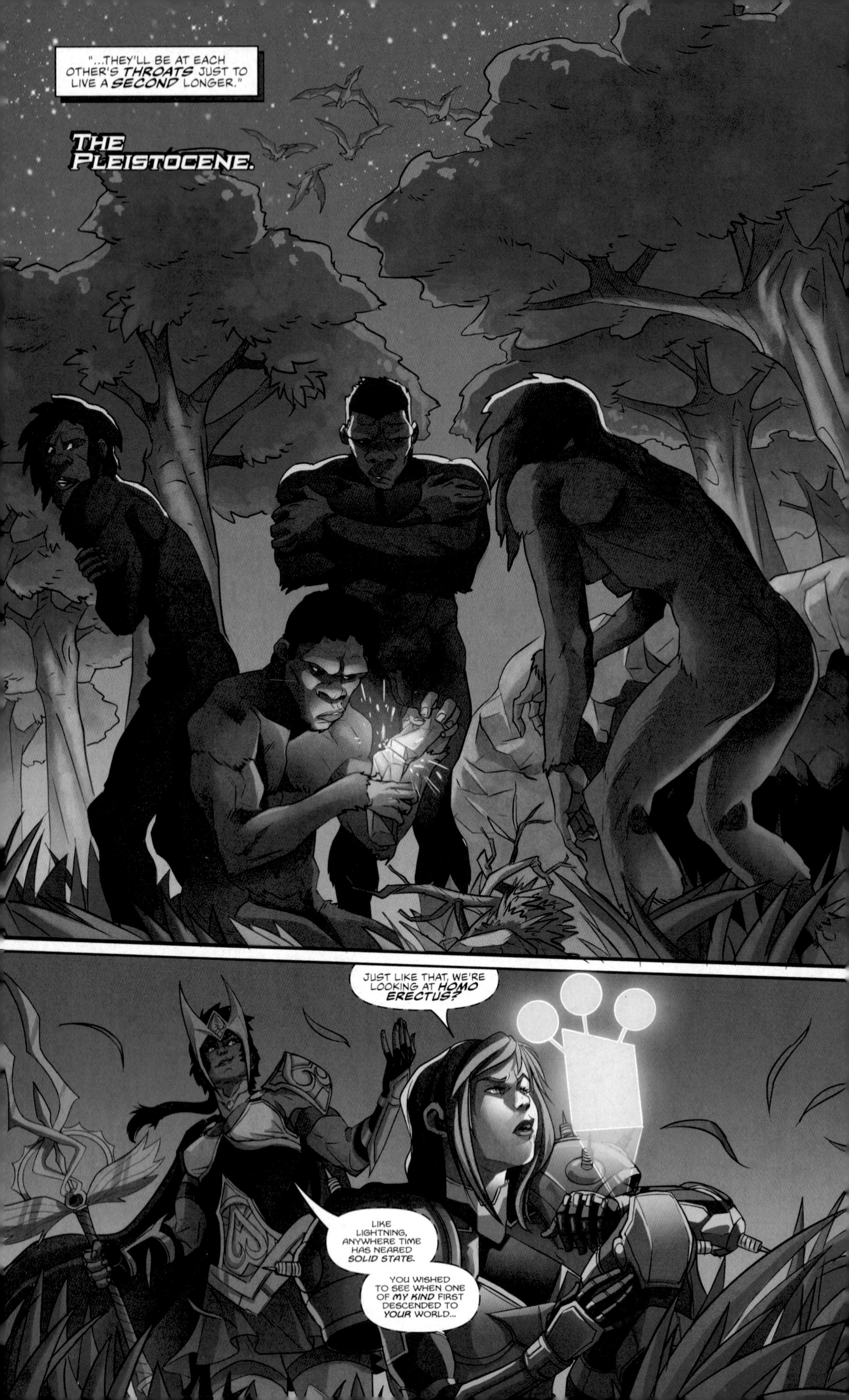
"...THEY'LL BE AT EACH OTHER'S THROATS JUST TO LIVE A SECOND LONGER."
THE PLEISTOCENE.
JUST LIKE THAT, WE'RE LOOKING AT HOMO ERECTUS?
LIKE LIGHTNING, ANYWHERE TIME HAS NEARED SOLID STATE.
YOU WISHED TO SEE WHEN ONE OF MY KIND FIRST DESCENDED TO YOUR WORLD...

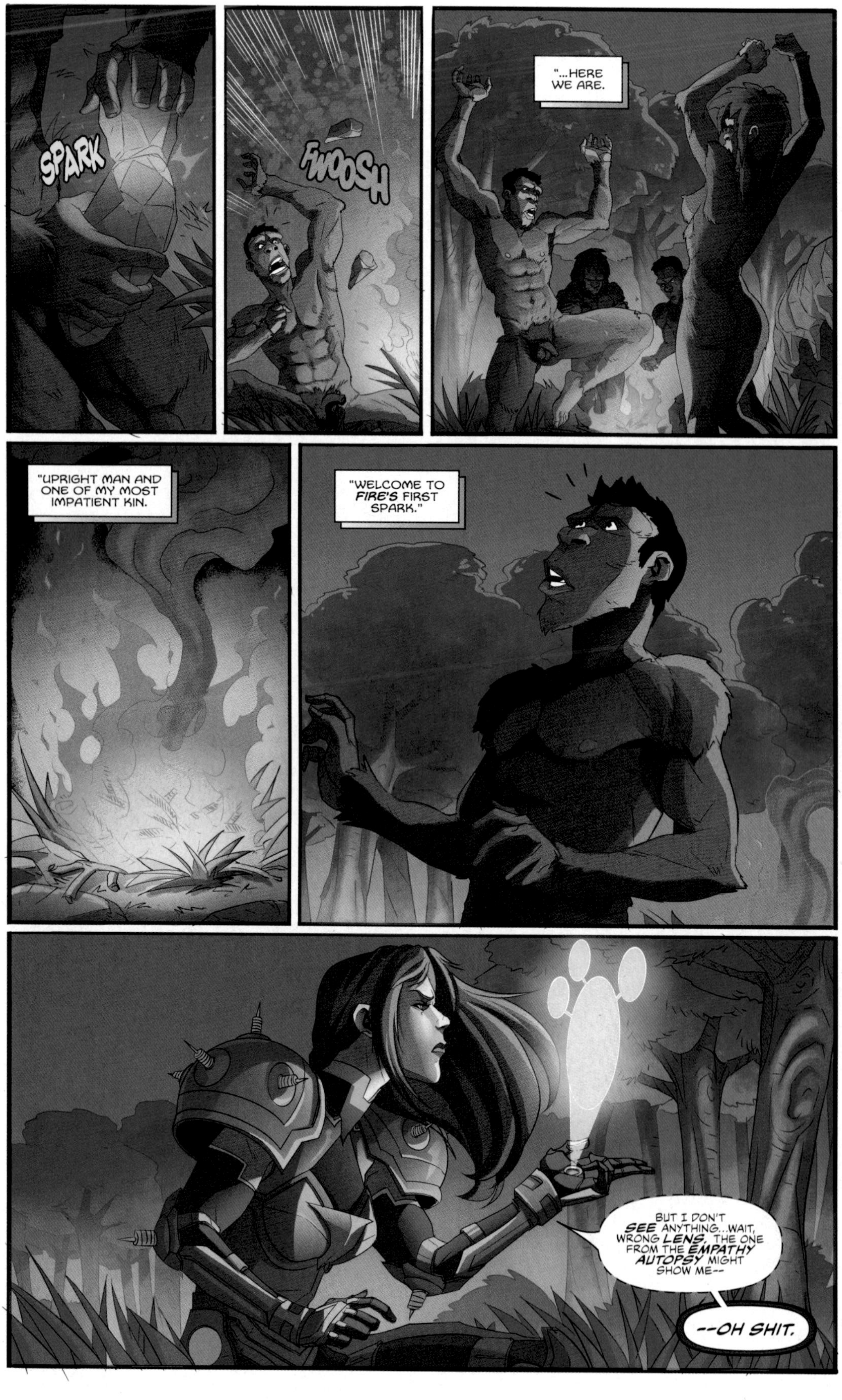
SPARK
FWOOSH
"...HERE WE ARE.
"UPRIGHT MAN AND ONE OF MY MOST IMPATIENT KIN.
"WELCOME TO FIRE'S FIRST SPARK."
BUT I DON'T SEE ANYTHING...WAIT, WRONG LENS. THE ONE FROM THE EMPATHY AUTOPSY MIGHT SHOW ME--
--OH SHIT.

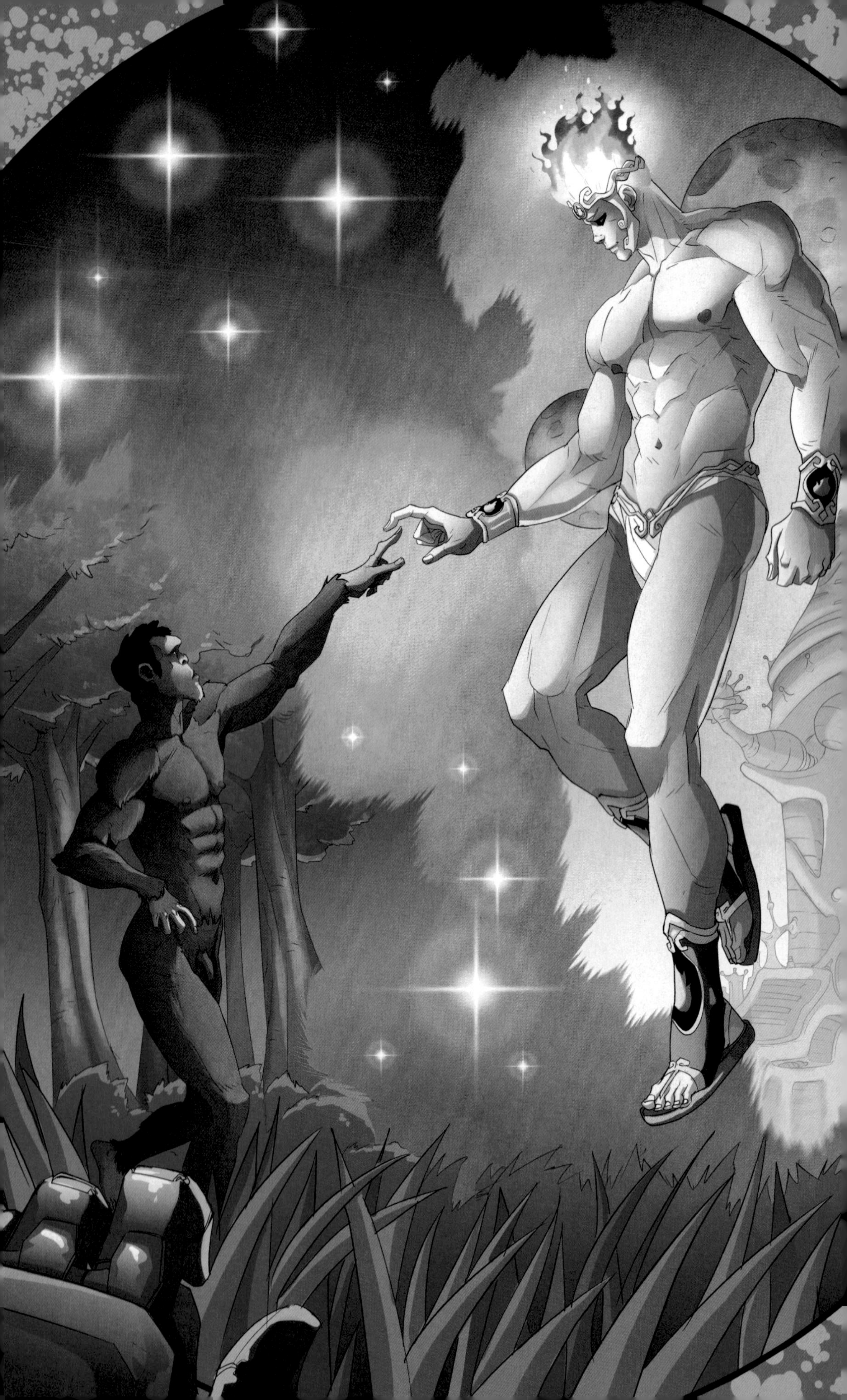

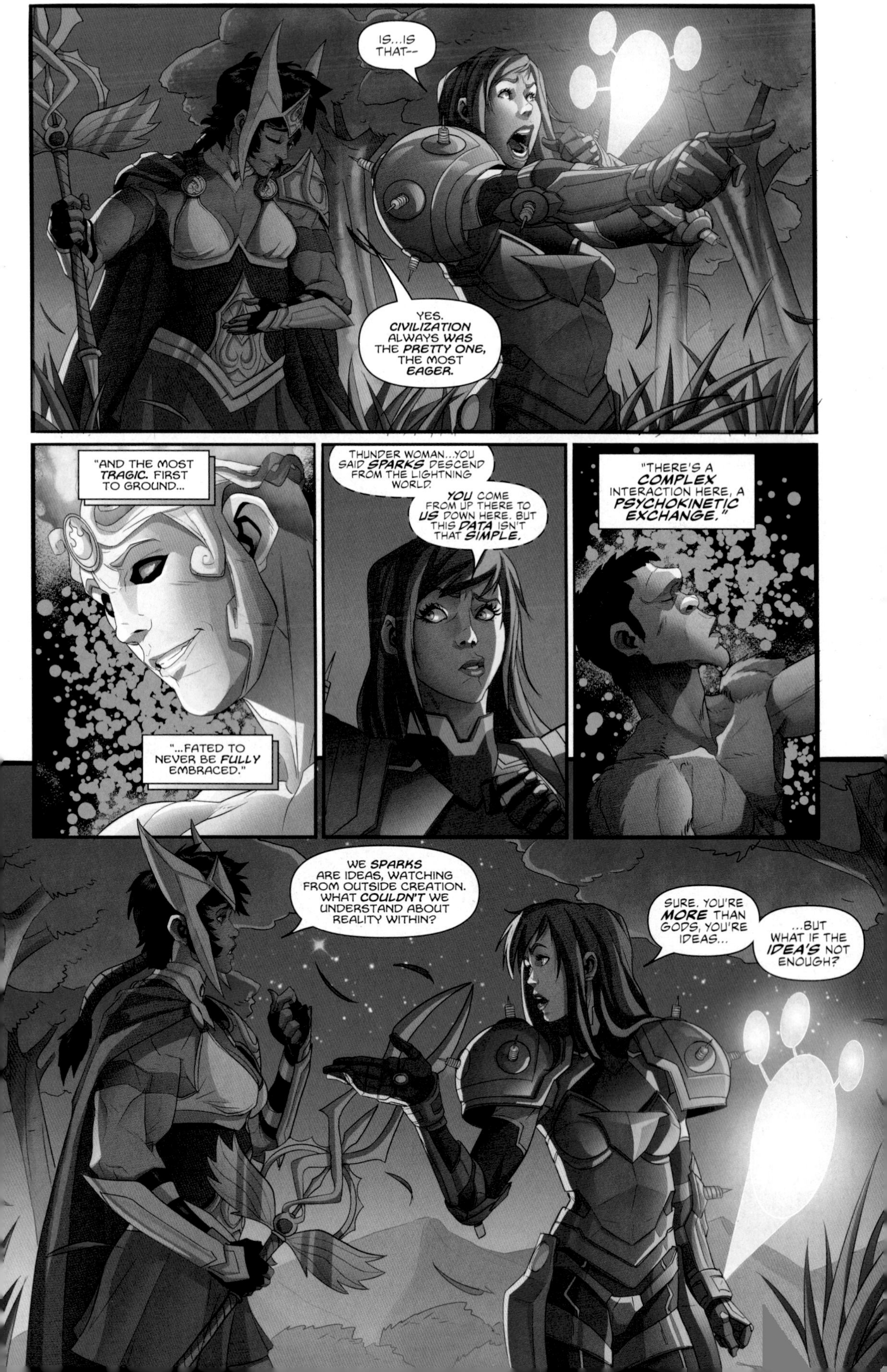
IS...IS THAT--
YES. CIVILIZATION ALWAYS WAS THE PRETTY ONE, THE MOST EAGER.
"AND THE MOST TRAGIC. FIRST TO GROUND...
"...FATED TO NEVER BE FULLY EMBRACED."
THUNDER WOMAN...YOU SAID SPARKS DESCEND FROM THE LIGHTNING WORLD.
YOU COME FROM UP THERE TO US DOWN HERE. BUT THIS DATA ISN'T THAT SIMPLE.
"THERE'S A COMPLEX INTERACTION HERE, A PSYCHOKINETIC EXCHANGE."
WE SPARKS ARE IDEAS, WATCHING FROM OUTSIDE CREATION. WHAT COULDN'T WE UNDERSTAND ABOUT REALITY WITHIN?
SURE. YOU'RE MORE THAN GODS, YOU'RE IDEAS...
...BUT WHAT IF THE IDEA'S NOT ENOUGH?

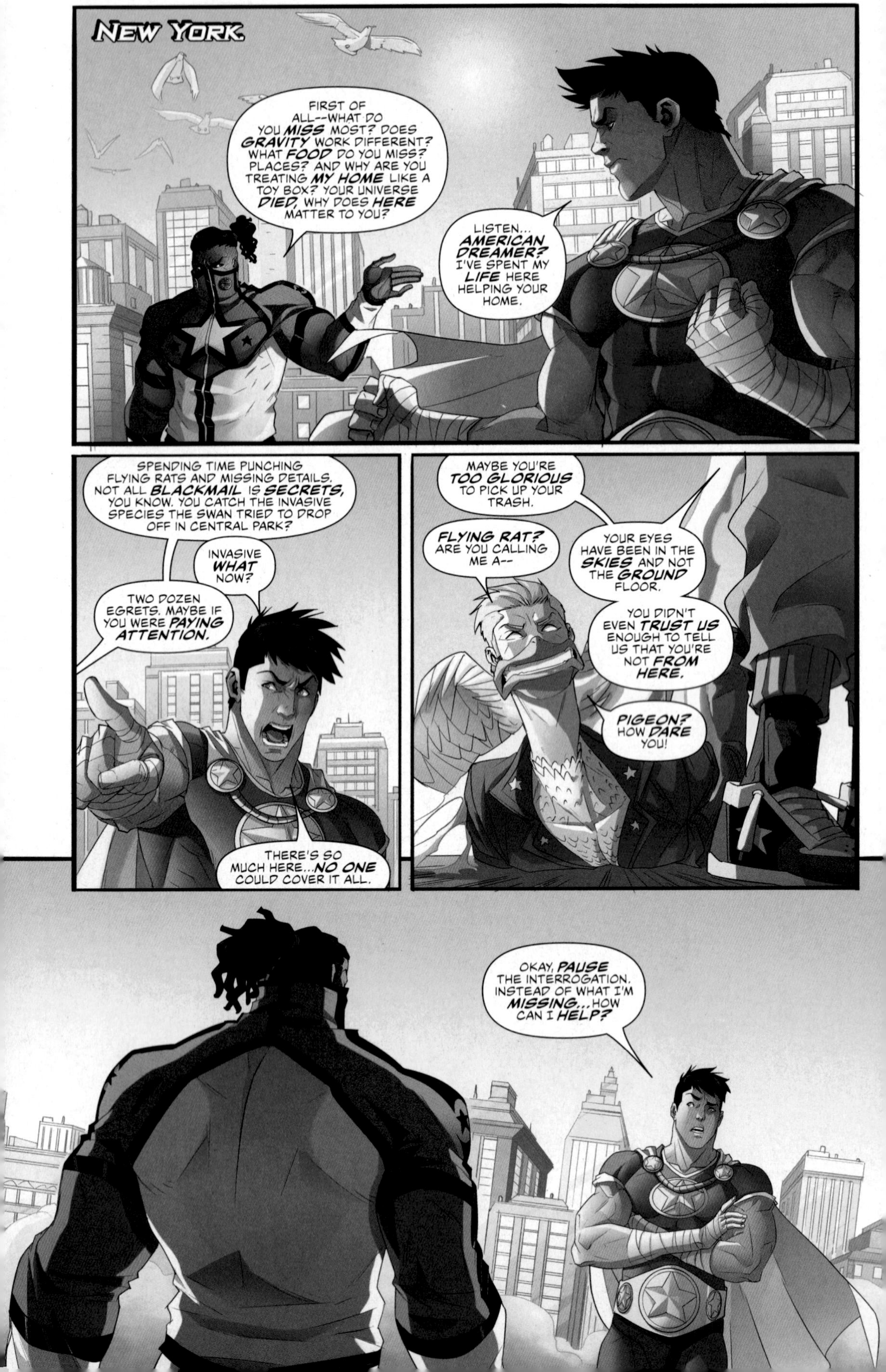
NEW YORK.
FIRST OF ALL--WHAT DO YOU MISS MOST? DOES GRAVITY WORK DIFFERENT? WHAT FOOD DO YOU MISS? PLACES? AND WHY ARE YOU TREATING MY HOME LIKE A TOY BOX? YOUR UNIVERSE DIED, WHY DOES HERE MATTER TO YOU?
LISTEN... AMERICAN DREAMER? I'VE SPENT MY LIFE HERE HELPING YOUR HOME.
SPENDING TIME PUNCHING FLYING RATS AND MISSING DETAILS. NOT ALL BLACKMAIL IS SECRETS, YOU KNOW. YOU CATCH THE INVASIVE SPECIES THE SWAN TRIED TO DROP OFF IN CENTRAL PARK?
INVASIVE WHAT NOW?
TWO DOZEN EGRETS. MAYBE IF YOU WERE PAYING ATTENTION.
THERE'S SO MUCH HERE...NO ONE COULD COVER IT ALL.
MAYBE YOU'RE TOO GLORIOUS TO PICK UP YOUR TRASH.
FLYING RAT? ARE YOU CALLING ME A--
YOUR EYES HAVE BEEN IN THE SKIES AND NOT THE GROUND FLOOR.
YOU DIDN'T EVEN TRUST US ENOUGH TO TELL US THAT YOU'RE NOT FROM HERE.
PIGEON? HOW DARE YOU!
OKAY, PAUSE THE INTERROGATION. INSTEAD OF WHAT I'M MISSING... HOW CAN I HELP?

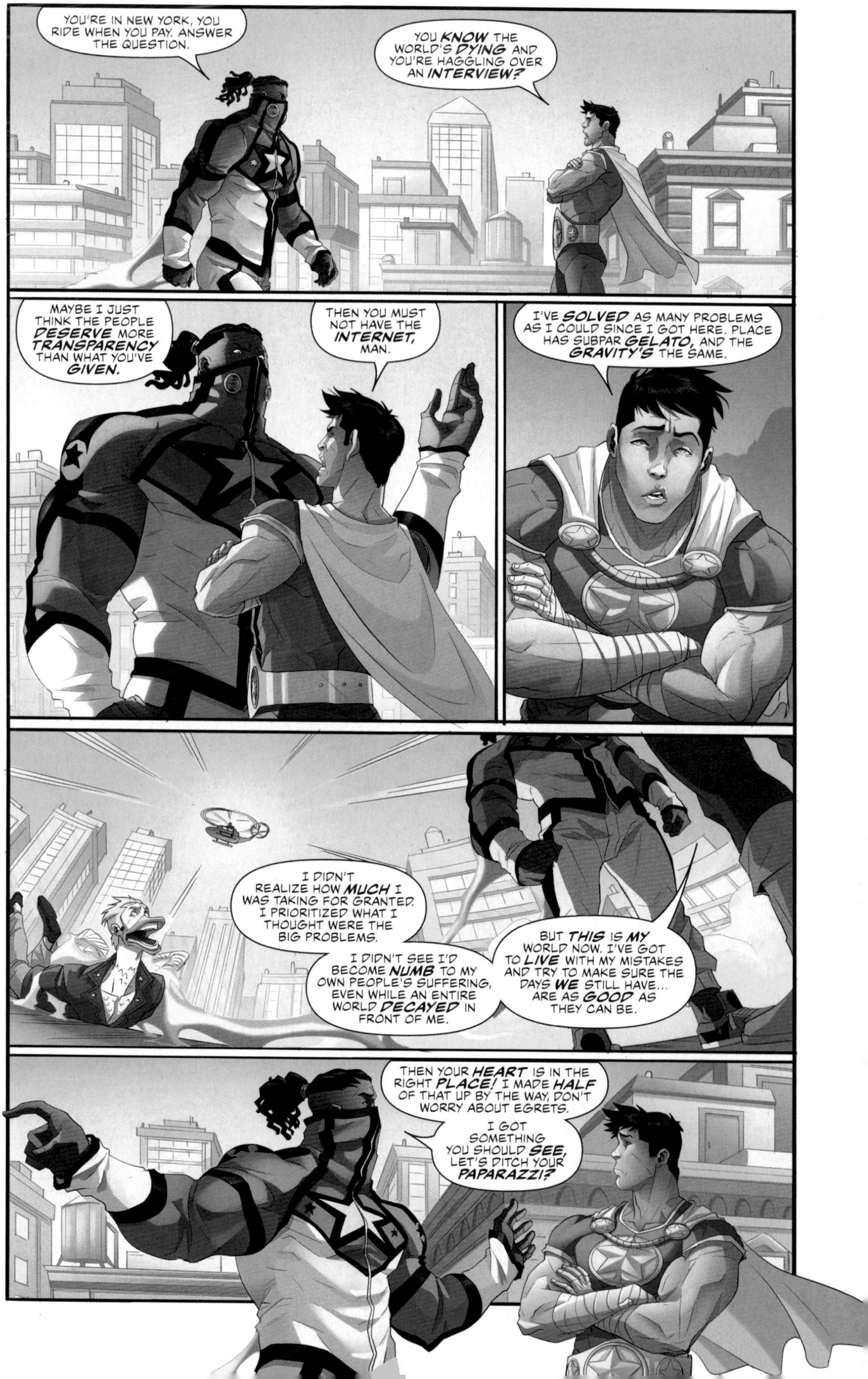
YOU'RE IN NEW YORK, YOU RIDE WHEN YOU PAY. ANSWER THE QUESTION.
YOU KNOW THE WORLD'S DYING AND YOU'RE HAGGLING OVER AN INTERVIEW?
MAYBE I JUST THINK THE PEOPLE DESERVE MORE TRANSPARENCY THAN WHAT YOU'VE GIVEN.
THEN YOU MUST NOT HAVE THE INTERNET, MAN.
I'VE SOLVED AS MANY PROBLEMS AS I COULD SINCE I GOT HERE. PLACE HAS SUBPAR GELATO, AND THE GRAVITY'S THE SAME.
I DIDN'T REALIZE HOW MUCH I WAS TAKING FOR GRANTED. I PRIORITIZED WHAT I THOUGHT WERE THE BIG PROBLEMS.
I DIDN'T SEE I'D BECOME NUMB TO MY OWN PEOPLE'S SUFFERING, EVEN WHILE AN ENTIRE WORLD DECAYED IN FRONT OF ME.
BUT THIS IS MY WORLD NOW. I'VE GOT TO LIVE WITH MY MISTAKES AND TRY TO MAKE SURE THE DAYS WE STILL HAVE... ARE AS GOOD AS THEY CAN BE.
THEN YOUR HEART IS IN THE RIGHT PLACE! I MADE HALF OF THAT UP BY THE WAY, DON'T WORRY ABOUT EGRETS.
I GOT SOMETHING YOU SHOULD SEE, LET'S DITCH YOUR PAPARAZZI?

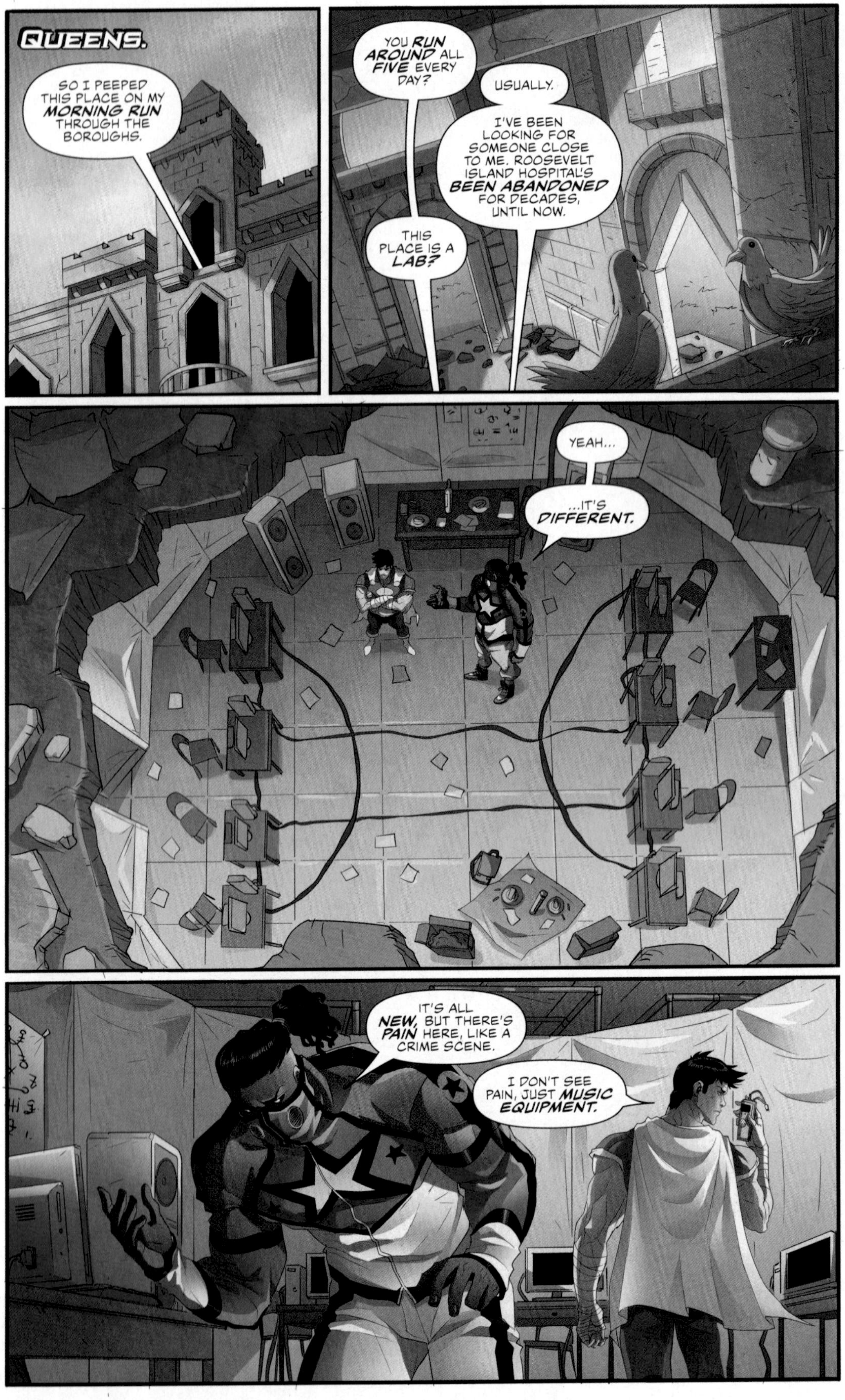
QUEENS.
SO I PEEPED THIS PLACE ON MY MORNING RUN THROUGH THE BOROUGHS.
YOU RUN AROUND ALL FIVE EVERY DAY?
USUALLY.
I'VE BEEN LOOKING FOR SOMEONE CLOSE TO ME. ROOSEVELT ISLAND HOSPITAL'S BEEN ABANDONED FOR DECADES, UNTIL NOW.
THIS PLACE IS A LAB?
YEAH...
...IT'S DIFFERENT.
IT'S ALL NEW, BUT THERE'S PAIN HERE, LIKE A CRIME SCENE.
I DON'T SEE PAIN, JUST MUSIC EQUIPMENT.

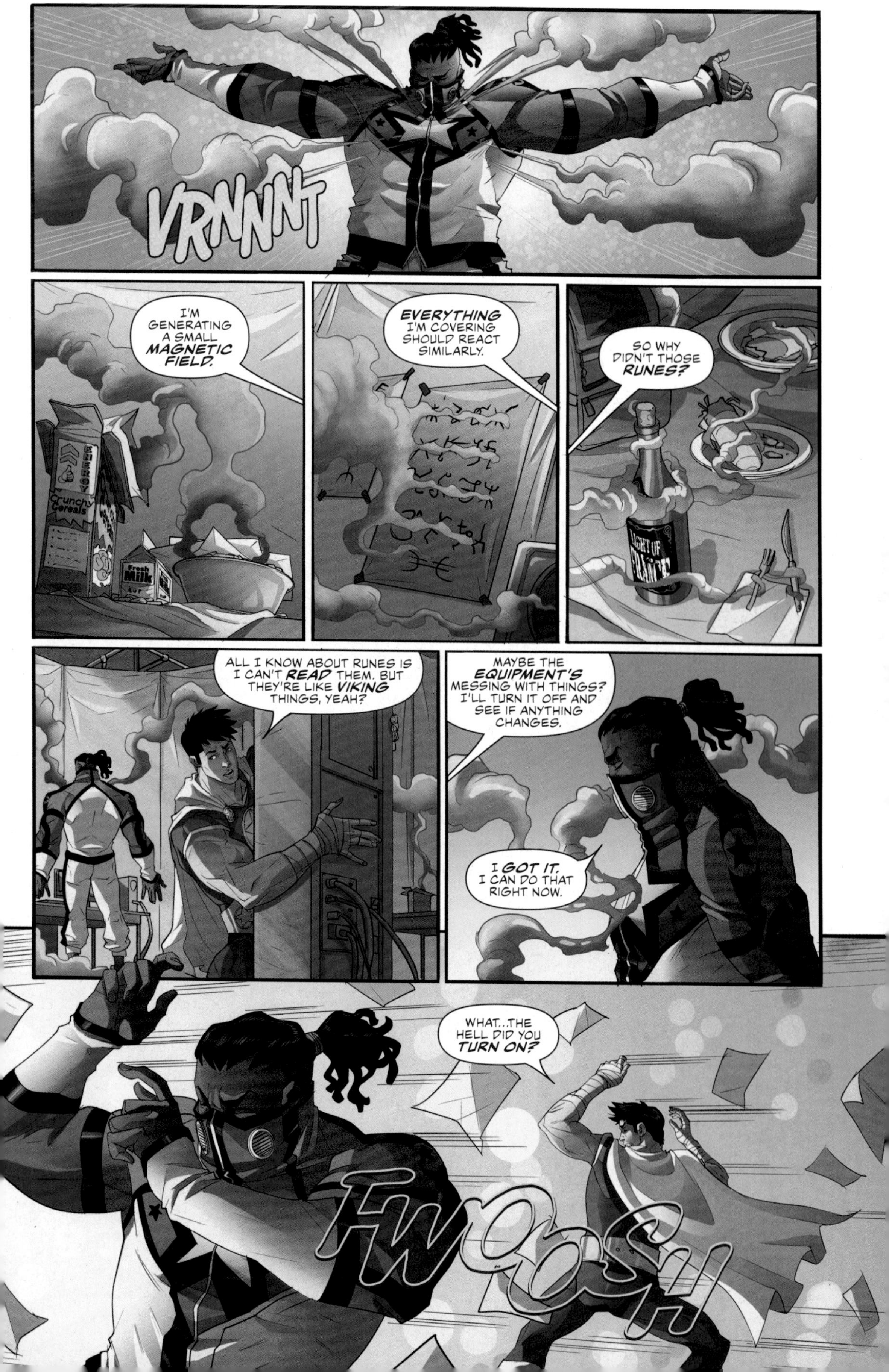
VRNNNT
I'M GENERATING A SMALL MAGNETIC FIELD.
EVERYTHING I'M COVERING SHOULD REACT SIMILARLY.
SO WHY DIDN'T THOSE RUNES?
ALL I KNOW ABOUT RUNES IS I CAN'T READ THEM. BUT THEY'RE LIKE VIKING THINGS, YEAH?
MAYBE THE EQUIPMENT'S MESSING WITH THINGS? I'LL TURN IT OFF AND SEE IF ANYTHING CHANGES.
I GOT IT. I CAN DO THAT RIGHT NOW.
WHAT...THE HELL DID YOU TURN ON?
FWOOSH

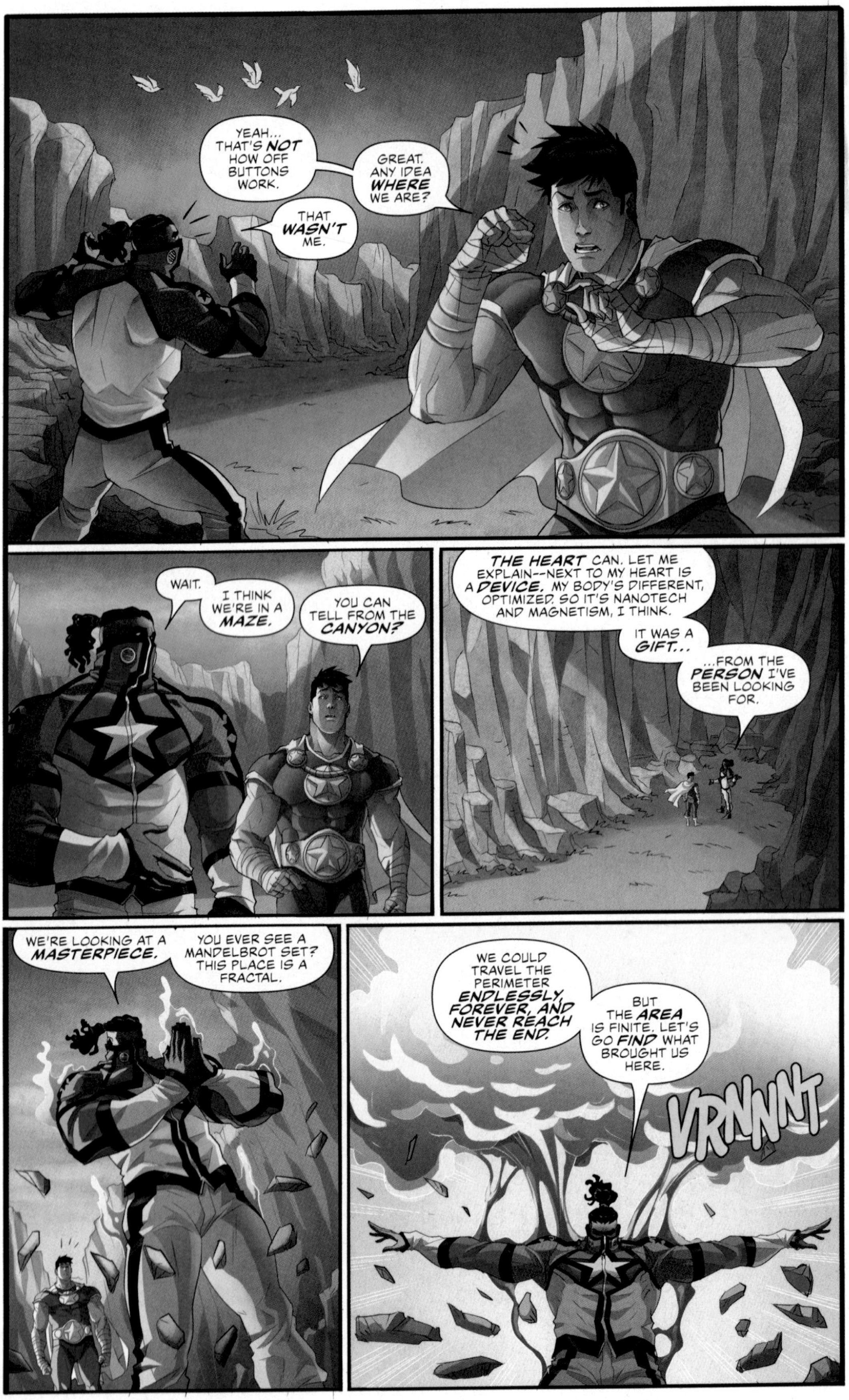
YEAH... THAT'S NOT HOW OFF BUTTONS WORK.
GREAT. ANY IDEA WHERE WE ARE?
THAT WASN'T ME.
WAIT.
I THINK WE'RE IN A MAZE.
YOU CAN TELL FROM THE CANYON?
THE HEART CAN. LET ME EXPLAIN--NEXT TO MY HEART IS A DEVICE. MY BODY'S DIFFERENT, OPTIMIZED. SO IT'S NANOTECH AND MAGNETISM, I THINK.
IT WAS A GIFT...
...FROM THE PERSON I'VE BEEN LOOKING FOR.
WE'RE LOOKING AT A MASTERPIECE.
YOU EVER SEE A MANDELBROT SET? THIS PLACE IS A FRACTAL.
WE COULD TRAVEL THE PERIMETER ENDLESSLY, FOREVER, AND NEVER REACH THE END.
BUT THE AREA IS FINITE. LET'S GO FIND WHAT BROUGHT US HERE.
VRNNNT

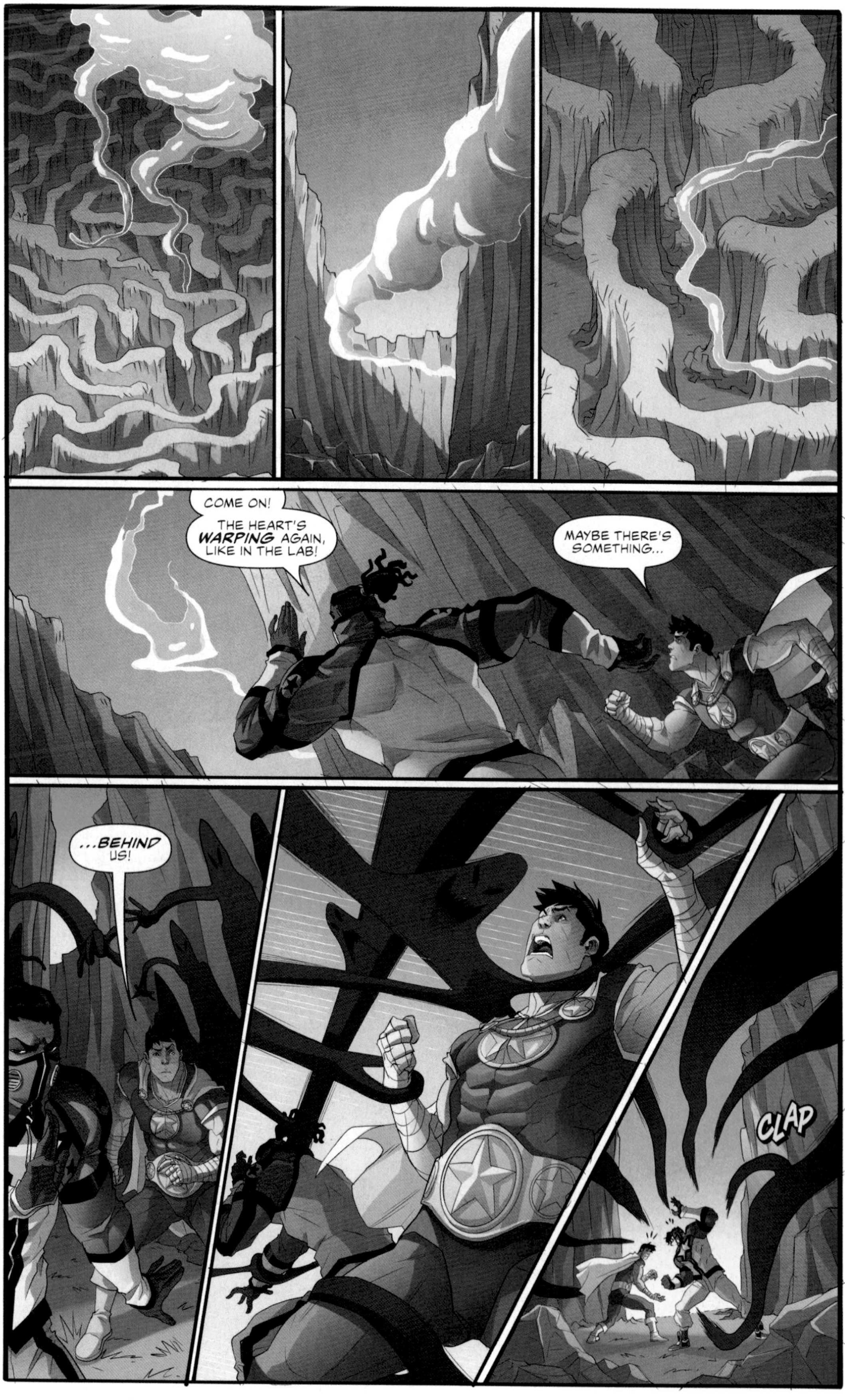
COME ON!
THE HEART'S WARPING AGAIN, LIKE IN THE LAB!
MAYBE THERE'S SOMETHING...
...BEHIND US!
CLAP

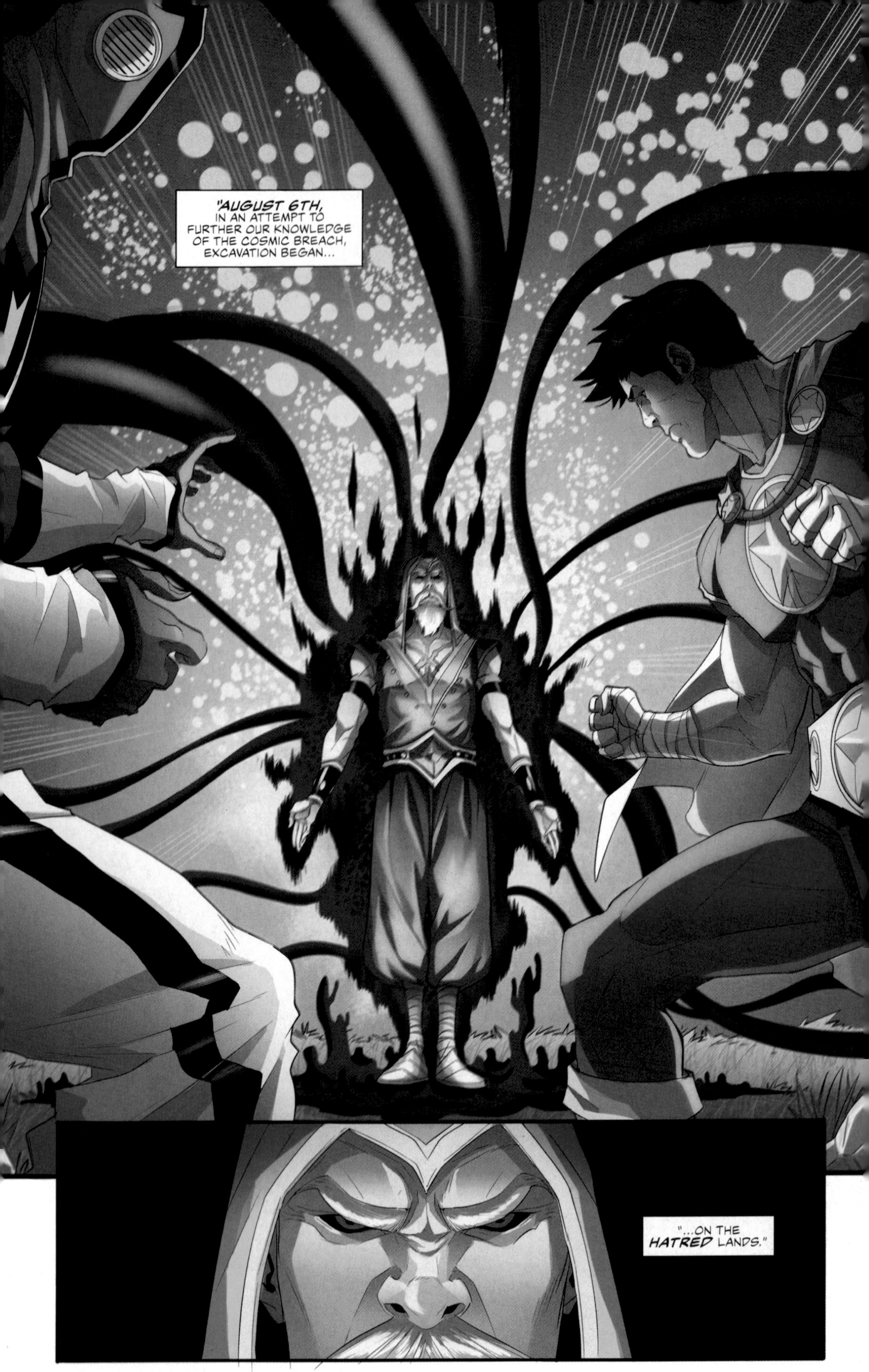
"AUGUST 6TH, IN AN ATTEMPT TO FURTHER OUR KNOWLEDGE OF THE COSMIC BREACH, EXCAVATION BEGAN...
"...ON THE HATRED LANDS."

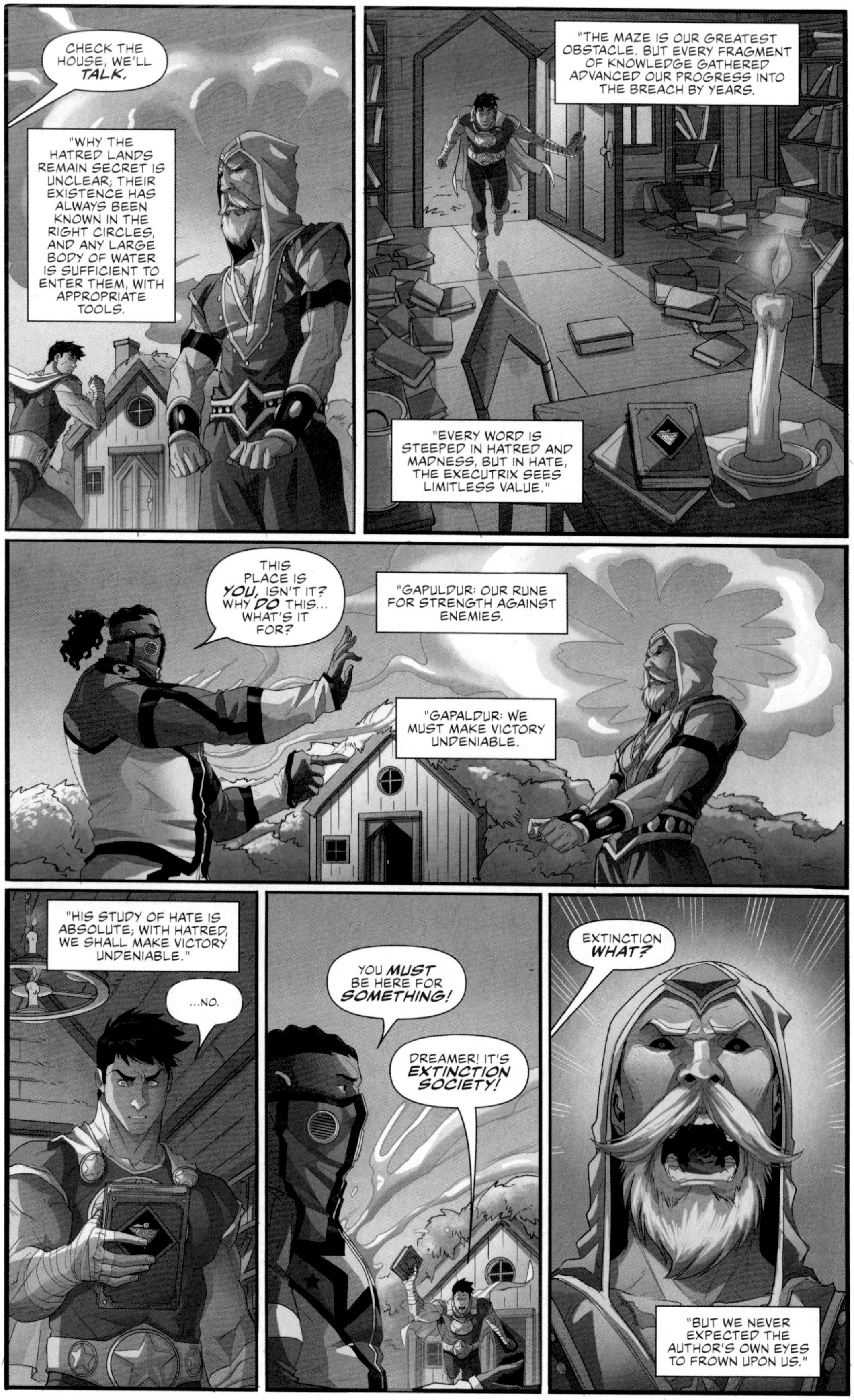
CHECK THE HOUSE, WE'LL TALK.
"WHY THE HATRED LANDS REMAIN SECRET IS UNCLEAR; THEIR EXISTENCE HAS ALWAYS BEEN KNOWN IN THE RIGHT CIRCLES, AND ANY LARGE BODY OF WATER IS SUFFICIENT TO ENTER THEM, WITH APPROPRIATE TOOLS.
"THE MAZE IS OUR GREATEST OBSTACLE. BUT EVERY FRAGMENT OF KNOWLEDGE GATHERED ADVANCED OUR PROGRESS INTO THE BREACH BY YEARS.
"EVERY WORD IS STEEPED IN HATRED AND MADNESS, BUT IN HATE, THE EXECUTRIX SEES LIMITLESS VALUE."
THIS PLACE IS YOU, ISN'T IT? WHY DO THIS... WHAT'S IT FOR?
"GAPULDUR: OUR RUNE FOR STRENGTH AGAINST ENEMIES.
"GAPALDUR: WE MUST MAKE VICTORY UNDENIABLE.
"HIS STUDY OF HATE IS ABSOLUTE; WITH HATRED, WE SHALL MAKE VICTORY UNDENIABLE."
...NO.
YOU MUST BE HERE FOR SOMETHING!
DREAMER! IT'S EXTINCTION SOCIETY!
EXTINCTION WHAT?
"BUT WE NEVER EXPECTED THE AUTHOR'S OWN EYES TO FROWN UPON US."

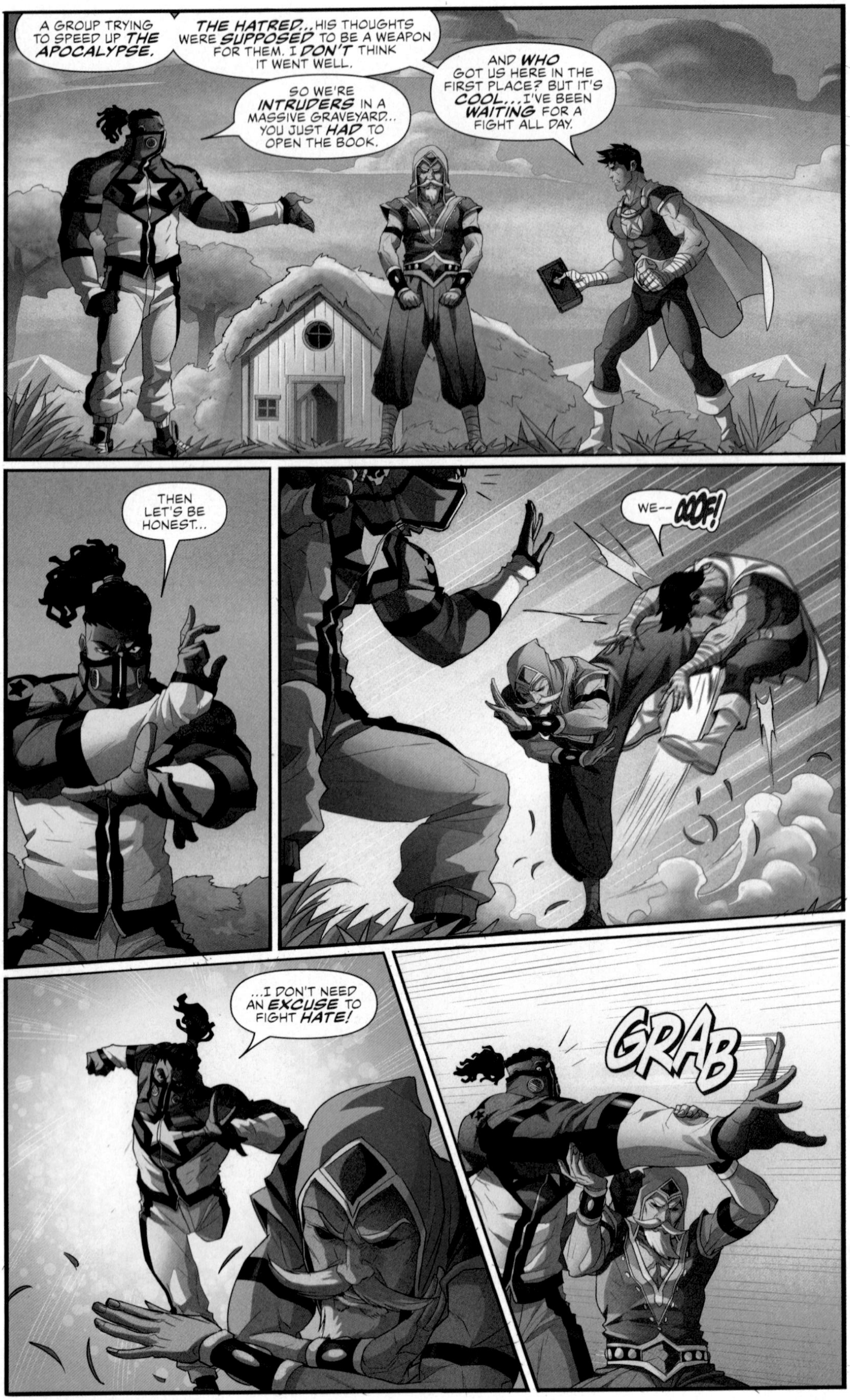
A GROUP TRYING TO SPEED UP THE APOCALYPSE.
THE HATRED... HIS THOUGHTS WERE SUPPOSED TO BE A WEAPON FOR THEM. I DON'T THINK IT WENT WELL.
SO WE'RE INTRUDERS IN A MASSIVE GRAVEYARD... YOU JUST HAD TO OPEN THE BOOK.
AND WHO GOT US HERE IN THE FIRST PLACE? BUT IT'S COOL... I'VE BEEN WAITING FOR A FIGHT ALL DAY.
THEN LET'S BE HONEST...
WE-- OOOF!
...I DON'T NEED AN EXCUSE TO FIGHT HATE!
GRAB

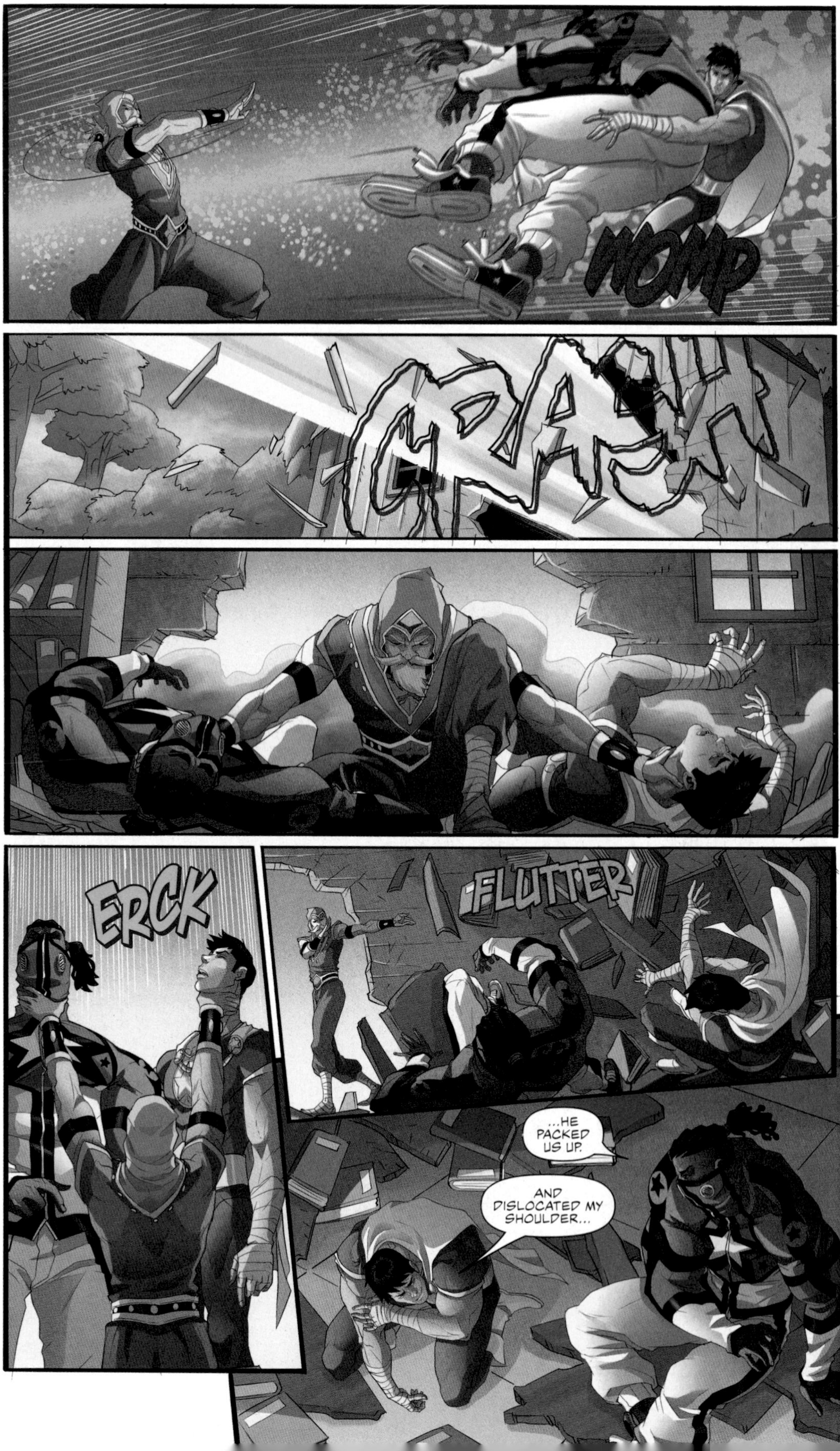
WOMP
CRASH
ERCK
FLUTTER
...HE PACKED US UP.
AND DISLOCATED MY SHOULDER...

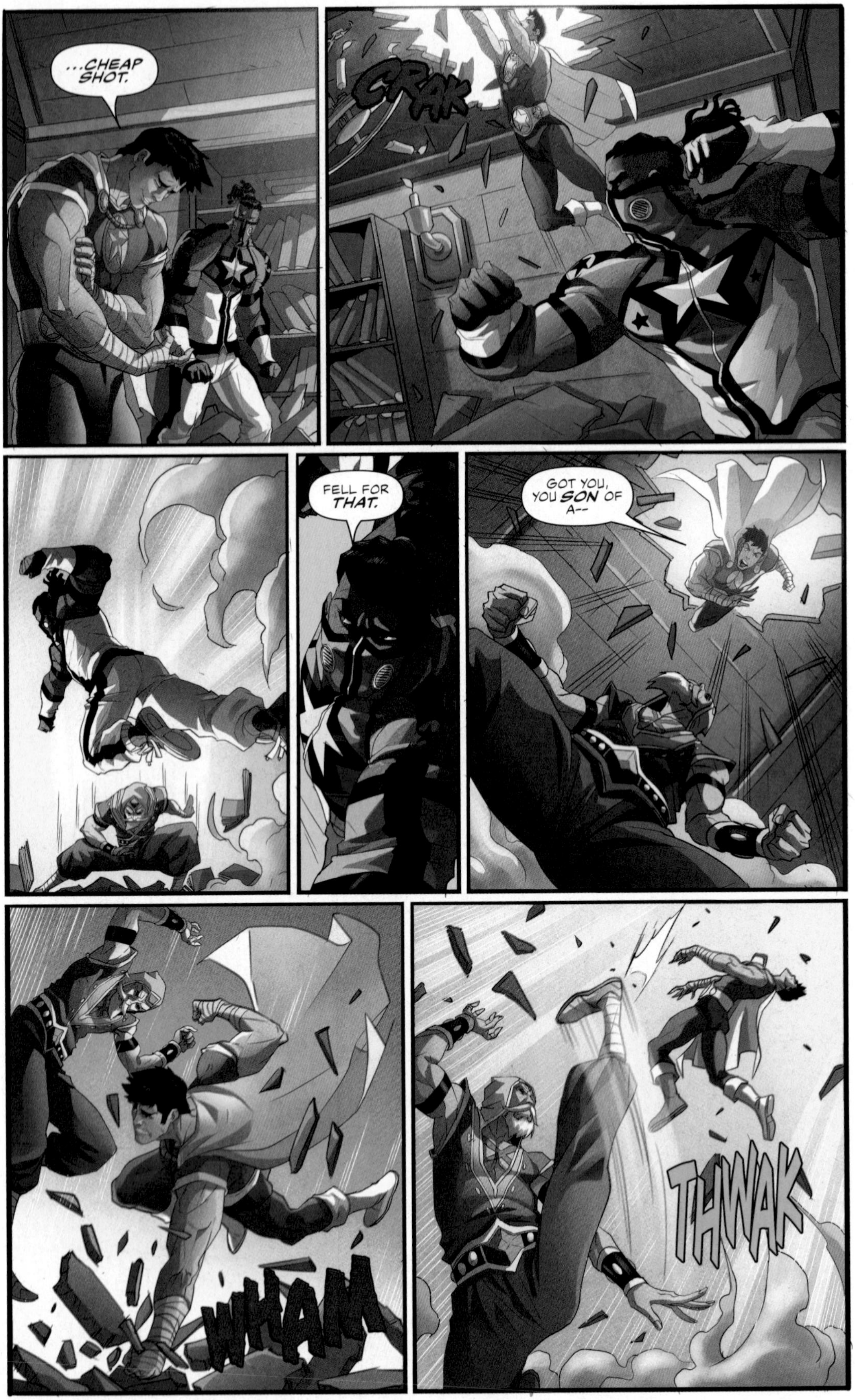
...CHEAP SHOT.
CRAK
FELL FOR THAT.
GOT YOU, YOU SON OF A--
WHAM
THWAK

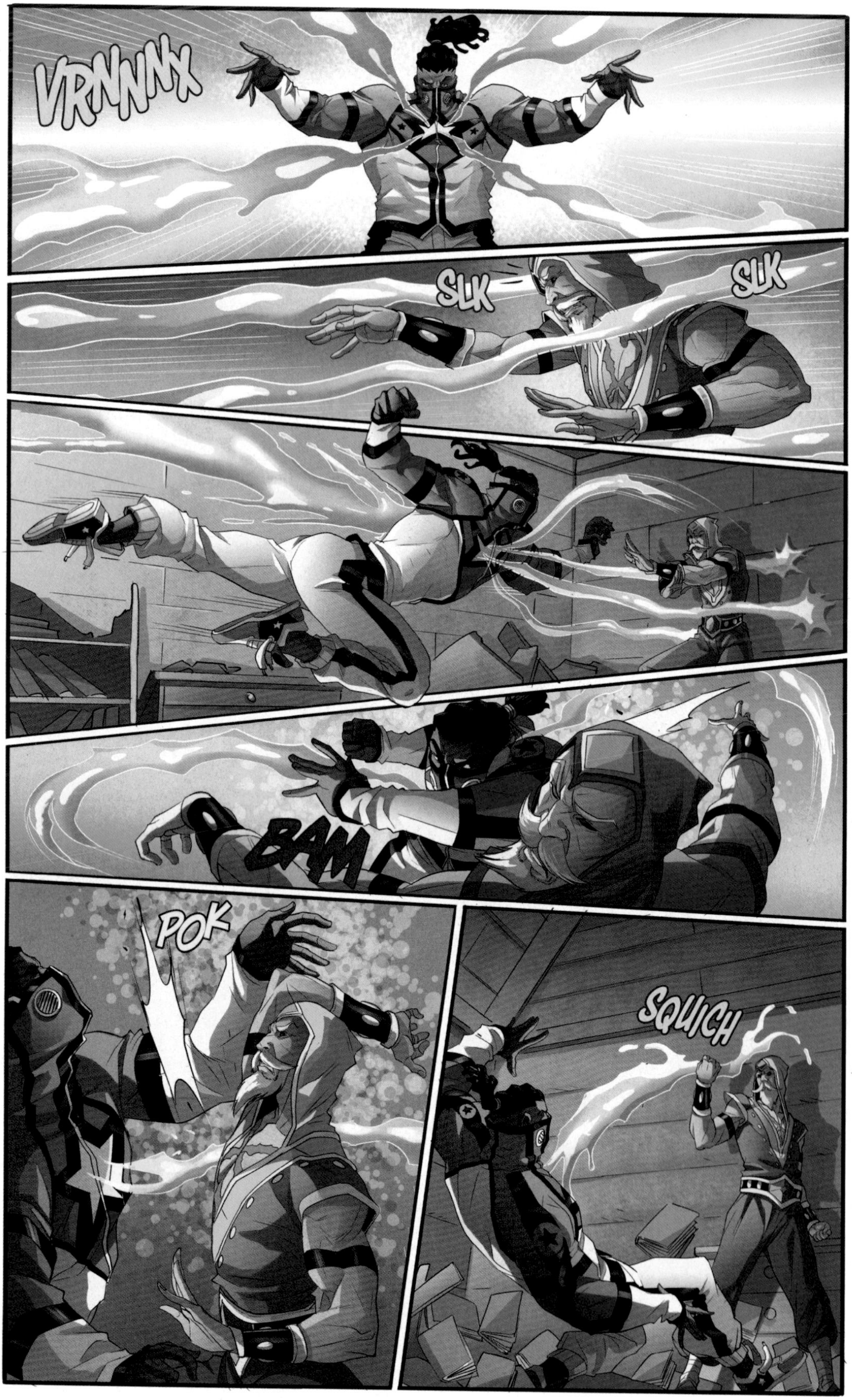
VRNNNX
SLK
SLK
BAM
POK
SQUICH

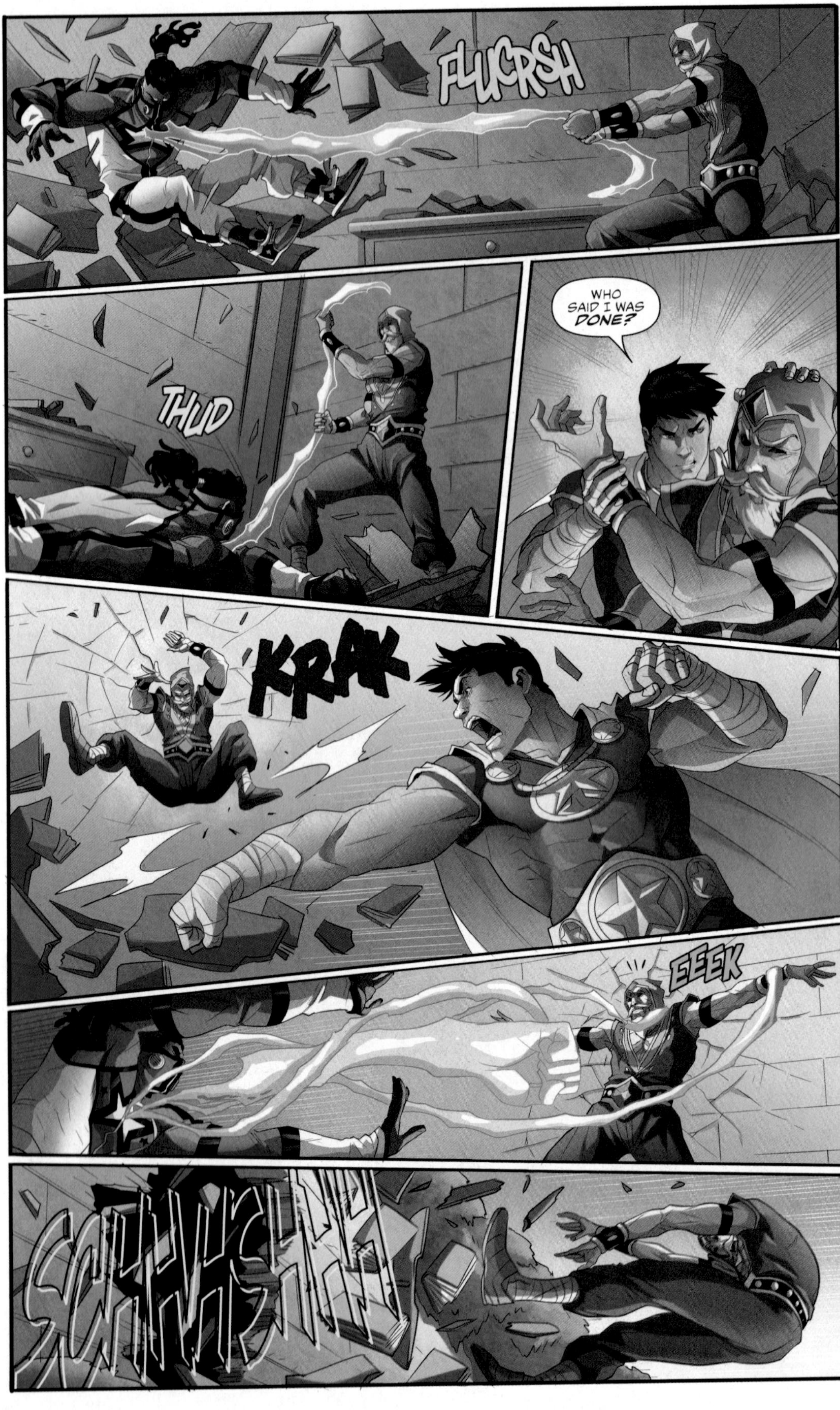
FLUCRSH
THUD
WHO SAID I WAS DONE?
KRAK
EEEK

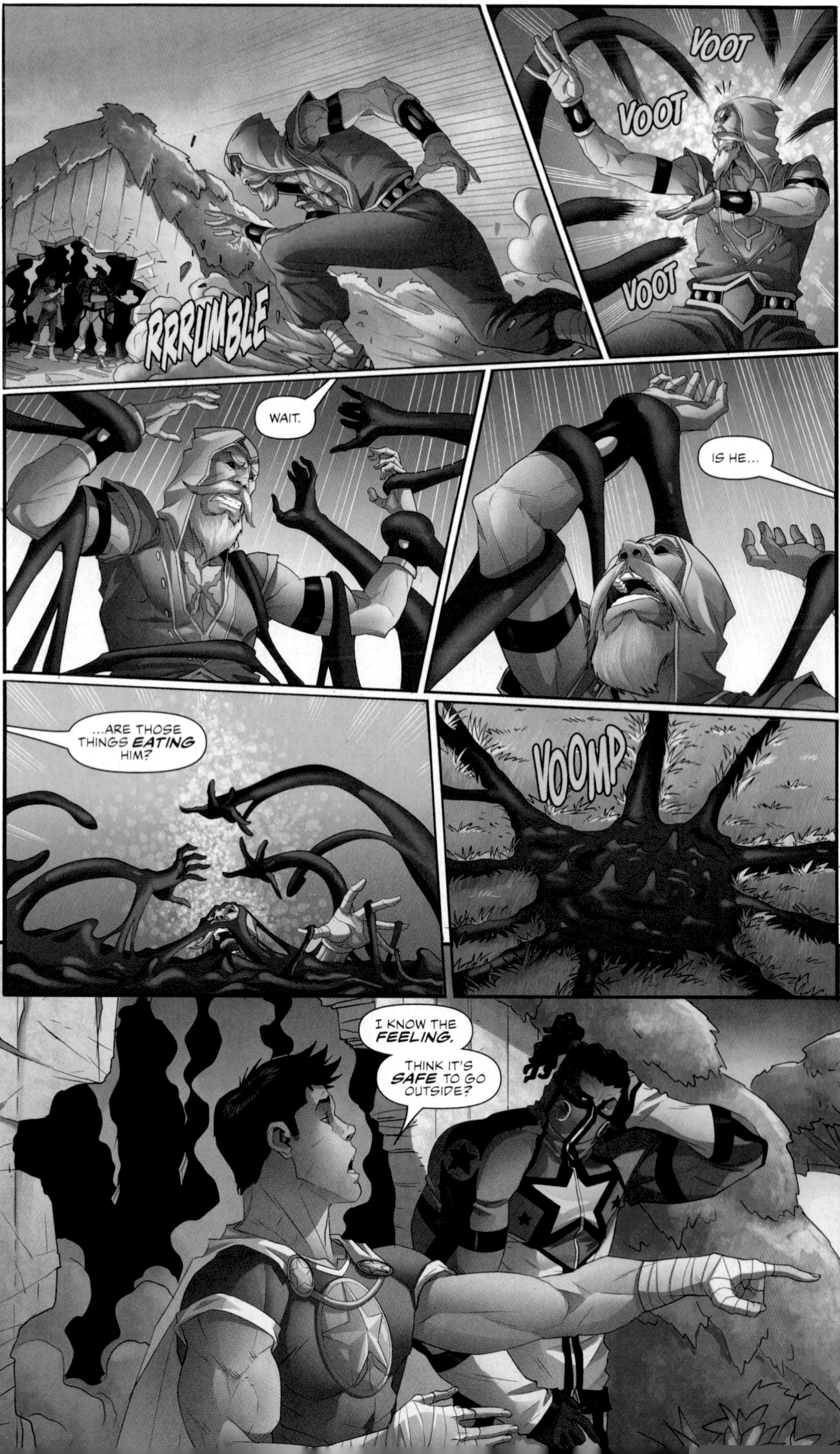
RRRUMBLE
VOOT
VOOT
VOOT
WAIT.
IS HE...
...ARE THOSE THINGS EATING HIM?
VOOMP
I KNOW THE FEELING.
THINK IT'S SAFE TO GO OUTSIDE?

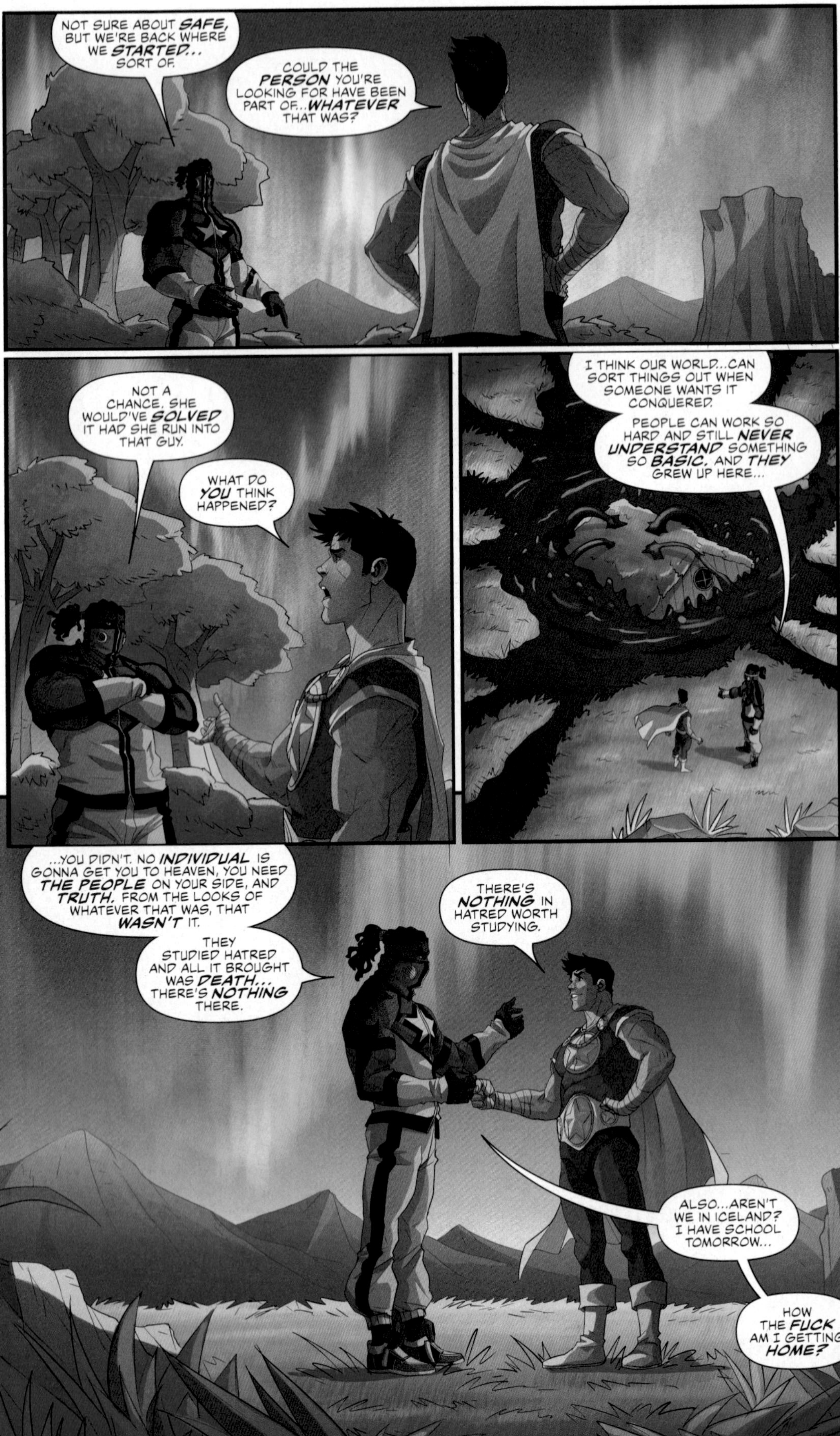
NOT SURE ABOUT SAFE, BUT WE'RE BACK WHERE WE STARTED... SORT OF.
COULD THE PERSON YOU'RE LOOKING FOR HAVE BEEN PART OF...WHATEVER THAT WAS?
NOT A CHANCE. SHE WOULD'VE SOLVED IT HAD SHE RUN INTO THAT GUY.
WHAT DO YOU THINK HAPPENED?
I THINK OUR WORLD...CAN SORT THINGS OUT WHEN SOMEONE WANTS IT CONQUERED.
PEOPLE CAN WORK SO HARD AND STILL NEVER UNDERSTAND SOMETHING SO BASIC. AND THEY GREW UP HERE...
...YOU DIDN'T. NO INDIVIDUAL IS GONNA GET YOU TO HEAVEN. YOU NEED THE PEOPLE ON YOUR SIDE, AND TRUTH. FROM THE LOOKS OF WHATEVER THAT WAS, THAT WASN'T IT.
THEY STUDIED HATRED AND ALL IT BROUGHT WAS DEATH... THERE'S NOTHING THERE.
THERE'S NOTHING IN HATRED WORTH STUDYING.
ALSO...AREN'T WE IN ICELAND? I HAVE SCHOOL TOMORROW...
HOW THE FUCK AM I GETTING HOME?

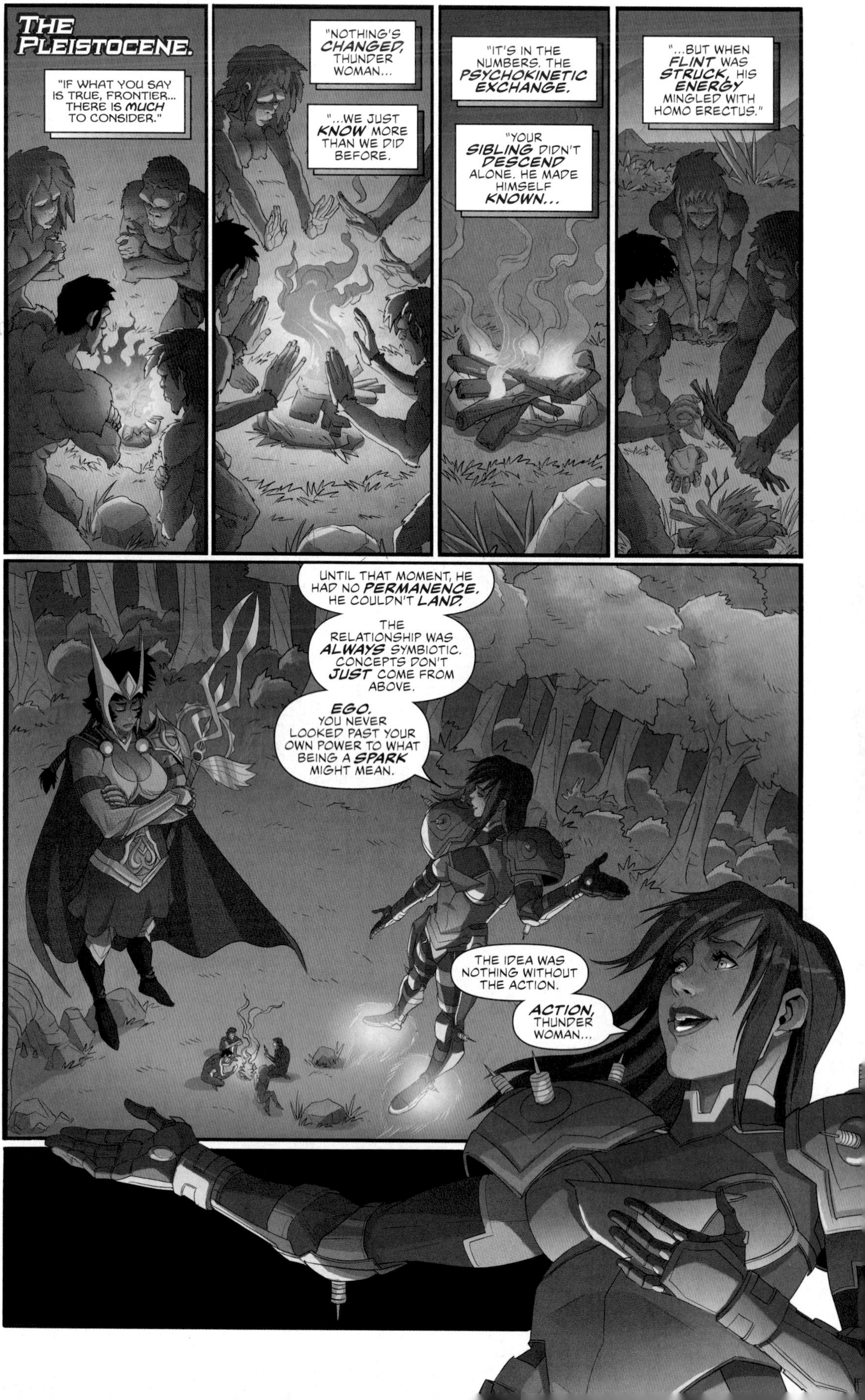
THE PLEISTOCENE.
"IF WHAT YOU SAY IS TRUE, FRONTIER... THERE IS MUCH TO CONSIDER."
"NOTHING'S CHANGED, THUNDER WOMAN...
"...WE JUST KNOW MORE THAN WE DID BEFORE.
"IT'S IN THE NUMBERS. THE PSYCHOKINETIC EXCHANGE.
"YOUR SIBLING DIDN'T DESCEND ALONE. HE MADE HIMSELF KNOWN...
"...BUT WHEN FLINT WAS STRUCK, HIS ENERGY MINGLED WITH HOMO ERECTUS."
UNTIL THAT MOMENT, HE HAD NO PERMANENCE. HE COULDN'T LAND.
THE RELATIONSHIP WAS ALWAYS SYMBIOTIC. CONCEPTS DON'T JUST COME FROM ABOVE.
EGO. YOU NEVER LOOKED PAST YOUR OWN POWER TO WHAT BEING A SPARK MIGHT MEAN.
THE IDEA WAS NOTHING WITHOUT THE ACTION.
ACTION, THUNDER WOMAN...

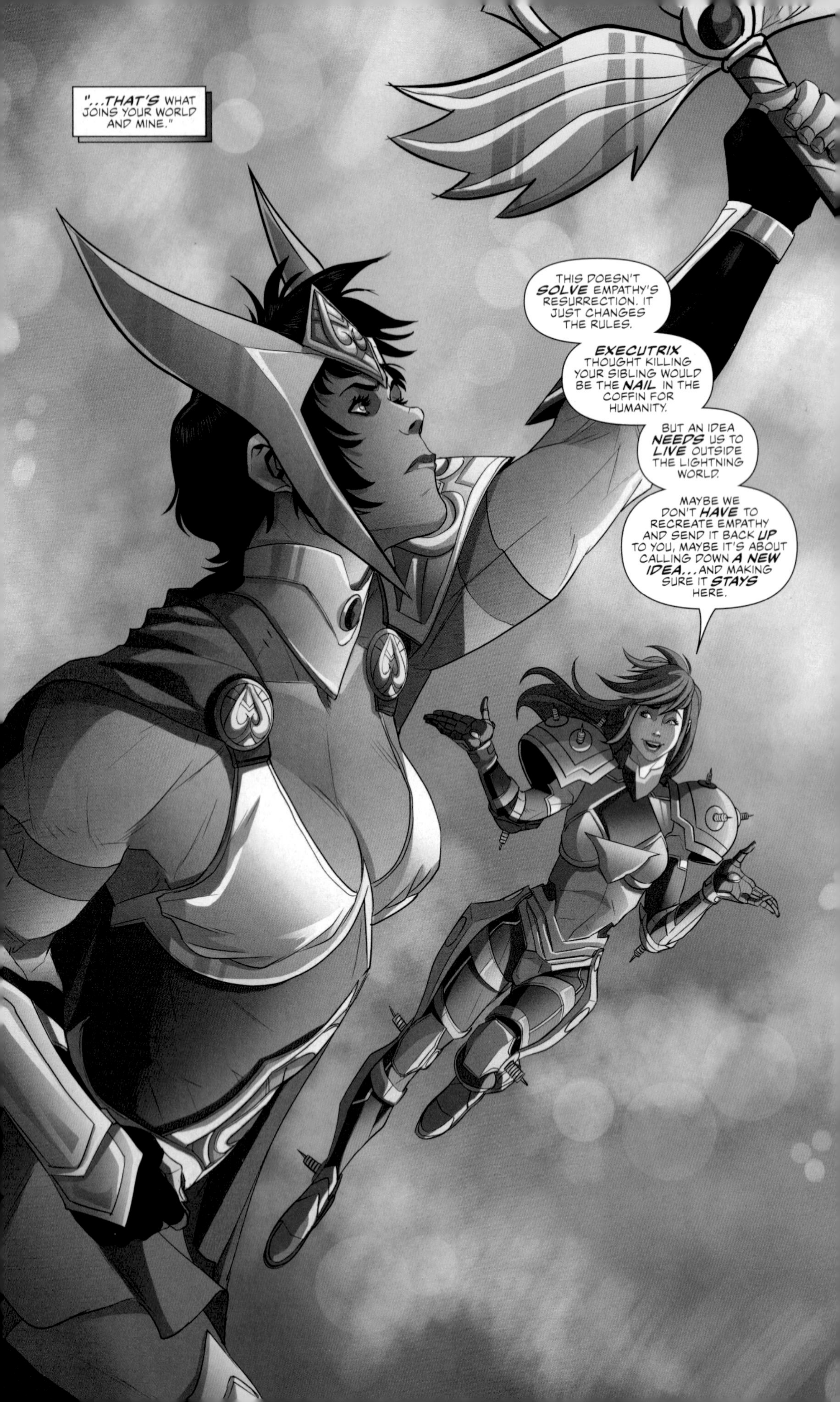
"...THAT'S WHAT JOINS YOUR WORLD AND MINE."
THIS DOESN'T SOLVE EMPATHY'S RESURRECTION. IT JUST CHANGES THE RULES.
EXECUTRIX THOUGHT KILLING YOUR SIBLING WOULD BE THE NAIL IN THE COFFIN FOR HUMANITY.
BUT AN IDEA NEEDS US TO LIVE OUTSIDE THE LIGHTNING WORLD.
MAYBE WE DON'T HAVE TO RECREATE EMPATHY AND SEND IT BACK UP TO YOU, MAYBE IT'S ABOUT CALLING DOWN A NEW IDEA...AND MAKING SURE IT STAYS HERE.

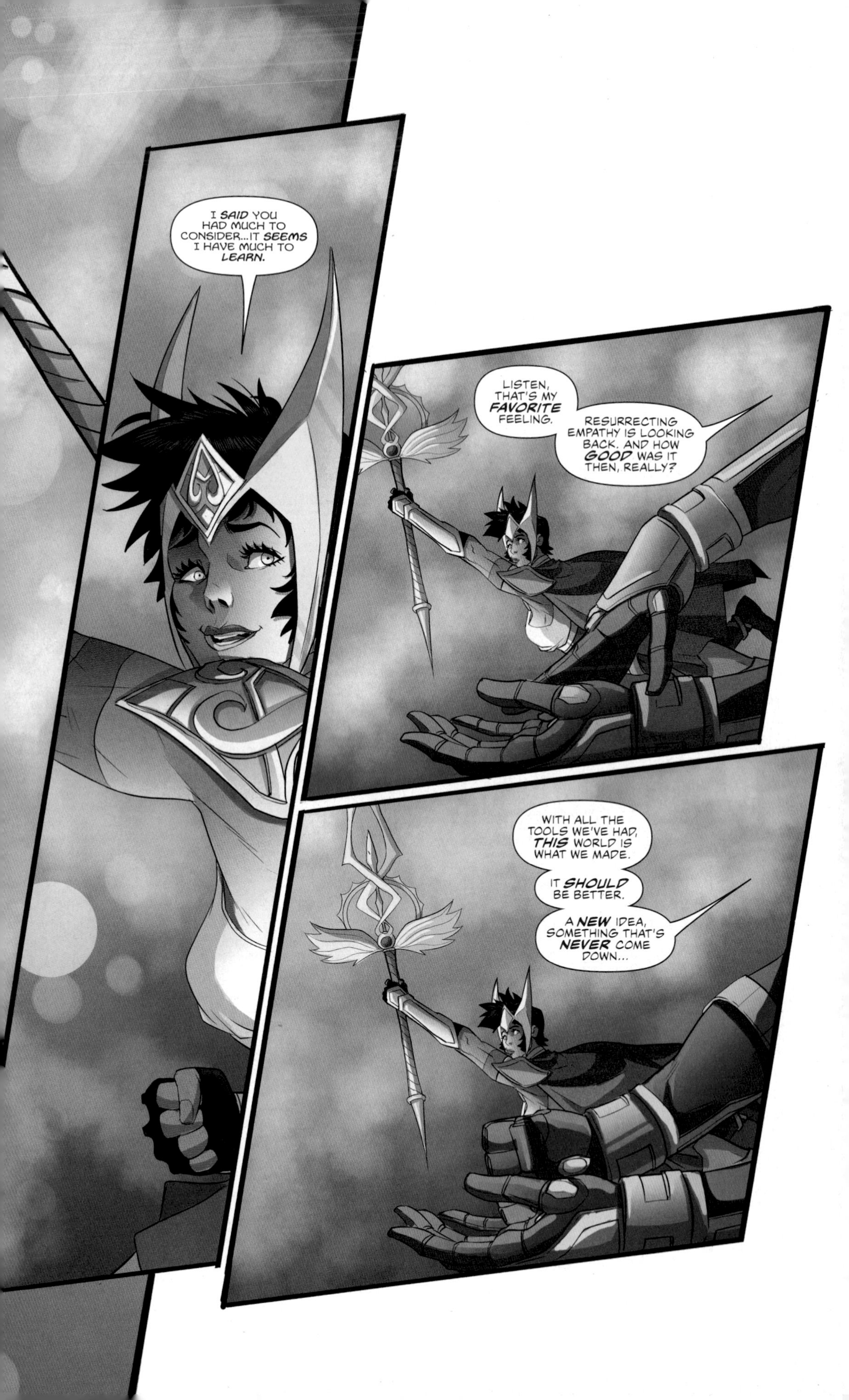

I SAID YOU HAD MUCH TO CONSIDER...IT SEEMS I HAVE MUCH TO LEARN.
LISTEN, THAT'S MY FAVORITE FEELING.
RESURRECTING EMPATHY IS LOOKING BACK. AND HOW GOOD WAS IT THEN, REALLY?
WITH ALL THE TOOLS WE'VE HAD, THIS WORLD IS WHAT WE MADE.
IT SHOULD BE BETTER.
A NEW IDEA, SOMETHING THAT'S NEVER COME DOWN...

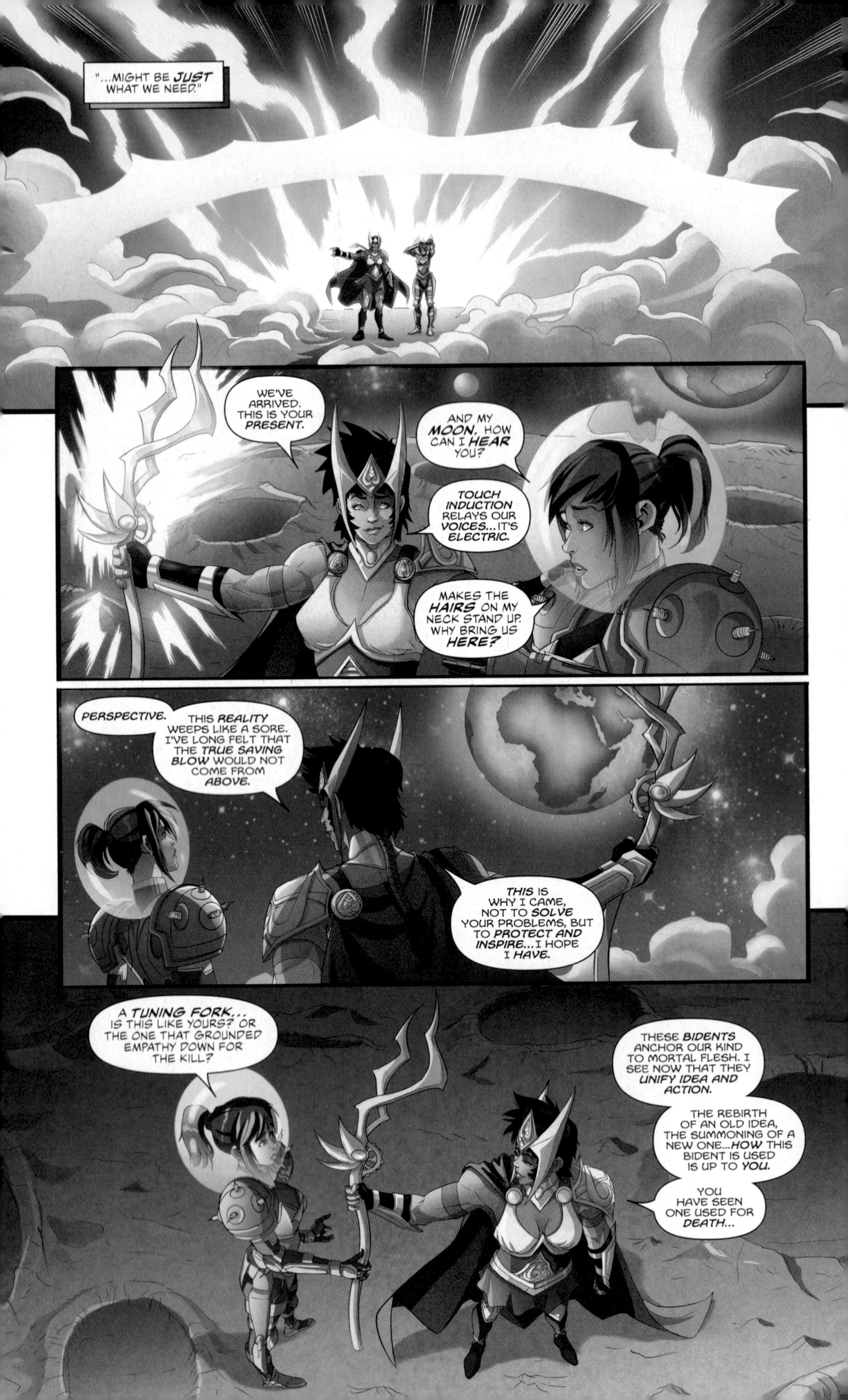
"...MIGHT BE JUST WHAT WE NEED."
WE'VE ARRIVED. THIS IS YOUR PRESENT.
AND MY MOON. HOW CAN I HEAR YOU?
TOUCH INDUCTION RELAYS OUR VOICES... IT'S ELECTRIC.
MAKES THE HAIRS ON MY NECK STAND UP. WHY BRING US HERE?
PERSPECTIVE.
THIS REALITY WEEPS LIKE A SORE. I'VE LONG FELT THAT THE TRUE SAVING BLOW WOULD NOT COME FROM ABOVE.
THIS IS WHY I CAME, NOT TO SOLVE YOUR PROBLEMS, BUT TO PROTECT AND INSPIRE... I HOPE I HAVE.
A TUNING FORK... IS THIS LIKE YOURS? OR THE ONE THAT GROUNDED EMPATHY DOWN FOR THE KILL?
THESE BIDENTS ANCHOR OUR KIND TO MORTAL FLESH. I SEE NOW THAT THEY UNIFY IDEA AND ACTION.
THE REBIRTH OF AN OLD IDEA, THE SUMMONING OF A NEW ONE... HOW THIS BIDENT IS USED IS UP TO YOU.
YOU HAVE SEEN ONE USED FOR DEATH...

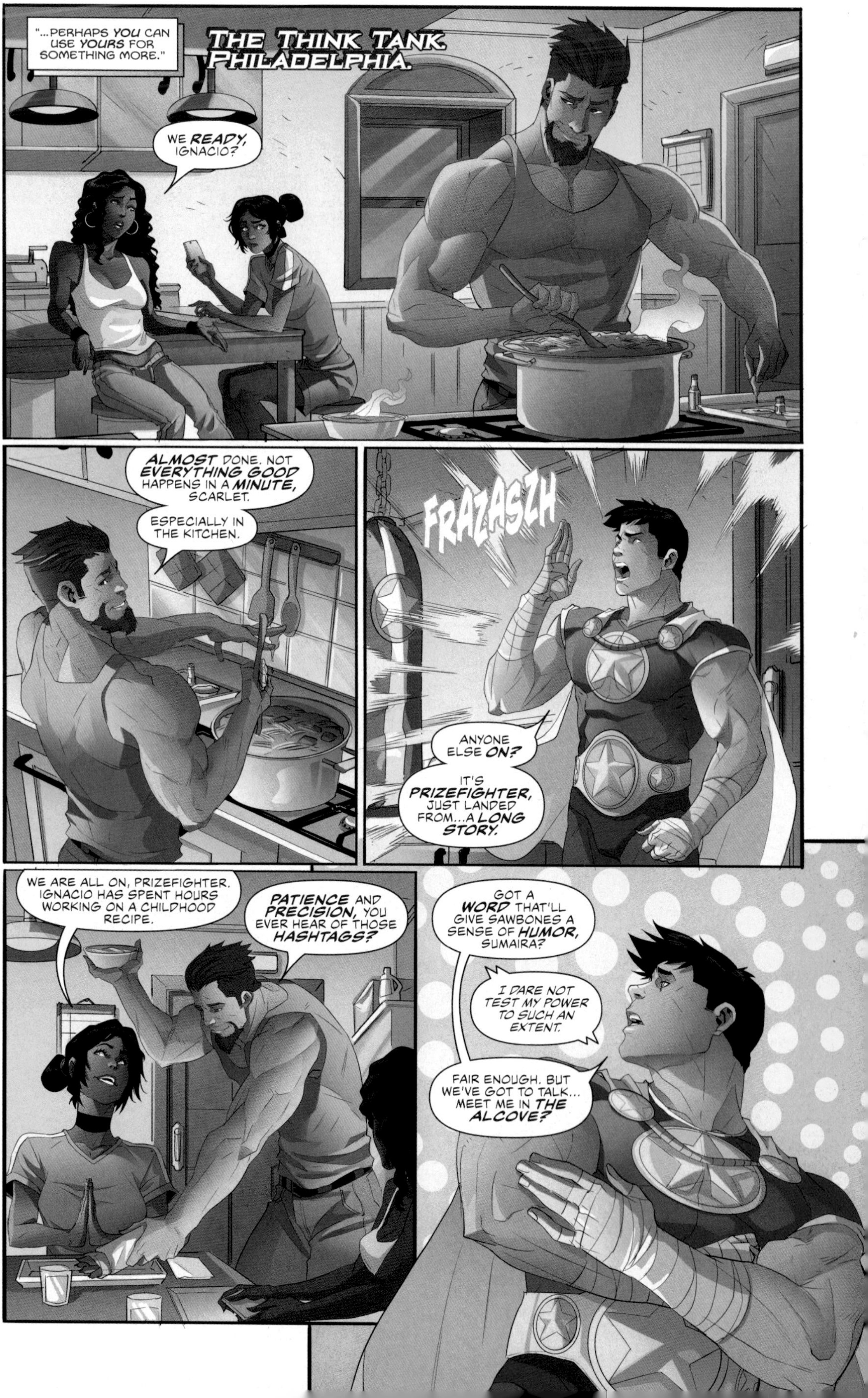
"...PERHAPS YOU CAN USE YOURS FOR SOMETHING MORE."
THE THINK TANK. PHILADELPHIA.
WE READY, IGNACIO?
ALMOST DONE. NOT EVERYTHING GOOD HAPPENS IN A MINUTE, SCARLET.
ESPECIALLY IN THE KITCHEN.
FRAZASZH
ANYONE ELSE ON?
IT'S PRIZEFIGHTER, JUST LANDED FROM...A LONG STORY.
WE ARE ALL ON, PRIZEFIGHTER. IGNACIO HAS SPENT HOURS WORKING ON A CHILDHOOD RECIPE.
PATIENCE AND PRECISION, YOU EVER HEAR OF THOSE HASHTAGS?
GOT A WORD THAT'LL GIVE SAWBONES A SENSE OF HUMOR, SUMAIRA?
I DARE NOT TEST MY POWER TO SUCH AN EXTENT.
FAIR ENOUGH. BUT WE'VE GOT TO TALK... MEET ME IN THE ALCOVE?

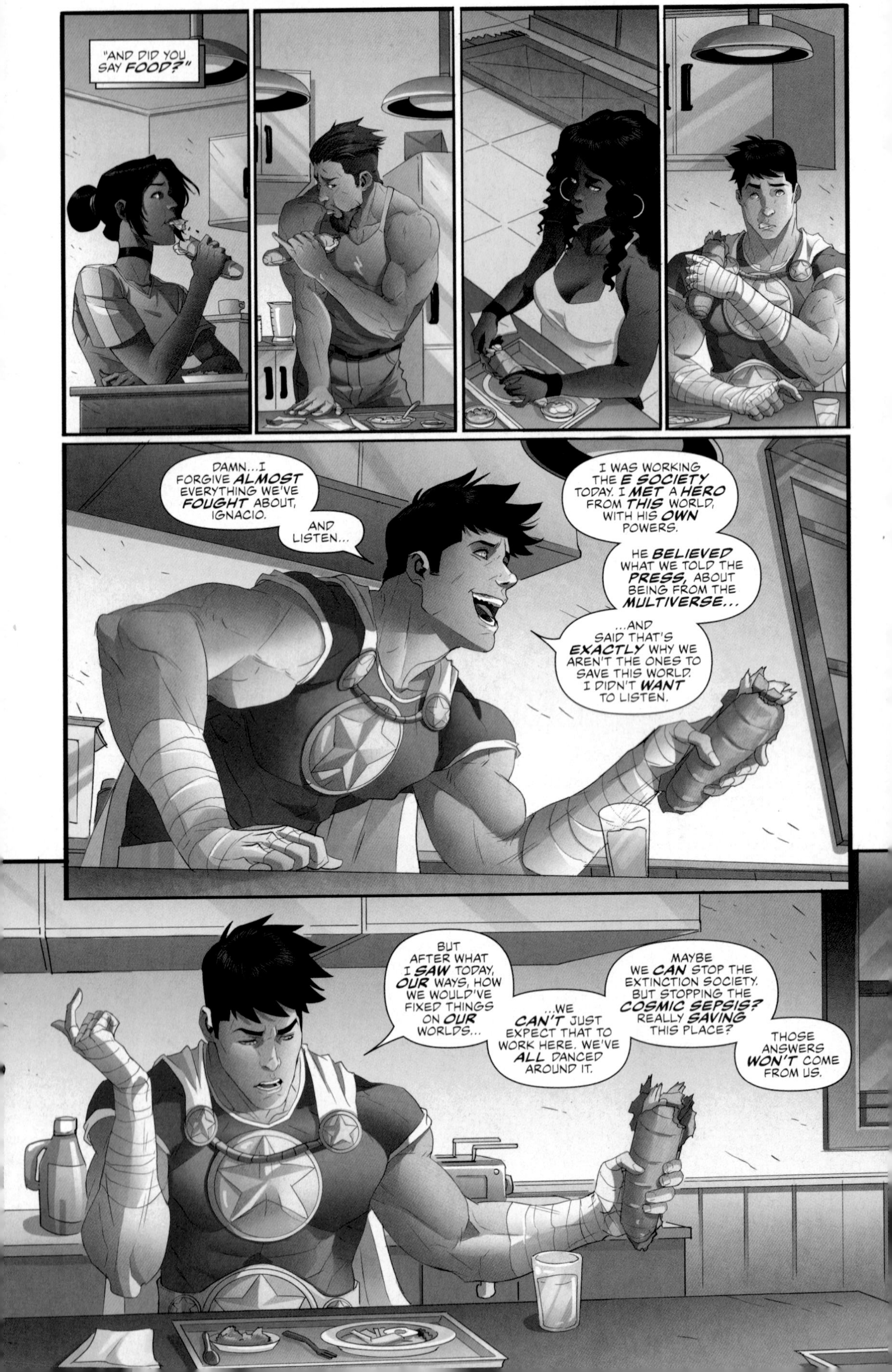
"AND DID YOU SAY FOOD?"
DAMN...I FORGIVE ALMOST EVERYTHING WE'VE FOUGHT ABOUT, IGNACIO.
AND LISTEN...
I WAS WORKING THE E SOCIETY TODAY. I MET A HERO FROM THIS WORLD, WITH HIS OWN POWERS.
HE BELIEVED WHAT WE TOLD THE PRESS, ABOUT BEING FROM THE MULTIVERSE...
...AND SAID THAT'S EXACTLY WHY WE AREN'T THE ONES TO SAVE THIS WORLD. I DIDN'T WANT TO LISTEN.
BUT AFTER WHAT I SAW TODAY, OUR WAYS, HOW WE WOULD'VE FIXED THINGS ON OUR WORLDS...
...WE CAN'T JUST EXPECT THAT TO WORK HERE. WE'VE ALL DANCED AROUND IT.
MAYBE WE CAN STOP THE EXTINCTION SOCIETY. BUT STOPPING THE COSMIC SEPSIS? REALLY SAVING THIS PLACE?
THOSE ANSWERS WON'T COME FROM US.

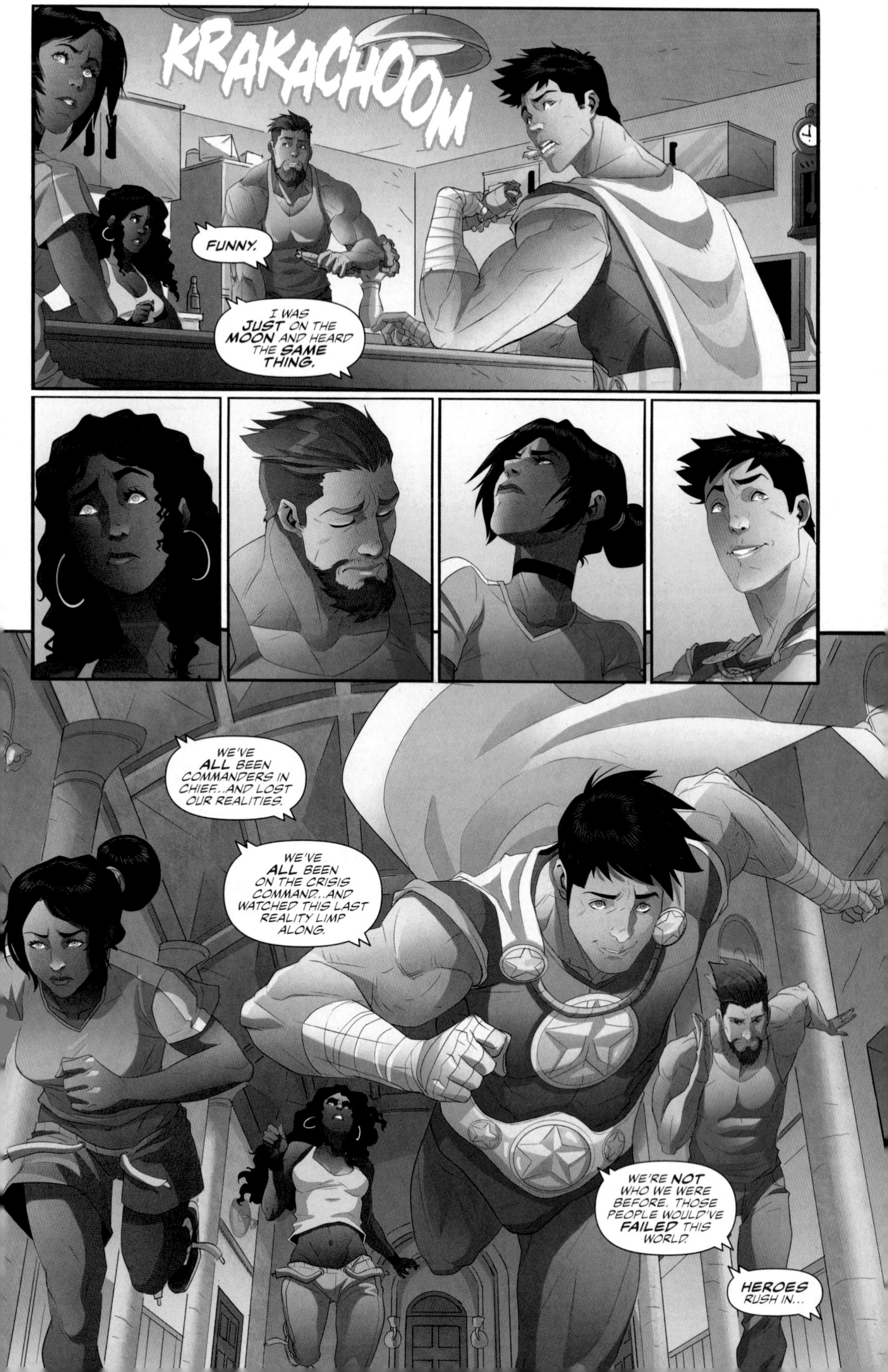
KRAKACHOOM
FUNNY.
I WAS JUST ON THE MOON AND HEARD THE SAME THING.
WE'VE ALL BEEN COMMANDERS IN CHIEF...AND LOST OUR REALITIES.
WE'VE ALL BEEN ON THE CRISIS COMMAND...AND WATCHED THIS LAST REALITY LIMP ALONG.
WE'RE NOT WHO WE WERE BEFORE. THOSE PEOPLE WOULD'VE FAILED THIS WORLD.
HEROES RUSH IN...

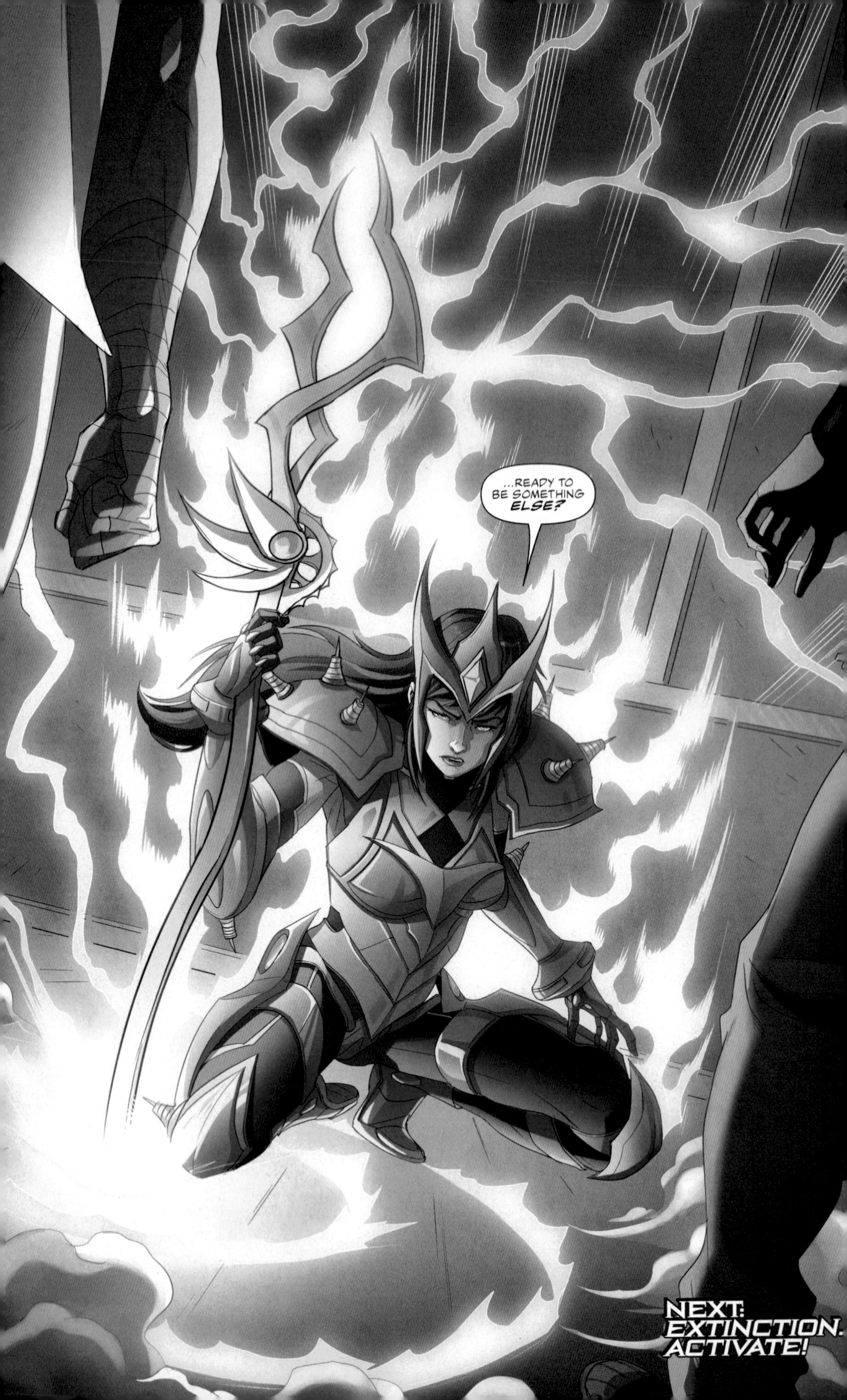
...READY TO BE SOMETHING ELSE?
NEXT: EXTINCTION. ACTIVATE!

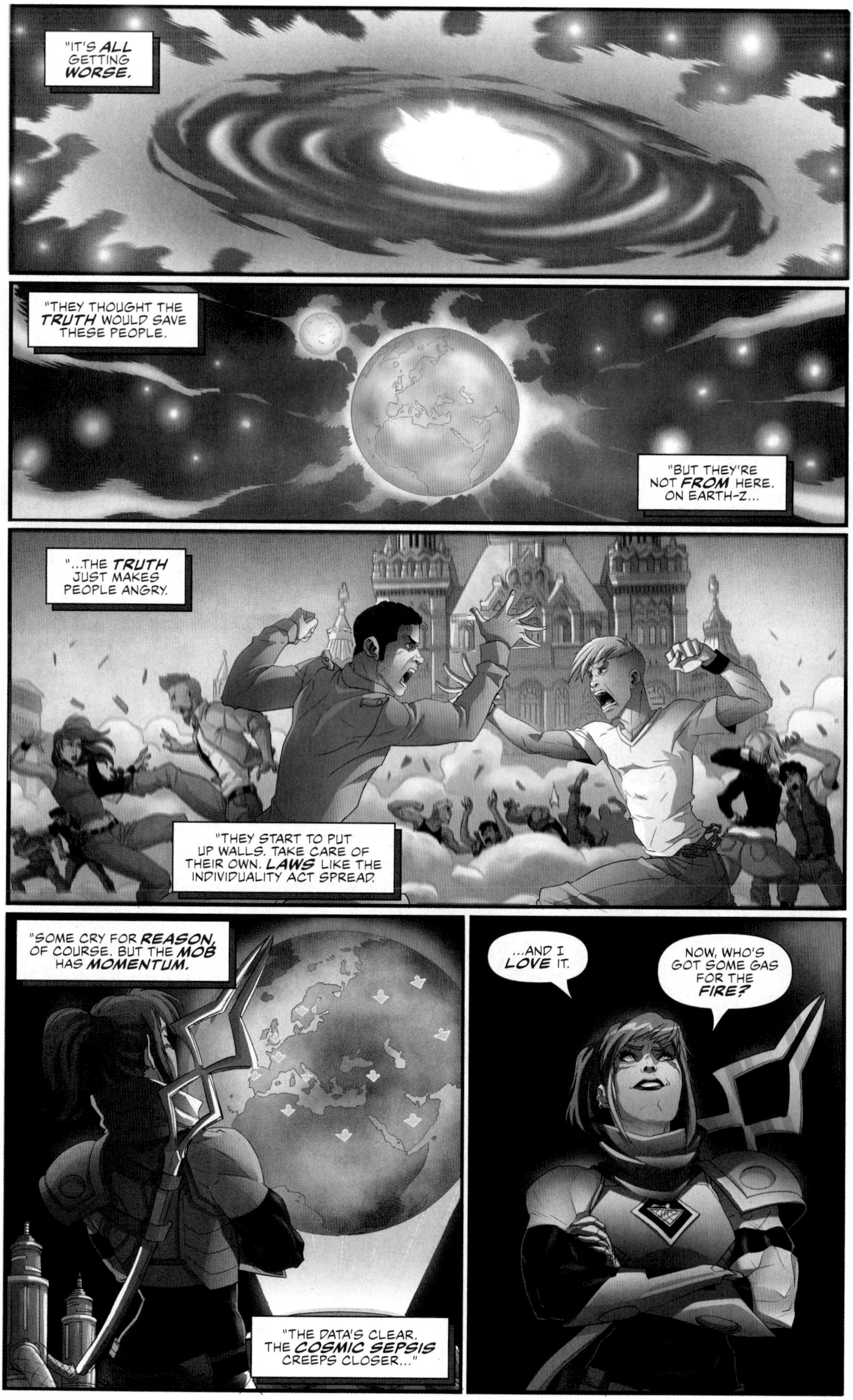
"IT'S ALL GETTING WORSE.
"THEY THOUGHT THE TRUTH WOULD SAVE THESE PEOPLE.
"BUT THEY'RE NOT FROM HERE. ON EARTH-Z...
"...THE TRUTH JUST MAKES PEOPLE ANGRY.
"THEY START TO PUT UP WALLS. TAKE CARE OF THEIR OWN. LAWS LIKE THE INDIVIDUALITY ACT SPREAD.
"SOME CRY FOR REASON, OF COURSE. BUT THE MOB HAS MOMENTUM.
"THE DATA'S CLEAR. THE COSMIC SEPSIS CREEPS CLOSER..."
...AND I LOVE IT.
NOW, WHO'S GOT SOME GAS FOR THE FIRE?

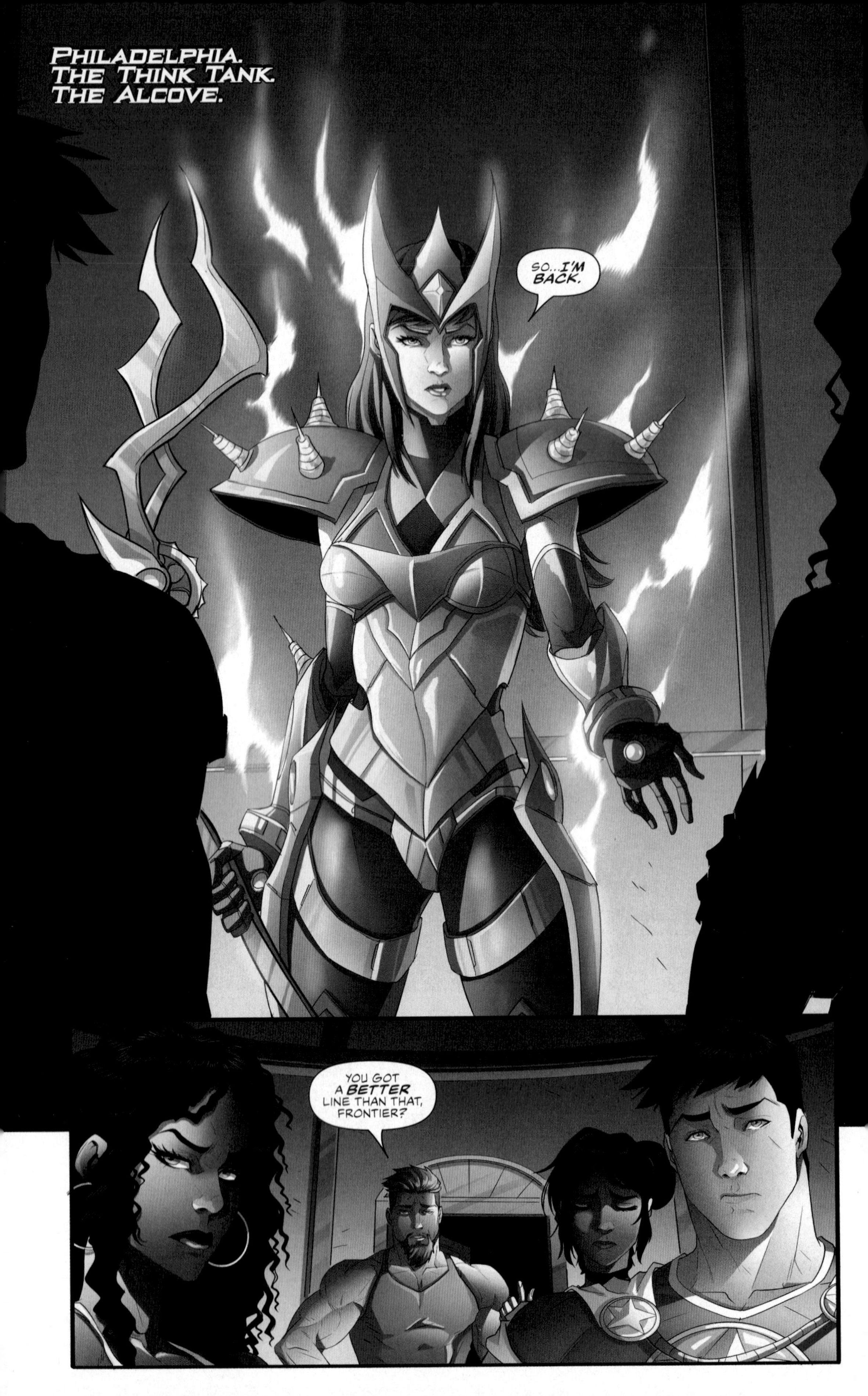
PHILADELPHIA.
THE THINK TANK.
THE ALCOVE.
SO...I'M BACK.
YOU GOT A BETTER LINE THAN THAT, FRONTIER?

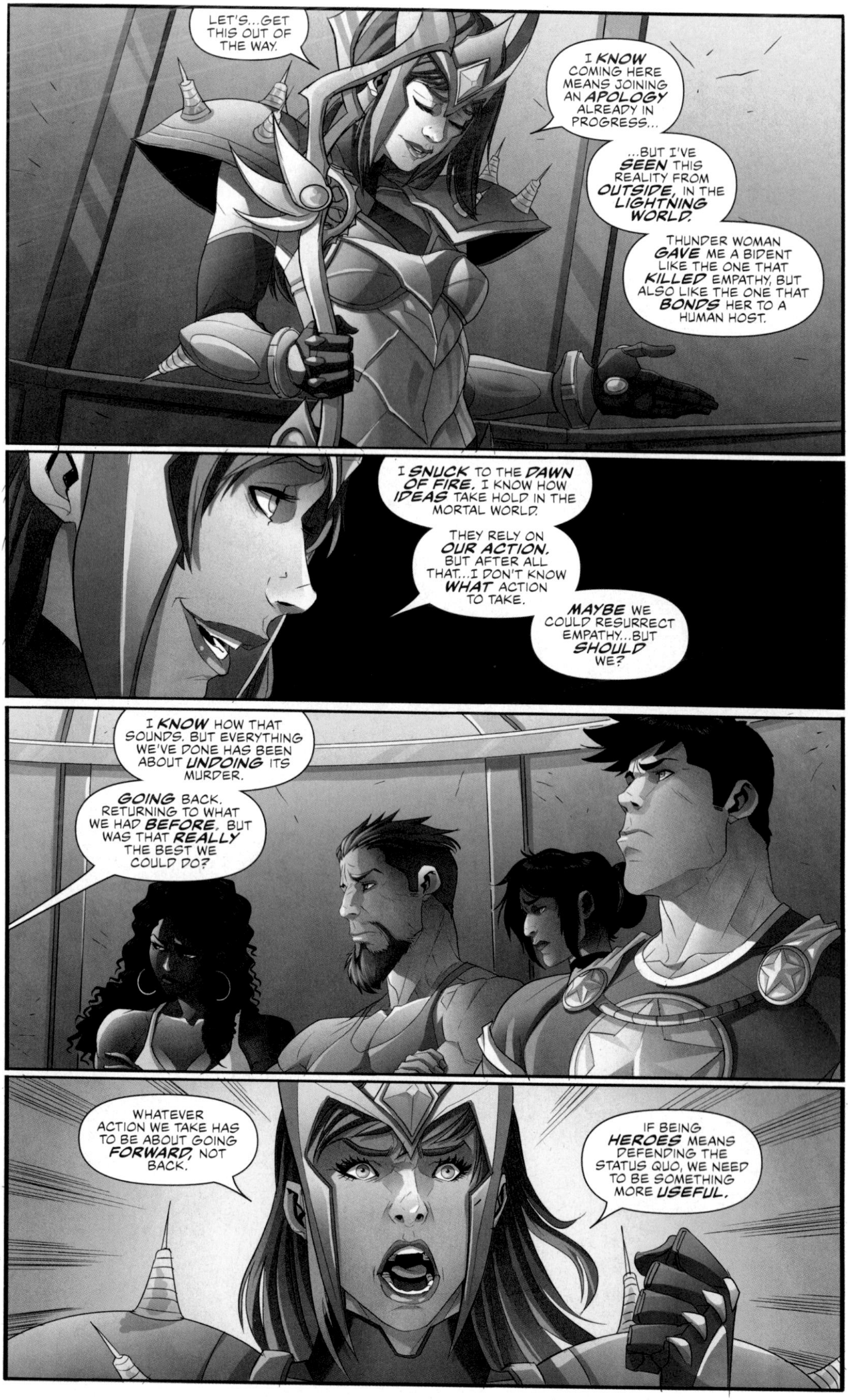
LET'S...GET THIS OUT OF THE WAY.
I KNOW COMING HERE MEANS JOINING AN APOLOGY ALREADY IN PROGRESS...
...BUT I'VE SEEN THIS REALITY FROM OUTSIDE, IN THE LIGHTNING WORLD.
THUNDER WOMAN GAVE ME A BIDENT LIKE THE ONE THAT KILLED EMPATHY, BUT ALSO LIKE THE ONE THAT BONDS HER TO A HUMAN HOST.
I SNUCK TO THE DAWN OF FIRE. I KNOW HOW IDEAS TAKE HOLD IN THE MORTAL WORLD.
THEY RELY ON OUR ACTION, BUT AFTER ALL THAT...I DON'T KNOW WHAT ACTION TO TAKE.
MAYBE WE COULD RESURRECT EMPATHY...BUT SHOULD WE?
I KNOW HOW THAT SOUNDS. BUT EVERYTHING WE'VE DONE HAS BEEN ABOUT UNDOING ITS MURDER.
GOING BACK. RETURNING TO WHAT WE HAD BEFORE. BUT WAS THAT REALLY THE BEST WE COULD DO?
WHATEVER ACTION WE TAKE HAS TO BE ABOUT GOING FORWARD, NOT BACK.
IF BEING HEROES MEANS DEFENDING THE STATUS QUO, WE NEED TO BE SOMETHING MORE USEFUL.

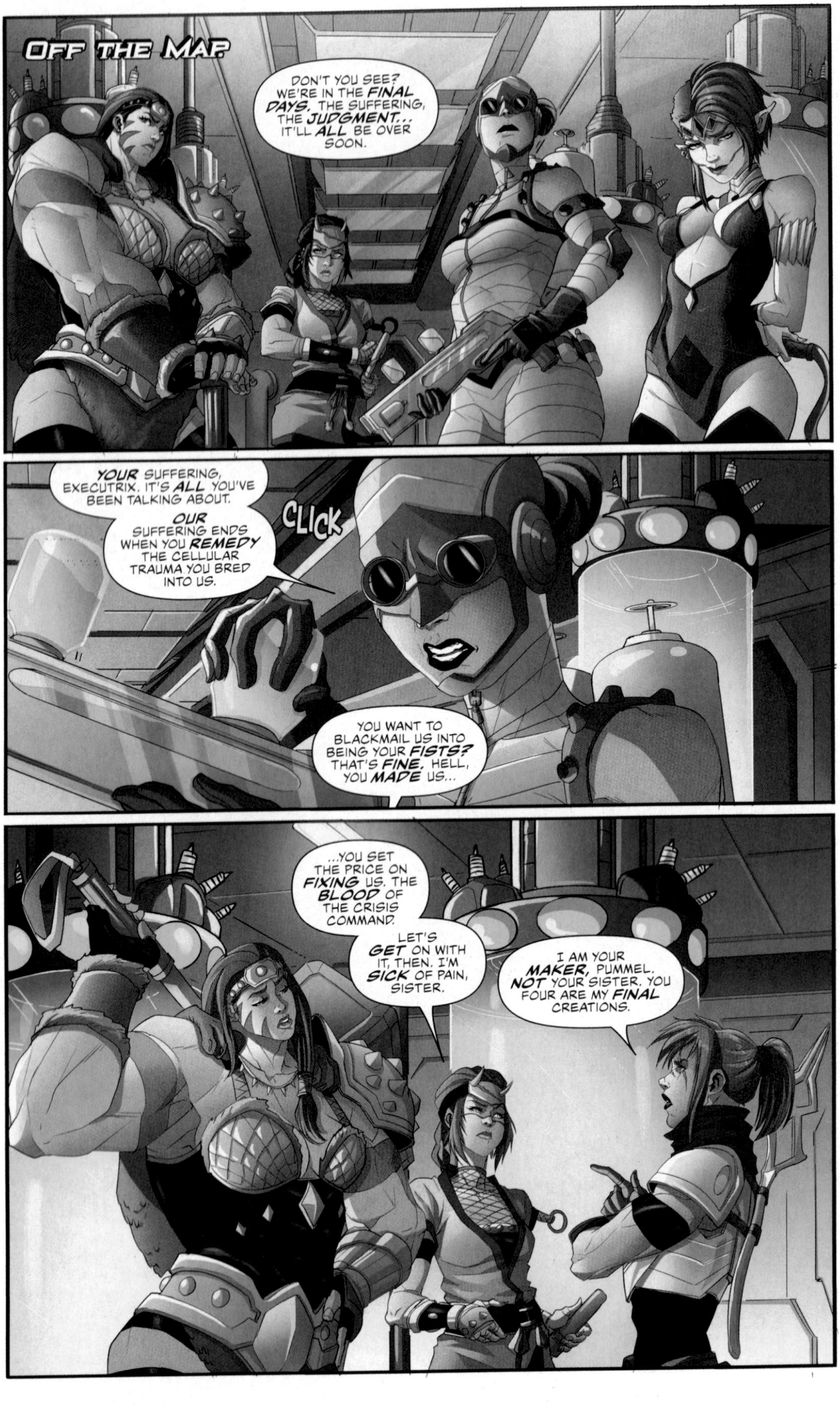
OFF THE MAP
DON'T YOU SEE? WE'RE IN THE FINAL DAYS. THE SUFFERING, THE JUDGMENT... IT'LL ALL BE OVER SOON.
YOUR SUFFERING, EXECUTRIX. IT'S ALL YOU'VE BEEN TALKING ABOUT.
OUR SUFFERING ENDS WHEN YOU REMEDY THE CELLULAR TRAUMA YOU BRED INTO US.
CLICK
YOU WANT TO BLACKMAIL US INTO BEING YOUR FISTS? THAT'S FINE. HELL, YOU MADE US...
...YOU SET THE PRICE ON FIXING US. THE BLOOD OF THE CRISIS COMMAND.
LET'S GET ON WITH IT, THEN. I'M SICK OF PAIN, SISTER.
I AM YOUR MAKER, PUMMEL. NOT YOUR SISTER. YOU FOUR ARE MY FINAL CREATIONS.

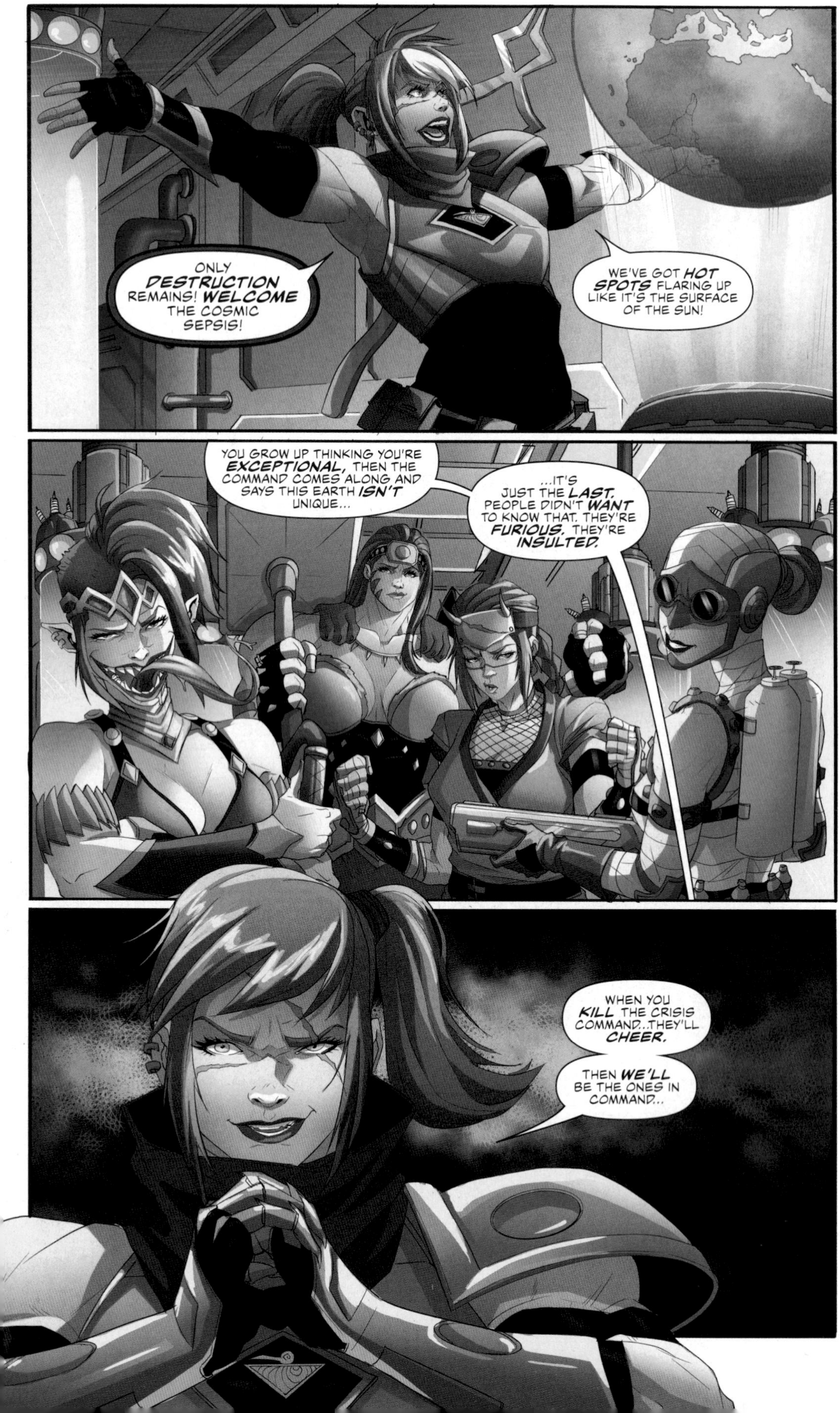
ONLY DESTRUCTION REMAINS! WELCOME THE COSMIC SEPSIS!
WE'VE GOT HOT SPOTS FLARING UP LIKE IT'S THE SURFACE OF THE SUN!
YOU GROW UP THINKING YOU'RE EXCEPTIONAL, THEN THE COMMAND COMES ALONG AND SAYS THIS EARTH ISN'T UNIQUE...
...IT'S JUST THE LAST. PEOPLE DIDN'T WANT TO KNOW THAT. THEY'RE FURIOUS. THEY'RE INSULTED.
WHEN YOU KILL THE CRISIS COMMAND..THEY'LL CHEER.
THEN WE'LL BE THE ONES IN COMMAND...

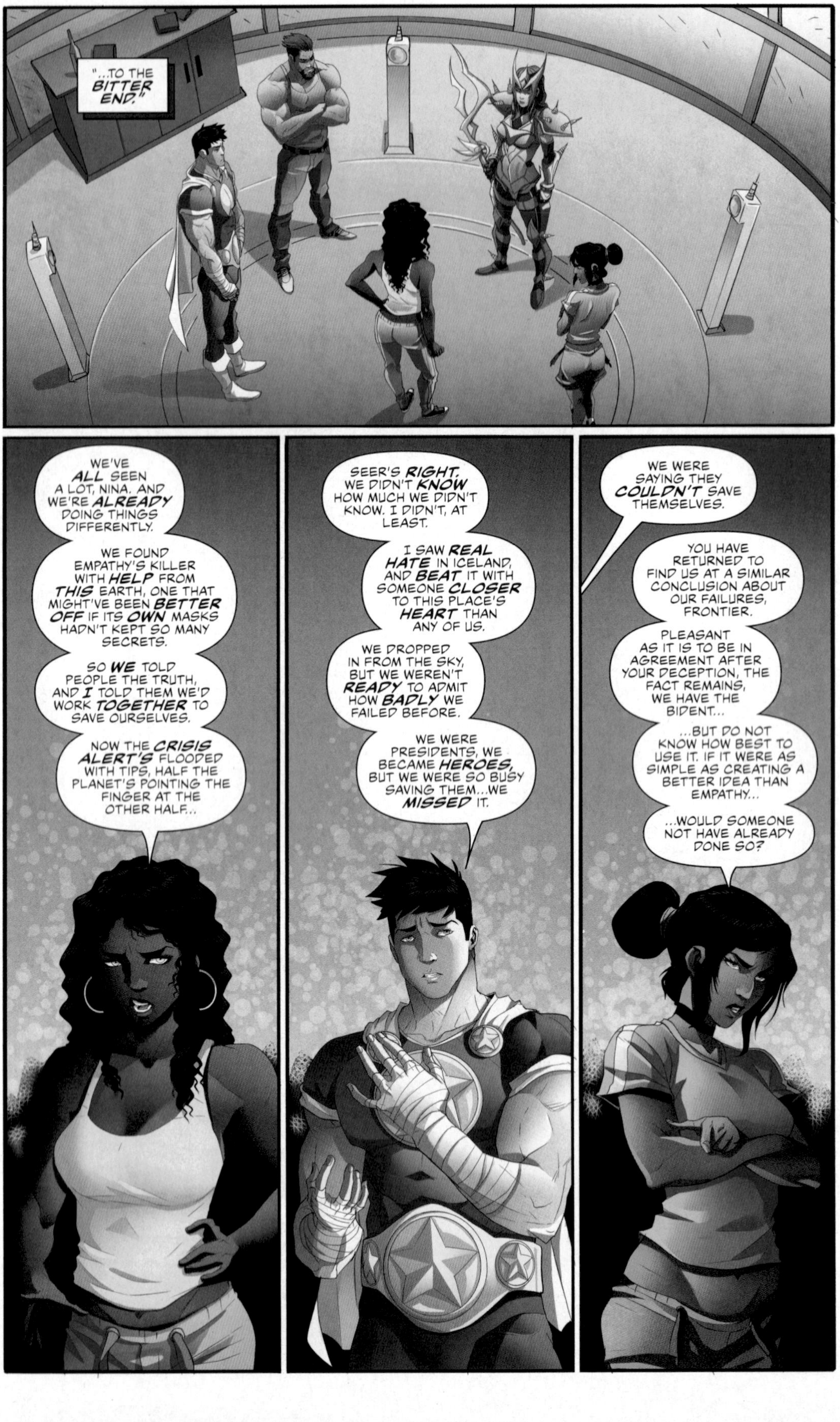

"...TO THE BITTER END."
WE'VE ALL SEEN A LOT, NINA. AND WE'RE ALREADY DOING THINGS DIFFERENTLY.
WE FOUND EMPATHY'S KILLER WITH HELP FROM THIS EARTH, ONE THAT MIGHT'VE BEEN BETTER OFF IF ITS OWN MASKS HADN'T KEPT SO MANY SECRETS.
SO WE TOLD PEOPLE THE TRUTH, AND I TOLD THEM WE'D WORK TOGETHER TO SAVE OURSELVES.
NOW THE CRISIS ALERT'S FLOODED WITH TIPS, HALF THE PLANET'S POINTING THE FINGER AT THE OTHER HALF...
SEER'S RIGHT. WE DIDN'T KNOW HOW MUCH WE DIDN'T KNOW. I DIDN'T, AT LEAST.
I SAW REAL HATE IN ICELAND, AND BEAT IT WITH SOMEONE CLOSER TO THIS PLACE'S HEART THAN ANY OF US.
WE DROPPED IN FROM THE SKY, BUT WE WEREN'T READY TO ADMIT HOW BADLY WE FAILED BEFORE.
WE WERE PRESIDENTS, WE BECAME HEROES, BUT WE WERE SO BUSY SAVING THEM...WE MISSED IT.
WE WERE SAYING THEY COULDN'T SAVE THEMSELVES.
YOU HAVE RETURNED TO FIND US AT A SIMILAR CONCLUSION ABOUT OUR FAILURES, FRONTIER.
PLEASANT AS IT IS TO BE IN AGREEMENT AFTER YOUR DECEPTION, THE FACT REMAINS, WE HAVE THE BIDENT...
...BUT DO NOT KNOW HOW BEST TO USE IT. IF IT WERE AS SIMPLE AS CREATING A BETTER IDEA THAN EMPATHY...
...WOULD SOMEONE NOT HAVE ALREADY DONE SO?

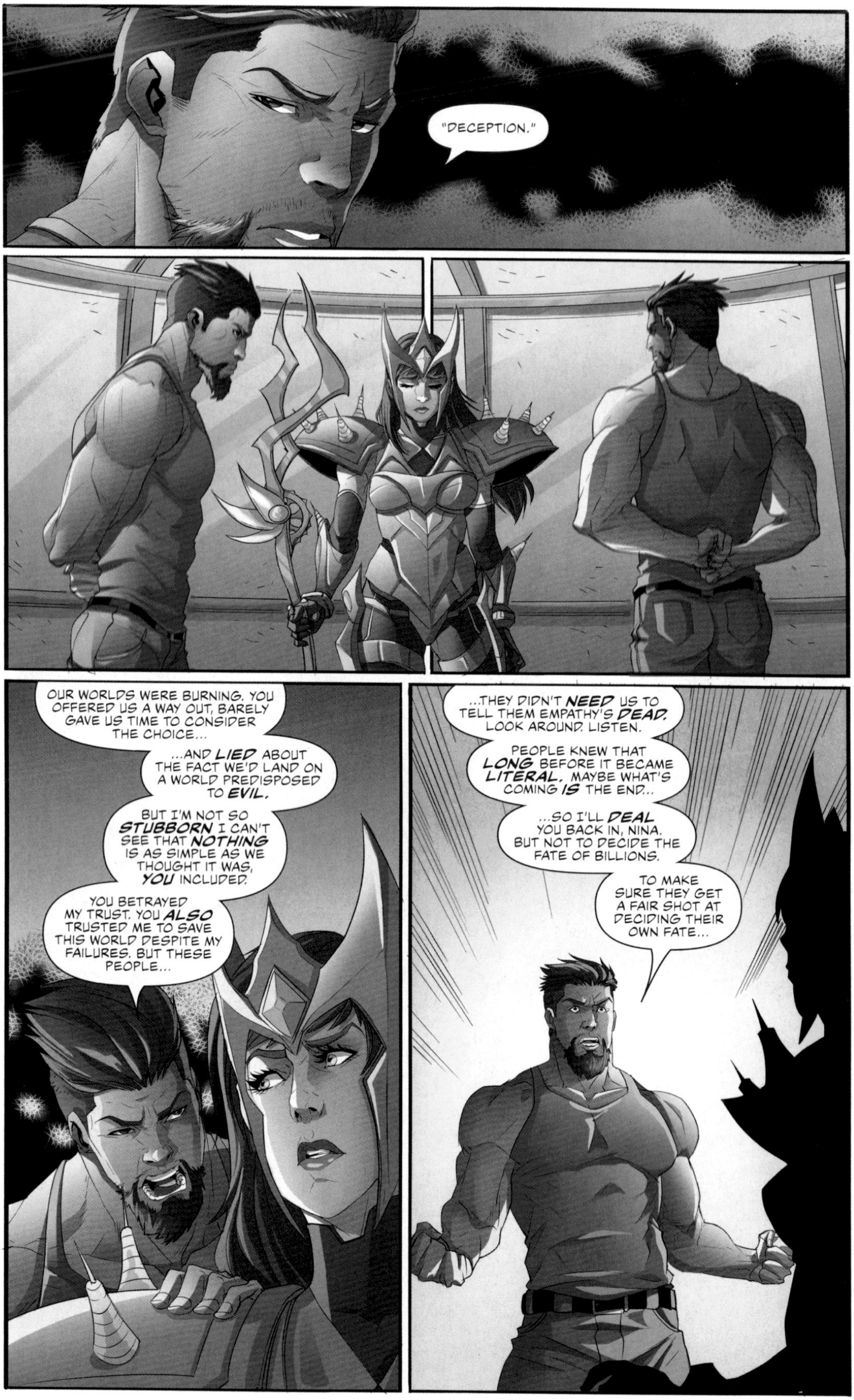
"DECEPTION."
OUR WORLDS WERE BURNING. YOU OFFERED US A WAY OUT, BARELY GAVE US TIME TO CONSIDER THE CHOICE...
...AND LIED ABOUT THE FACT WE'D LAND ON A WORLD PREDISPOSED TO EVIL.
BUT I'M NOT SO STUBBORN I CAN'T SEE THAT NOTHING IS AS SIMPLE AS WE THOUGHT IT WAS, YOU INCLUDED.
YOU BETRAYED MY TRUST. YOU ALSO TRUSTED ME TO SAVE THIS WORLD DESPITE MY FAILURES. BUT THESE PEOPLE...
...THEY DIDN'T NEED US TO TELL THEM EMPATHY'S DEAD. LOOK AROUND. LISTEN.
PEOPLE KNEW THAT LONG BEFORE IT BECAME LITERAL. MAYBE WHAT'S COMING IS THE END...
...SO I'LL DEAL YOU BACK IN, NINA. BUT NOT TO DECIDE THE FATE OF BILLIONS.
TO MAKE SURE THEY GET A FAIR SHOT AT DECIDING THEIR OWN FATE...

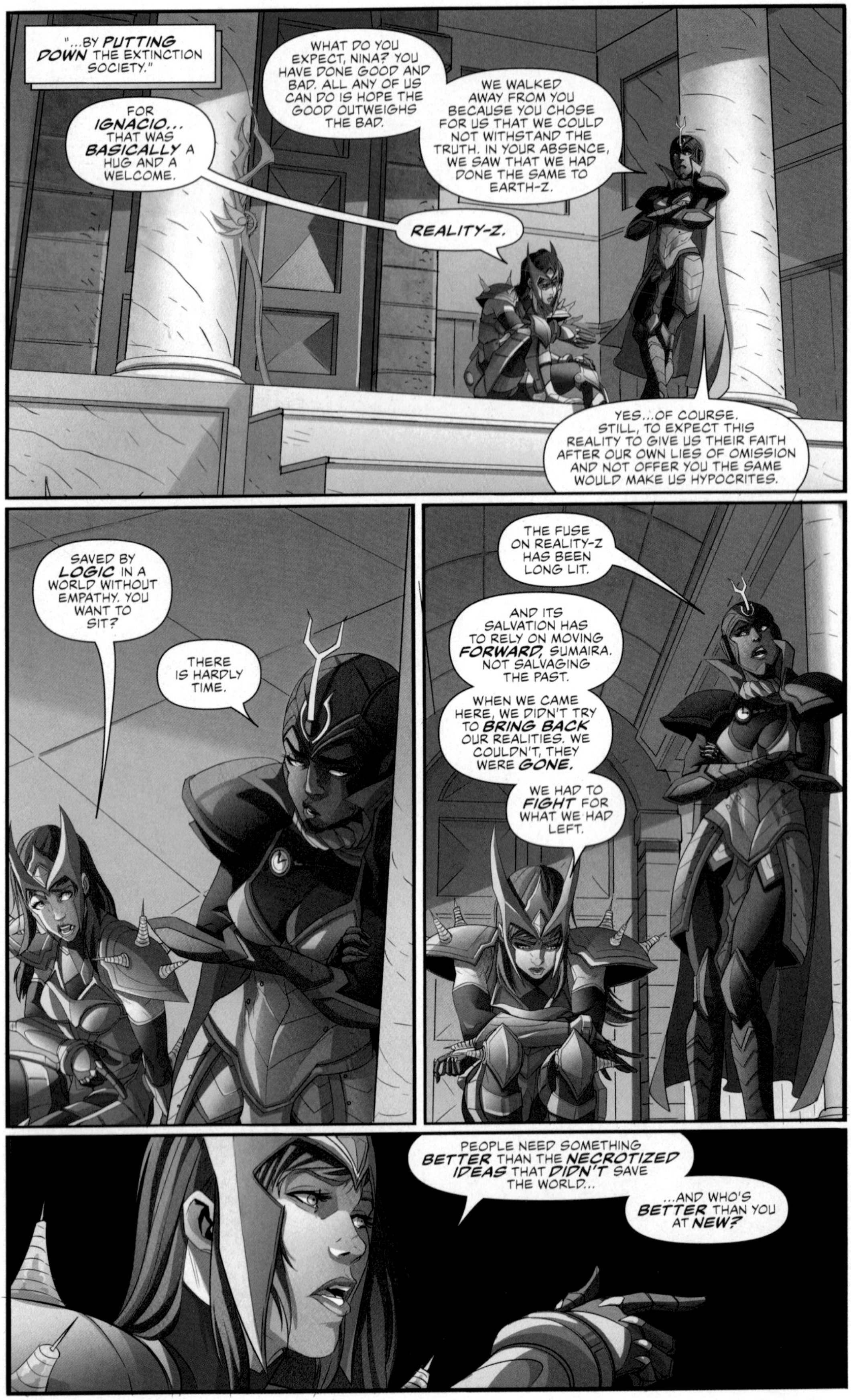
"...BY PUTTING DOWN THE EXTINCTION SOCIETY."
WHAT DO YOU EXPECT, NINA? YOU HAVE DONE GOOD AND BAD. ALL ANY OF US CAN DO IS HOPE THE GOOD OUTWEIGHS THE BAD.
FOR IGNACIO... THAT WAS BASICALLY A HUG AND A WELCOME.
WE WALKED AWAY FROM YOU BECAUSE YOU CHOSE FOR US THAT WE COULD NOT WITHSTAND THE TRUTH. IN YOUR ABSENCE, WE SAW THAT WE HAD DONE THE SAME TO EARTH-Z.
REALITY-Z.
YES...OF COURSE. STILL, TO EXPECT THIS REALITY TO GIVE US THEIR FAITH AFTER OUR OWN LIES OF OMISSION AND NOT OFFER YOU THE SAME WOULD MAKE US HYPOCRITES.
SAVED BY LOGIC IN A WORLD WITHOUT EMPATHY. YOU WANT TO SIT?
THERE IS HARDLY TIME.
THE FUSE ON REALITY-Z HAS BEEN LONG LIT.
AND ITS SALVATION HAS TO RELY ON MOVING FORWARD, SUMAIRA. NOT SALVAGING THE PAST.
WHEN WE CAME HERE, WE DIDN'T TRY TO BRING BACK OUR REALITIES. WE COULDN'T, THEY WERE GONE.
WE HAD TO FIGHT FOR WHAT WE HAD LEFT.
PEOPLE NEED SOMETHING BETTER THAN THE NECROTIZED IDEAS THAT DIDN'T SAVE THE WORLD...
...AND WHO'S BETTER THAN YOU AT NEW?

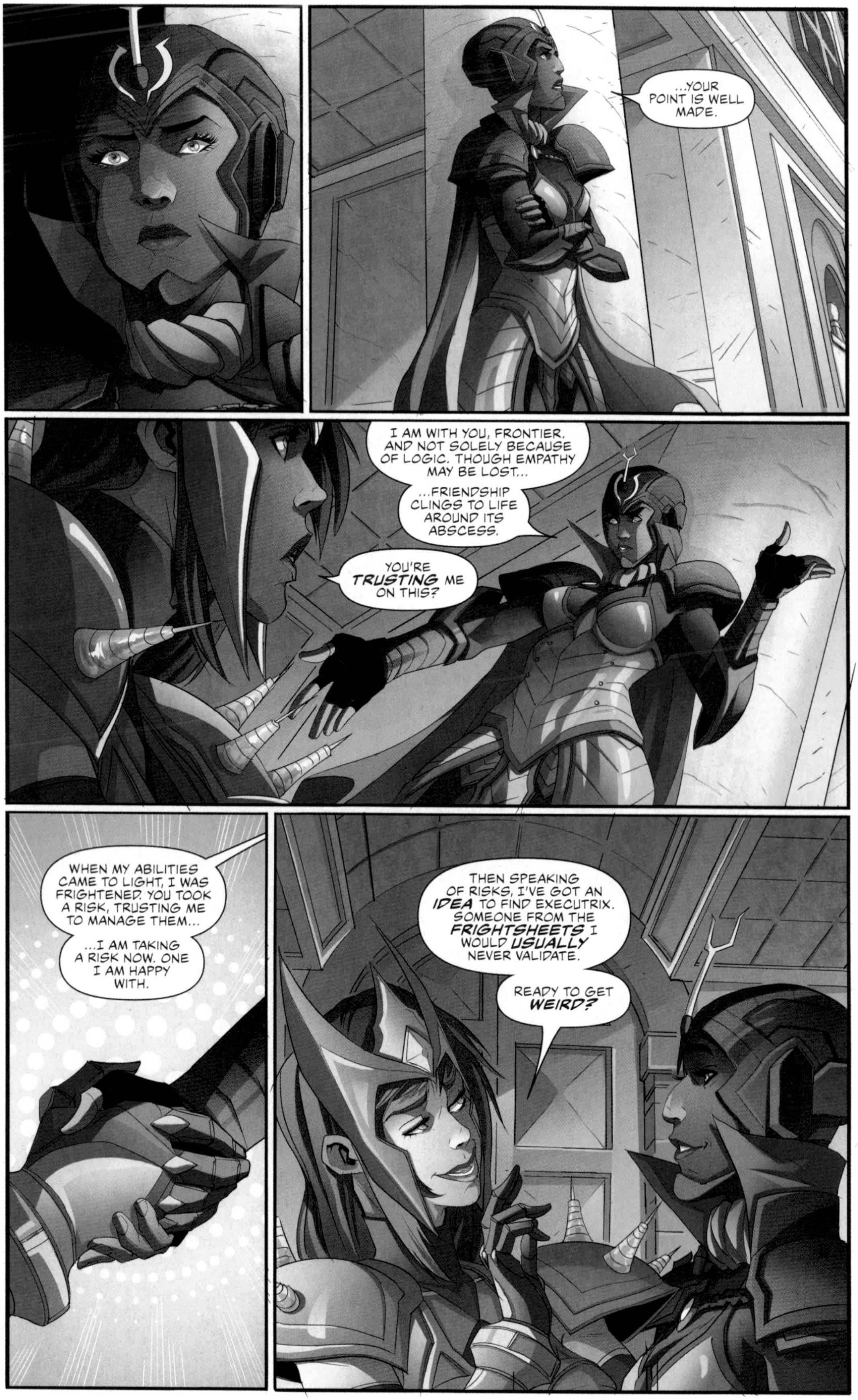
...YOUR POINT IS WELL MADE.
I AM WITH YOU, FRONTIER. AND NOT SOLELY BECAUSE OF LOGIC. THOUGH EMPATHY MAY BE LOST...
...FRIENDSHIP CLINGS TO LIFE AROUND ITS ABSCESS.
YOU'RE TRUSTING ME ON THIS?
WHEN MY ABILITIES CAME TO LIGHT, I WAS FRIGHTENED. YOU TOOK A RISK, TRUSTING ME TO MANAGE THEM...
...I AM TAKING A RISK NOW. ONE I AM HAPPY WITH.
THEN SPEAKING OF RISKS, I'VE GOT AN IDEA TO FIND EXECUTRIX. SOMEONE FROM THE FRIGHTSHEETS I WOULD USUALLY NEVER VALIDATE.
READY TO GET WEIRD?

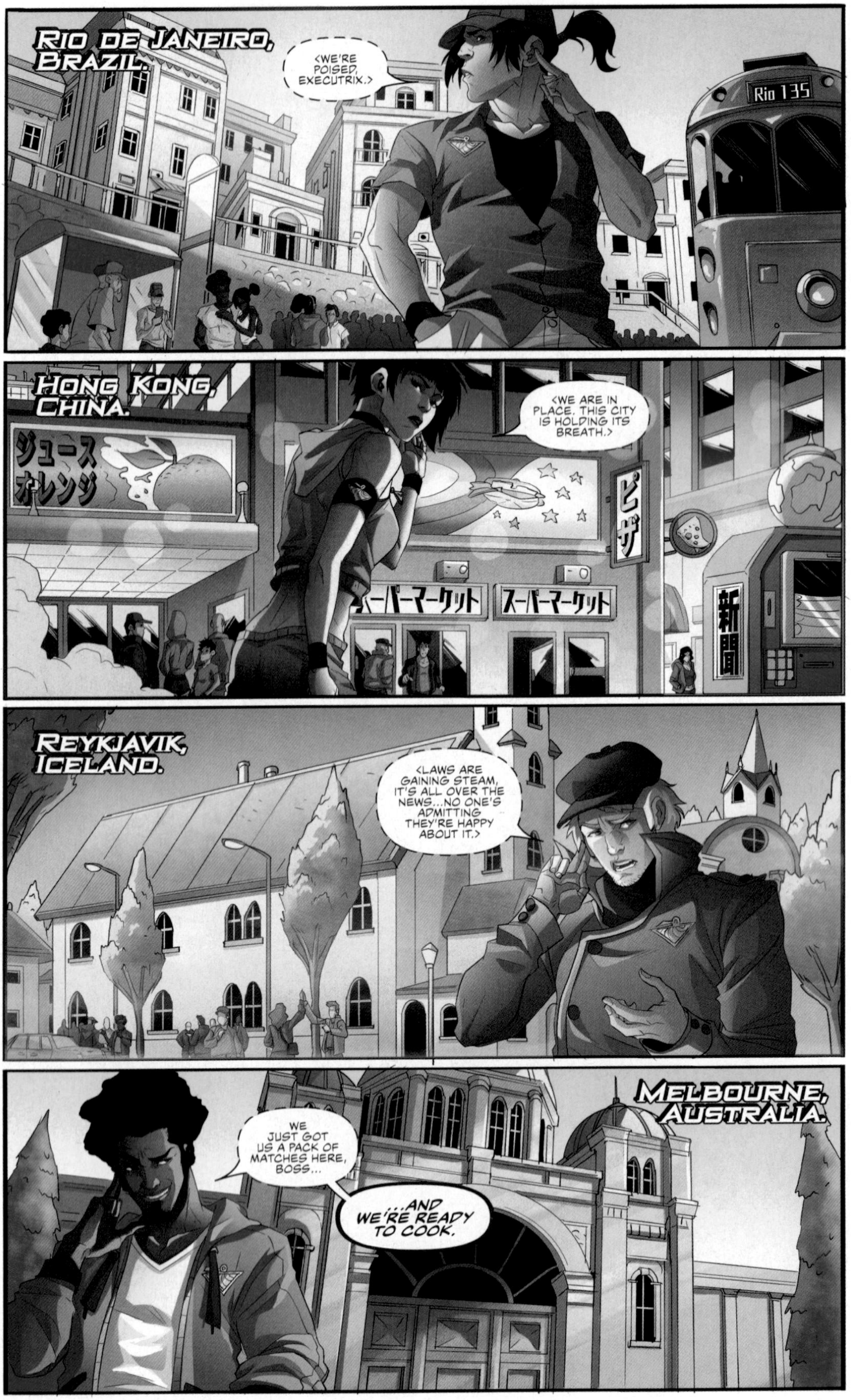
RIO DE JANEIRO, BRAZIL.
<WE'RE POISED, EXECUTRIX.>
Rio 135
HONG KONG, CHINA.
ジュース
オレンジ
<WE ARE IN PLACE. THIS CITY IS HOLDING ITS BREATH.>
ピザ
スーパーマーケット
スーパーマーケット
新聞
REYKJAVIK, ICELAND.
<LAWS ARE GAINING STEAM, IT'S ALL OVER THE NEWS...NO ONE'S ADMITTING THEY'RE HAPPY ABOUT IT.>
MELBOURNE, AUSTRALIA.
WE JUST GOT US A PACK OF MATCHES HERE, BOSS...
...AND WE'RE READY TO COOK.

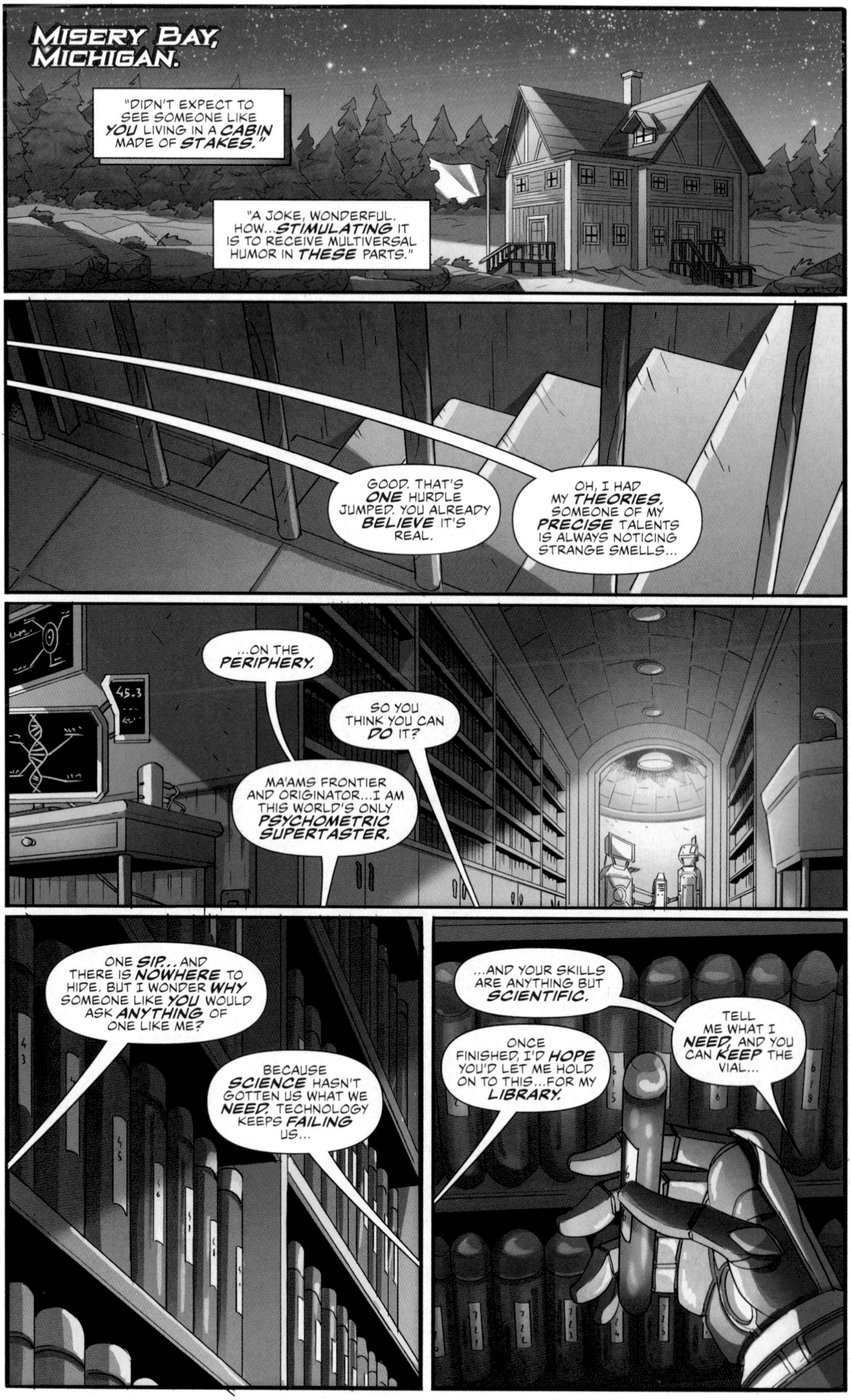
MISERY BAY, MICHIGAN.
"DIDN'T EXPECT TO SEE SOMEONE LIKE YOU LIVING IN A CABIN MADE OF STAKES."
"A JOKE, WONDERFUL. HOW...STIMULATING IT IS TO RECEIVE MULTIVERSAL HUMOR IN THESE PARTS."
GOOD. THAT'S ONE HURDLE JUMPED. YOU ALREADY BELIEVE IT'S REAL.
OH, I HAD MY THEORIES. SOMEONE OF MY PRECISE TALENTS IS ALWAYS NOTICING STRANGE SMELLS...
...ON THE PERIPHERY.
SO YOU THINK YOU CAN DO IT?
MA'AMS FRONTIER AND ORIGINATOR...I AM THIS WORLD'S ONLY PSYCHOMETRIC SUPERTASTER.
ONE SIP... AND THERE IS NOWHERE TO HIDE. BUT I WONDER WHY SOMEONE LIKE YOU WOULD ASK ANYTHING OF ONE LIKE ME?
BECAUSE SCIENCE HASN'T GOTTEN US WHAT WE NEED. TECHNOLOGY KEEPS FAILING US...
...AND YOUR SKILLS ARE ANYTHING BUT SCIENTIFIC.
TELL ME WHAT I NEED, AND YOU CAN KEEP THE VIAL...
ONCE FINISHED, I'D HOPE YOU'D LET ME HOLD ON TO THIS...FOR MY LIBRARY.

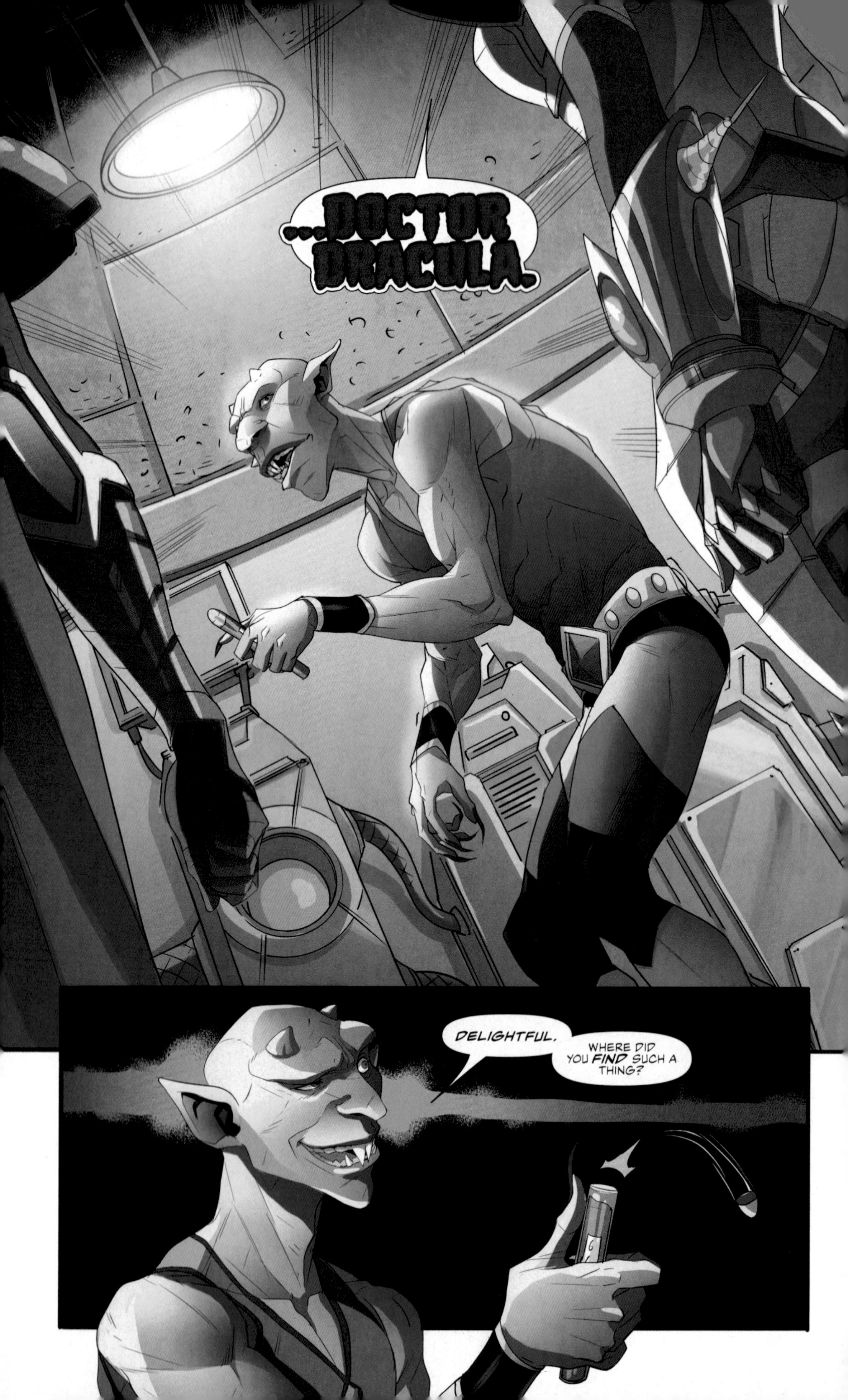
...DOCTOR DRACULA.
DELIGHTFUL.
WHERE DID YOU FIND SUCH A THING?

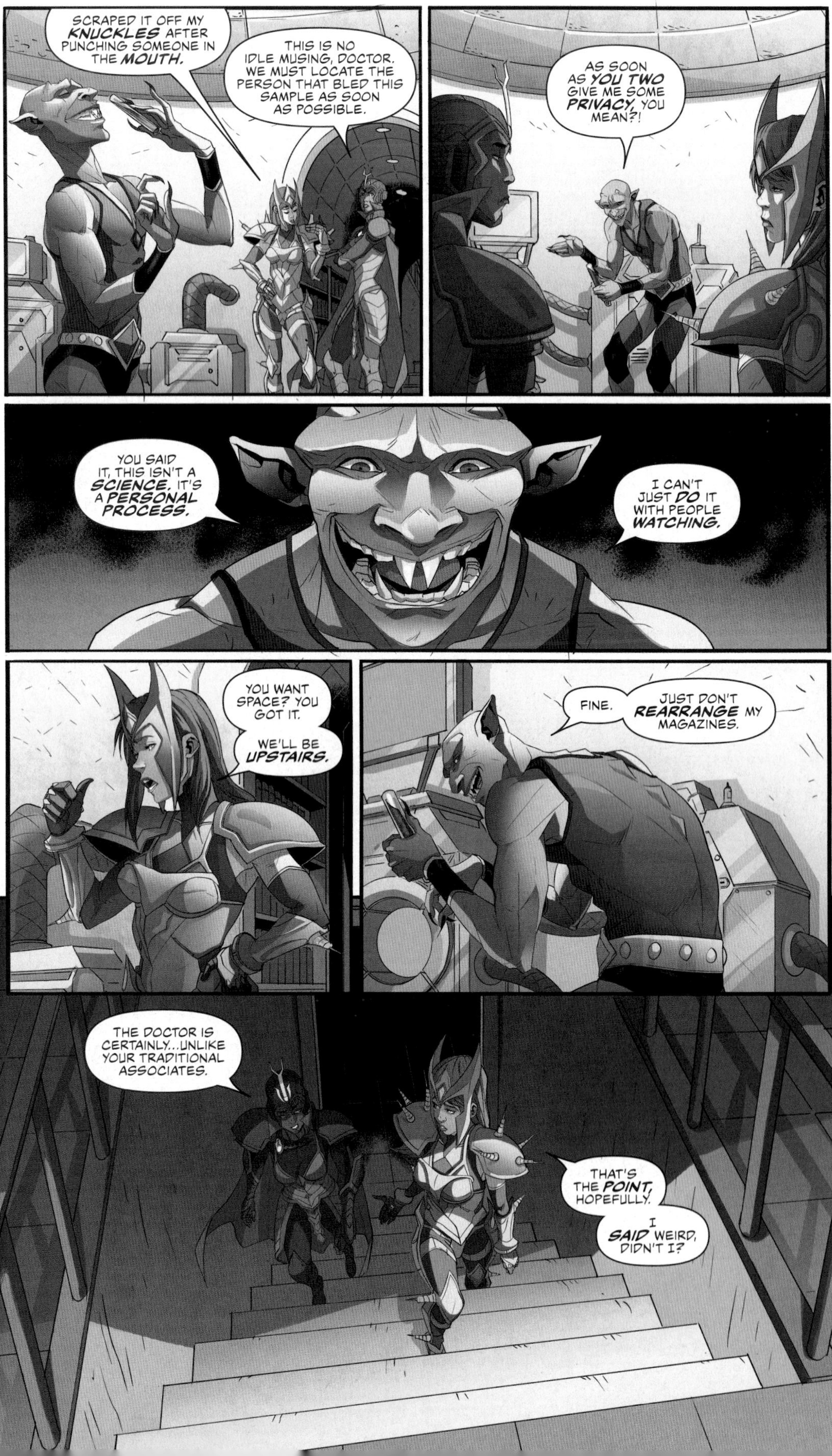
SCRAPED IT OFF MY KNUCKLES AFTER PUNCHING SOMEONE IN THE MOUTH.
THIS IS NO IDLE MUSING, DOCTOR. WE MUST LOCATE THE PERSON THAT BLED THIS SAMPLE AS SOON AS POSSIBLE.
AS SOON AS YOU TWO GIVE ME SOME PRIVACY, YOU MEAN?!
YOU SAID IT, THIS ISN'T A SCIENCE. IT'S A PERSONAL PROCESS.
I CAN'T JUST DO IT WITH PEOPLE WATCHING.
YOU WANT SPACE? YOU GOT IT.
WE'LL BE UPSTAIRS.
FINE.
JUST DON'T REARRANGE MY MAGAZINES.
THE DOCTOR IS CERTAINLY...UNLIKE YOUR TRADITIONAL ASSOCIATES.
THAT'S THE POINT, HOPEFULLY.
I SAID WEIRD, DIDN'T I?

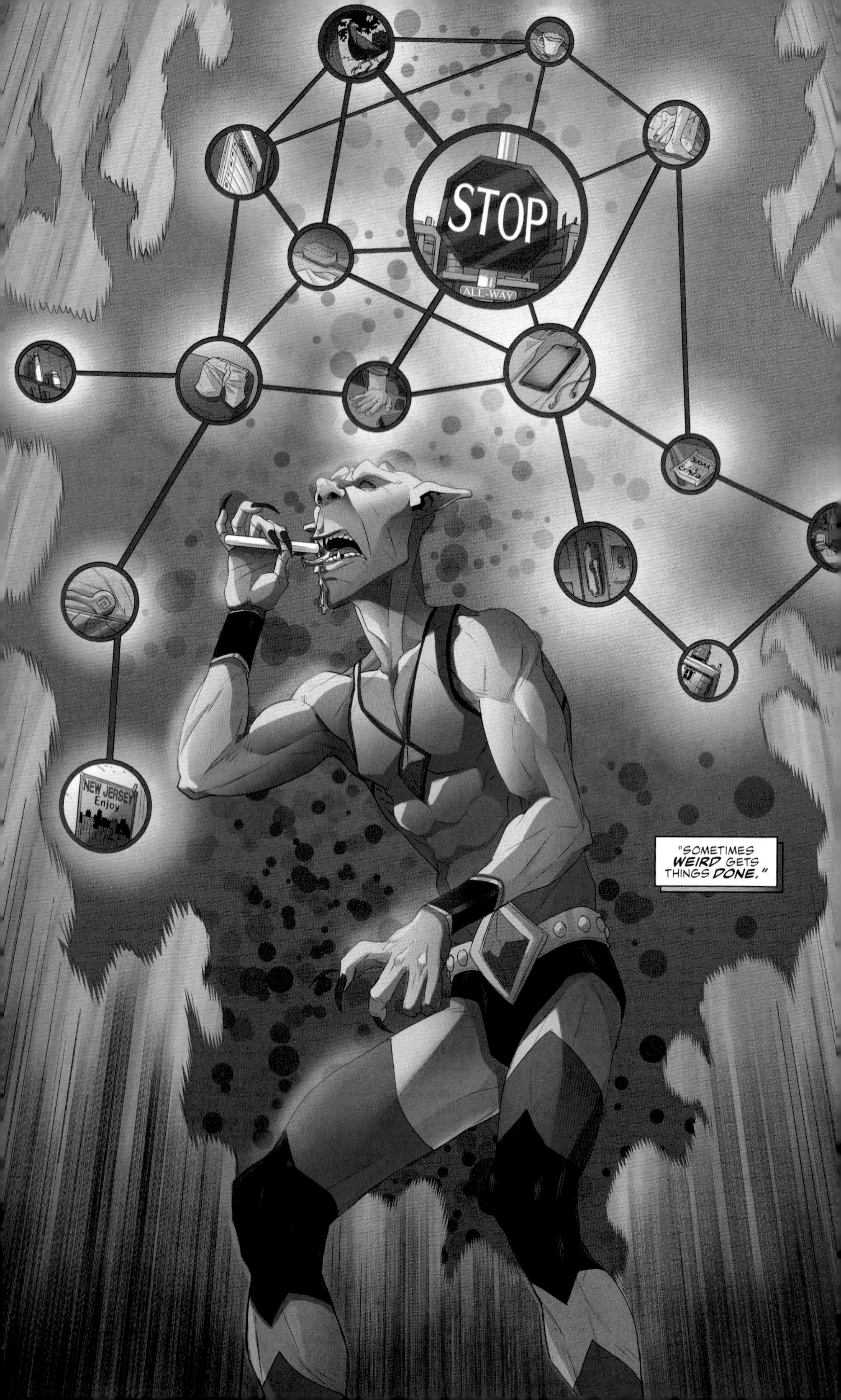
STOP
ALL-WAY
NEW JERSEY
Enjoy
"SOMETIMES WEIRD GETS THINGS DONE."

IT IS SO QUIET. WHAT DO YOU THINK HE IS DOING DOWN THERE?

SOMETHING PRIVATE AND WILDLY IRRATIONAL. I'M TRYING TO JUST FOCUS ON THE *RESULTS.*

THEN *FOCUS* NO LONGER.

THAT WAS BRIEF.

NOT *EVERY* TALENT TAKES TIME.

THE SAMPLE WAS QUITE *UNIQUE.* A CORE *UNQUESTIONABLY* BORN FROM *THIS* WORLD'S TERROIR, ALL ITS EMOTIONAL AND SOCIAL HALLMARKS. BUT *NOTES TOO* OF SOMETHING I'VE NEVER *TASTED* ON THE FRINGE.

ANOTHER PLANET? ANOTHER *REALITY?* I'VE TASTED *MANY* EXTRATERRESTRIAL BOUQUETS, AND *THIS* WAS--

THE *RESULTS,* DOCTOR. NOT THE *REVIEW.*

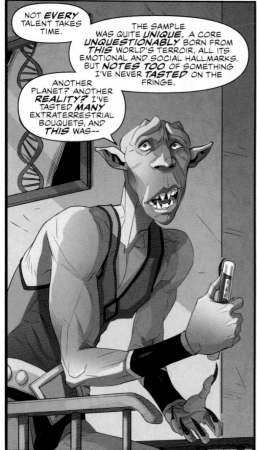

OH, SHE'S BEEN *ALL OVER* THIS PLANET. BUT HER STEPS WEREN'T *HARD* TO FOLLOW. SHE LEFT MANY TRAILS...

...AND THEY *ALL* DISAPPEAR AT THE EXACT SAME POINT. SHALL I WRITE IT DOWN?

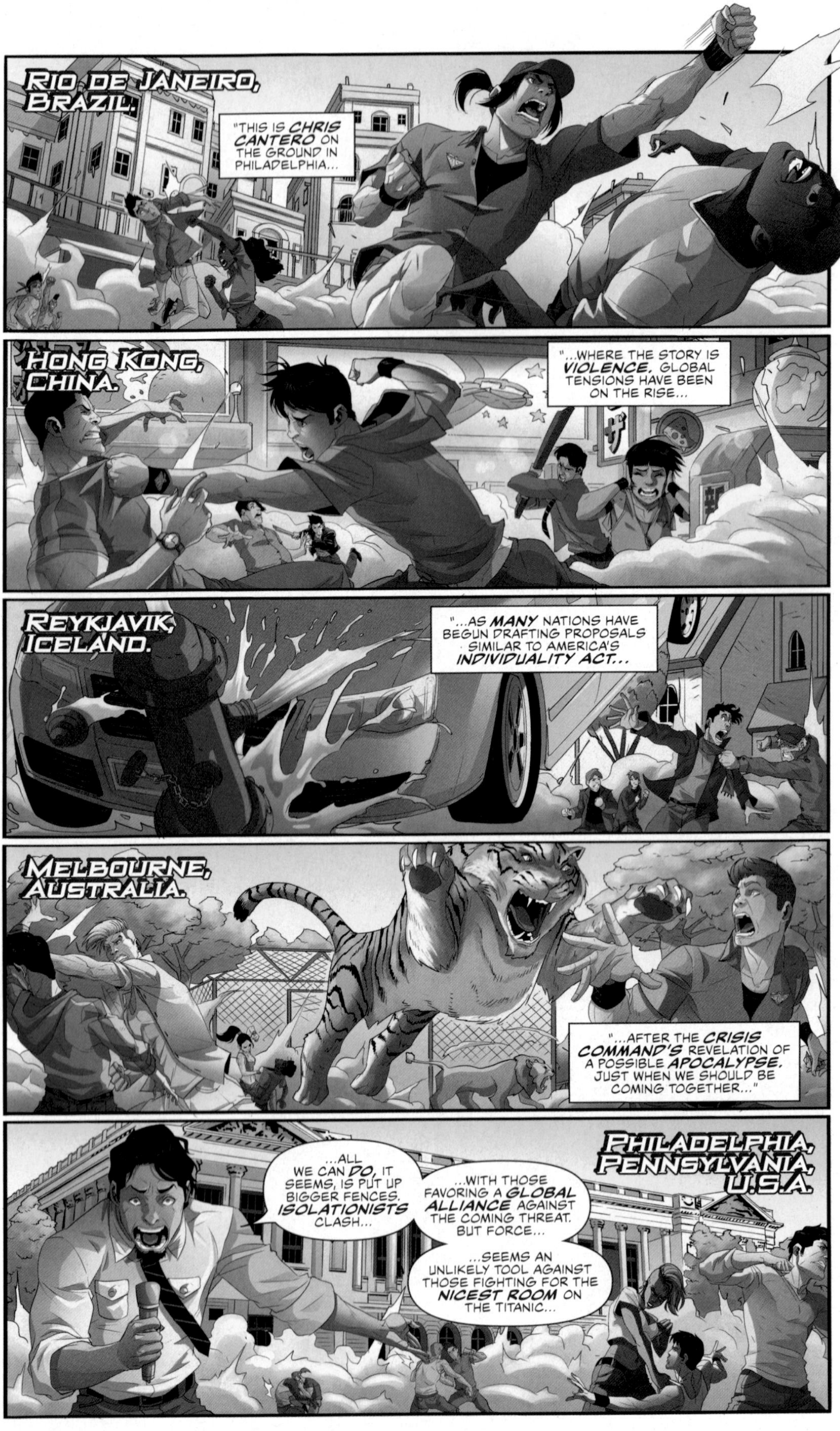
RIO DE JANEIRO, BRAZIL.
"THIS IS CHRIS CANTERO ON THE GROUND IN PHILADELPHIA...
HONG KONG, CHINA.
"...WHERE THE STORY IS VIOLENCE. GLOBAL TENSIONS HAVE BEEN ON THE RISE...
REYKJAVIK, ICELAND.
"...AS MANY NATIONS HAVE BEGUN DRAFTING PROPOSALS SIMILAR TO AMERICA'S INDIVIDUALITY ACT...
MELBOURNE, AUSTRALIA.
"...AFTER THE CRISIS COMMAND'S REVELATION OF A POSSIBLE APOCALYPSE. JUST WHEN WE SHOULD BE COMING TOGETHER..."
PHILADELPHIA, PENNSYLVANIA, U.S.A.
...ALL WE CAN DO, IT SEEMS, IS PUT UP BIGGER FENCES. ISOLATIONISTS CLASH...
...WITH THOSE FAVORING A GLOBAL ALLIANCE AGAINST THE COMING THREAT. BUT FORCE...
...SEEMS AN UNLIKELY TOOL AGAINST THOSE FIGHTING FOR THE NICEST ROOM ON THE TITANIC...

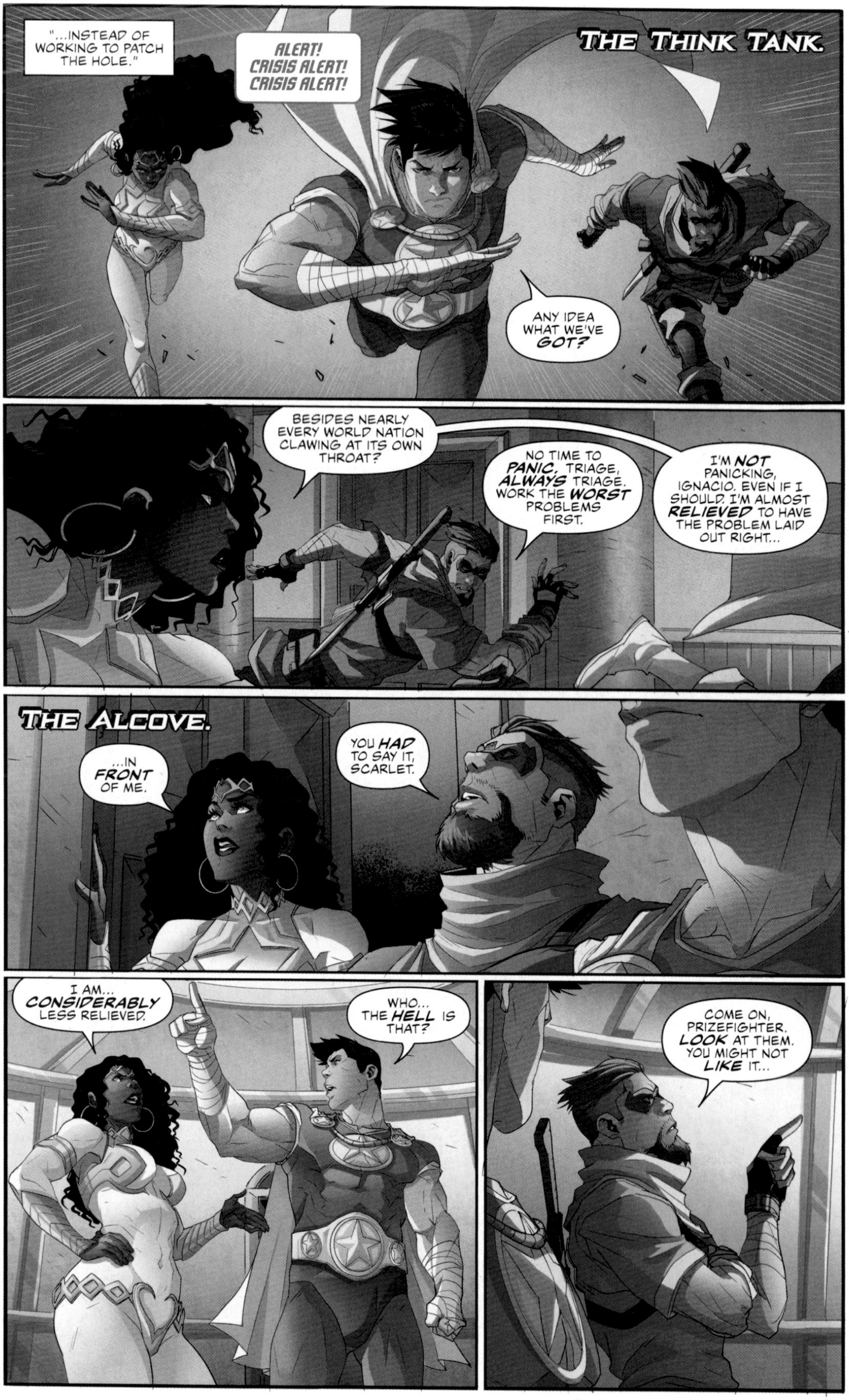

"...INSTEAD OF WORKING TO PATCH THE HOLE."
ALERT! CRISIS ALERT! CRISIS ALERT!
THE THINK TANK.
ANY IDEA WHAT WE'VE GOT?
BESIDES NEARLY EVERY WORLD NATION CLAWING AT ITS OWN THROAT?
NO TIME TO PANIC. TRIAGE, ALWAYS TRIAGE. WORK THE WORST PROBLEMS FIRST.
I'M NOT PANICKING, IGNACIO. EVEN IF I SHOULD. I'M ALMOST RELIEVED TO HAVE THE PROBLEM LAID OUT RIGHT...
THE ALCOVE.
...IN FRONT OF ME.
YOU HAD TO SAY IT, SCARLET.
I AM... CONSIDERABLY LESS RELIEVED.
WHO... THE HELL IS THAT?
COME ON, PRIZEFIGHTER. LOOK AT THEM. YOU MIGHT NOT LIKE IT...

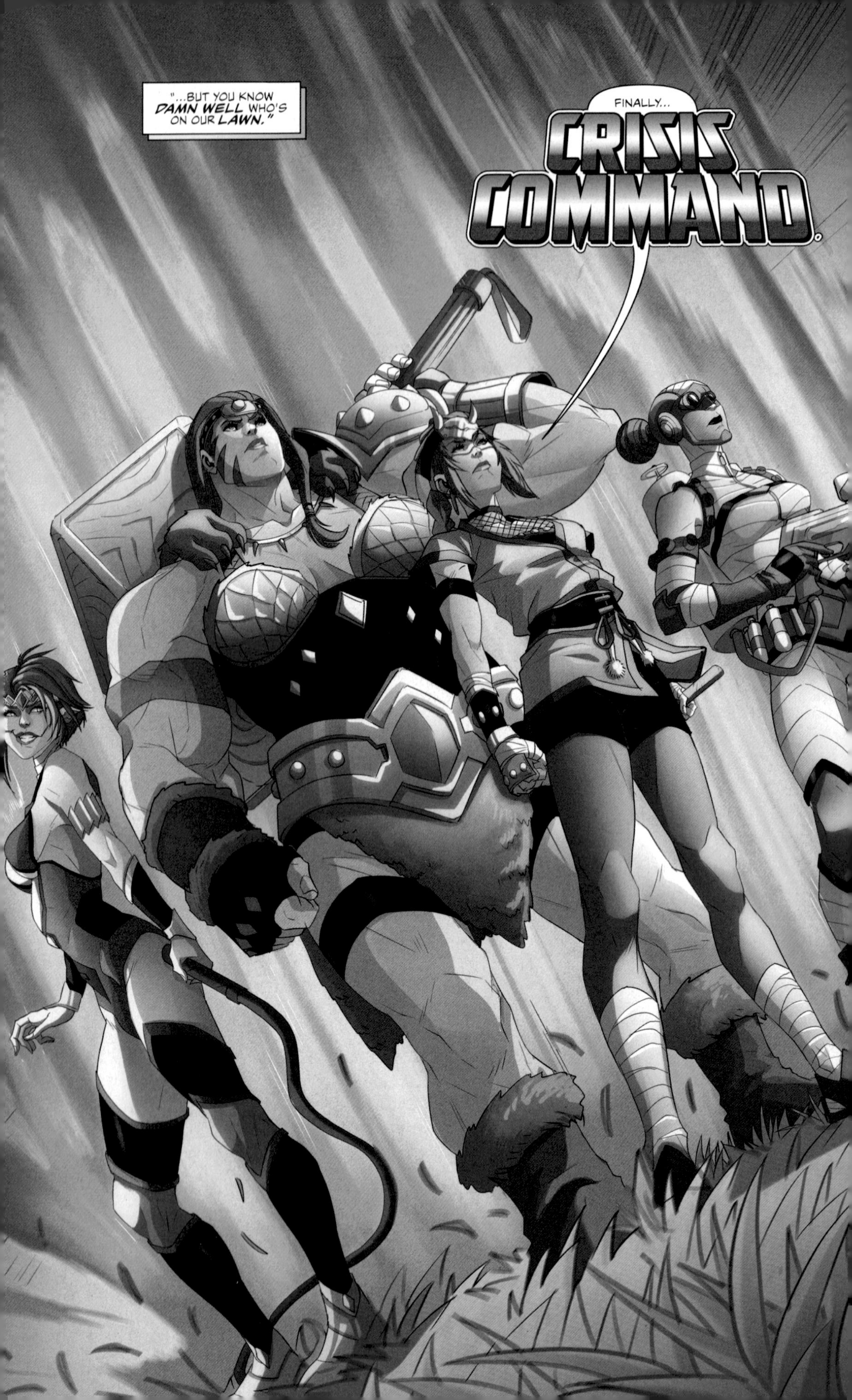

"...BUT YOU KNOW DAMN WELL WHO'S ON OUR LAWN."
FINALLY...
CRISIS COMMAND.

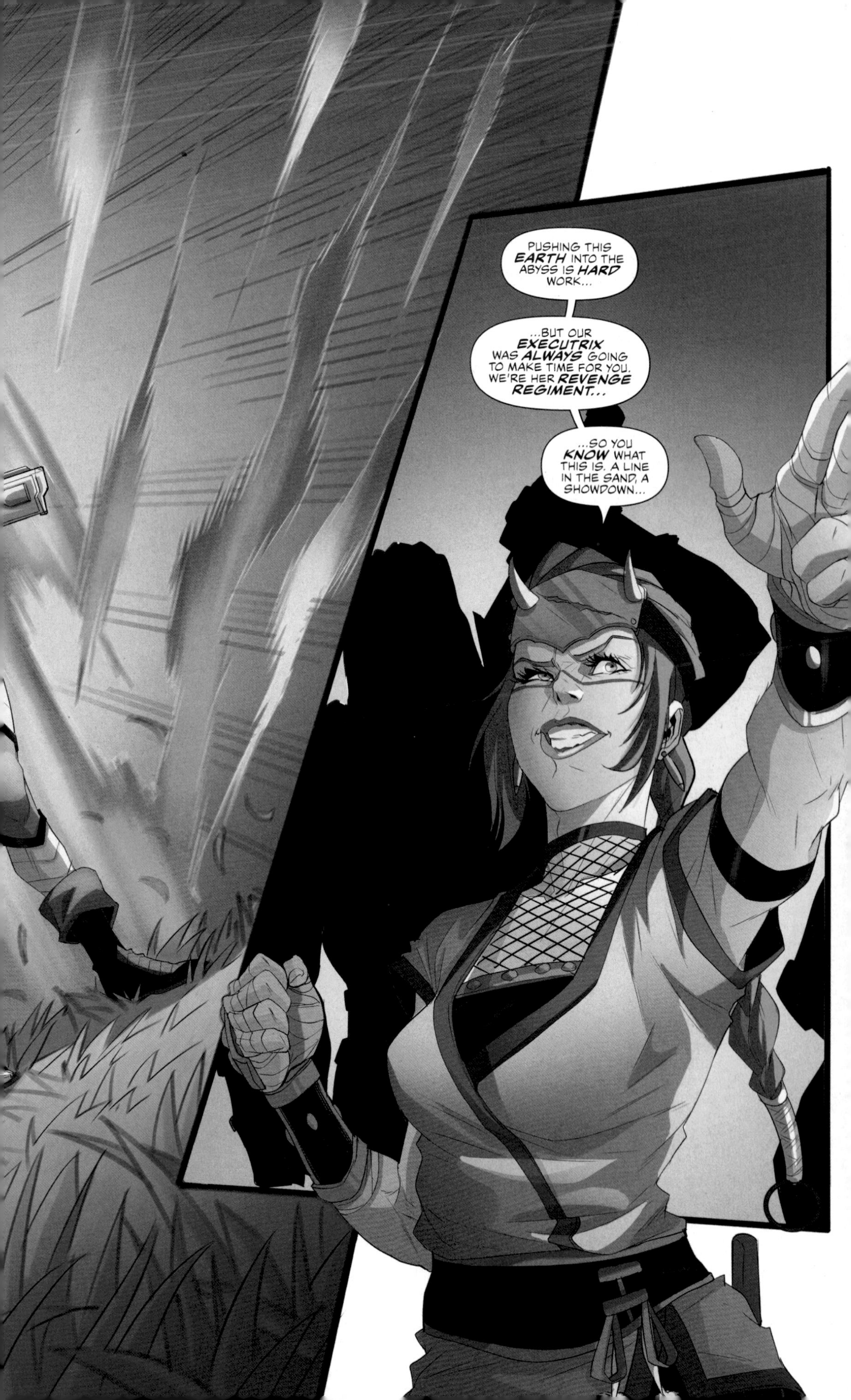
PUSHING THIS EARTH INTO THE ABYSS IS HARD WORK...
...BUT OUR EXECUTRIX WAS ALWAYS GOING TO MAKE TIME FOR YOU. WE'RE HER REVENGE REGIMENT...
...SO YOU KNOW WHAT THIS IS. A LINE IN THE SAND, A SHOWDOWN...

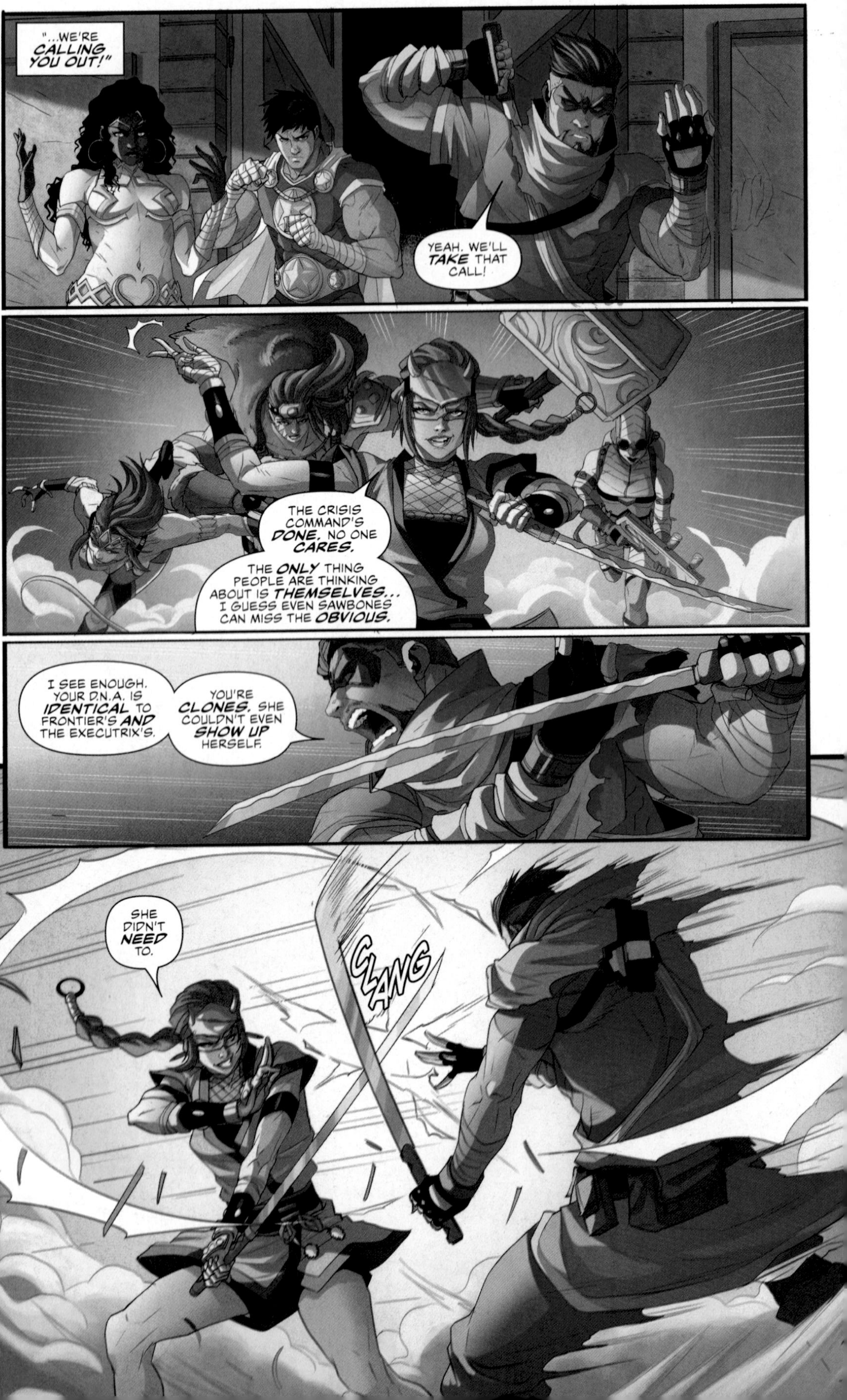
"...WE'RE CALLING YOU OUT!"
YEAH. WE'LL TAKE THAT CALL!
THE CRISIS COMMAND'S DONE. NO ONE CARES.
THE ONLY THING PEOPLE ARE THINKING ABOUT IS THEMSELVES... I GUESS EVEN SAWBONES CAN MISS THE OBVIOUS.
I SEE ENOUGH. YOUR D.N.A. IS IDENTICAL TO FRONTIER'S AND THE EXECUTRIX'S.
YOU'RE CLONES. SHE COULDN'T EVEN SHOW UP HERSELF.
SHE DIDN'T NEED TO.
CLANG

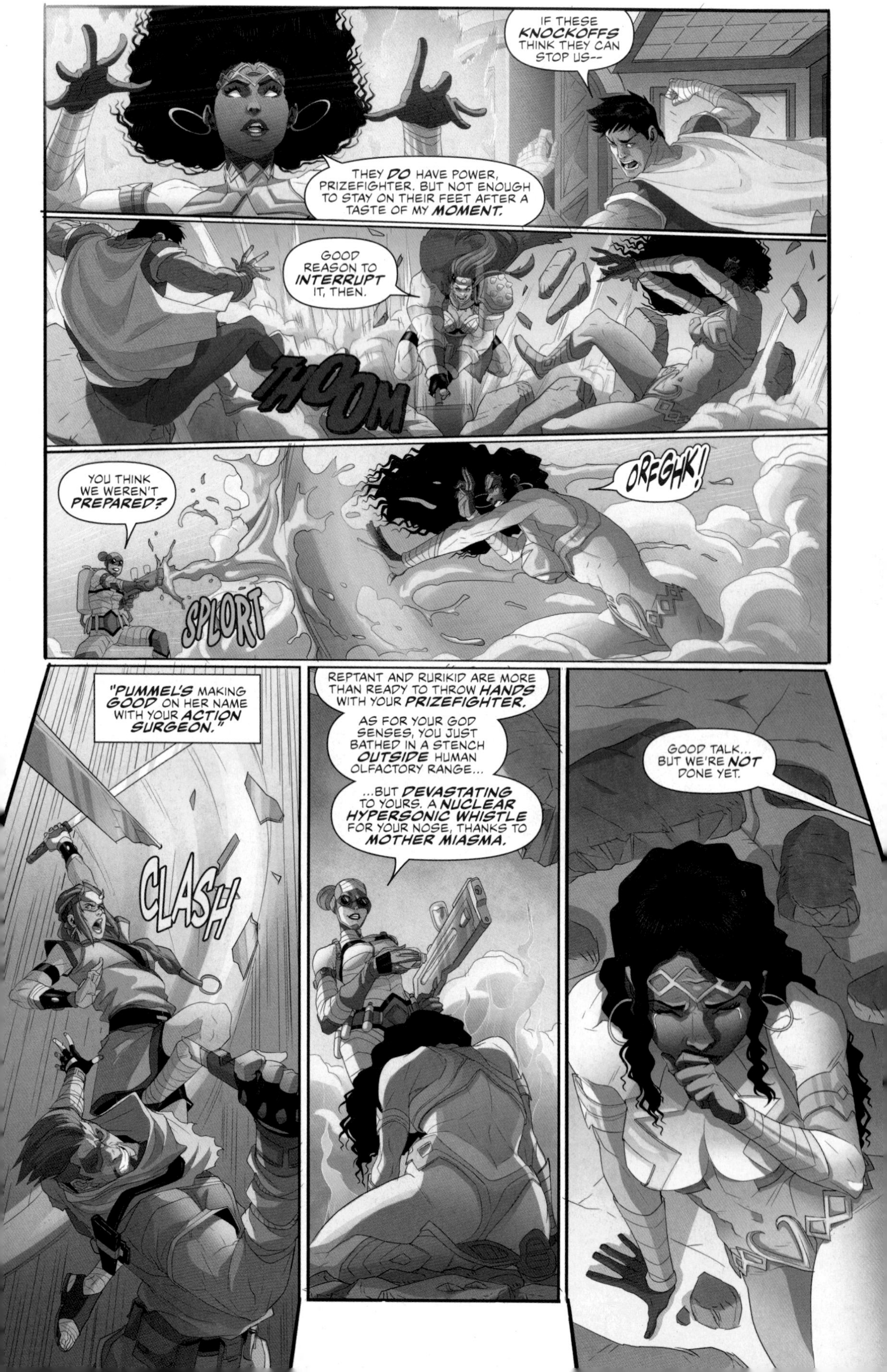
IF THESE KNOCKOFFS THINK THEY CAN STOP US--
THEY DO HAVE POWER, PRIZEFIGHTER. BUT NOT ENOUGH TO STAY ON THEIR FEET AFTER A TASTE OF MY MOMENT.
GOOD REASON TO INTERRUPT IT, THEN.
THOOOM
YOU THINK WE WEREN'T PREPARED?
ORFGHK!
SPLORT
"PUMMEL'S MAKING GOOD ON HER NAME WITH YOUR ACTION SURGEON."
CLASH
REPTANT AND RURIKID ARE MORE THAN READY TO THROW HANDS WITH YOUR PRIZEFIGHTER.
AS FOR YOUR GOD SENSES, YOU JUST BATHED IN A STENCH OUTSIDE HUMAN OLFACTORY RANGE...
...BUT DEVASTATING TO YOURS. A NUCLEAR HYPERSONIC WHISTLE FOR YOUR NOSE, THANKS TO MOTHER MIASMA.
GOOD TALK... BUT WE'RE NOT DONE YET.

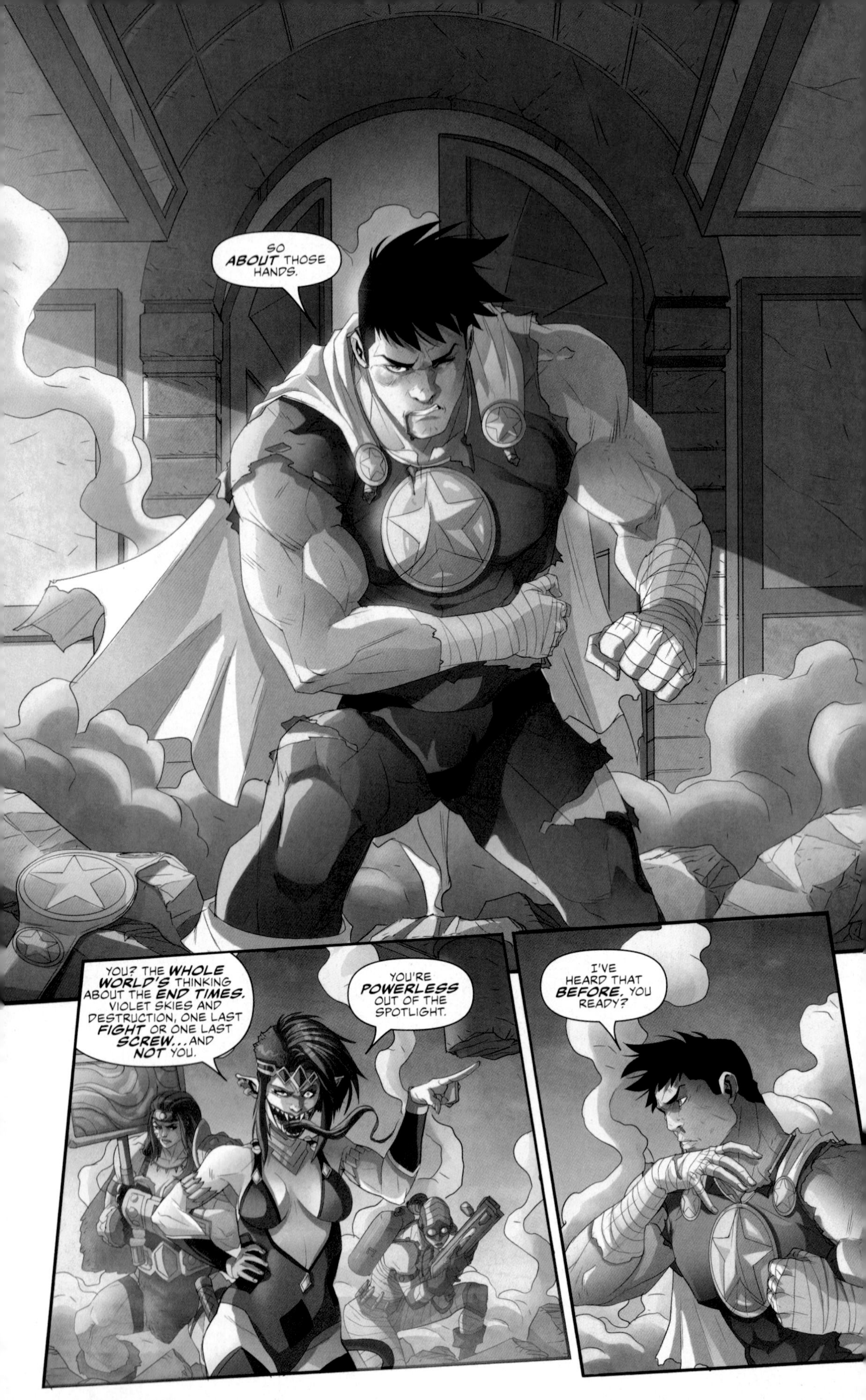
SO ABOUT THOSE HANDS.
YOU? THE WHOLE WORLD'S THINKING ABOUT THE END TIMES. VIOLET SKIES AND DESTRUCTION, ONE LAST FIGHT OR ONE LAST SCREW...AND NOT YOU.
YOU'RE POWERLESS OUT OF THE SPOTLIGHT.
I'VE HEARD THAT BEFORE. YOU READY?

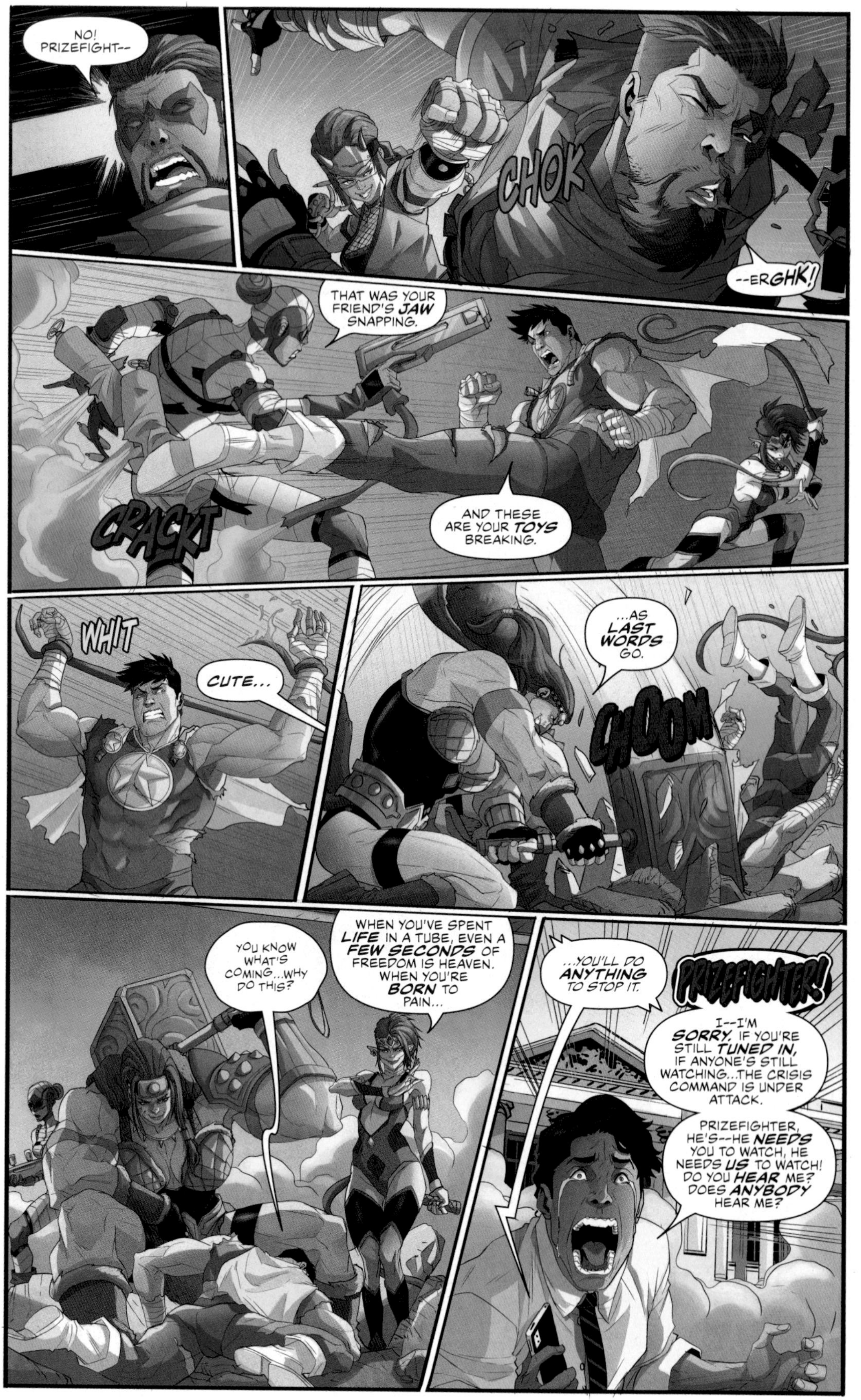
NO! PRIZEFIGHT--
CHOK
--ERGHK!
THAT WAS YOUR FRIEND'S JAW SNAPPING.
CRACKT
AND THESE ARE YOUR TOYS BREAKING.
WHIT
CUTE...
...AS LAST WORDS GO.
CHOOM
YOU KNOW WHAT'S COMING...WHY DO THIS?
WHEN YOU'VE SPENT LIFE IN A TUBE, EVEN A FEW SECONDS OF FREEDOM IS HEAVEN. WHEN YOU'RE BORN TO PAIN...
...YOU'LL DO ANYTHING TO STOP IT.
PRIZEFIGHTER!
I--I'M SORRY. IF YOU'RE STILL TUNED IN, IF ANYONE'S STILL WATCHING...THE CRISIS COMMAND IS UNDER ATTACK.
PRIZEFIGHTER, HE'S--HE NEEDS YOU TO WATCH, HE NEEDS US TO WATCH! DO YOU HEAR ME? DOES ANYBODY HEAR ME?

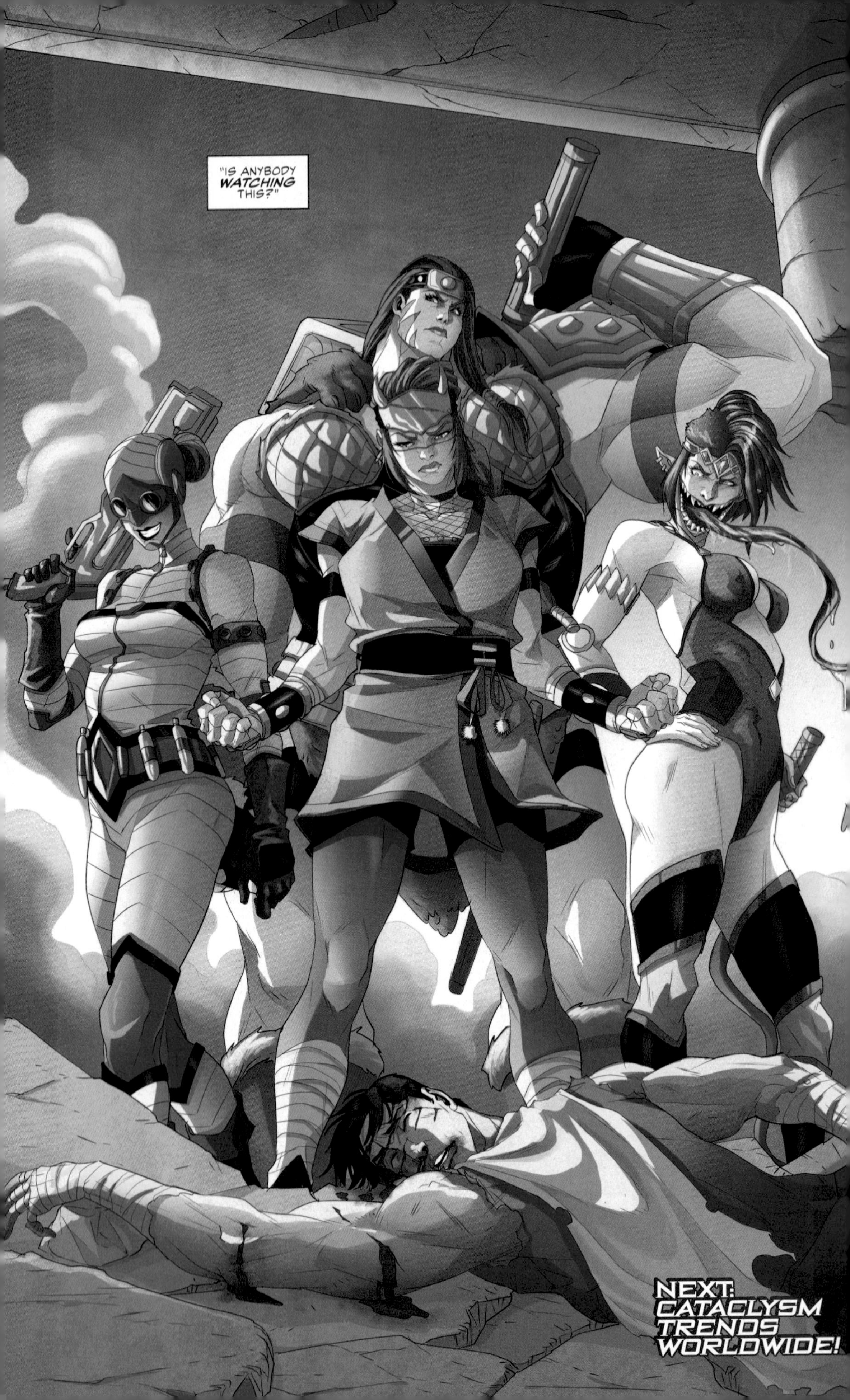
"IS ANYBODY WATCHING THIS?"
NEXT: CATACLYSM TRENDS WORLDWIDE!

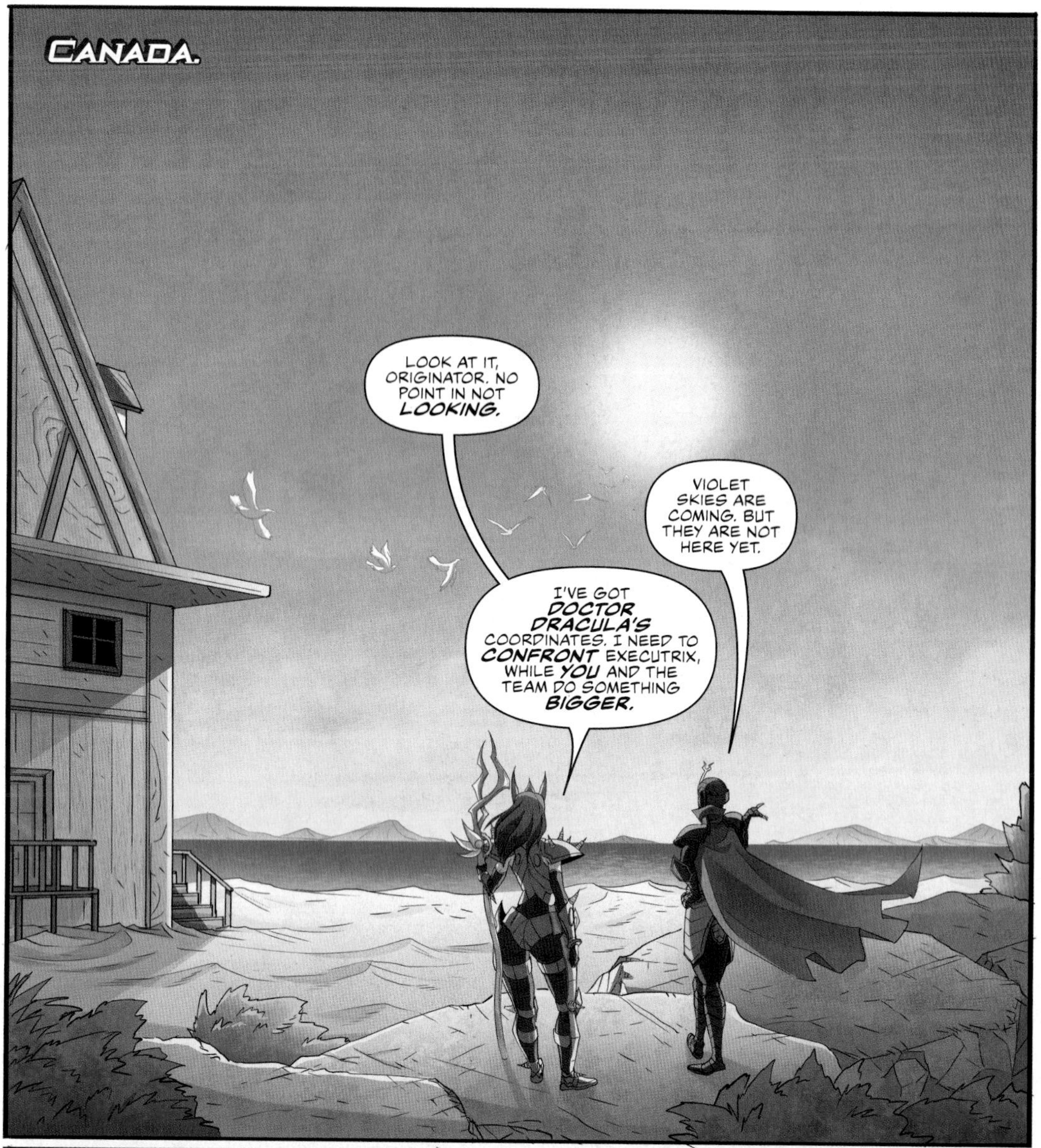
CANADA.
LOOK AT IT, ORIGINATOR. NO POINT IN NOT LOOKING.
VIOLET SKIES ARE COMING. BUT THEY ARE NOT HERE YET.
I'VE GOT DOCTOR DRACULA'S COORDINATES. I NEED TO CONFRONT EXECUTRIX, WHILE YOU AND THE TEAM DO SOMETHING BIGGER.
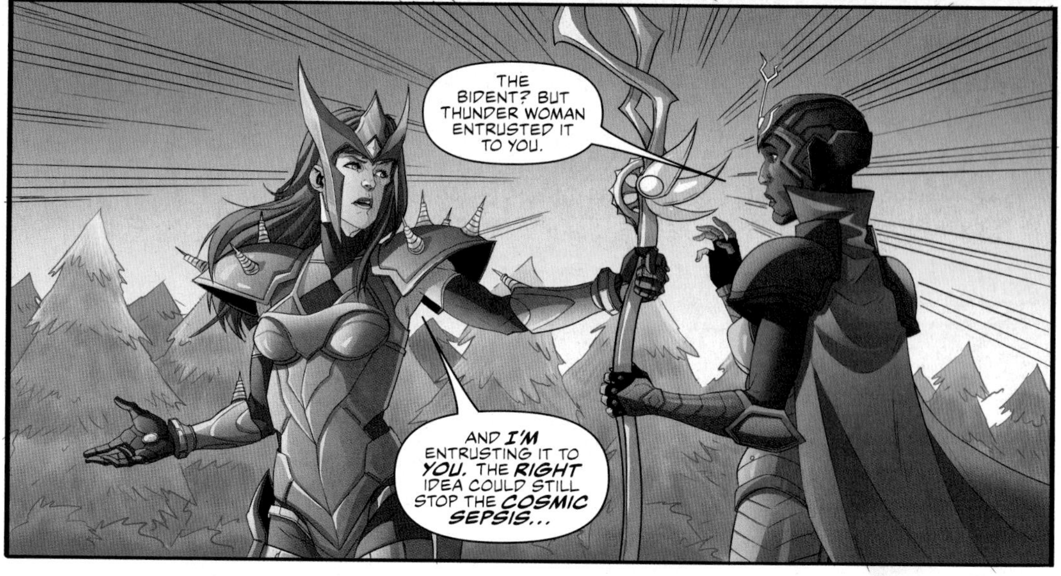
THE BIDENT? BUT THUNDER WOMAN ENTRUSTED IT TO YOU.
AND I'M ENTRUSTING IT TO YOU. THE RIGHT IDEA COULD STILL STOP THE COSMIC SEPSIS...

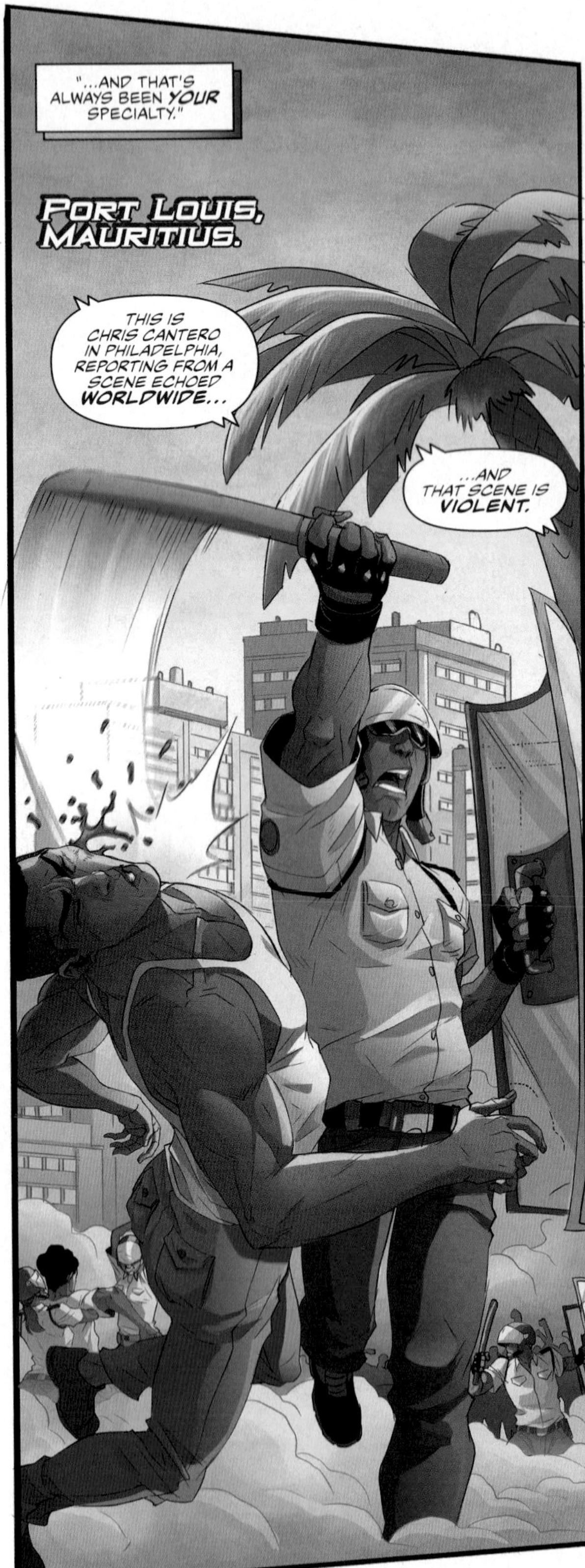
"...AND THAT'S ALWAYS BEEN YOUR SPECIALTY."
PORT LOUIS, MAURITIUS.
THIS IS CHRIS CANTERO IN PHILADELPHIA, REPORTING FROM A SCENE ECHOED WORLDWIDE...
...AND THAT SCENE IS VIOLENT.

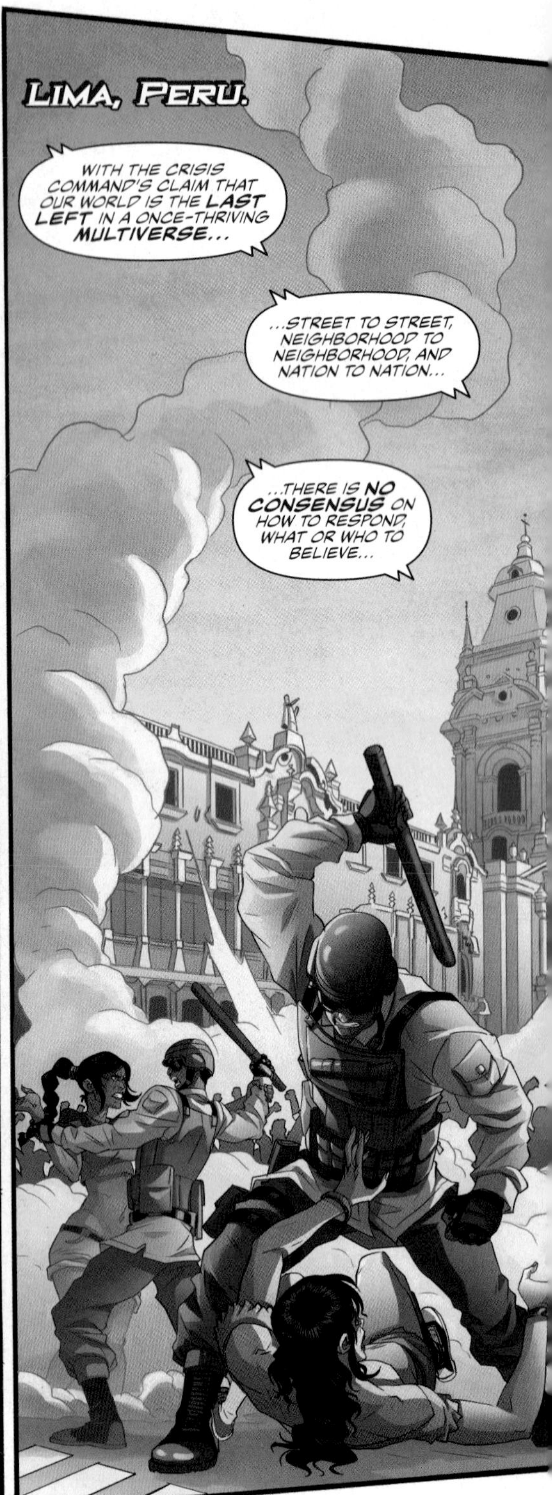
LIMA, PERU.
WITH THE CRISIS COMMAND'S CLAIM THAT OUR WORLD IS THE LAST LEFT IN A ONCE-THRIVING MULTIVERSE...
...STREET TO STREET, NEIGHBORHOOD TO NEIGHBORHOOD, AND NATION TO NATION...
...THERE IS NO CONSENSUS ON HOW TO RESPOND, WHAT OR WHO TO BELIEVE...

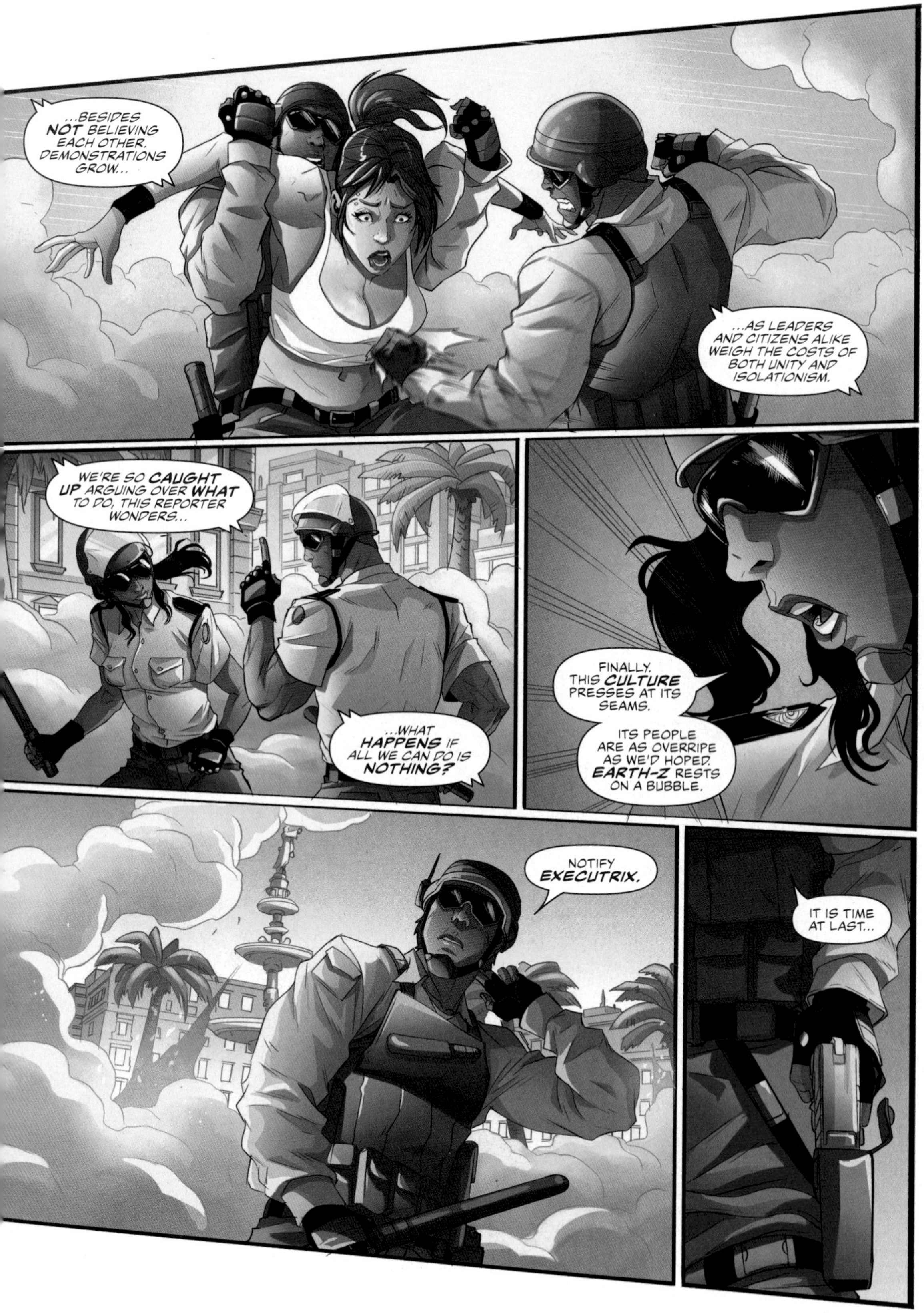
...BESIDES NOT BELIEVING EACH OTHER, DEMONSTRATIONS GROW...
...AS LEADERS AND CITIZENS ALIKE WEIGH THE COSTS OF BOTH UNITY AND ISOLATIONISM.
WE'RE SO CAUGHT UP ARGUING OVER WHAT TO DO, THIS REPORTER WONDERS...
...WHAT HAPPENS IF ALL WE CAN DO IS NOTHING?
FINALLY. THIS CULTURE PRESSES AT ITS SEAMS.
ITS PEOPLE ARE AS OVERRIPE AS WE'D HOPED. EARTH-Z RESTS ON A BUBBLE.
NOTIFY EXECUTRIX.
IT IS TIME AT LAST...

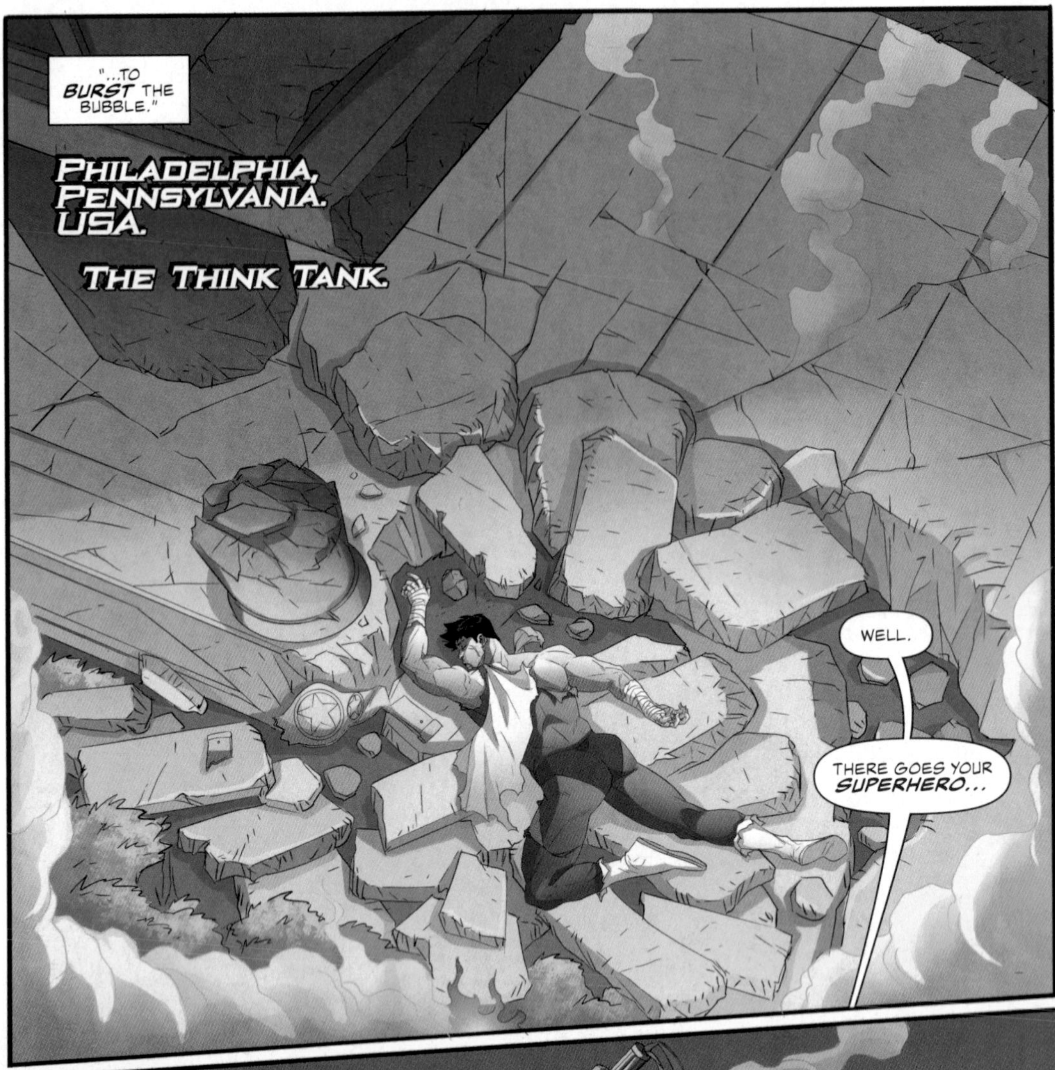
"...TO BURST THE BUBBLE."
PHILADELPHIA, PENNSYLVANIA. USA.
THE THINK TANK.
WELL.
THERE GOES YOUR SUPERHERO...

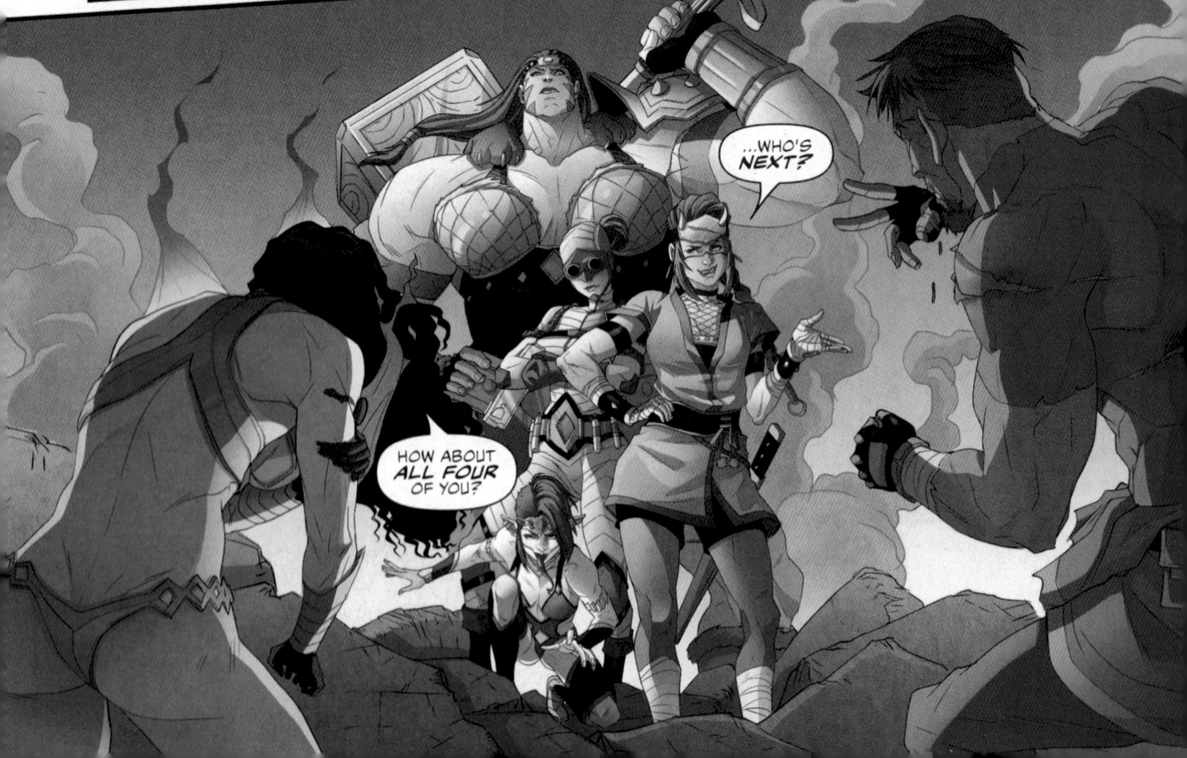
...WHO'S NEXT?
HOW ABOUT ALL FOUR OF YOU?

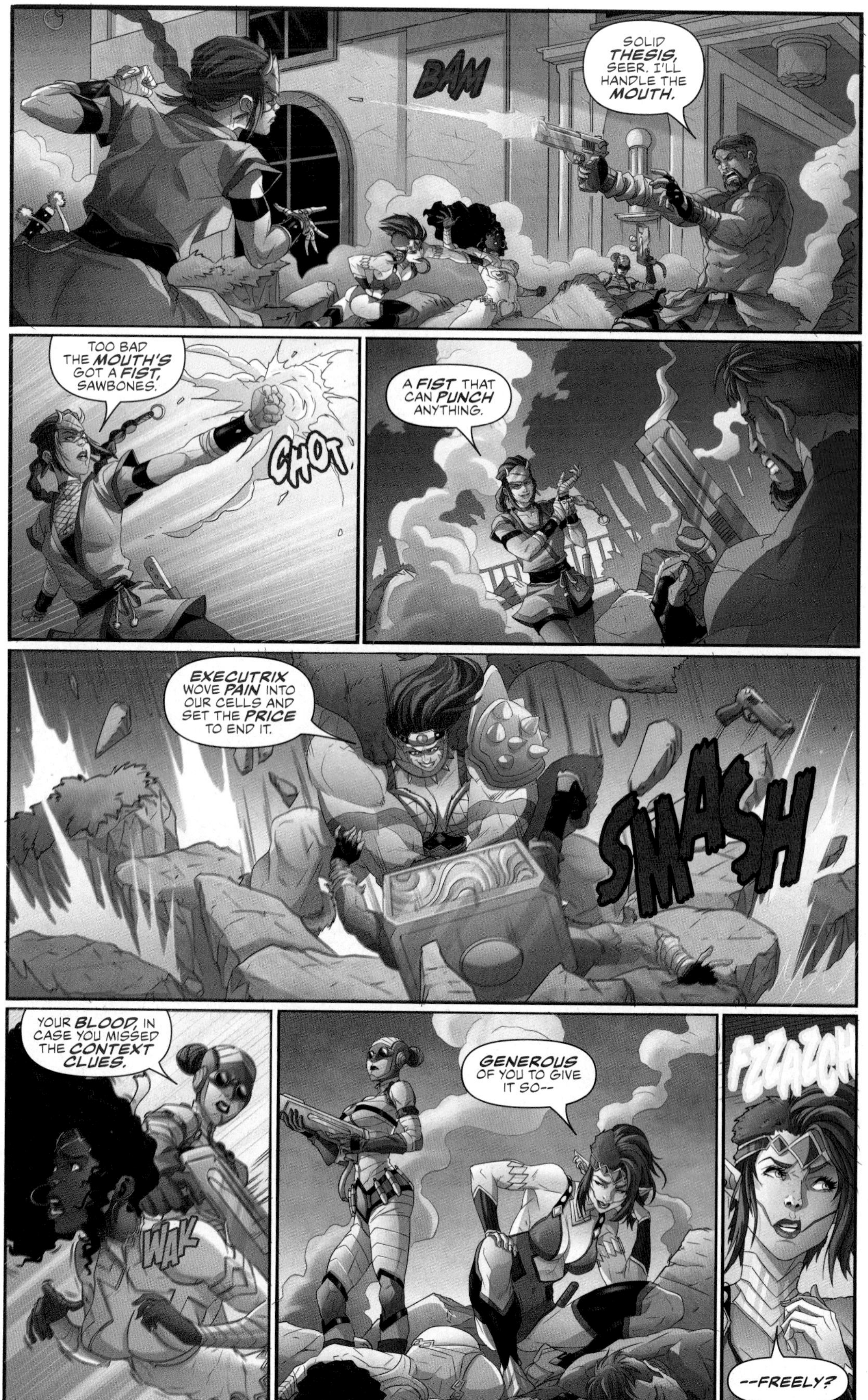
BAM
SOLID THESIS, SEER. I'LL HANDLE THE MOUTH.
TOO BAD THE MOUTH'S GOT A FIST, SAWBONES.
CHOT
A FIST THAT CAN PUNCH ANYTHING.
EXECUTRIX WOVE PAIN INTO OUR CELLS AND SET THE PRICE TO END IT.
SMASH
YOUR BLOOD, IN CASE YOU MISSED THE CONTEXT CLUES.
WAK
GENEROUS OF YOU TO GIVE IT SO--
FZZAZCH
--FREELY?

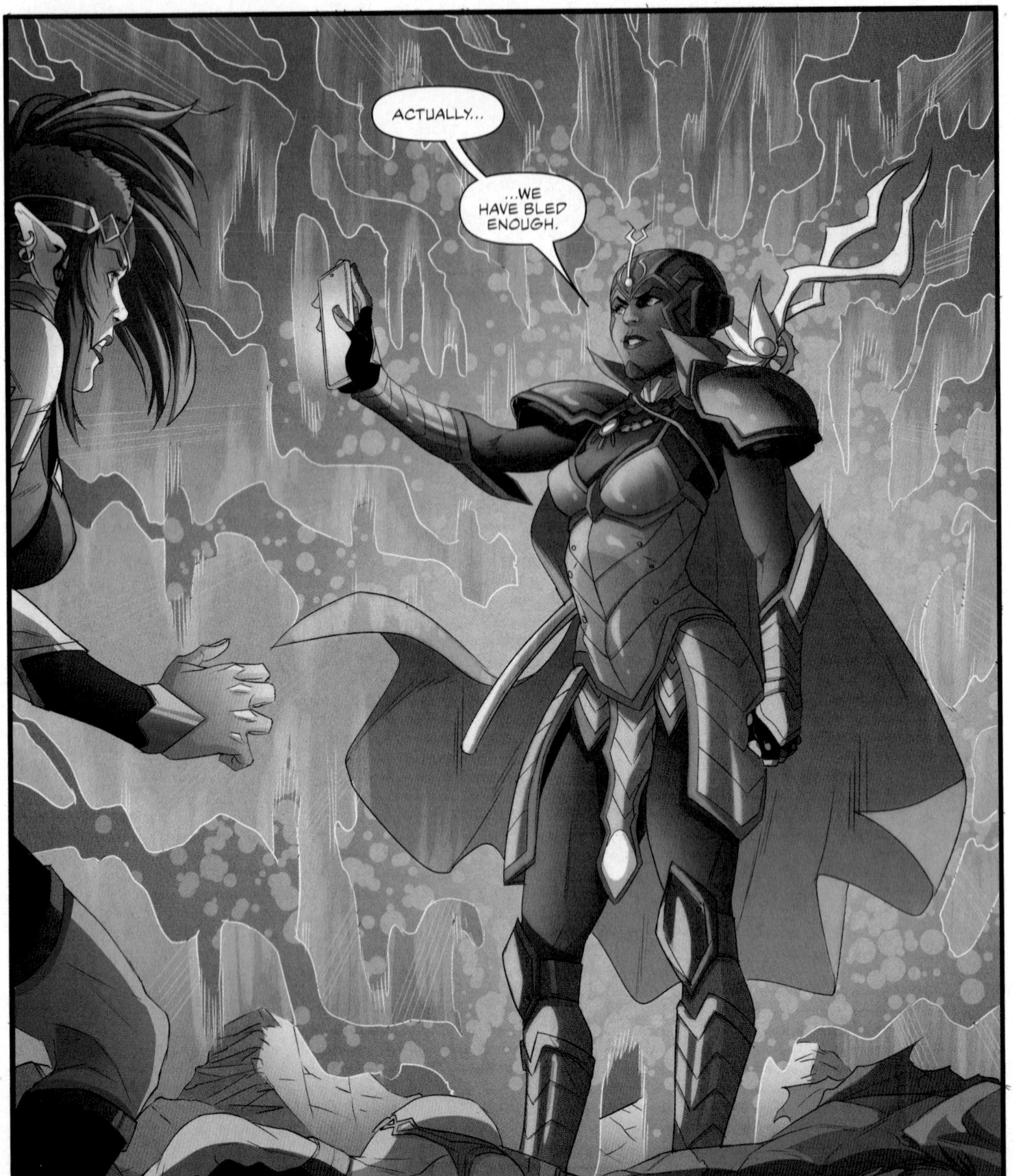
ACTUALLY...
...WE HAVE BLED ENOUGH.

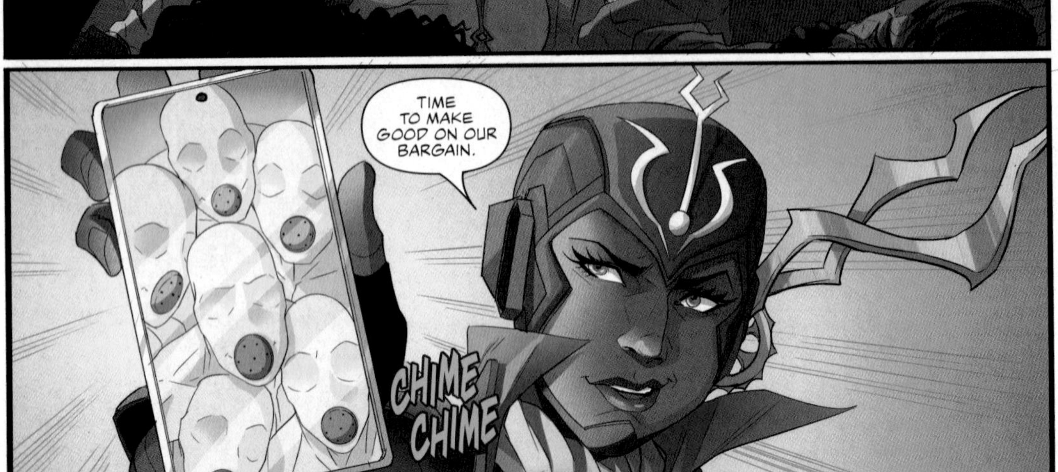
TIME TO MAKE GOOD ON OUR BARGAIN.
CHIME CHIME

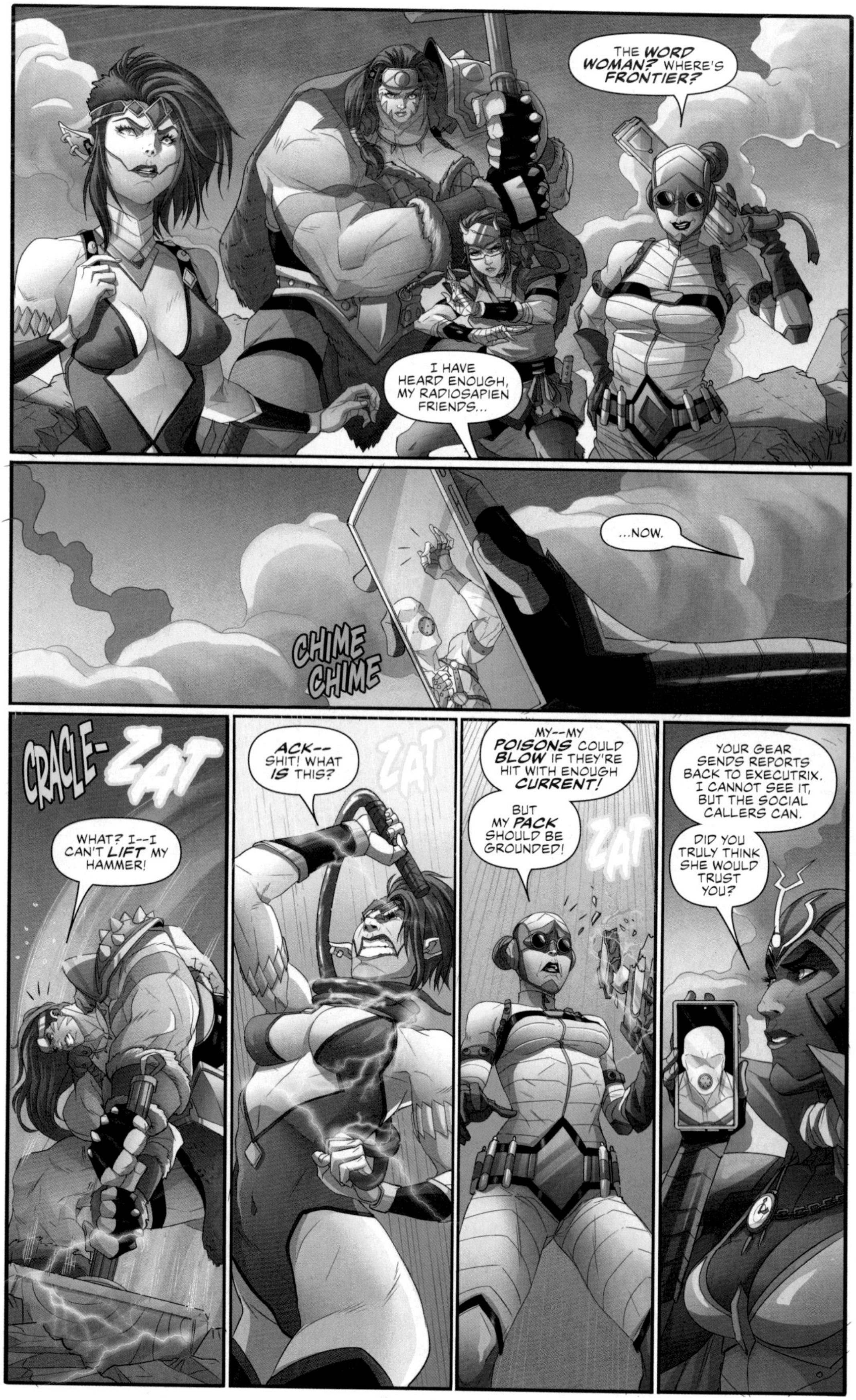
THE WORD WOMAN? WHERE'S FRONTIER?
I HAVE HEARD ENOUGH, MY RADIOSAPIEN FRIENDS...
...NOW.
CHIME CHIME
CRACLE-ZAT
WHAT? I--I CAN'T LIFT MY HAMMER!
ACK--SHIT! WHAT IS THIS?
ZAT
MY--MY POISONS COULD BLOW IF THEY'RE HIT WITH ENOUGH CURRENT!
BUT MY PACK SHOULD BE GROUNDED!
ZAT
YOUR GEAR SENDS REPORTS BACK TO EXECUTRIX. I CANNOT SEE IT, BUT THE SOCIAL CALLERS CAN.
DID YOU TRULY THINK SHE WOULD TRUST YOU?

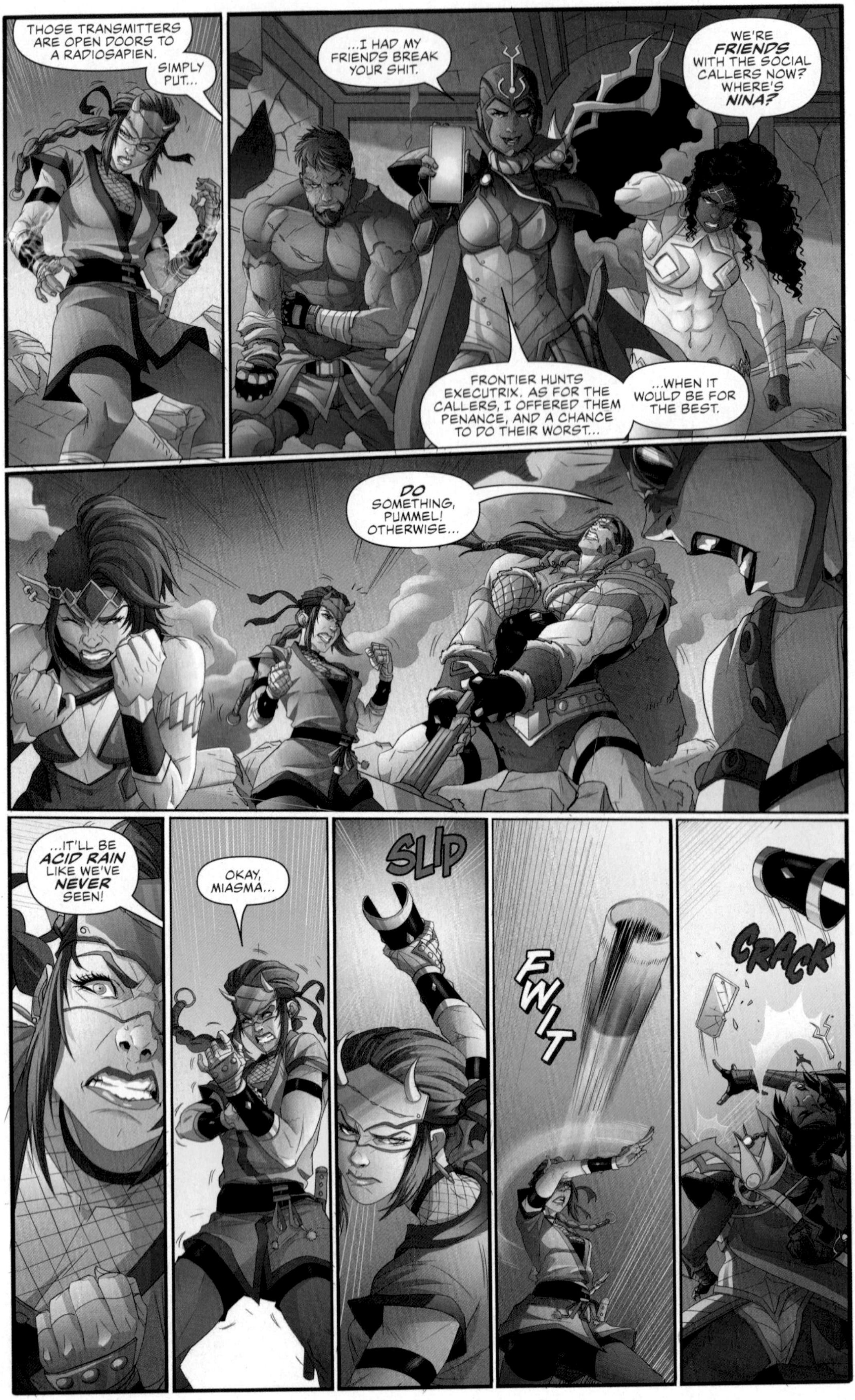
THOSE TRANSMITTERS ARE OPEN DOORS TO A RADIOSAPIEN.
SIMPLY PUT...
...I HAD MY FRIENDS BREAK YOUR SHIT.
WE'RE FRIENDS WITH THE SOCIAL CALLERS NOW? WHERE'S NINA?
FRONTIER HUNTS EXECUTRIX. AS FOR THE CALLERS, I OFFERED THEM PENANCE, AND A CHANCE TO DO THEIR WORST...
...WHEN IT WOULD BE FOR THE BEST.
DO SOMETHING, PUMMEL! OTHERWISE...
...IT'LL BE ACID RAIN LIKE WE'VE NEVER SEEN!
OKAY, MIASMA...
SLIP
FWIT
CRACK

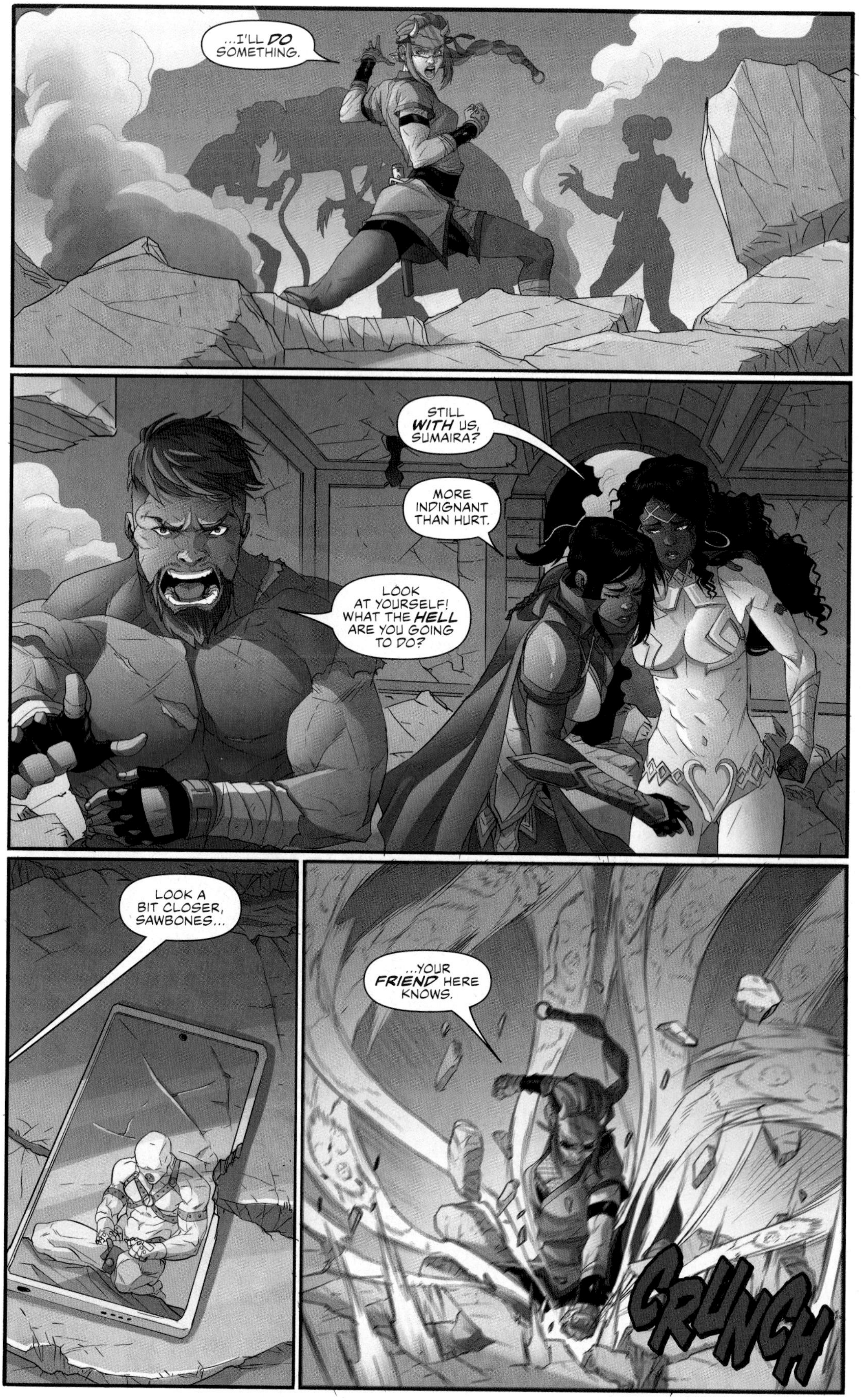
...I'LL DO SOMETHING.
STILL WITH US, SUMAIRA?
MORE INDIGNANT THAN HURT.
LOOK AT YOURSELF! WHAT THE HELL ARE YOU GOING TO DO?
LOOK A BIT CLOSER, SAWBONES...
...YOUR FRIEND HERE KNOWS.
CRUNCH

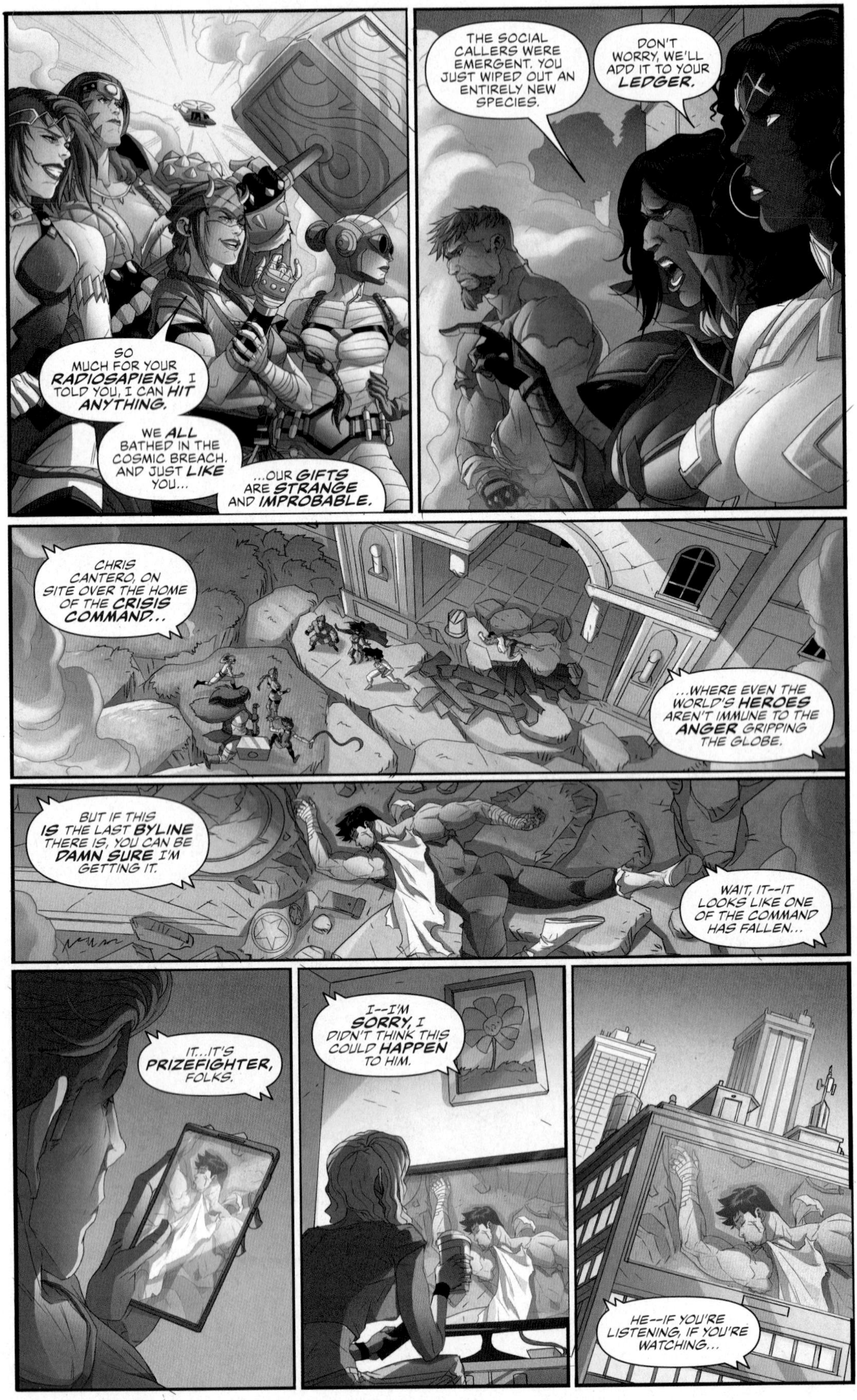
SO MUCH FOR YOUR RADIOSAPIENS. I TOLD YOU, I CAN HIT ANYTHING.
WE ALL BATHED IN THE COSMIC BREACH. AND JUST LIKE YOU...
...OUR GIFTS ARE STRANGE AND IMPROBABLE.
THE SOCIAL CALLERS WERE EMERGENT. YOU JUST WIPED OUT AN ENTIRELY NEW SPECIES.
DON'T WORRY, WE'LL ADD IT TO YOUR LEDGER.
CHRIS CANTERO, ON SITE OVER THE HOME OF THE CRISIS COMMAND...
...WHERE EVEN THE WORLD'S HEROES AREN'T IMMUNE TO THE ANGER GRIPPING THE GLOBE.
BUT IF THIS IS THE LAST BYLINE THERE IS, YOU CAN BE DAMN SURE I'M GETTING IT.
WAIT, IT--IT LOOKS LIKE ONE OF THE COMMAND HAS FALLEN...
IT...IT'S PRIZEFIGHTER, FOLKS.
I--I'M SORRY, I DIDN'T THINK THIS COULD HAPPEN TO HIM.
HE--IF YOU'RE LISTENING, IF YOU'RE WATCHING...

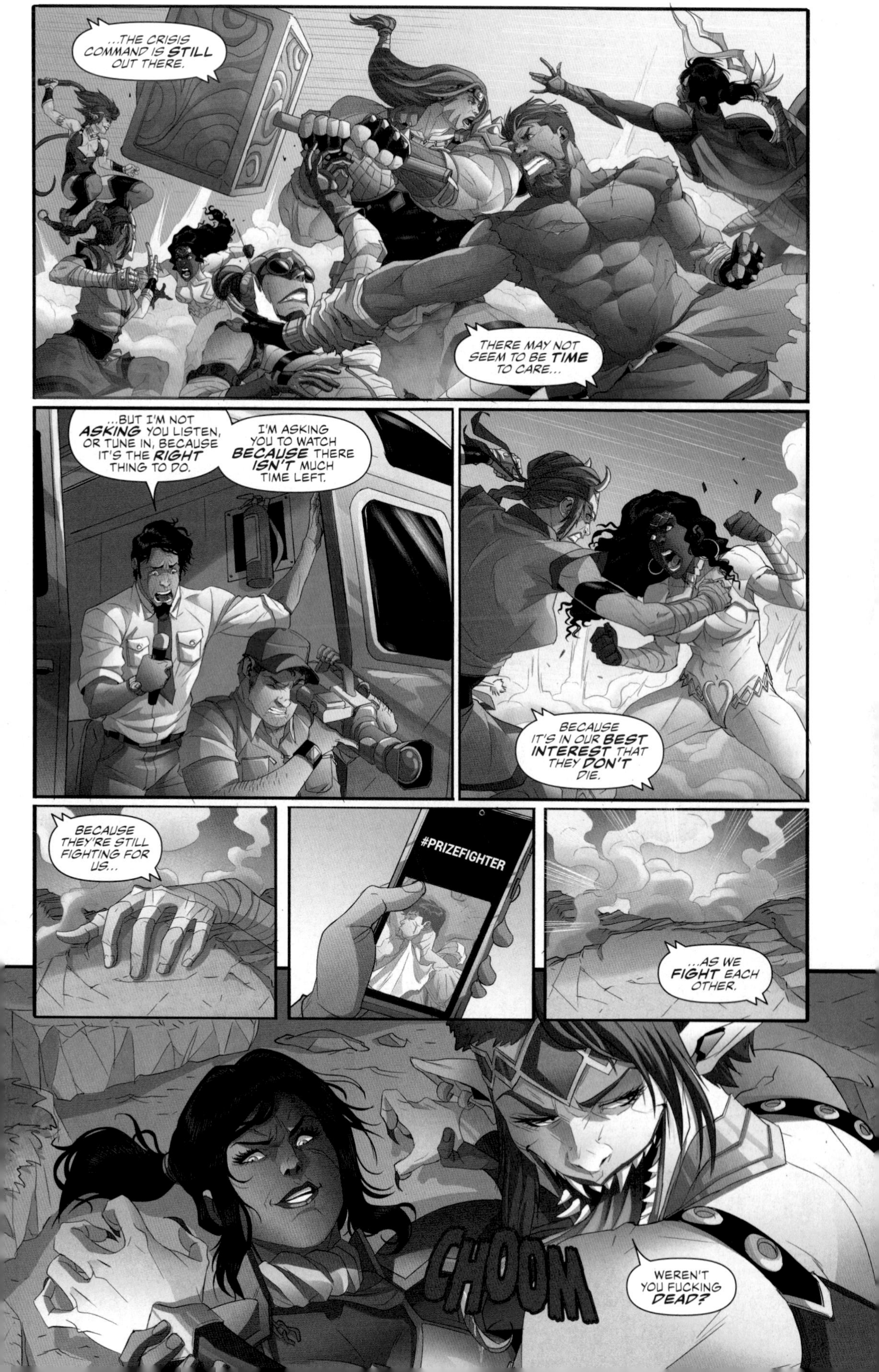
...THE CRISIS COMMAND IS STILL OUT THERE.
THERE MAY NOT SEEM TO BE TIME TO CARE...
...BUT I'M NOT ASKING YOU LISTEN, OR TUNE IN, BECAUSE IT'S THE RIGHT THING TO DO.
I'M ASKING YOU TO WATCH BECAUSE THERE ISN'T MUCH TIME LEFT.
BECAUSE IT'S IN OUR BEST INTEREST THAT THEY DON'T DIE.
BECAUSE THEY'RE STILL FIGHTING FOR US...
#PRIZEFIGHTER
...AS WE FIGHT EACH OTHER.
CHOOM
WEREN'T YOU FUCKING DEAD?

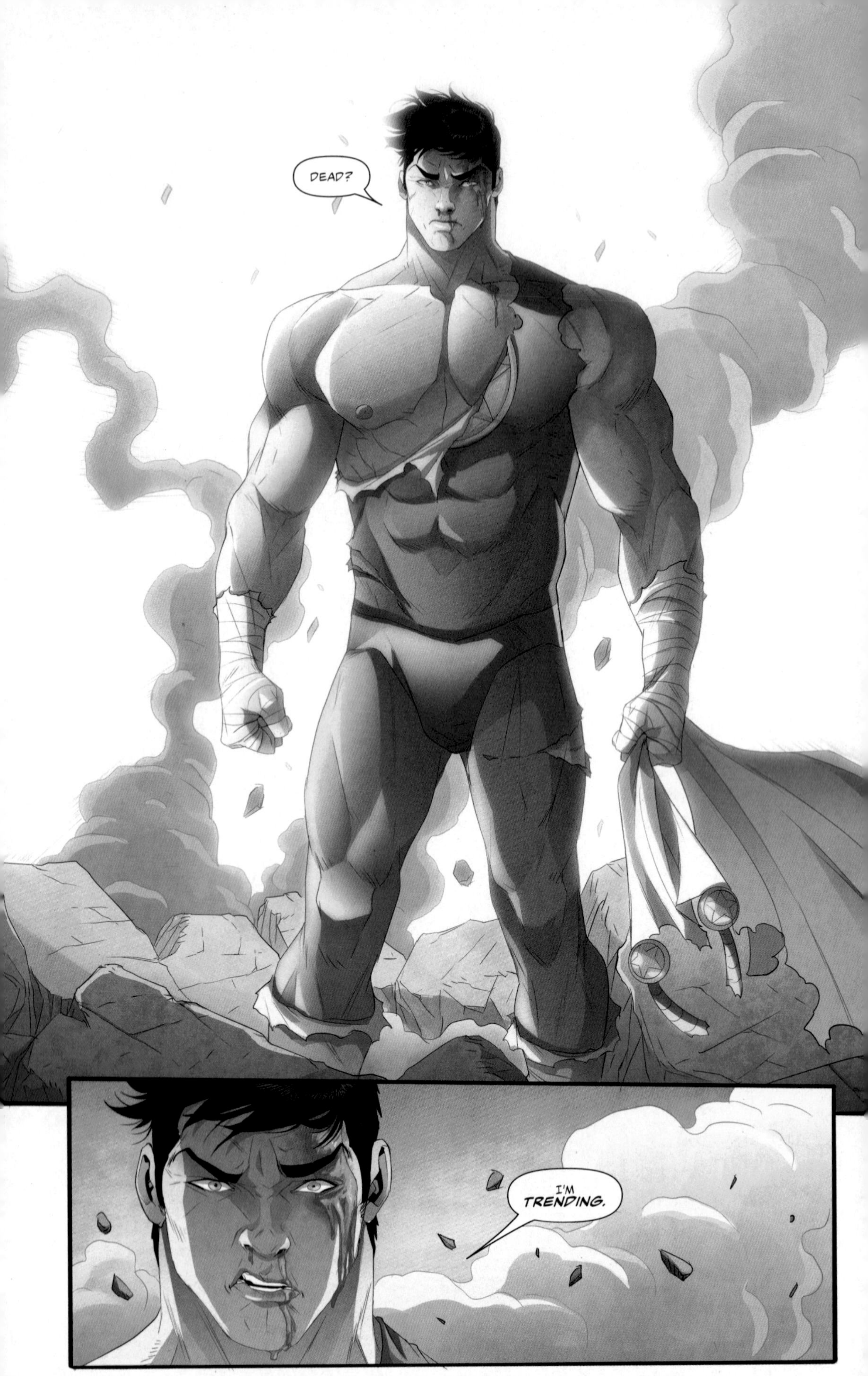
DEAD?
I'M TRENDING.

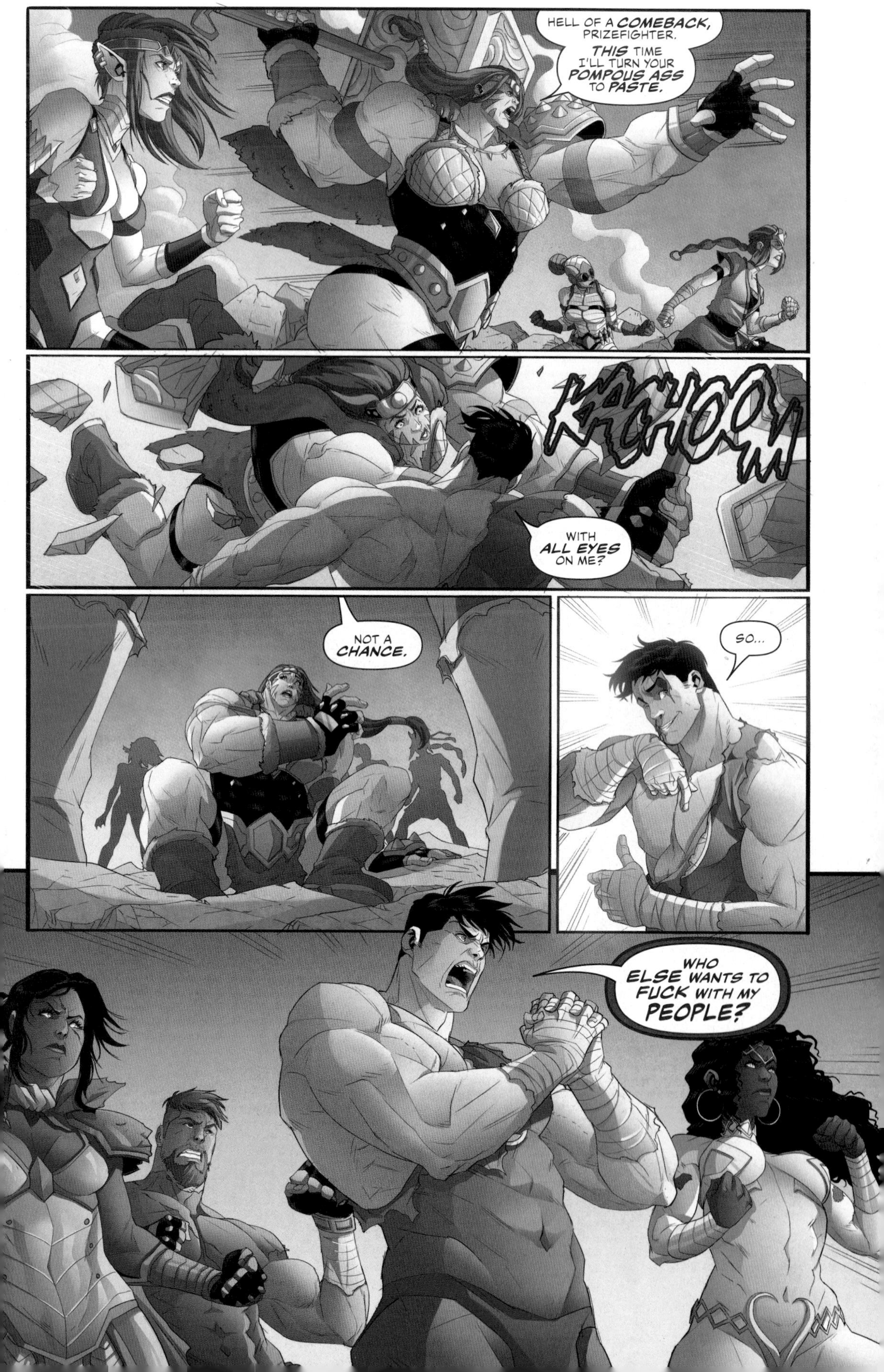
HELL OF A COMEBACK, PRIZEFIGHTER.
THIS TIME I'LL TURN YOUR POMPOUS ASS TO PASTE.
KRCHOOM
WITH ALL EYES ON ME?
NOT A CHANCE.
SO...
WHO ELSE WANTS TO FUCK WITH MY PEOPLE?

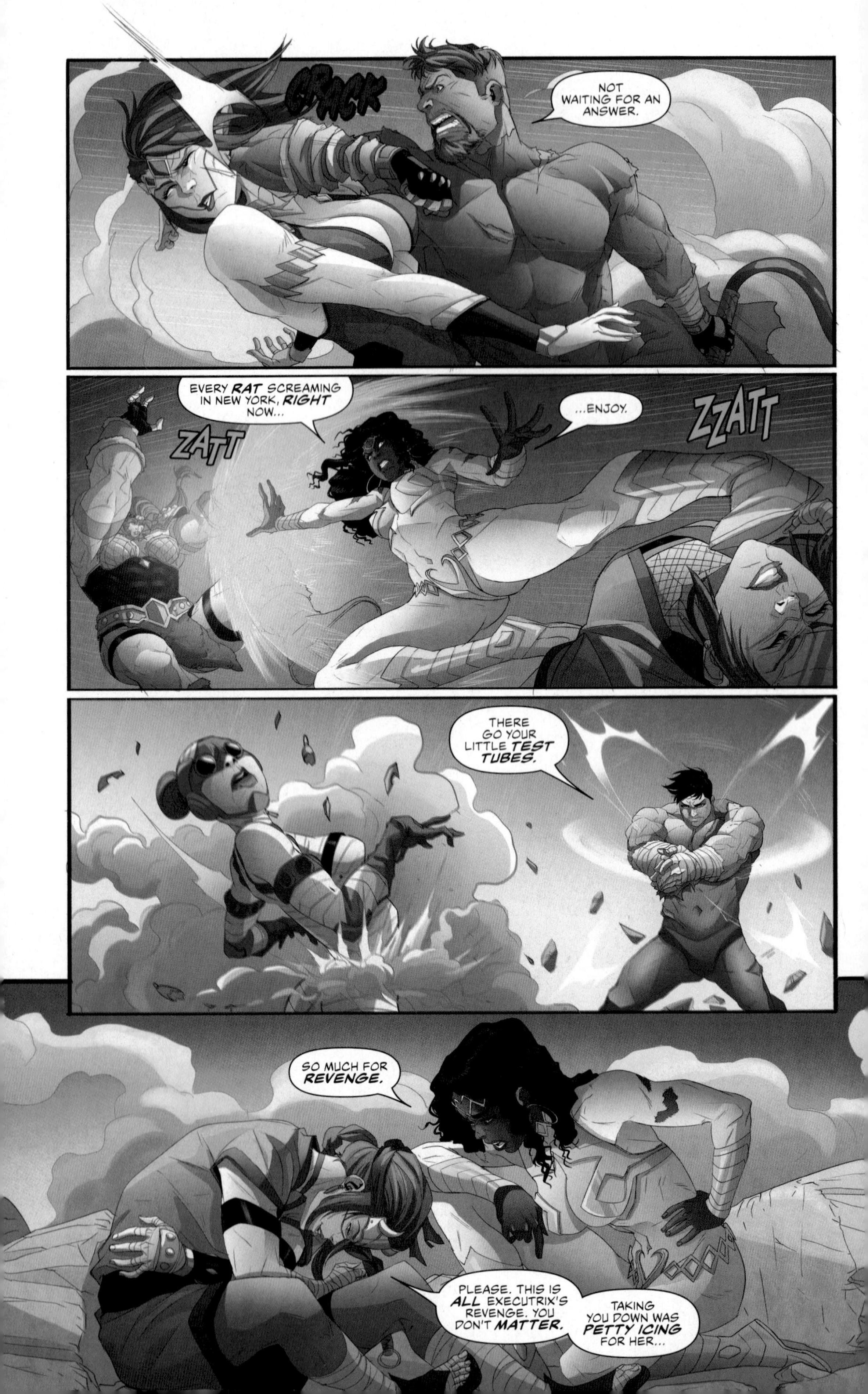
CRACK
NOT WAITING FOR AN ANSWER.
EVERY RAT SCREAMING IN NEW YORK, RIGHT NOW...
ZATT
...ENJOY.
ZZATT
THERE GO YOUR LITTLE TEST TUBES.
SO MUCH FOR REVENGE.
PLEASE. THIS IS ALL EXECUTRIX'S REVENGE. YOU DON'T MATTER.
TAKING YOU DOWN WAS PETTY ICING FOR HER...

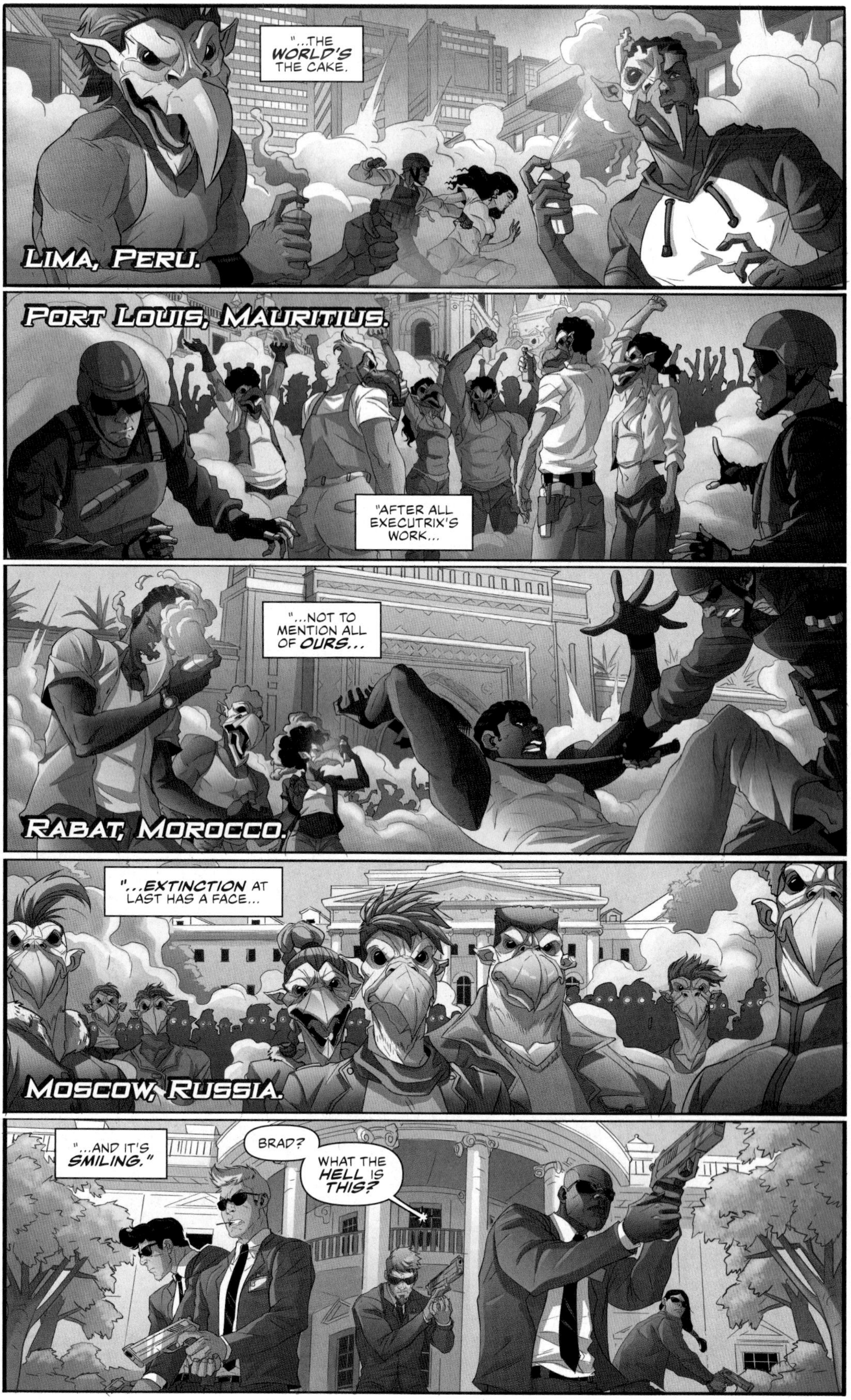
"...THE WORLD'S THE CAKE.
LIMA, PERU.
PORT LOUIS, MAURITIUS.
"AFTER ALL EXECUTRIX'S WORK...
"...NOT TO MENTION ALL OF OURS...
RABAT, MOROCCO.
"...EXTINCTION AT LAST HAS A FACE...
MOSCOW, RUSSIA.
"...AND IT'S SMILING."
BRAD?
WHAT THE HELL IS THIS?

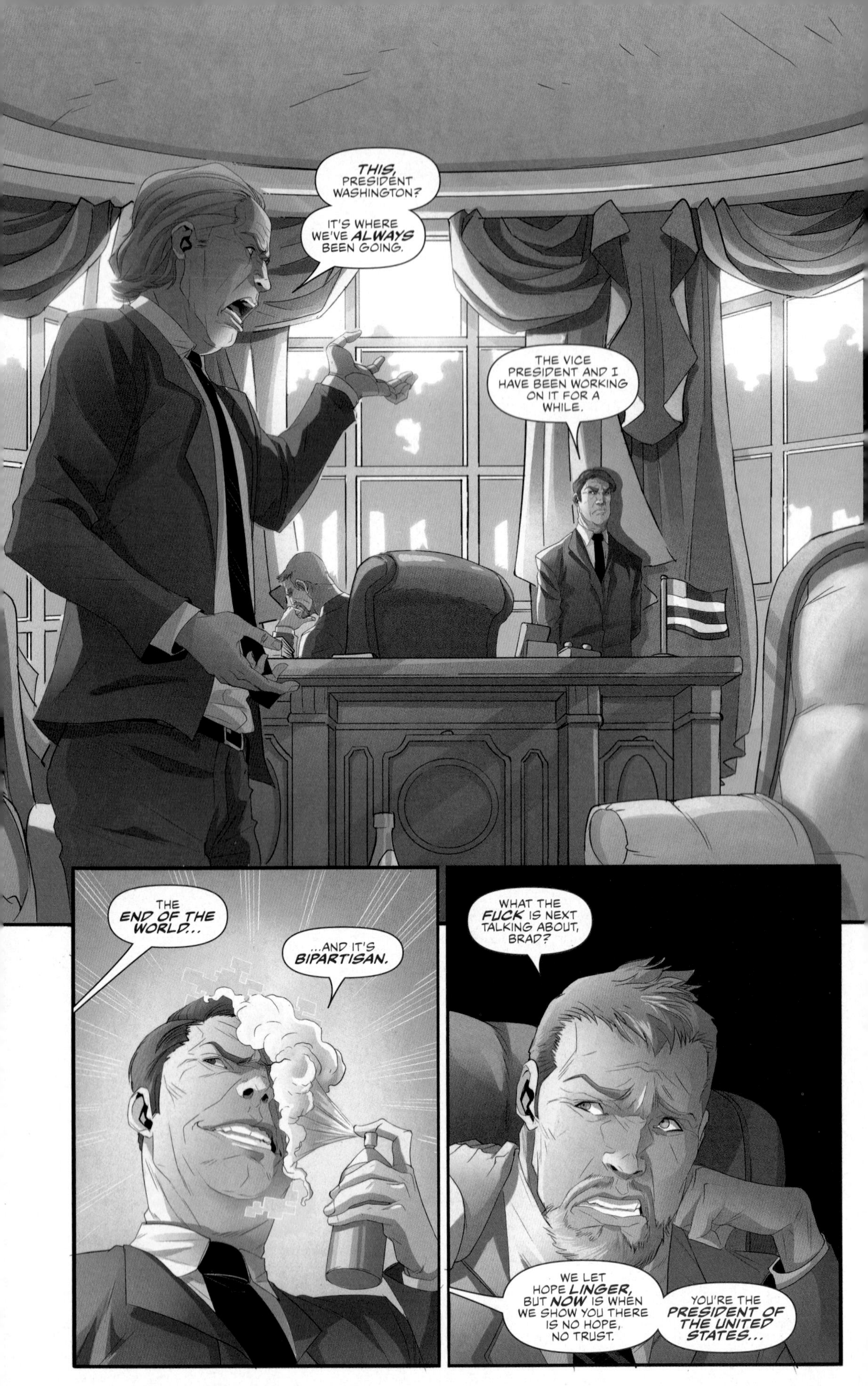
THIS, PRESIDENT WASHINGTON?
IT'S WHERE WE'VE ALWAYS BEEN GOING.
THE VICE PRESIDENT AND I HAVE BEEN WORKING ON IT FOR A WHILE.
THE END OF THE WORLD...
...AND IT'S BIPARTISAN.
WHAT THE FUCK IS NEXT TALKING ABOUT, BRAD?
YOU'RE THE PRESIDENT OF THE UNITED STATES...
WE LET HOPE LINGER, BUT NOW IS WHEN WE SHOW YOU THERE IS NO HOPE, NO TRUST.

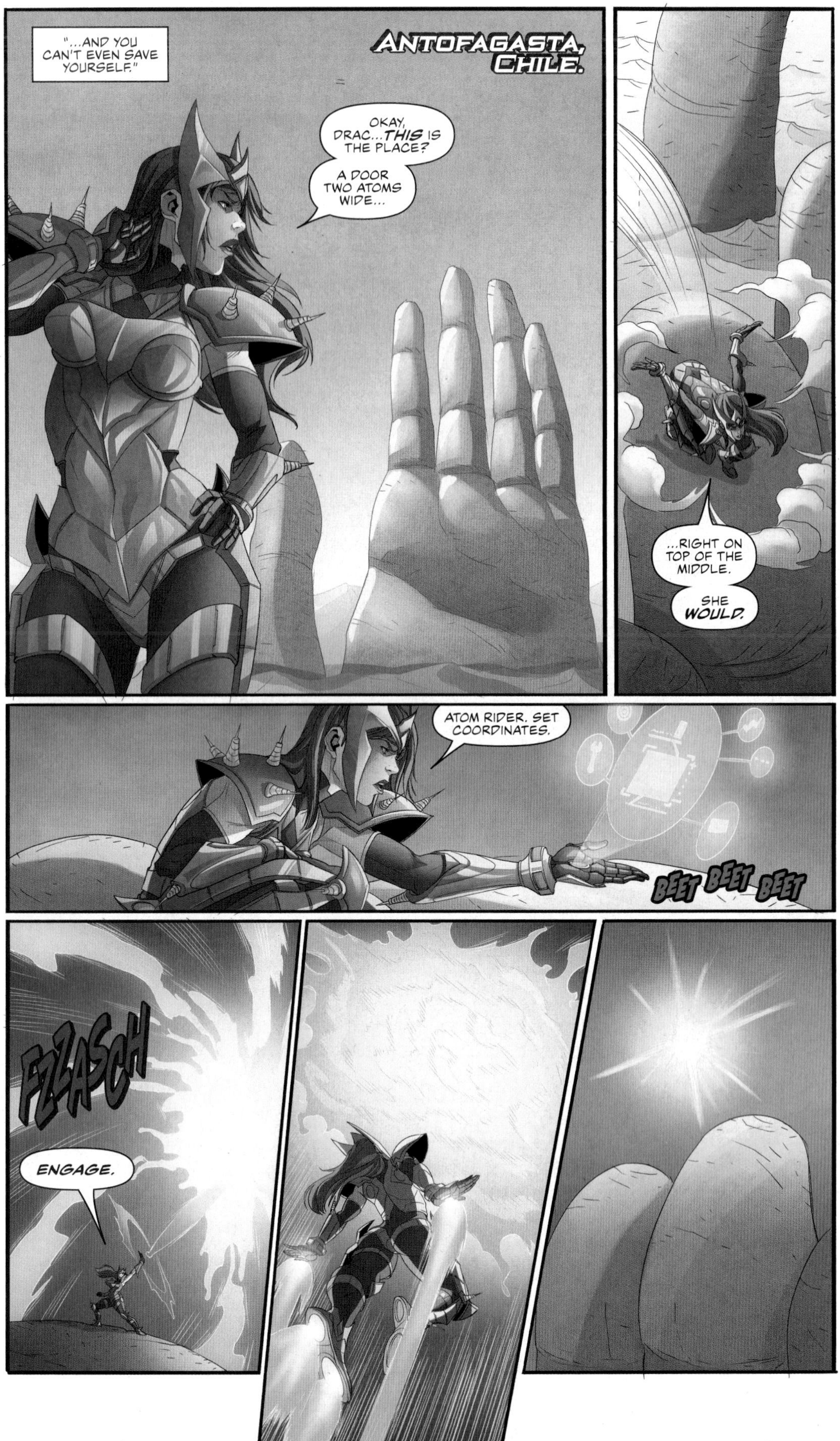
"...AND YOU CAN'T EVEN SAVE YOURSELF."
ANTOFAGASTA, CHILE.
OKAY, DRAC...THIS IS THE PLACE?
A DOOR TWO ATOMS WIDE...
...RIGHT ON TOP OF THE MIDDLE.
SHE WOULD.
ATOM RIDER. SET COORDINATES.
BEET BEET BEET
FZZASCH
ENGAGE.

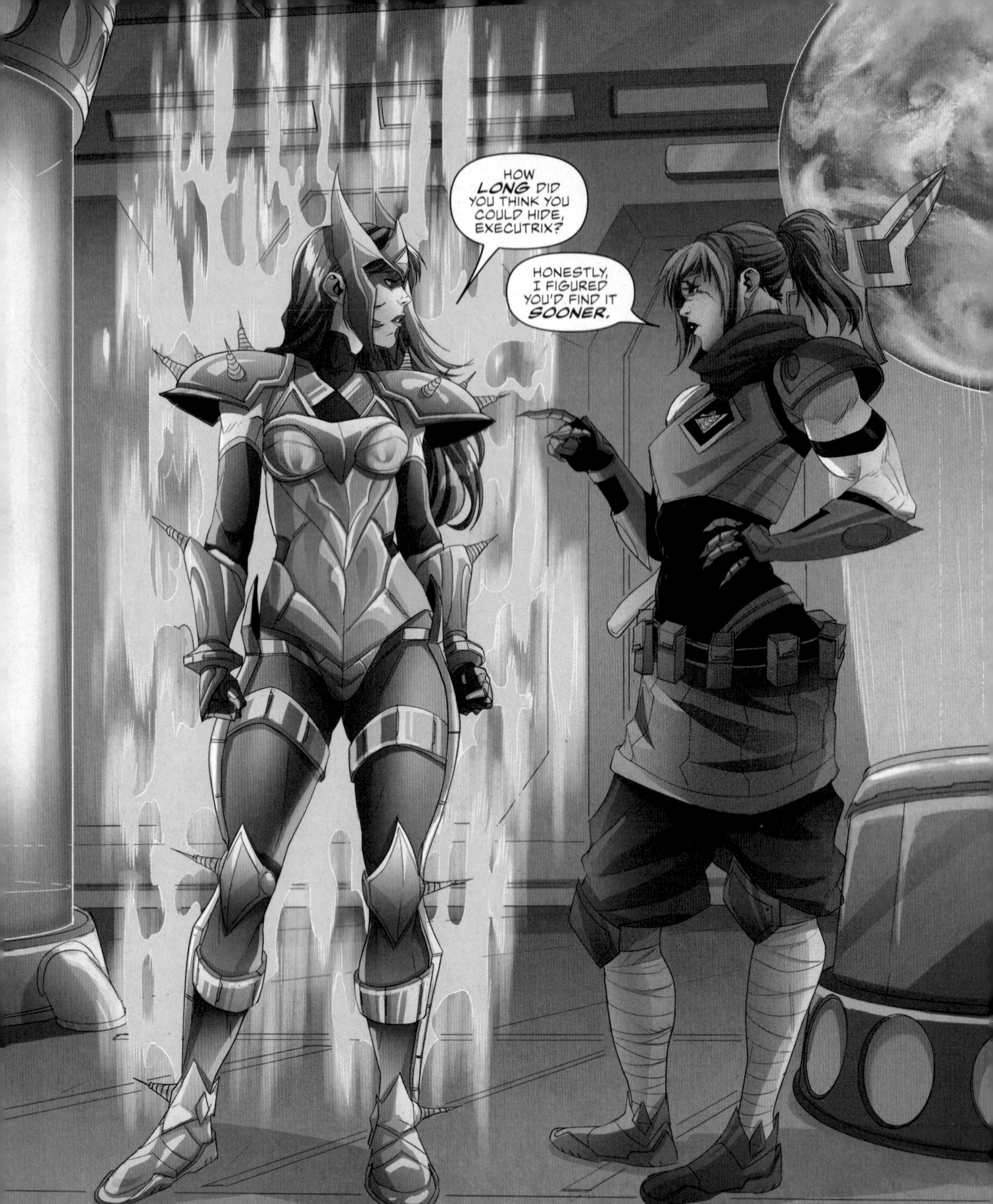
HOW LONG DID YOU THINK YOU COULD HIDE, EXECUTRIX?
HONESTLY, I FIGURED YOU'D FIND IT SOONER.

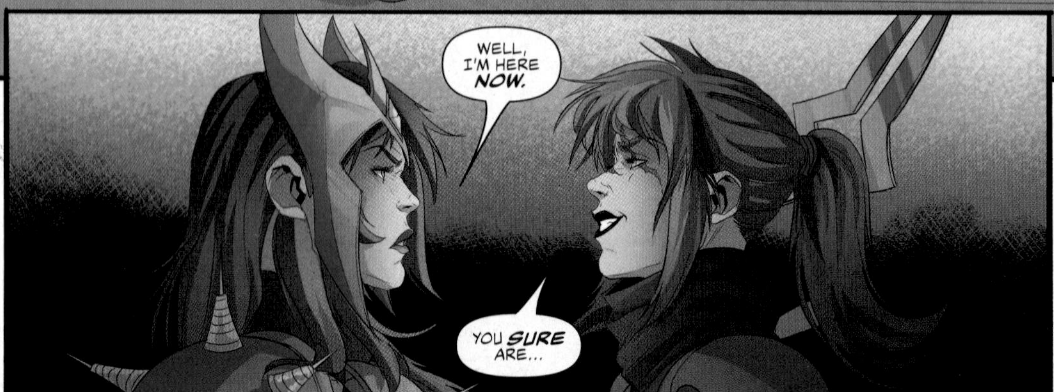
WELL, I'M HERE NOW.
YOU SURE ARE...

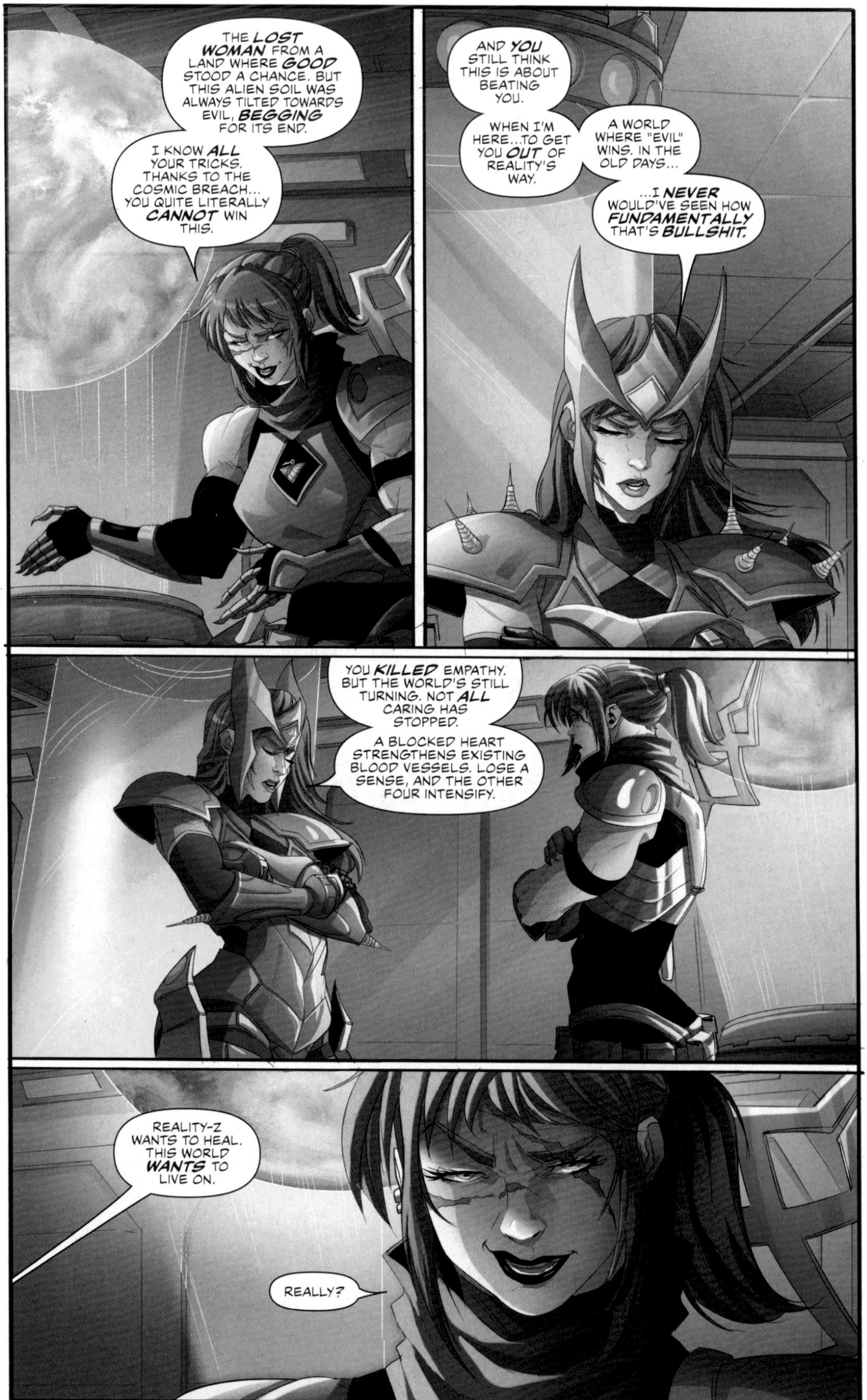
THE LOST WOMAN FROM A LAND WHERE GOOD STOOD A CHANCE. BUT THIS ALIEN SOIL WAS ALWAYS TILTED TOWARDS EVIL, BEGGING FOR ITS END.
I KNOW ALL YOUR TRICKS. THANKS TO THE COSMIC BREACH... YOU QUITE LITERALLY CANNOT WIN THIS.
AND YOU STILL THINK THIS IS ABOUT BEATING YOU.
WHEN I'M HERE...TO GET YOU OUT OF REALITY'S WAY.
A WORLD WHERE "EVIL" WINS. IN THE OLD DAYS...
...I NEVER WOULD'VE SEEN HOW FUNDAMENTALLY THAT'S BULLSHIT.
YOU KILLED EMPATHY. BUT THE WORLD'S STILL TURNING. NOT ALL CARING HAS STOPPED.
A BLOCKED HEART STRENGTHENS EXISTING BLOOD VESSELS. LOSE A SENSE, AND THE OTHER FOUR INTENSIFY.
REALITY-Z WANTS TO HEAL. THIS WORLD WANTS TO LIVE ON.
REALLY?

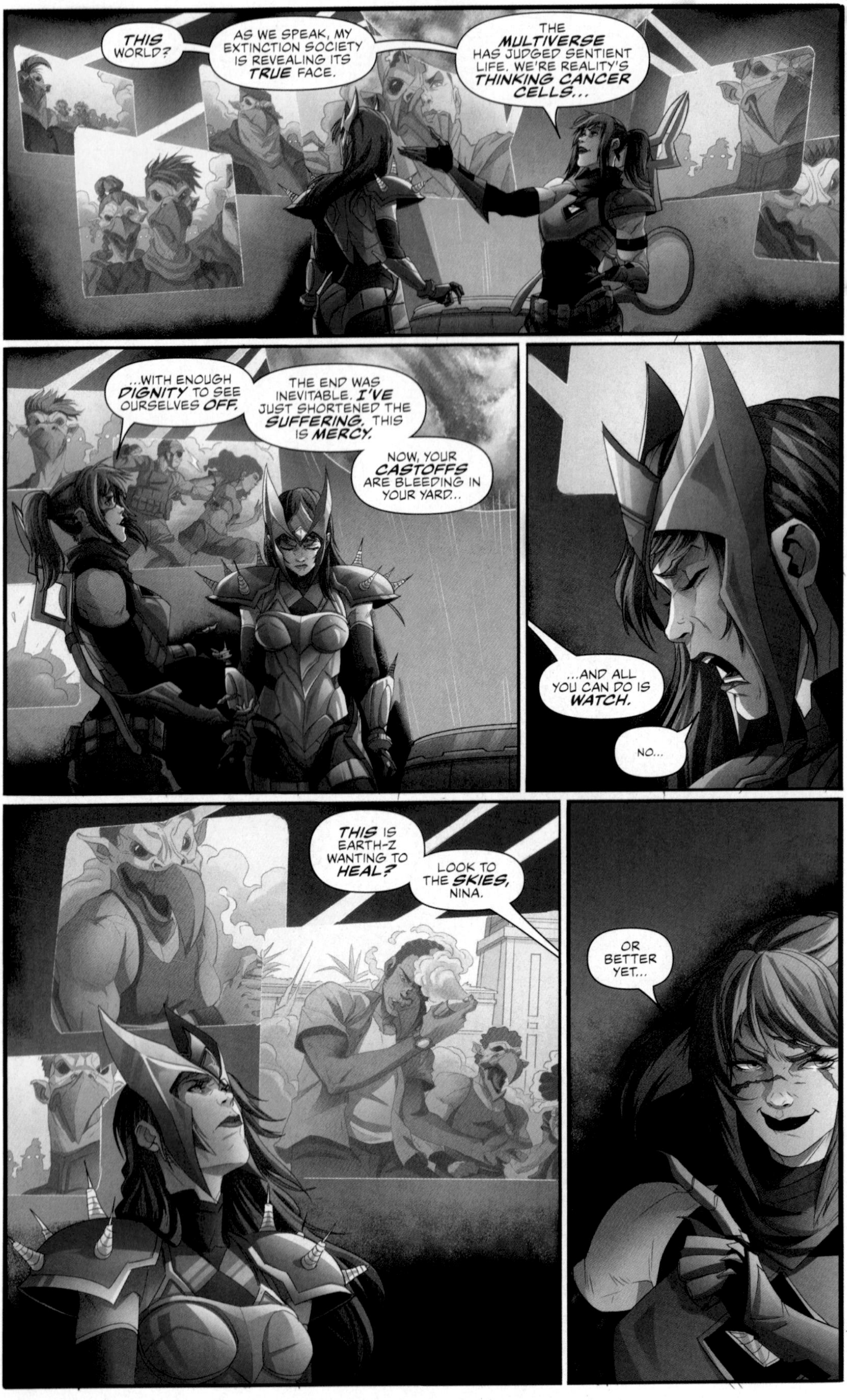

THIS WORLD?
AS WE SPEAK, MY EXTINCTION SOCIETY IS REVEALING ITS TRUE FACE.
THE MULTIVERSE HAS JUDGED SENTIENT LIFE. WE'RE REALITY'S THINKING CANCER CELLS...
...WITH ENOUGH DIGNITY TO SEE OURSELVES OFF.
THE END WAS INEVITABLE. I'VE JUST SHORTENED THE SUFFERING. THIS IS MERCY.
NOW, YOUR CASTOFFS ARE BLEEDING IN YOUR YARD...
...AND ALL YOU CAN DO IS WATCH.
NO...
THIS IS EARTH-Z WANTING TO HEAL?
LOOK TO THE SKIES, NINA.
OR BETTER YET...

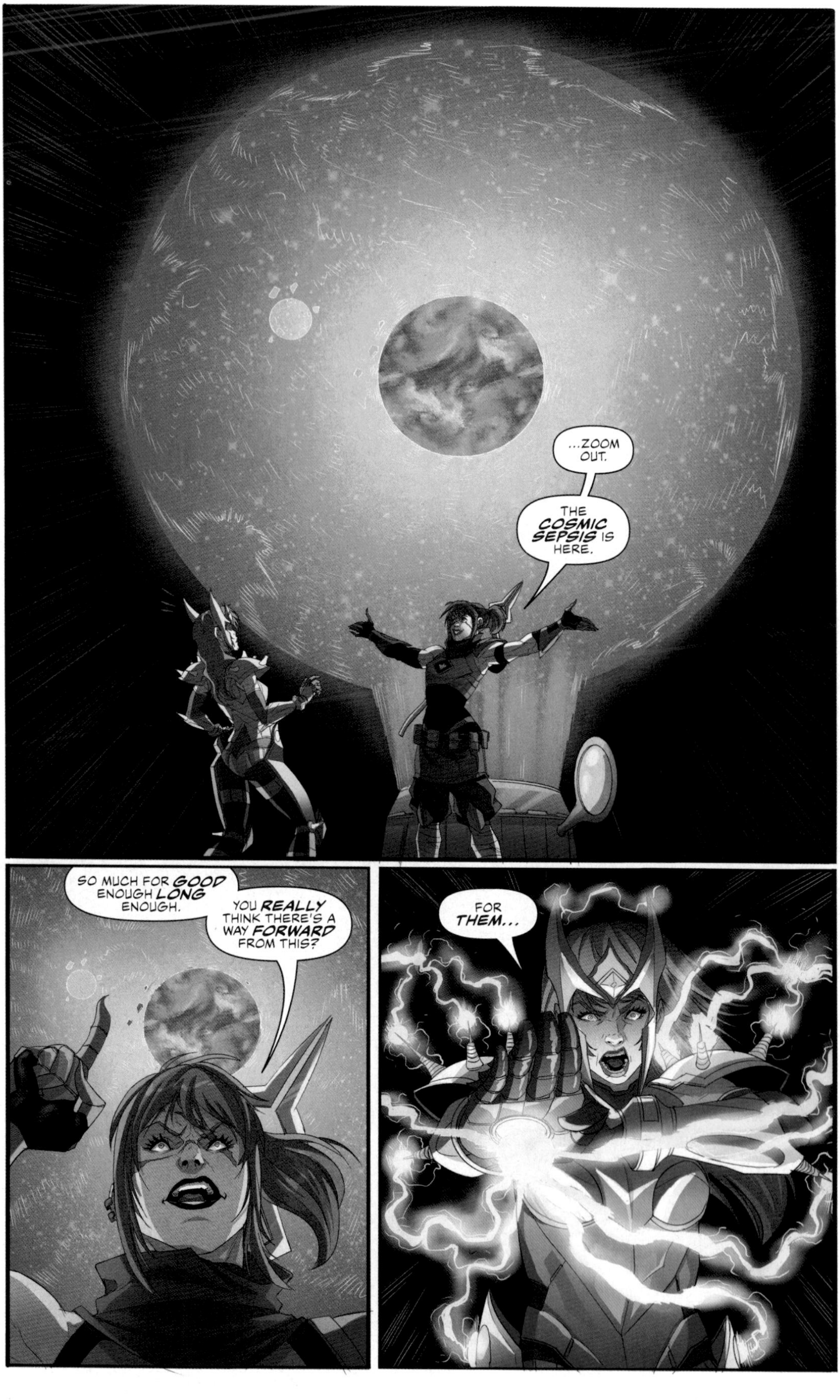
...ZOOM OUT.
THE COSMIC SEPSIS IS HERE.
SO MUCH FOR GOOD ENOUGH LONG ENOUGH.
YOU REALLY THINK THERE'S A WAY FORWARD FROM THIS?
FOR THEM...

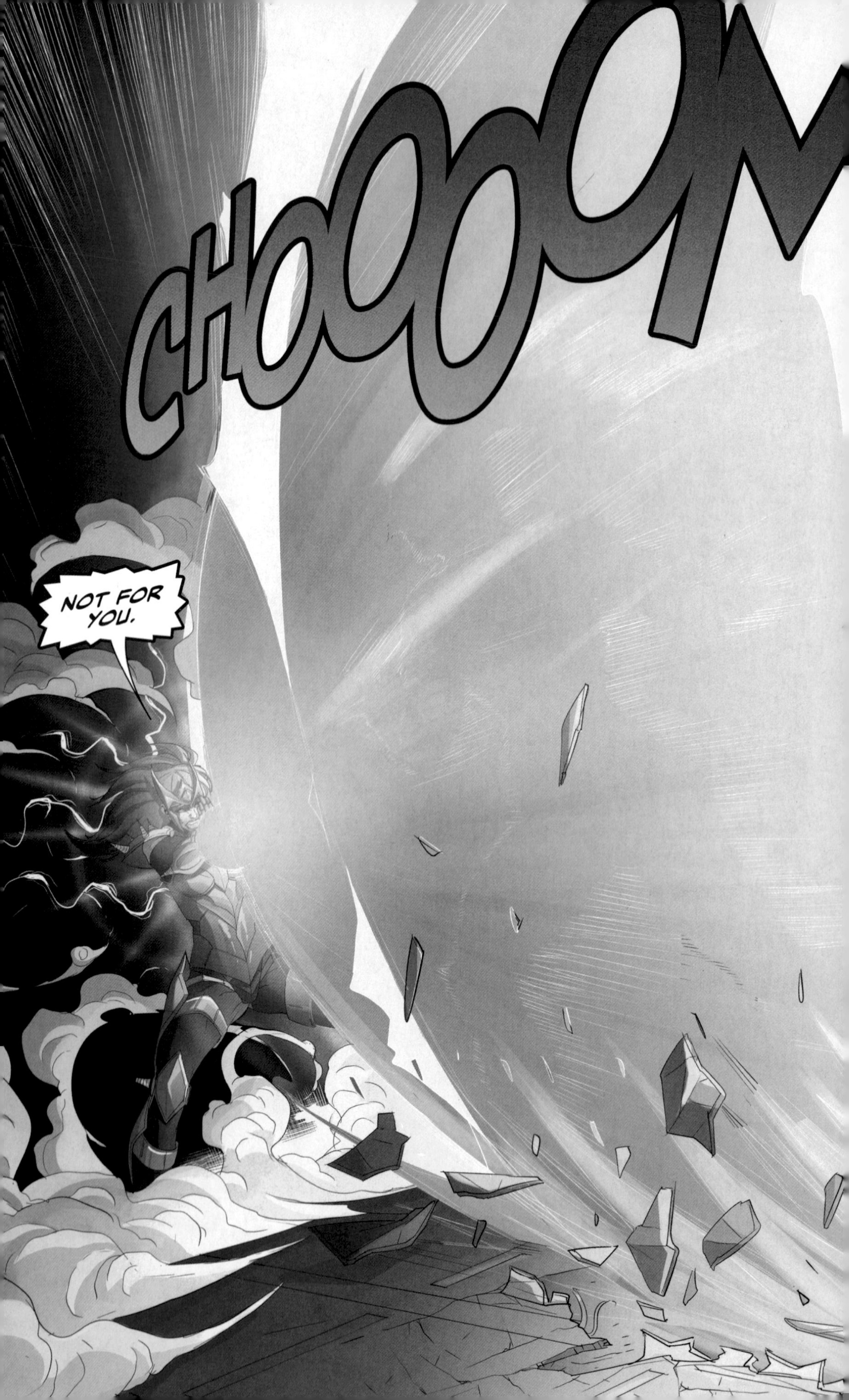
CHOOOOM
NOT FOR YOU.

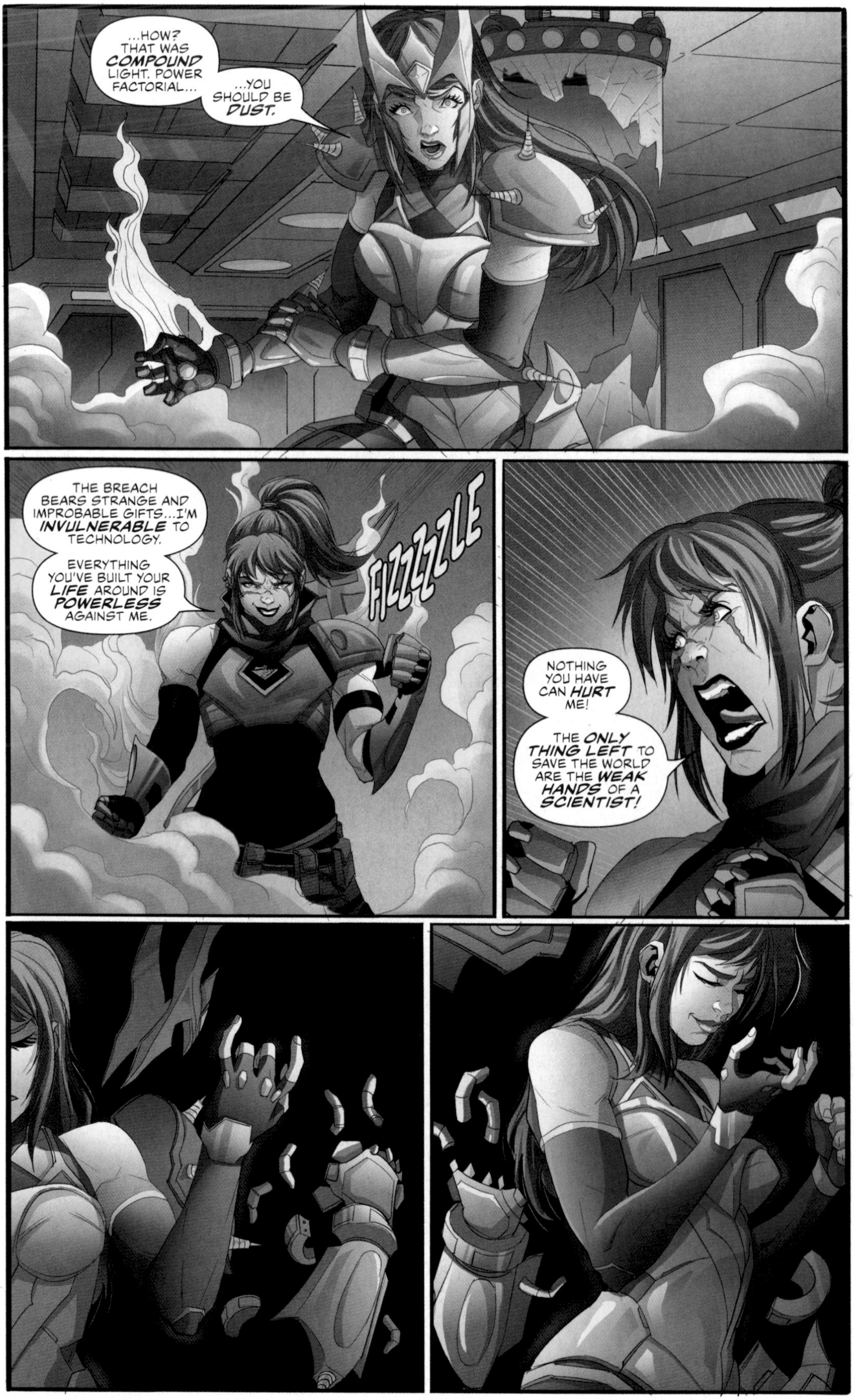
...HOW? THAT WAS COMPOUND LIGHT. POWER FACTORIAL...
...YOU SHOULD BE DUST.
THE BREACH BEARS STRANGE AND IMPROBABLE GIFTS...I'M INVULNERABLE TO TECHNOLOGY.
EVERYTHING YOU'VE BUILT YOUR LIFE AROUND IS POWERLESS AGAINST ME.
FIZZZZZLE
NOTHING YOU HAVE CAN HURT ME!
THE ONLY THING LEFT TO SAVE THE WORLD ARE THE WEAK HANDS OF A SCIENTIST!

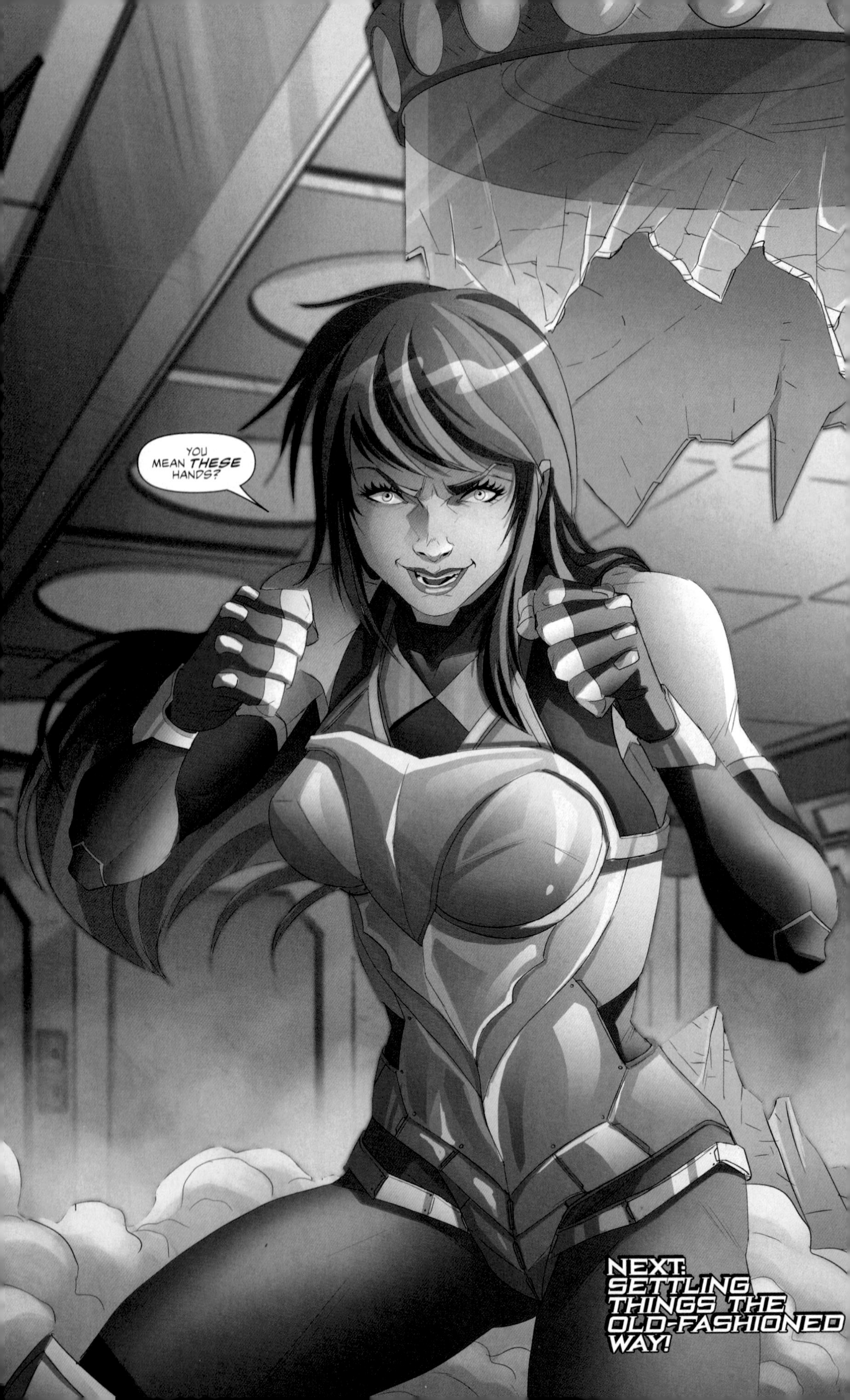
YOU MEAN THESE HANDS?
NEXT: SETTLING THINGS THE OLD-FASHIONED WAY!

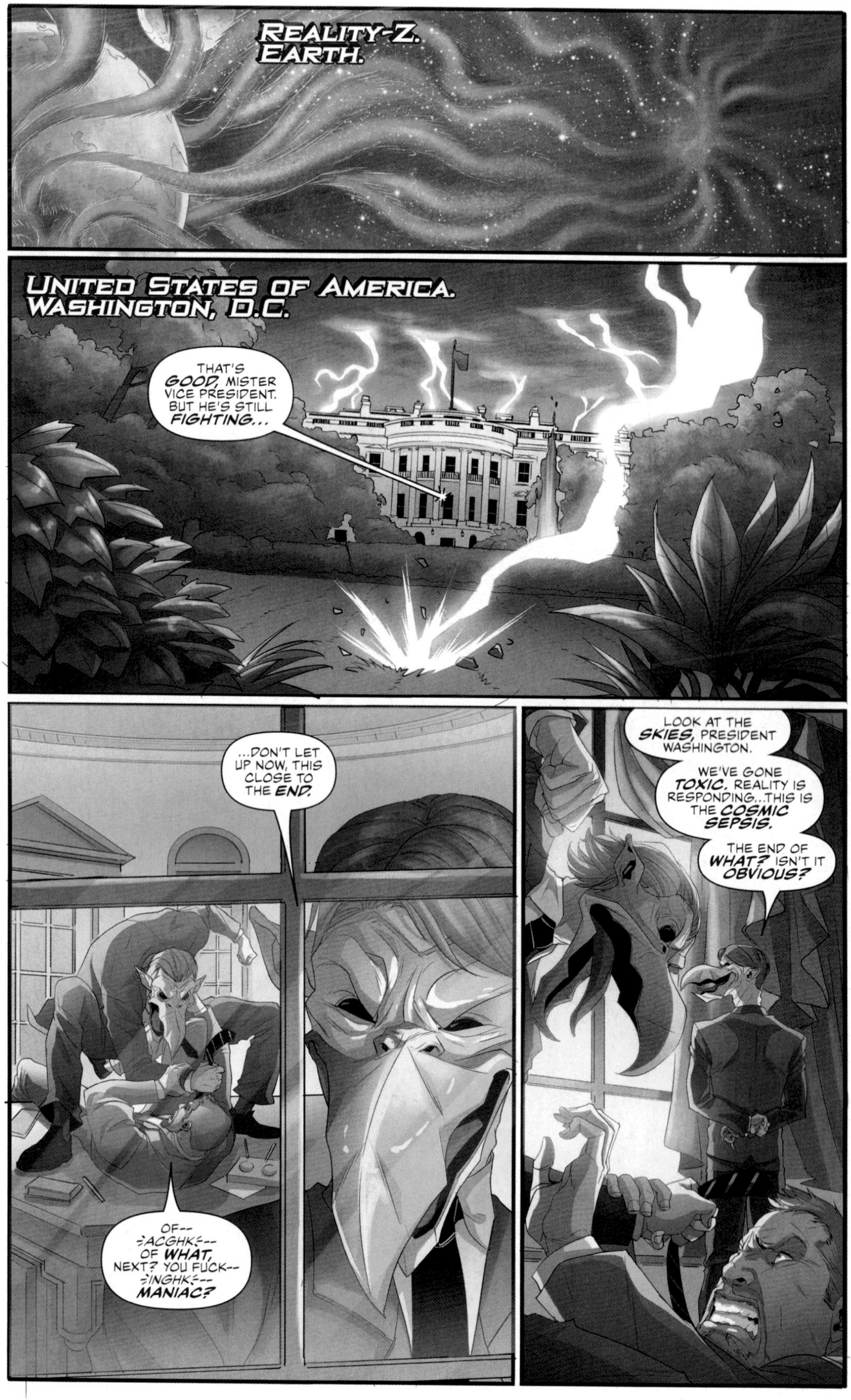
REALITY-Z.
EARTH.
UNITED STATES OF AMERICA.
WASHINGTON, D.C.
THAT'S GOOD, MISTER VICE PRESIDENT. BUT HE'S STILL FIGHTING...
...DON'T LET UP NOW, THIS CLOSE TO THE END.
OF-- ⇒ACGHK⇐-- OF WHAT, NEXT? YOU FUCK-- ⇒INGHK⇐-- MANIAC?
LOOK AT THE SKIES, PRESIDENT WASHINGTON.
WE'VE GONE TOXIC. REALITY IS RESPONDING...THIS IS THE COSMIC SEPSIS.
THE END OF WHAT? ISN'T IT OBVIOUS?

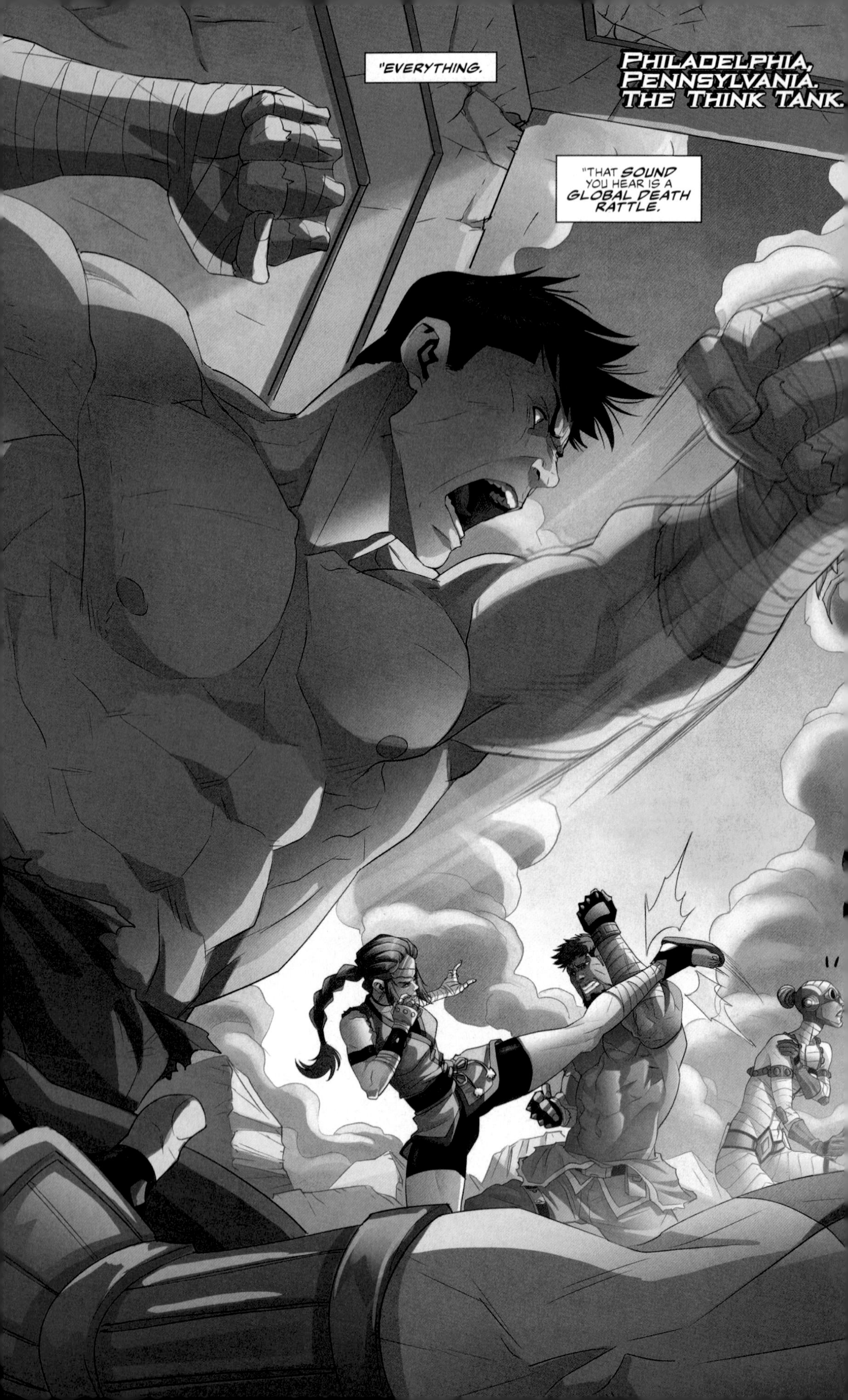
PHILADELPHIA, PENNSYLVANIA. THE THINK TANK.
"EVERYTHING.
"THAT SOUND YOU HEAR IS A GLOBAL DEATH RATTLE.

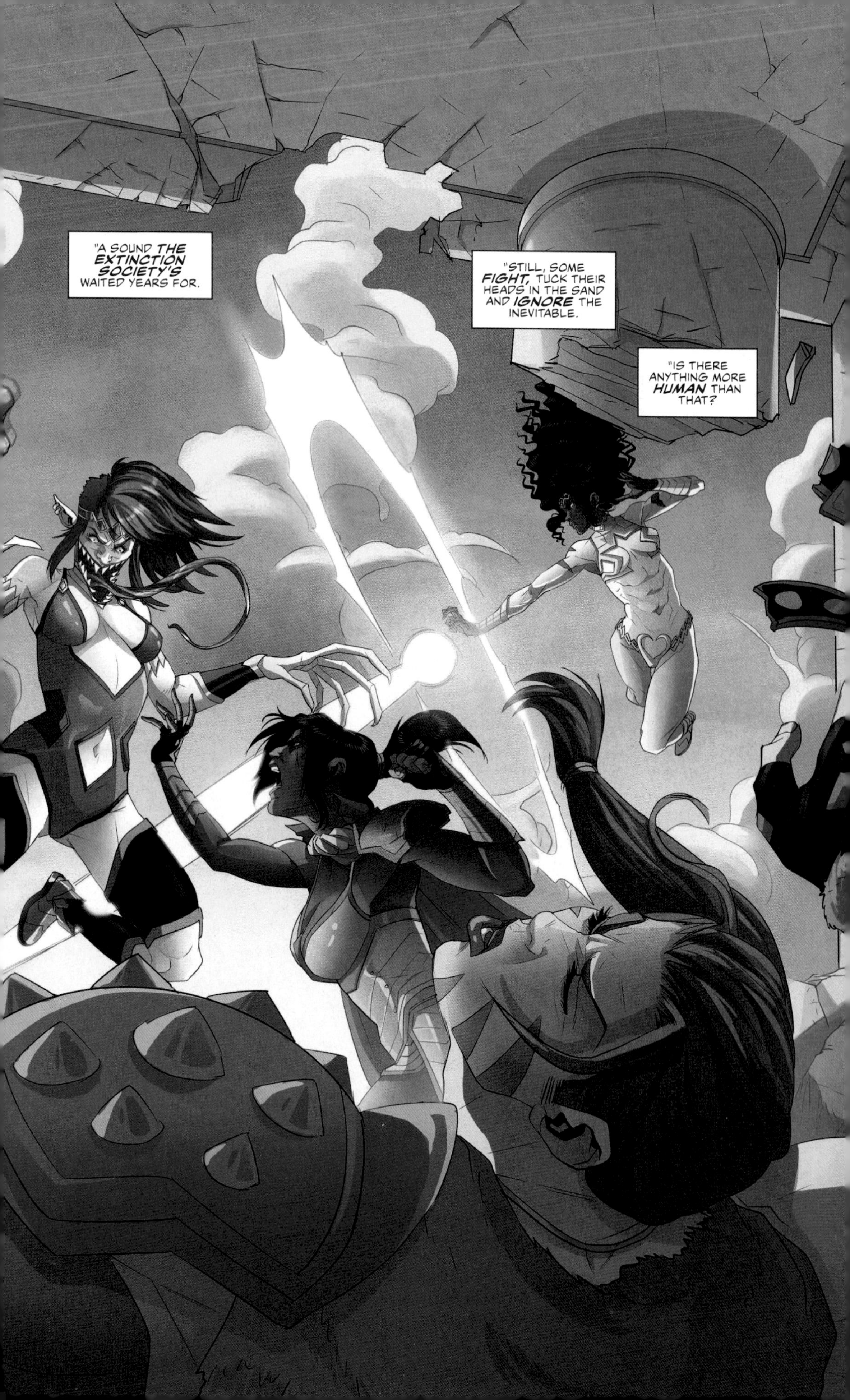
"A SOUND THE EXTINCTION SOCIETY'S WAITED YEARS FOR.
"STILL, SOME FIGHT, TUCK THEIR HEADS IN THE SAND AND IGNORE THE INEVITABLE.
"IS THERE ANYTHING MORE HUMAN THAN THAT?

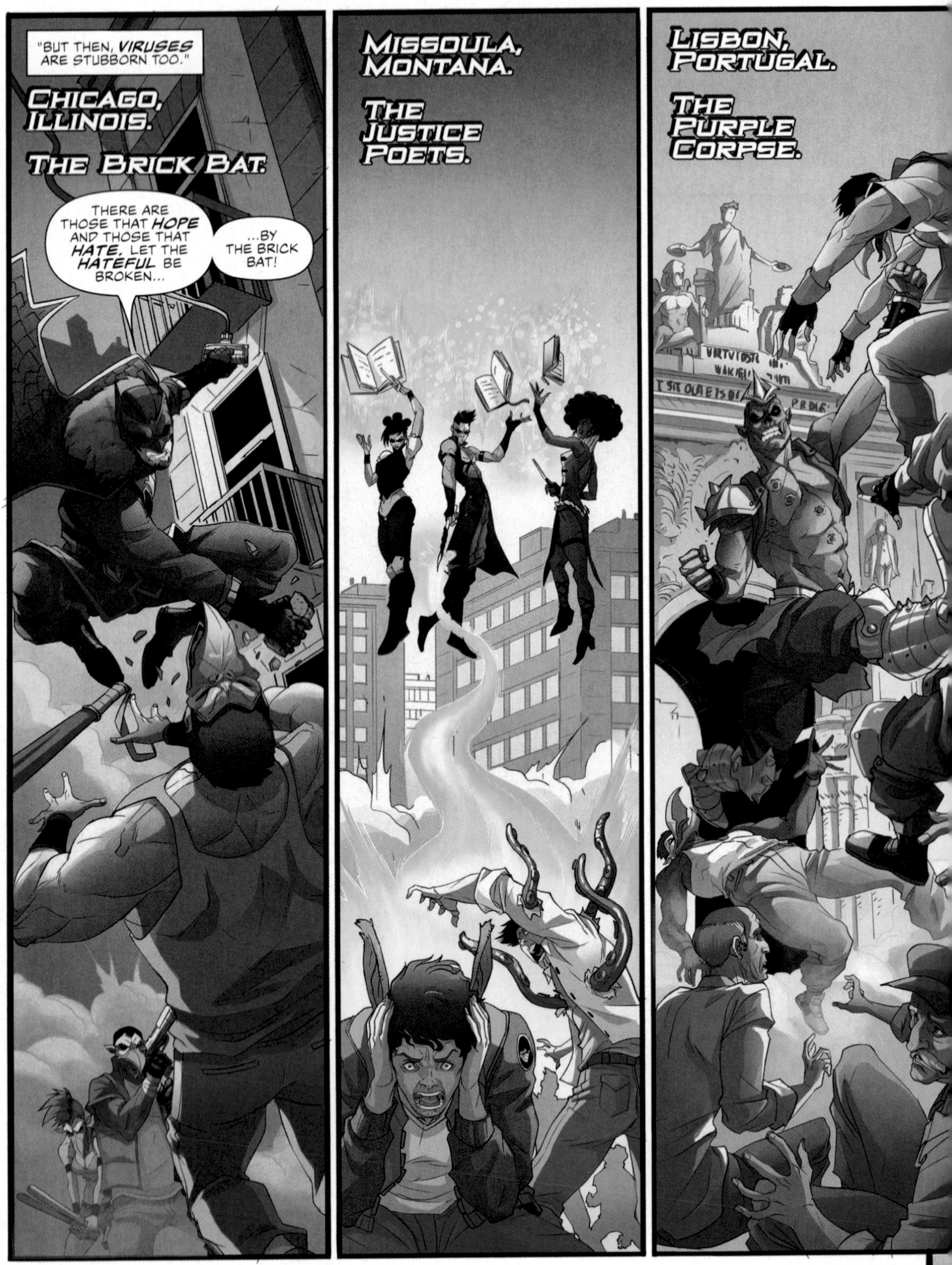
"BUT THEN, VIRUSES ARE STUBBORN TOO."
CHICAGO, ILLINOIS.
THE BRICK BAT.
THERE ARE THOSE THAT HOPE AND THOSE THAT HATE. LET THE HATEFUL BE BROKEN...
...BY THE BRICK BAT!
MISSOULA, MONTANA.
THE JUSTICE POETS.
LISBON, PORTUGAL.
THE PURPLE CORPSE.

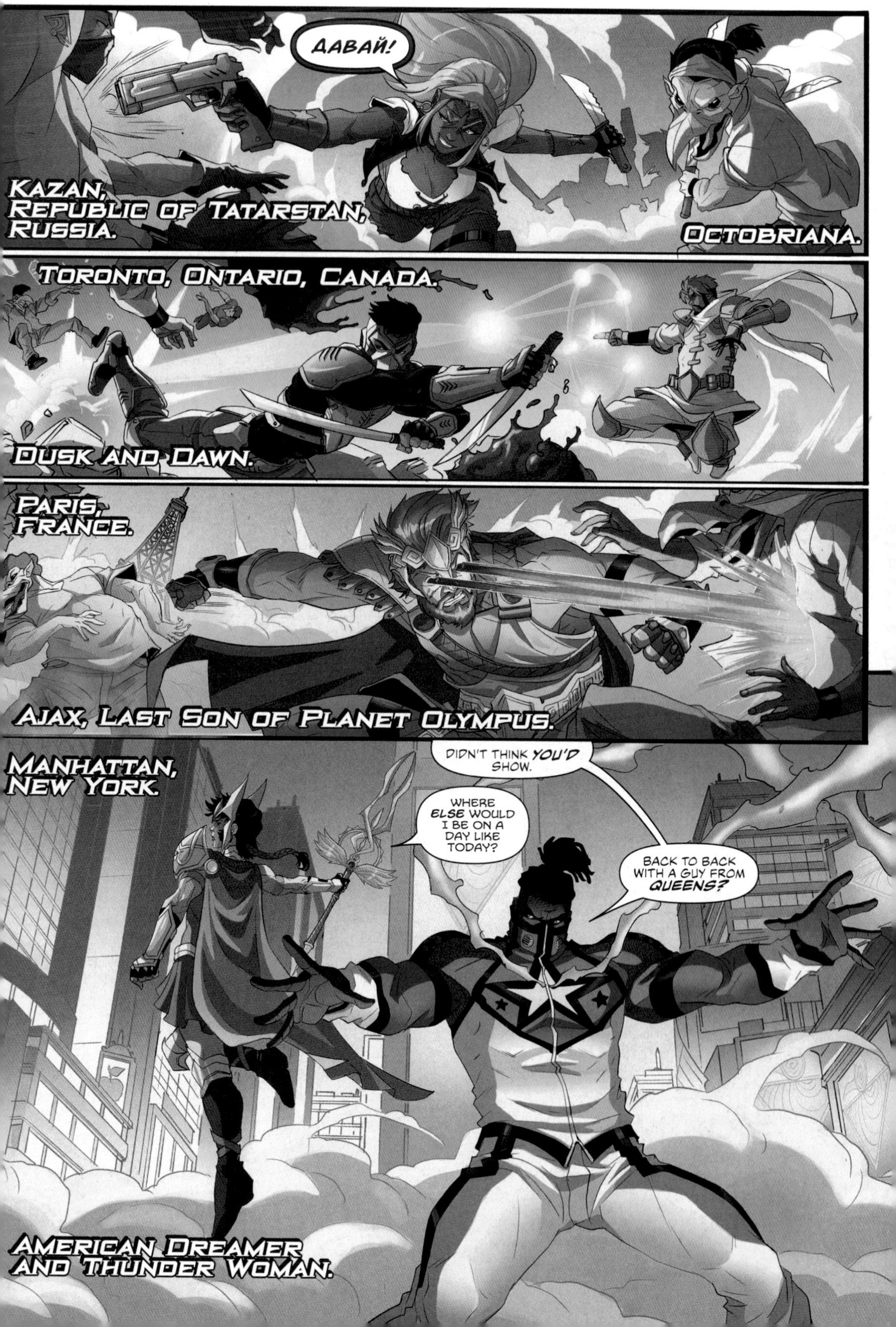
ДАВАЙ!
KAZAN, REPUBLIC OF TATARSTAN, RUSSIA.
OCTOBRIANA.
TORONTO, ONTARIO, CANADA.
DUSK AND DAWN.
PARIS, FRANCE.
AJAX, LAST SON OF PLANET OLYMPUS.
MANHATTAN, NEW YORK.
DIDN'T THINK YOU'D SHOW.
WHERE ELSE WOULD I BE ON A DAY LIKE TODAY?
BACK TO BACK WITH A GUY FROM QUEENS?
AMERICAN DREAMER AND THUNDER WOMAN.

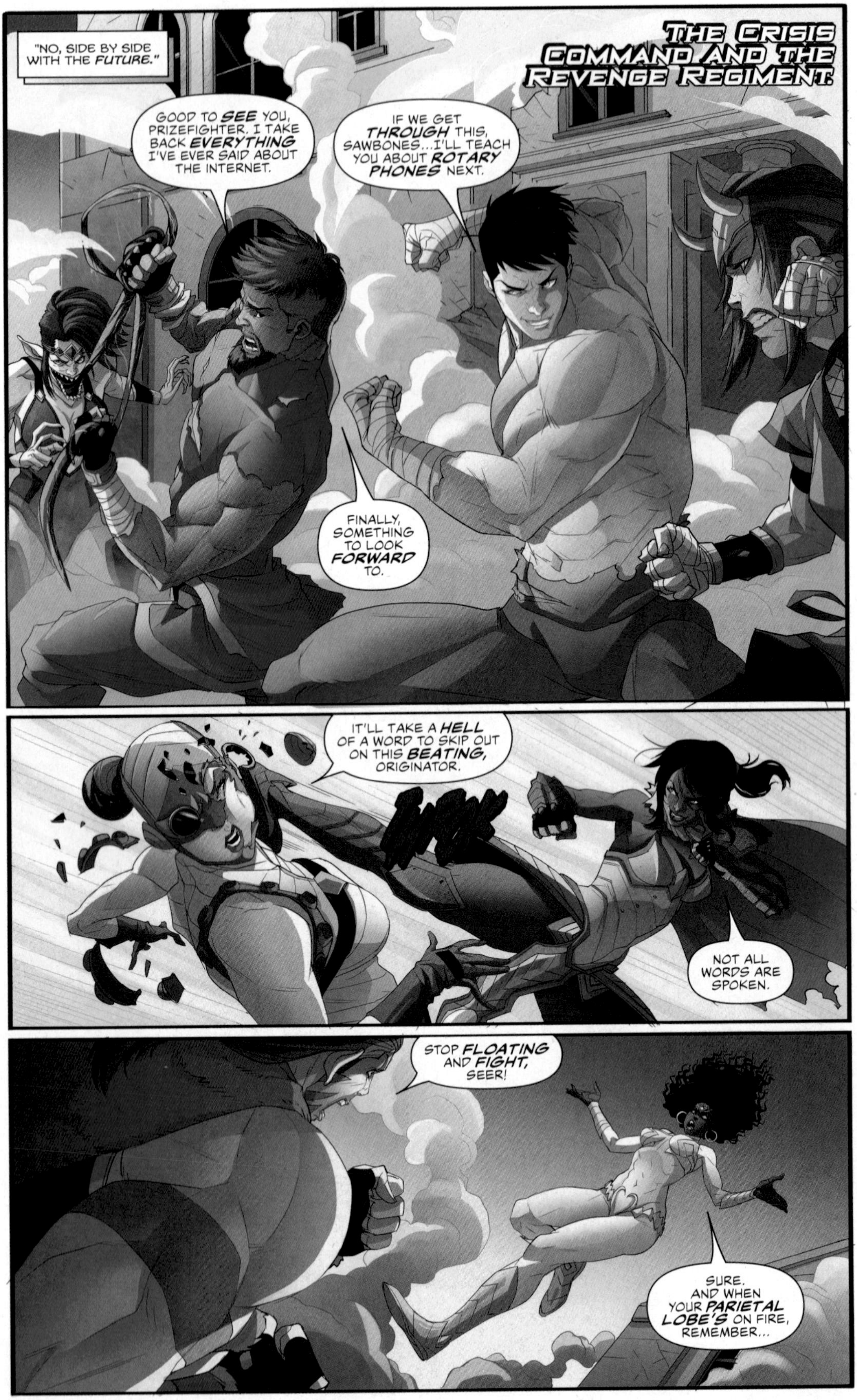
"NO, SIDE BY SIDE WITH THE FUTURE."
THE CRISIS COMMAND AND THE REVENGE REGIMENT.
GOOD TO SEE YOU, PRIZEFIGHTER. I TAKE BACK EVERYTHING I'VE EVER SAID ABOUT THE INTERNET.
IF WE GET THROUGH THIS, SAWBONES...I'LL TEACH YOU ABOUT ROTARY PHONES NEXT.
FINALLY, SOMETHING TO LOOK FORWARD TO.
IT'LL TAKE A HELL OF A WORD TO SKIP OUT ON THIS BEATING, ORIGINATOR.
NOT ALL WORDS ARE SPOKEN.
STOP FLOATING AND FIGHT, SEER!
SURE. AND WHEN YOUR PARIETAL LOBE'S ON FIRE, REMEMBER...

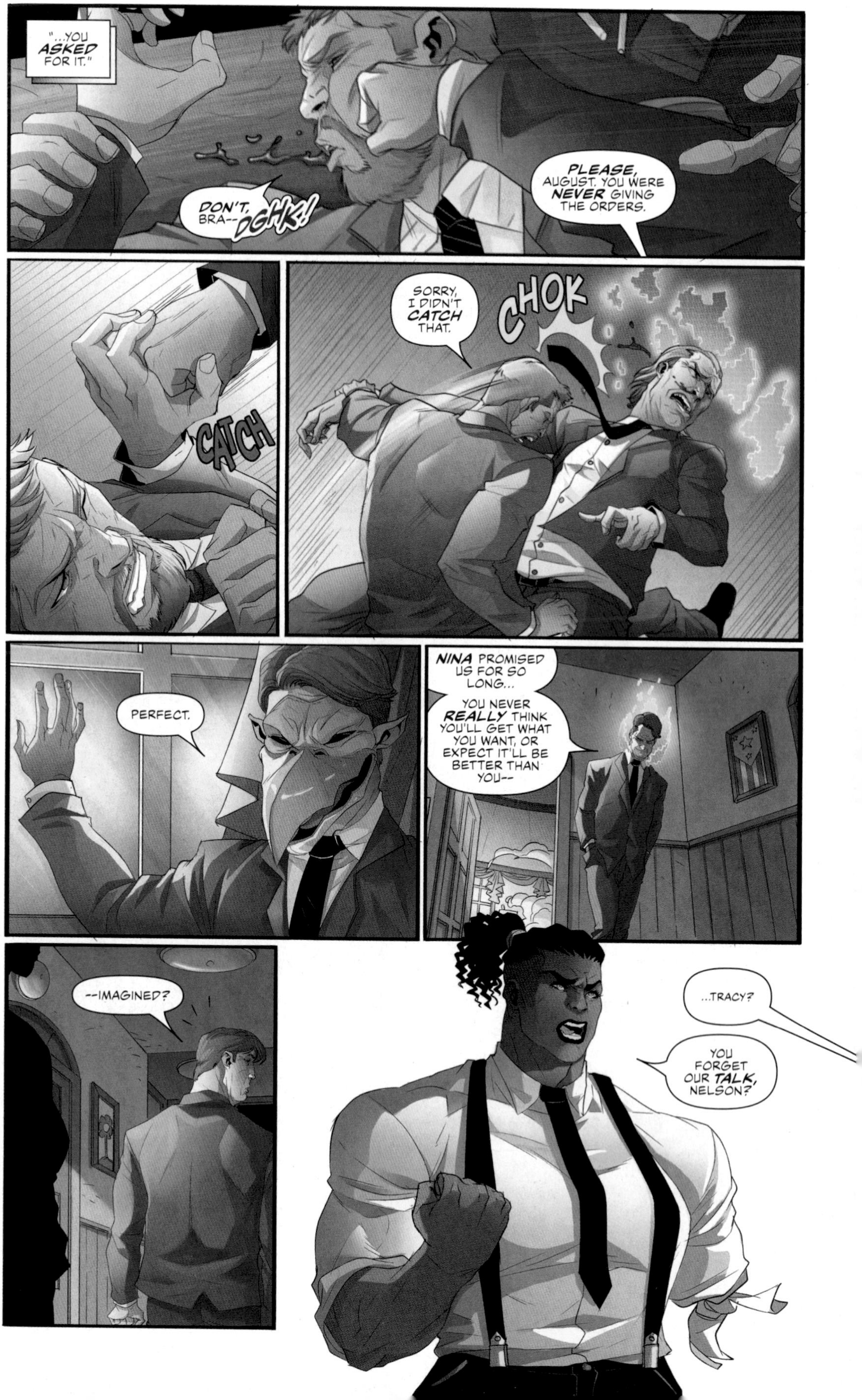
"...YOU ASKED FOR IT."
DON'T, BRA--DGHK!
PLEASE, AUGUST. YOU WERE NEVER GIVING THE ORDERS.
CATCH
SORRY, I DIDN'T CATCH THAT.
CHOK
PERFECT.
NINA PROMISED US FOR SO LONG...
YOU NEVER REALLY THINK YOU'LL GET WHAT YOU WANT, OR EXPECT IT'LL BE BETTER THAN YOU--
--IMAGINED?
...TRACY?
YOU FORGET OUR TALK, NELSON?

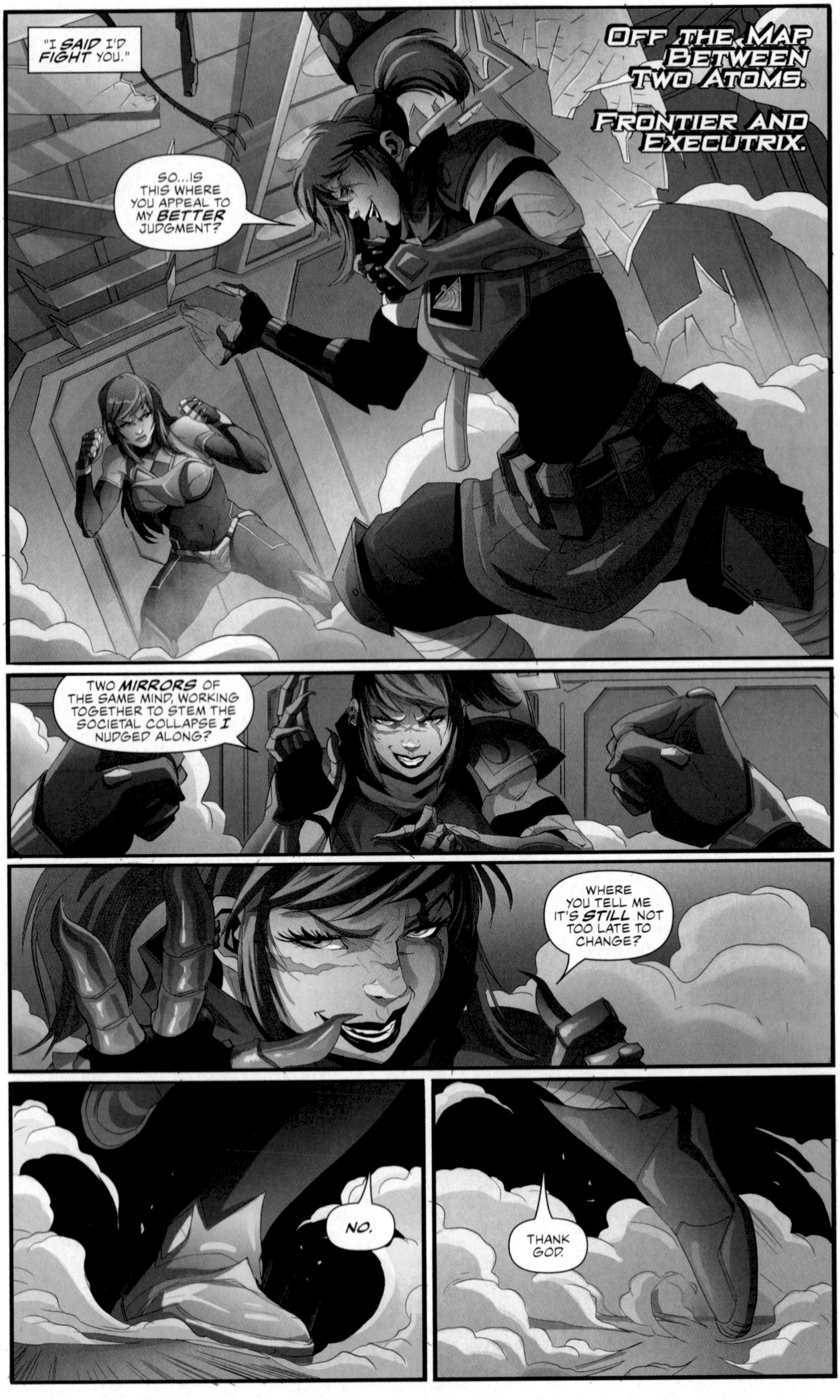
"I SAID I'D FIGHT YOU."
OFF THE MAP. BETWEEN TWO ATOMS.
FRONTIER AND EXECUTRIX.
SO...IS THIS WHERE YOU APPEAL TO MY BETTER JUDGMENT?
TWO MIRRORS OF THE SAME MIND, WORKING TOGETHER TO STEM THE SOCIETAL COLLAPSE I NUDGED ALONG?
WHERE YOU TELL ME IT'S STILL NOT TOO LATE TO CHANGE?
NO.
THANK GOD.

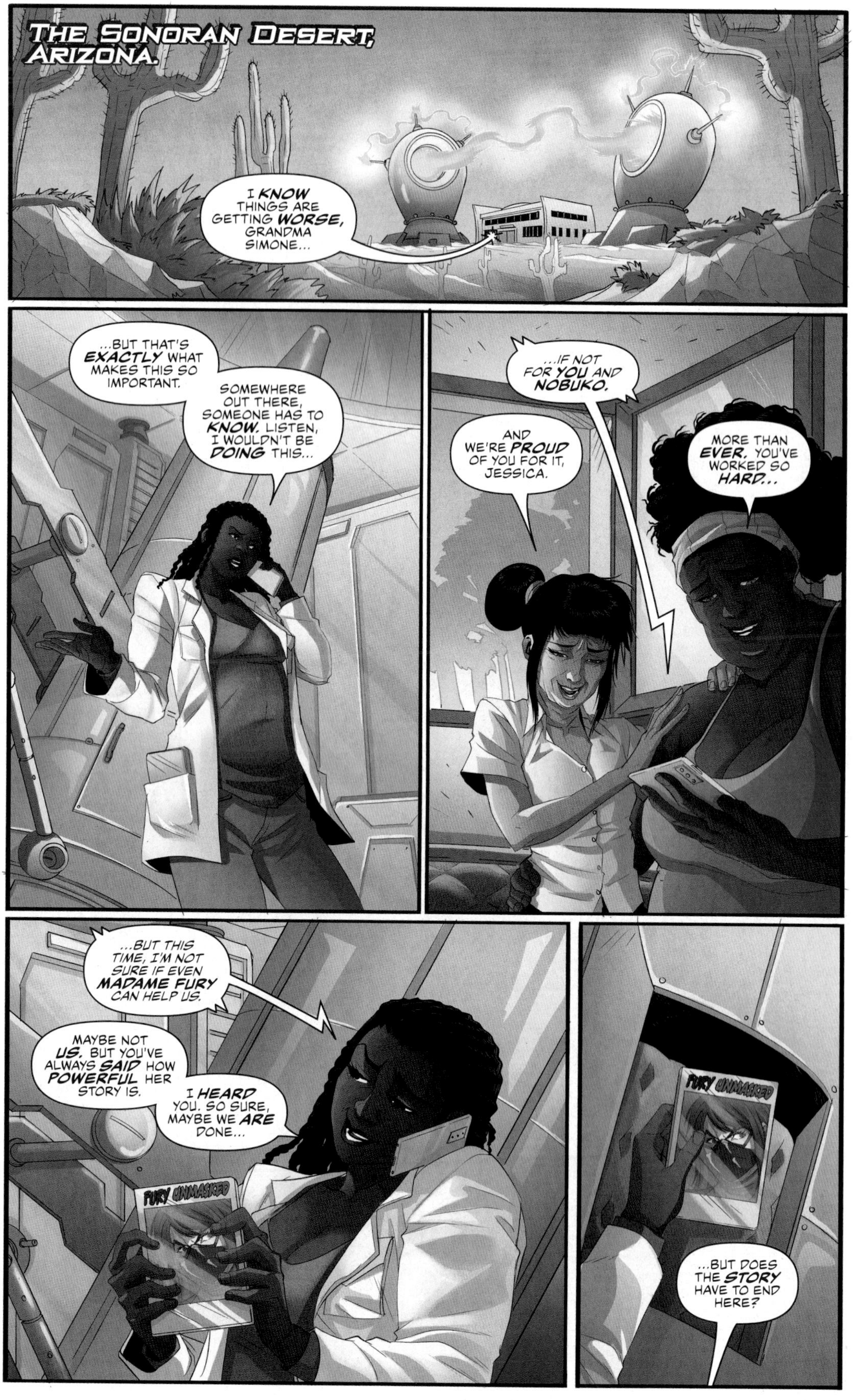
THE SONORAN DESERT, ARIZONA.
I KNOW THINGS ARE GETTING WORSE, GRANDMA SIMONE...
...BUT THAT'S EXACTLY WHAT MAKES THIS SO IMPORTANT.
SOMEWHERE OUT THERE, SOMEONE HAS TO KNOW. LISTEN, I WOULDN'T BE DOING THIS...
...IF NOT FOR YOU AND NOBUKO.
AND WE'RE PROUD OF YOU FOR IT, JESSICA.
MORE THAN EVER. YOU'VE WORKED SO HARD...
...BUT THIS TIME, I'M NOT SURE IF EVEN MADAME FURY CAN HELP US.
MAYBE NOT US. BUT YOU'VE ALWAYS SAID HOW POWERFUL HER STORY IS.
I HEARD YOU. SO SURE, MAYBE WE ARE DONE...
FURY UNMASKED
FURY UNMASKED
...BUT DOES THE STORY HAVE TO END HERE?

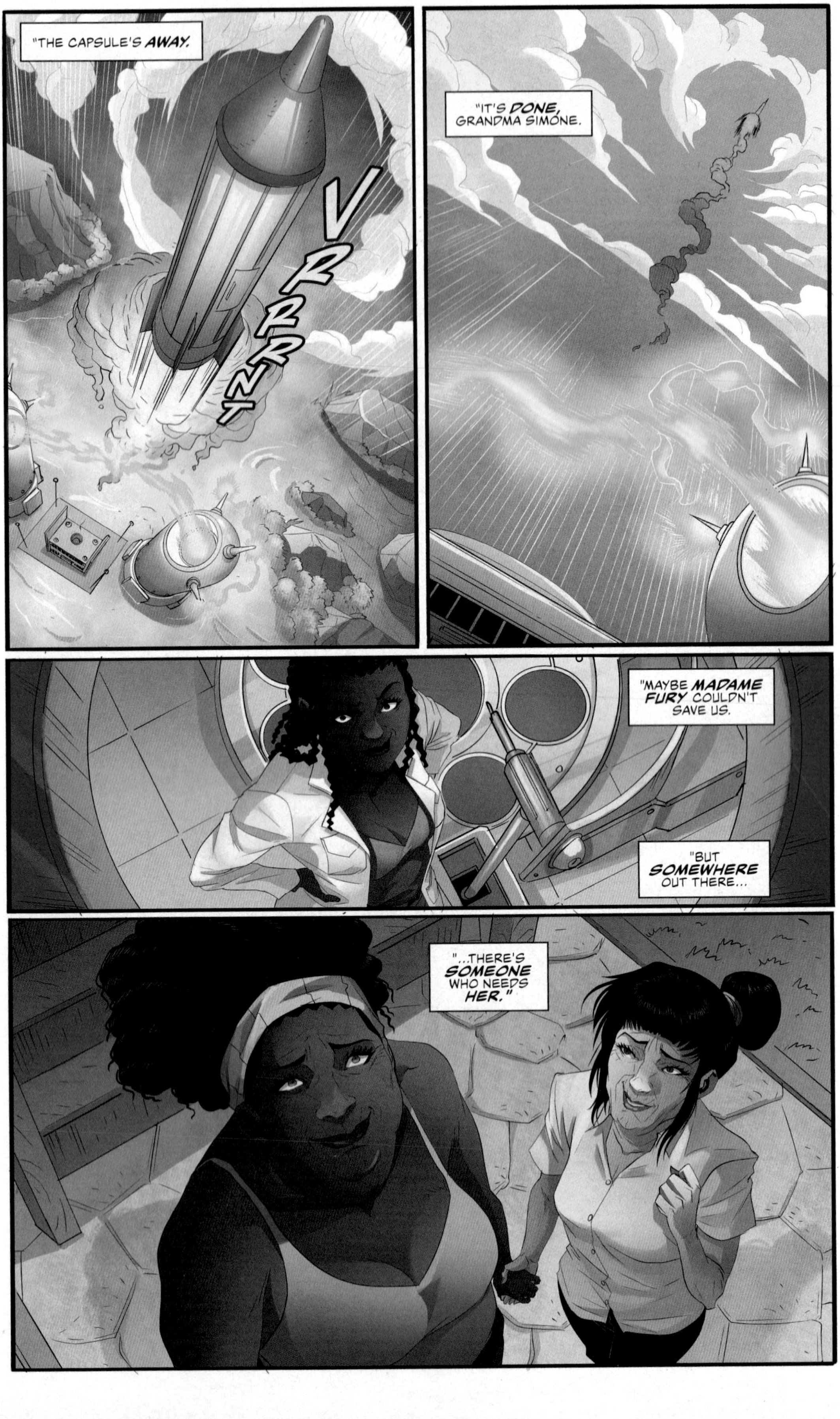
"THE CAPSULE'S AWAY.
VRRRNT
"IT'S DONE, GRANDMA SIMONE.
"MAYBE MADAME FURY COULDN'T SAVE US.
"BUT SOMEWHERE OUT THERE...
"...THERE'S SOMEONE WHO NEEDS HER."

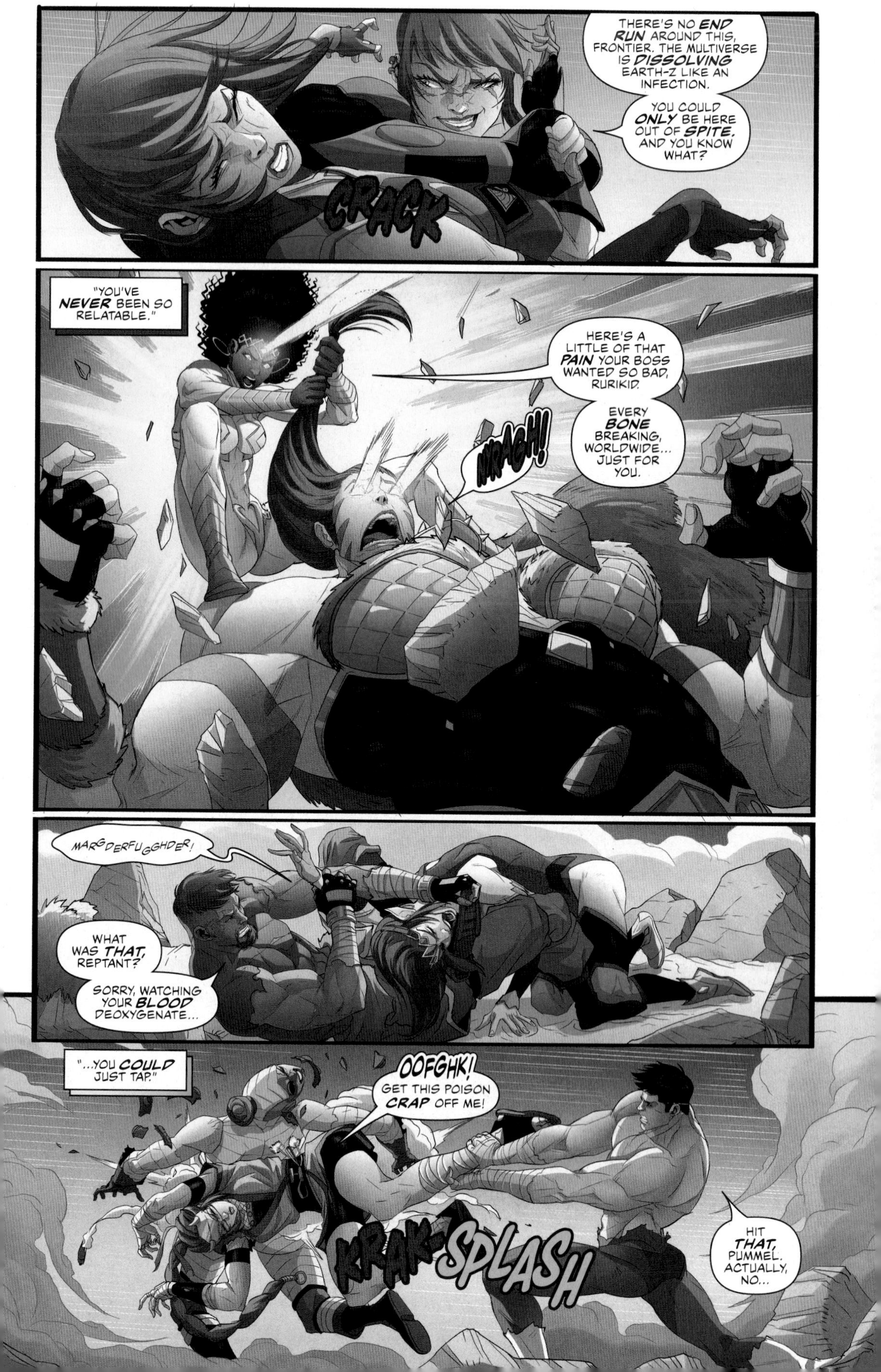

THERE'S NO END RUN AROUND THIS, FRONTIER. THE MULTIVERSE IS DISSOLVING EARTH-Z LIKE AN INFECTION.
YOU COULD ONLY BE HERE OUT OF SPITE. AND YOU KNOW WHAT?
CRACK
"YOU'VE NEVER BEEN SO RELATABLE."
HERE'S A LITTLE OF THAT PAIN YOUR BOSS WANTED SO BAD, RURIKID.
EVERY BONE BREAKING, WORLDWIDE... JUST FOR YOU.
NYRAGH!
MARGDERFUGGHDER!
WHAT WAS THAT, REPTANT?
SORRY, WATCHING YOUR BLOOD DEOXYGENATE...
"...YOU COULD JUST TAP."
OOFGHK! GET THIS POISON CRAP OFF ME!
KRAK-SPLASH
HIT THAT, PUMMEL. ACTUALLY, NO...

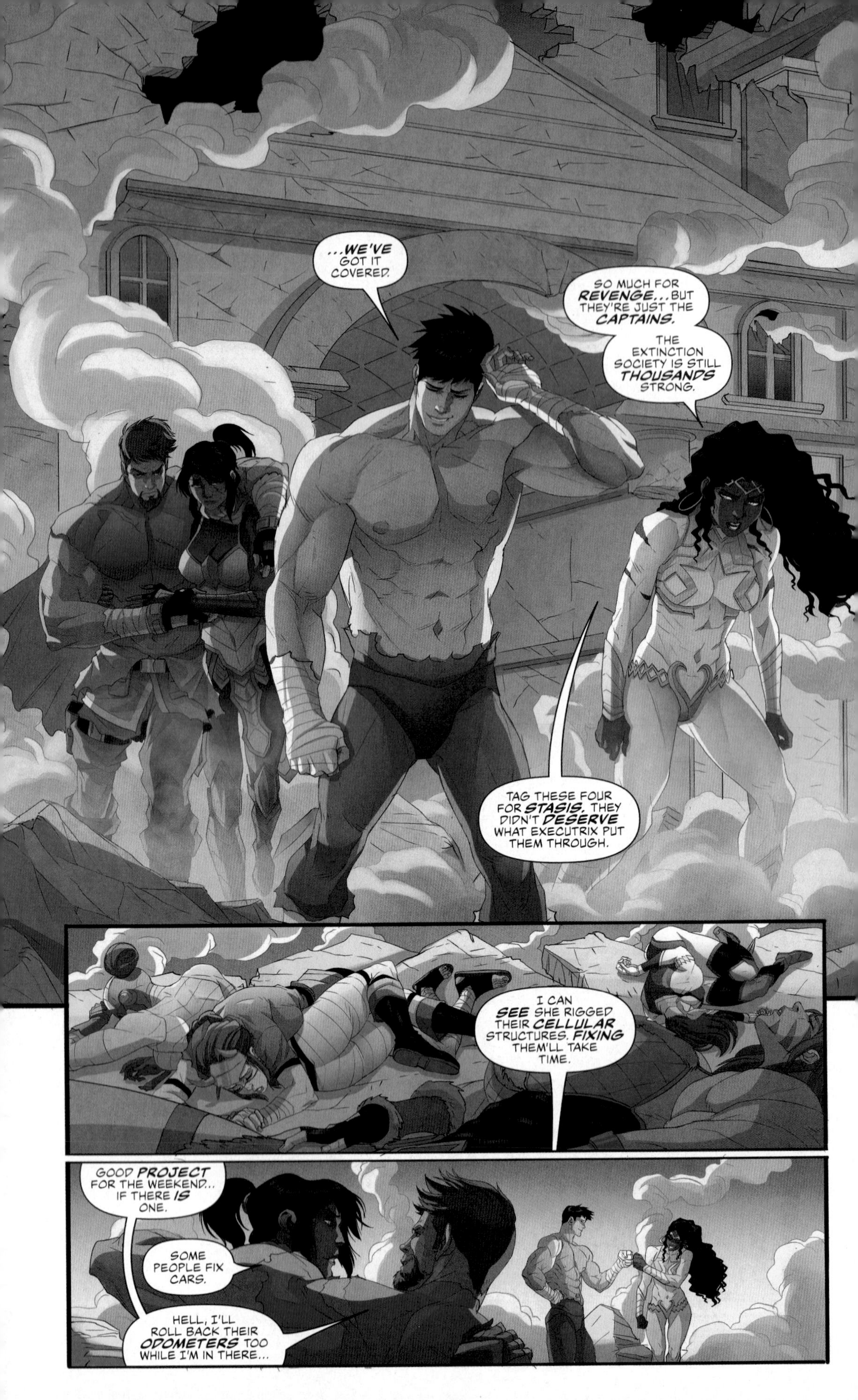
...WE'VE GOT IT COVERED.
SO MUCH FOR REVENGE... BUT THEY'RE JUST THE CAPTAINS.
THE EXTINCTION SOCIETY IS STILL THOUSANDS STRONG.
TAG THESE FOUR FOR STASIS. THEY DIDN'T DESERVE WHAT EXECUTRIX PUT THEM THROUGH.
I CAN SEE SHE RIGGED THEIR CELLULAR STRUCTURES. FIXING THEM'LL TAKE TIME.
GOOD PROJECT FOR THE WEEKEND... IF THERE IS ONE.
SOME PEOPLE FIX CARS.
HELL, I'LL ROLL BACK THEIR ODOMETERS TOO WHILE I'M IN THERE...

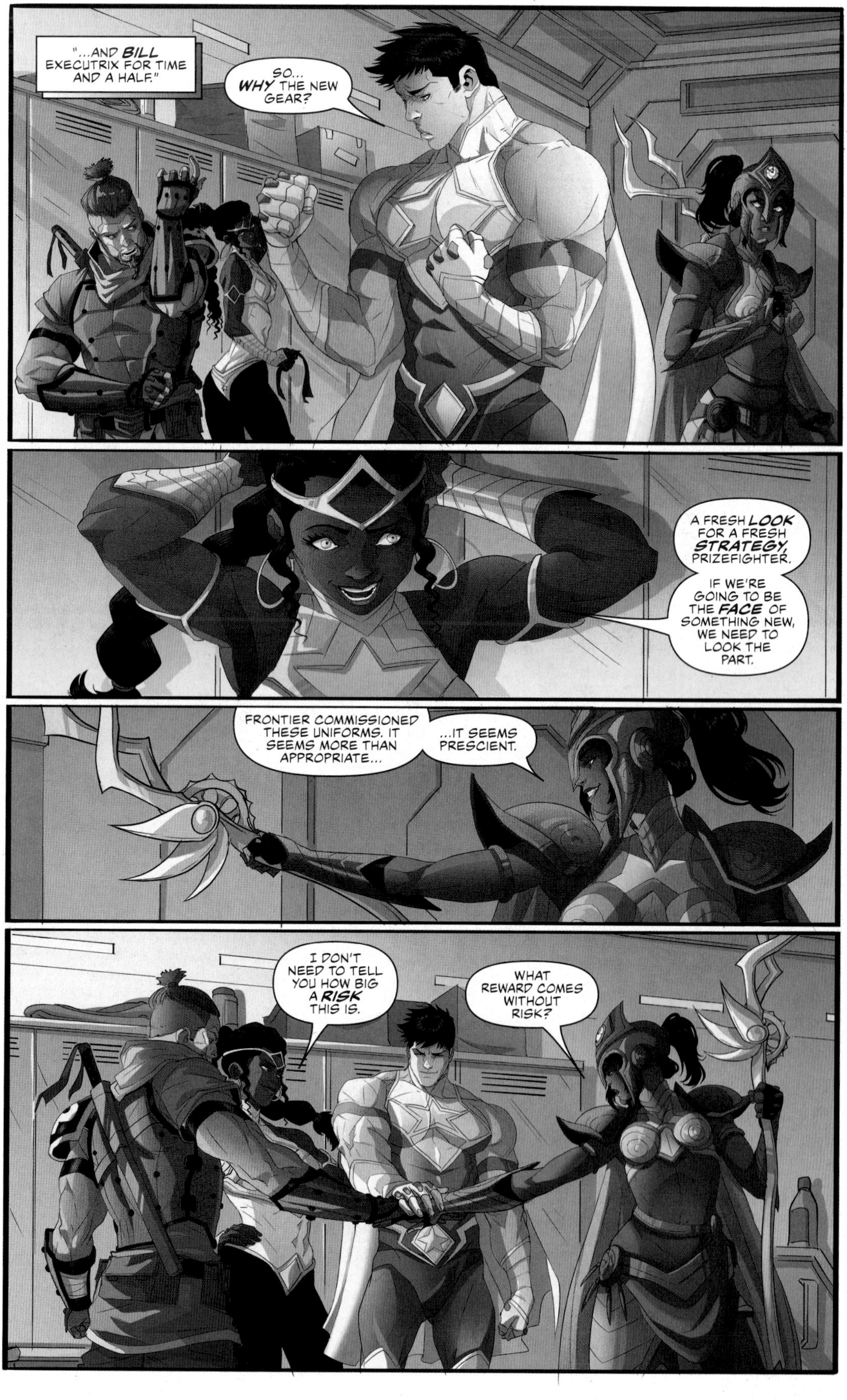
"...AND BILL EXECUTRIX FOR TIME AND A HALF."
SO... WHY THE NEW GEAR?
A FRESH LOOK FOR A FRESH STRATEGY, PRIZEFIGHTER.
IF WE'RE GOING TO BE THE FACE OF SOMETHING NEW, WE NEED TO LOOK THE PART.
FRONTIER COMMISSIONED THESE UNIFORMS. IT SEEMS MORE THAN APPROPRIATE...
...IT SEEMS PRESCIENT.
I DON'T NEED TO TELL YOU HOW BIG A RISK THIS IS.
WHAT REWARD COMES WITHOUT RISK?

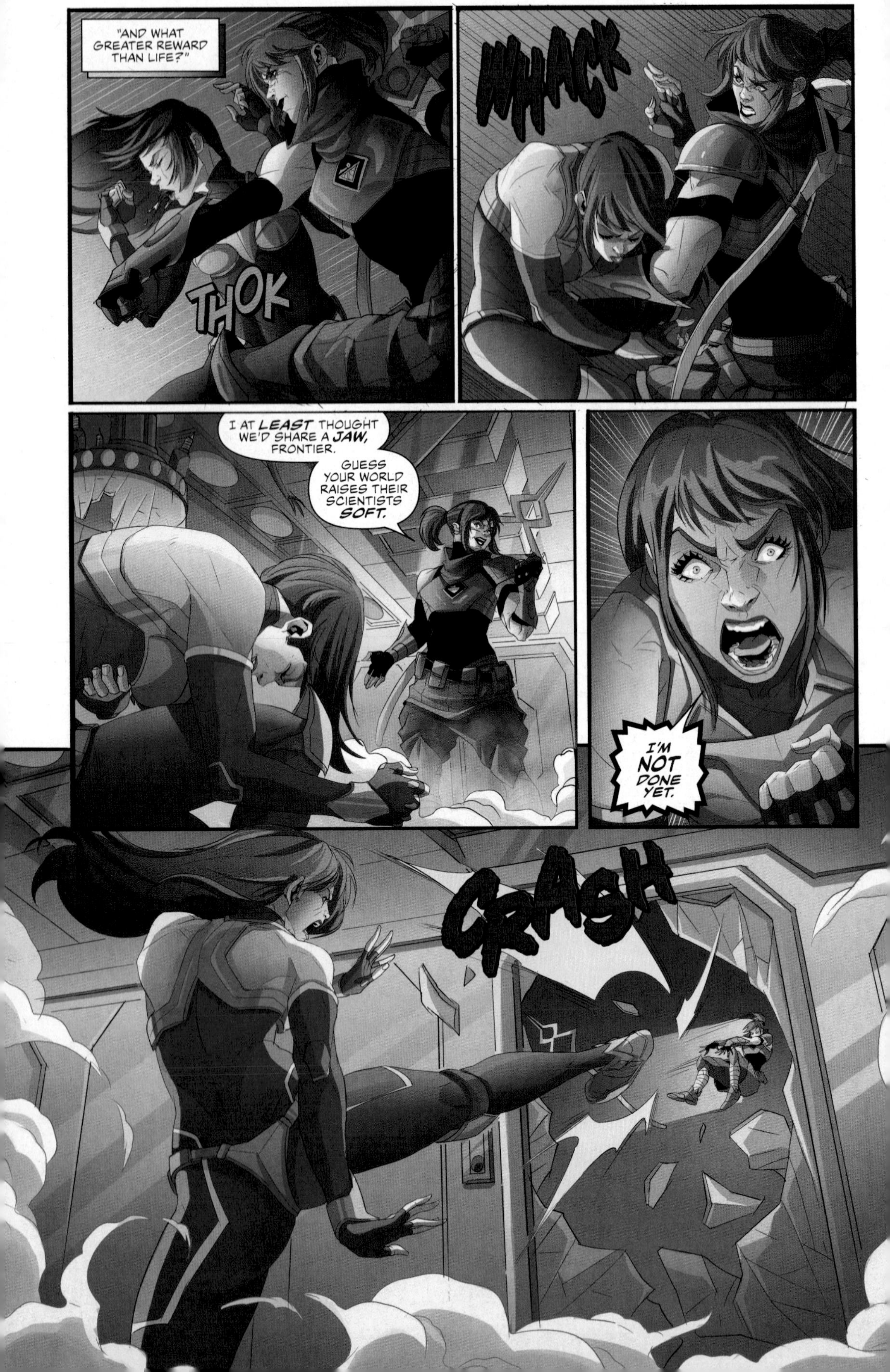
"AND WHAT GREATER REWARD THAN LIFE?"
THOK
WHACK
I AT LEAST THOUGHT WE'D SHARE A JAW, FRONTIER.
GUESS YOUR WORLD RAISES THEIR SCIENTISTS SOFT.
I'M NOT DONE YET.
CRASH

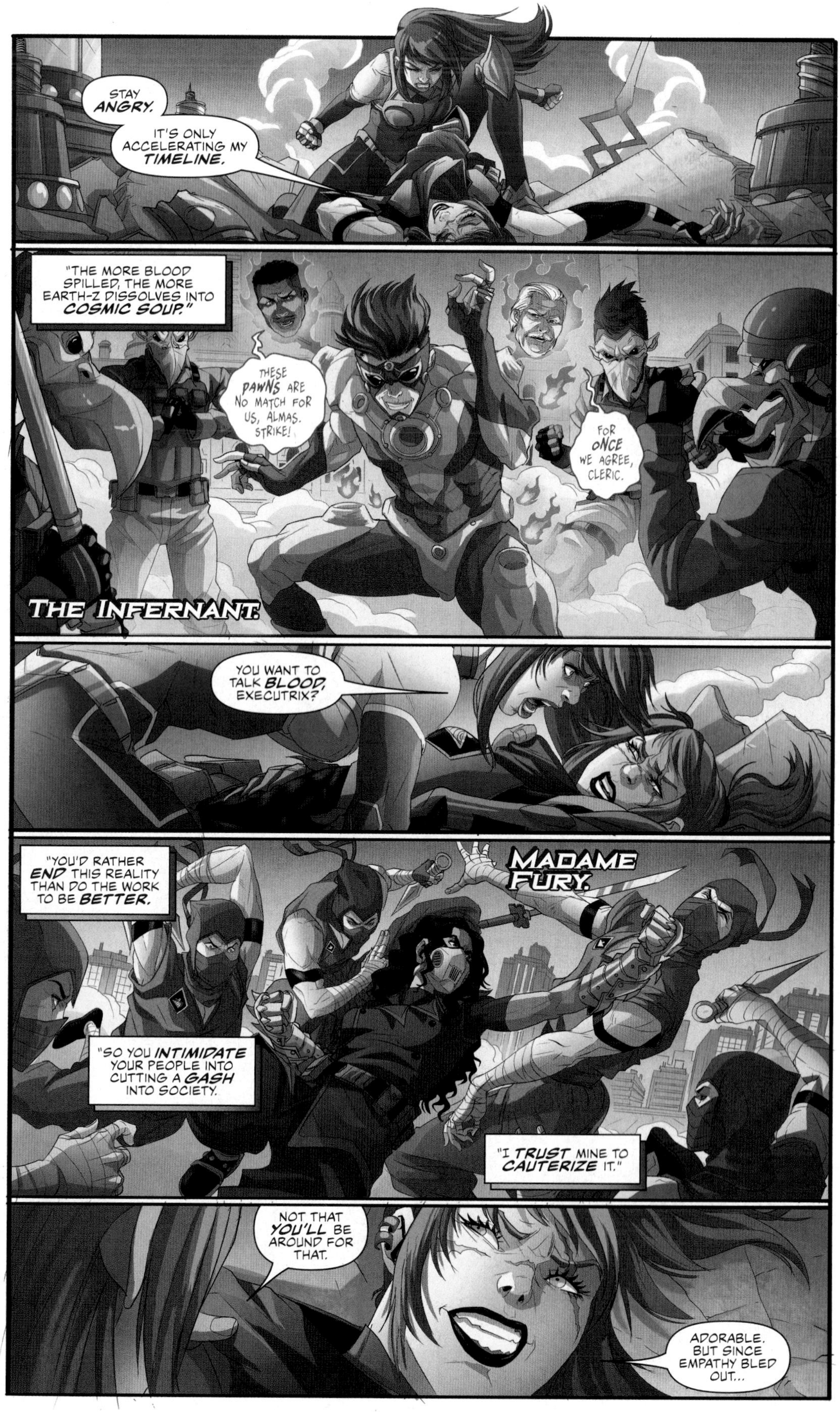
STAY ANGRY.
IT'S ONLY ACCELERATING MY TIMELINE.
"THE MORE BLOOD SPILLED, THE MORE EARTH-Z DISSOLVES INTO COSMIC SOUP."
THESE PAWNS ARE NO MATCH FOR US, ALMAS. STRIKE!
FOR ONCE WE AGREE, CLERIC.
THE INFERNANT.
YOU WANT TO TALK BLOOD, EXECUTRIX?
"YOU'D RATHER END THIS REALITY THAN DO THE WORK TO BE BETTER.
MADAME FURY.
"SO YOU INTIMIDATE YOUR PEOPLE INTO CUTTING A GASH INTO SOCIETY.
"I TRUST MINE TO CAUTERIZE IT."
NOT THAT YOU'LL BE AROUND FOR THAT.
ADORABLE. BUT SINCE EMPATHY BLED OUT...

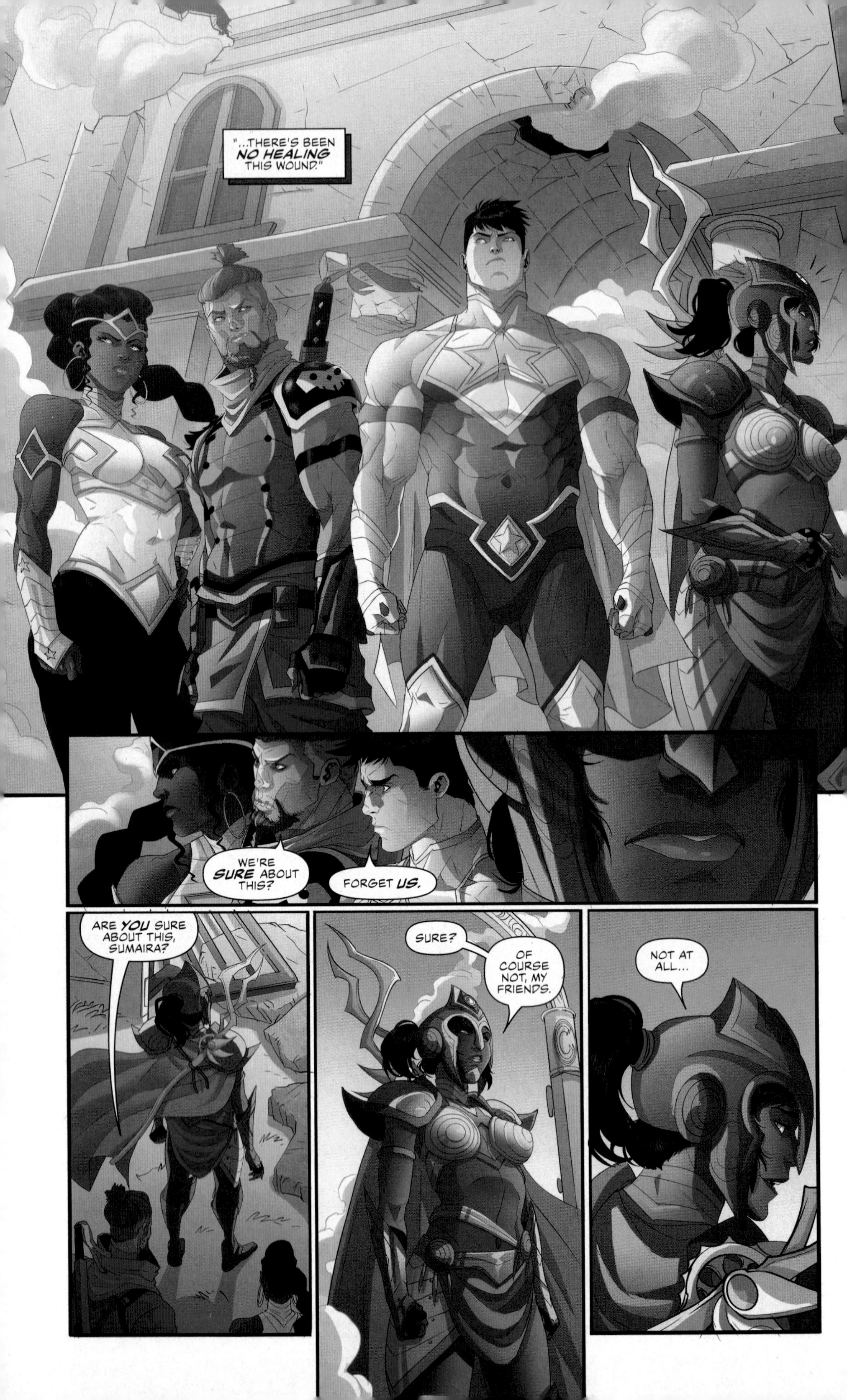
"...THERE'S BEEN NO HEALING THIS WOUND."
WE'RE SURE ABOUT THIS?
FORGET US.
ARE YOU SURE ABOUT THIS, SUMAIRA?
SURE?
OF COURSE NOT, MY FRIENDS.
NOT AT ALL...

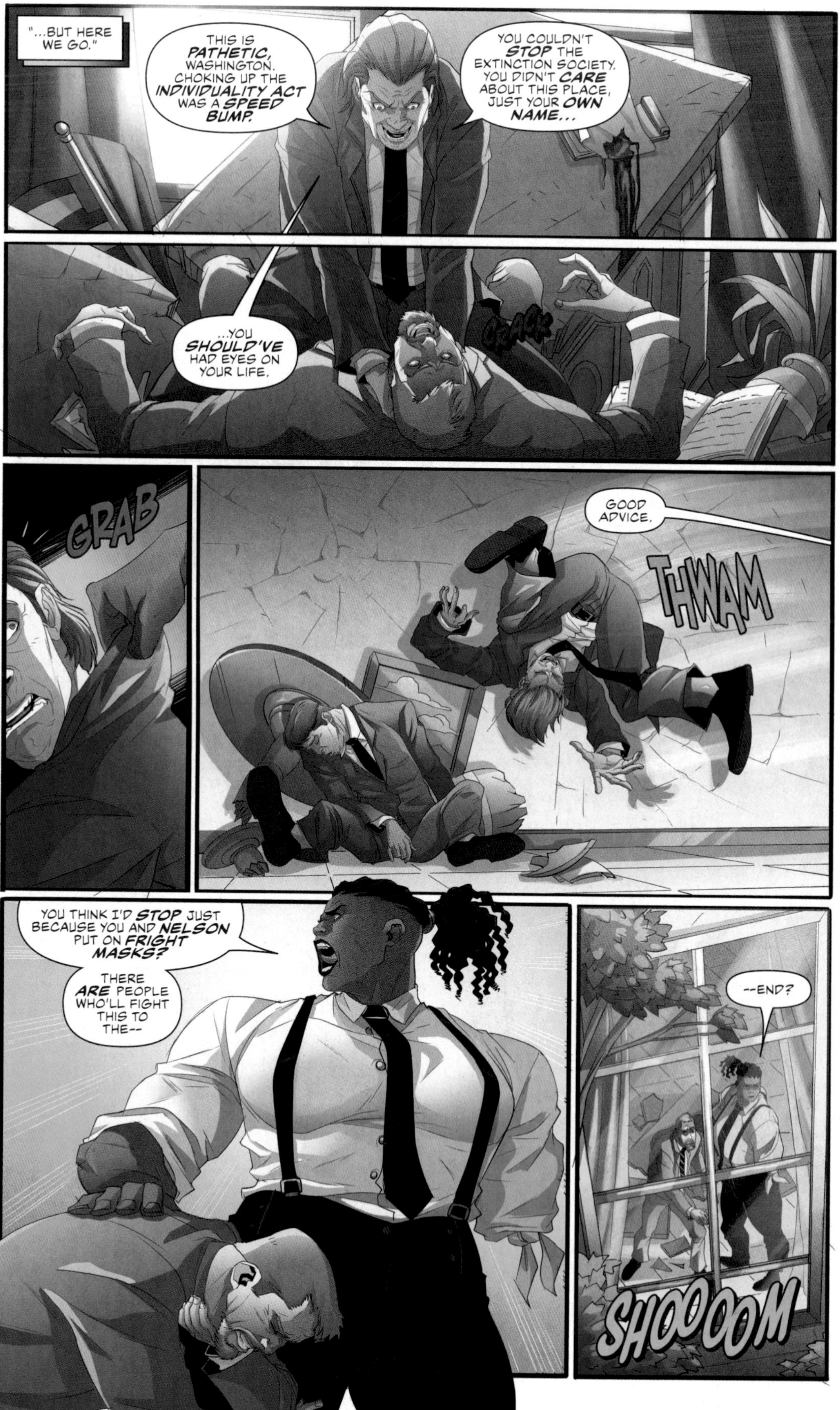
"...BUT HERE WE GO."
THIS IS PATHETIC, WASHINGTON. CHOKING UP THE INDIVIDUALITY ACT WAS A SPEED BUMP.
YOU COULDN'T STOP THE EXTINCTION SOCIETY. YOU DIDN'T CARE ABOUT THIS PLACE, JUST YOUR OWN NAME...
...YOU SHOULD'VE HAD EYES ON YOUR LIFE.
CRACK
GRAB
GOOD ADVICE.
THWAM
YOU THINK I'D STOP JUST BECAUSE YOU AND NELSON PUT ON FRIGHT MASKS?
THERE ARE PEOPLE WHO'LL FIGHT THIS TO THE--
--END?
SHOOOOOM

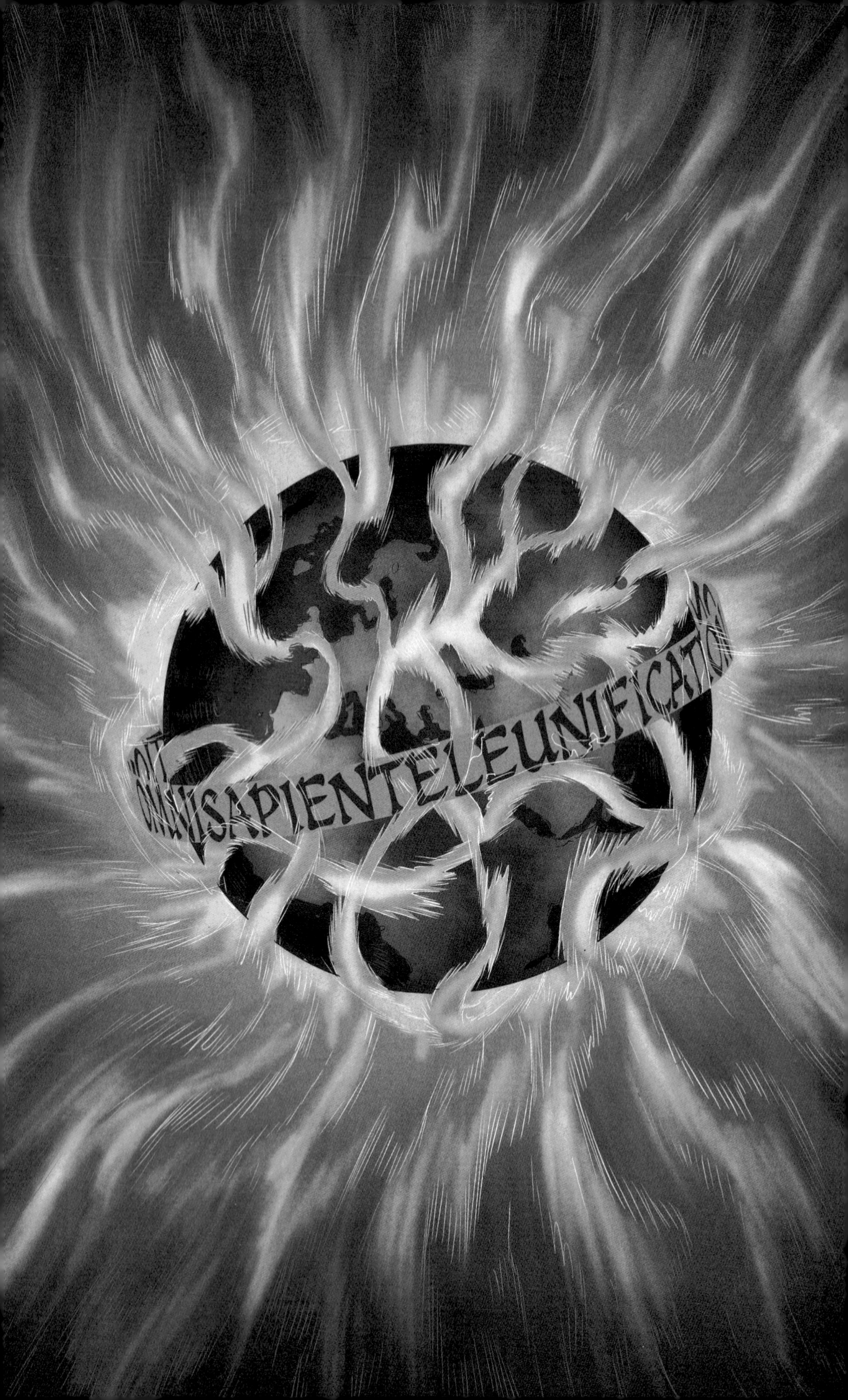
OMNISAPIENTELEUNIFICATIO

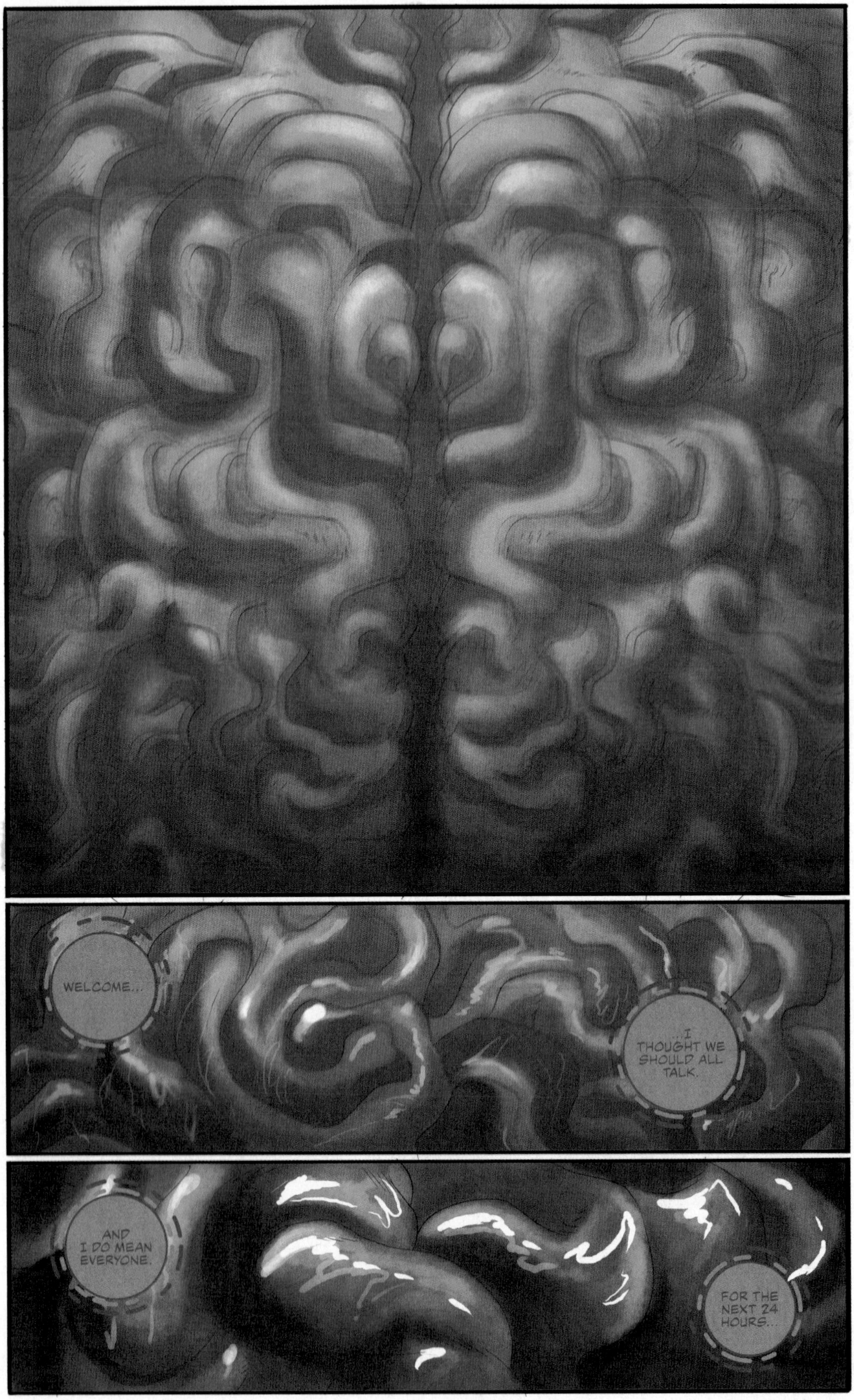
WELCOME...
...I THOUGHT WE SHOULD ALL TALK.
AND I DO MEAN EVERYONE.
FOR THE NEXT 24 HOURS...

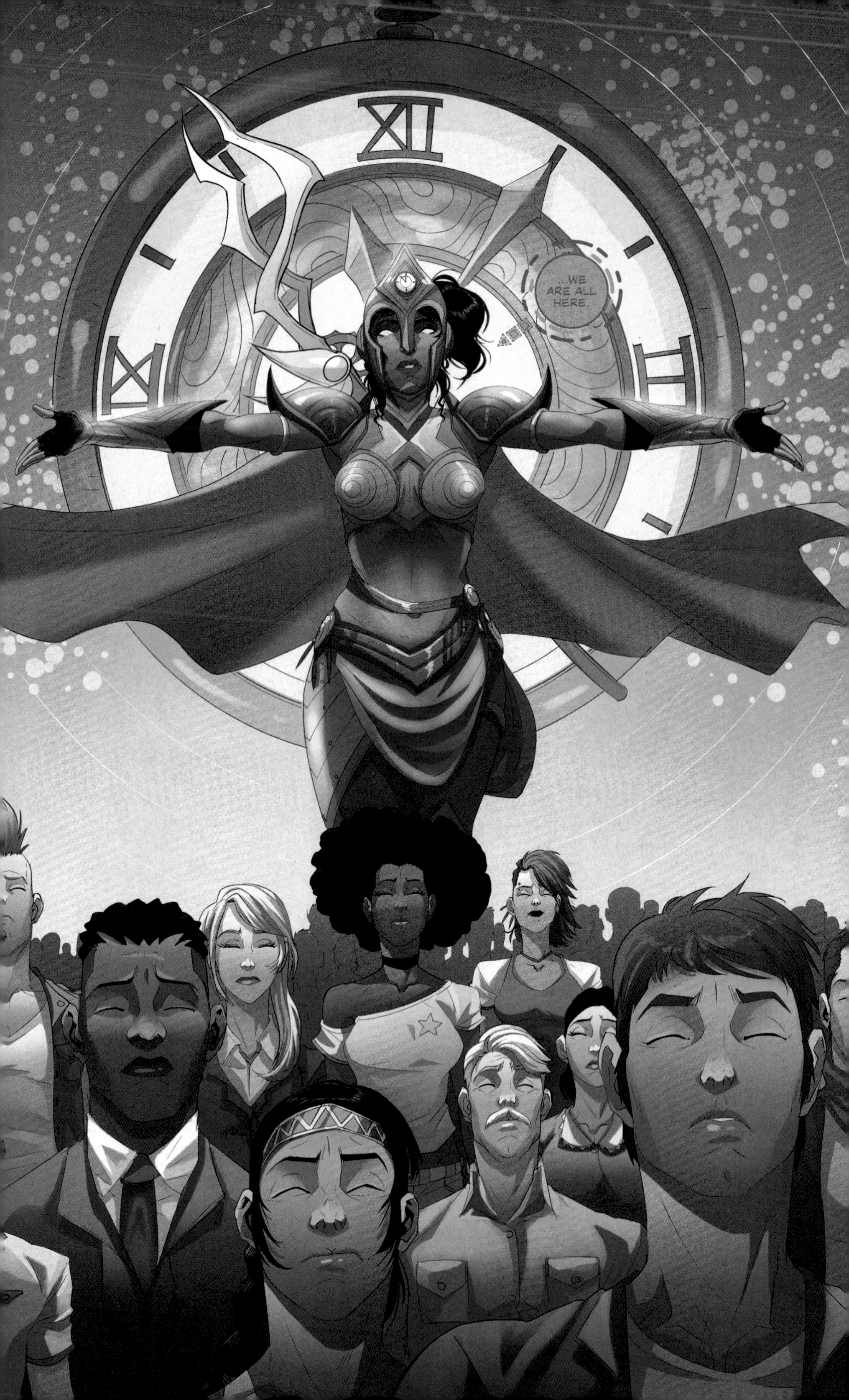
...WE ARE ALL HERE.

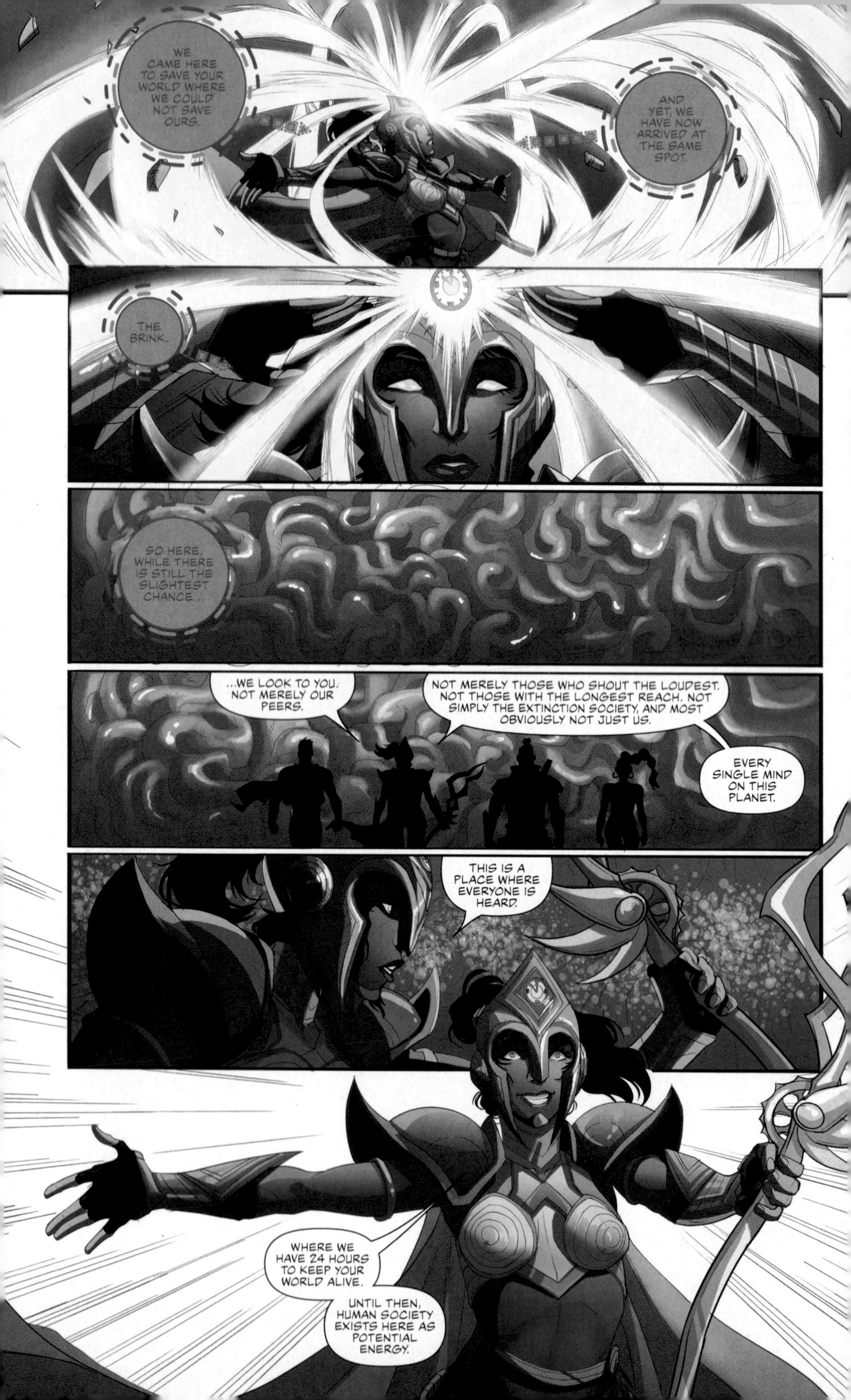
WE CAME HERE TO SAVE YOUR WORLD WHERE WE COULD NOT SAVE OURS.
AND YET, WE HAVE NOW ARRIVED AT THE SAME SPOT.
THE BRINK.
SO HERE, WHILE THERE IS STILL THE SLIGHTEST CHANCE...
...WE LOOK TO YOU. NOT MERELY OUR PEERS.
NOT MERELY THOSE WHO SHOUT THE LOUDEST. NOT THOSE WITH THE LONGEST REACH. NOT SIMPLY THE EXTINCTION SOCIETY, AND MOST OBVIOUSLY NOT JUST US.
EVERY SINGLE MIND ON THIS PLANET.
THIS IS A PLACE WHERE EVERYONE IS HEARD.
WHERE WE HAVE 24 HOURS TO KEEP YOUR WORLD ALIVE.
UNTIL THEN, HUMAN SOCIETY EXISTS HERE AS POTENTIAL ENERGY.

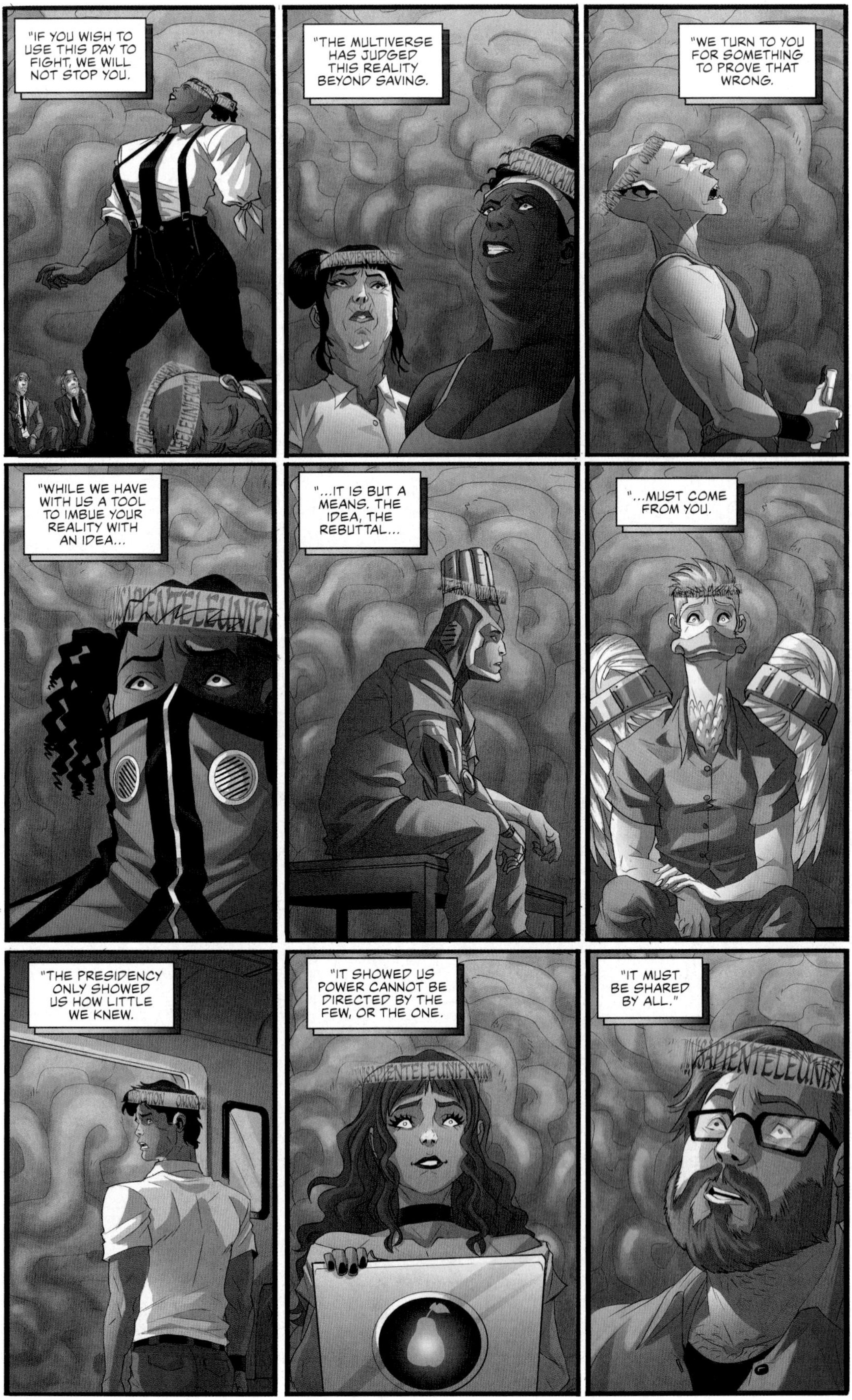
"IF YOU WISH TO USE THIS DAY TO FIGHT, WE WILL NOT STOP YOU.
"THE MULTIVERSE HAS JUDGED THIS REALITY BEYOND SAVING.
"WE TURN TO YOU FOR SOMETHING TO PROVE THAT WRONG.
"WHILE WE HAVE WITH US A TOOL TO IMBUE YOUR REALITY WITH AN IDEA...
"...IT IS BUT A MEANS. THE IDEA, THE REBUTTAL...
"...MUST COME FROM YOU.
"THE PRESIDENCY ONLY SHOWED US HOW LITTLE WE KNEW.
"IT SHOWED US POWER CANNOT BE DIRECTED BY THE FEW, OR THE ONE.
"IT MUST BE SHARED BY ALL."

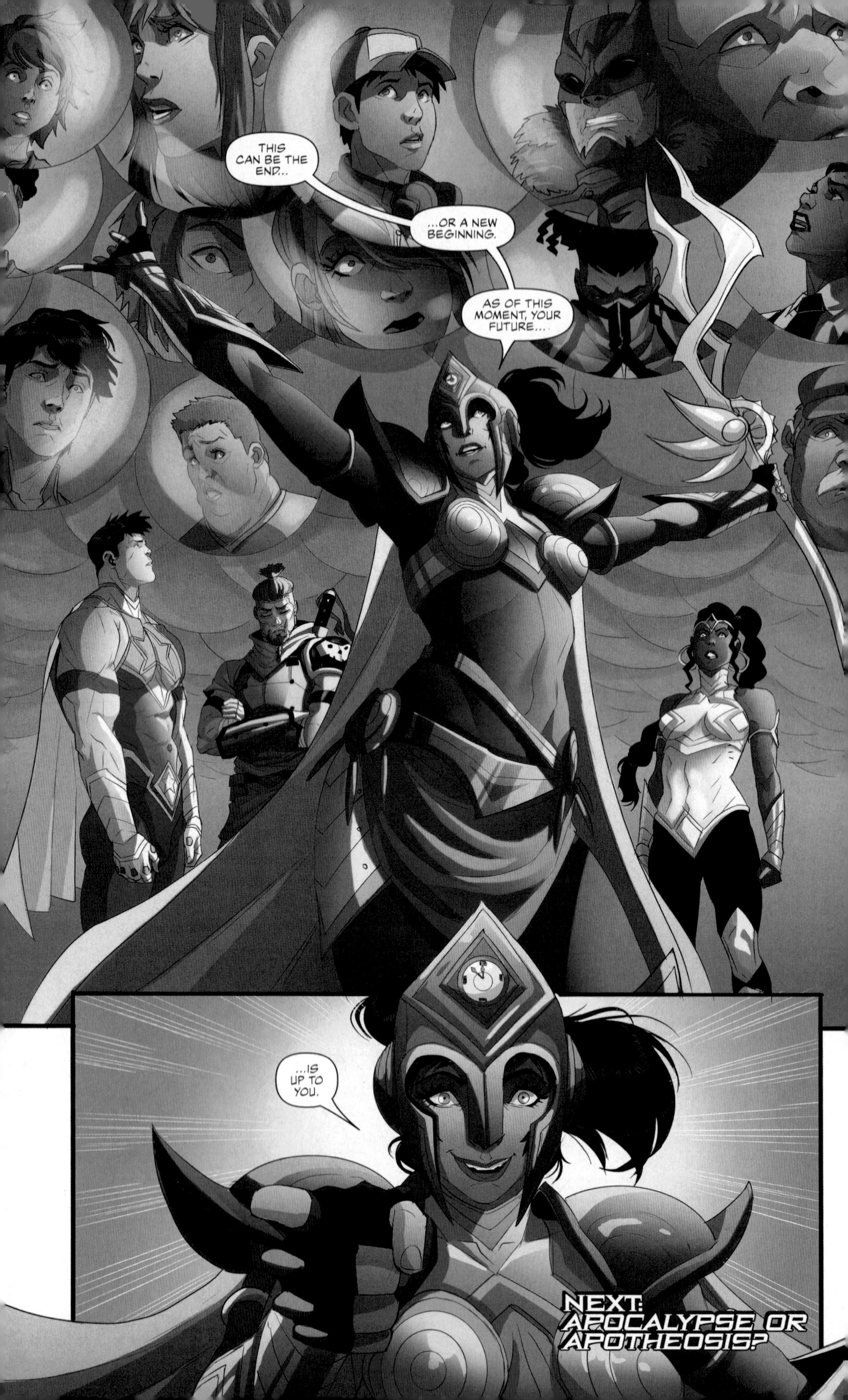
THIS CAN BE THE END...
...OR A NEW BEGINNING.
AS OF THIS MOMENT, YOUR FUTURE....
...IS UP TO YOU.
NEXT: APOCALYPSE OR APOTHEOSIS?

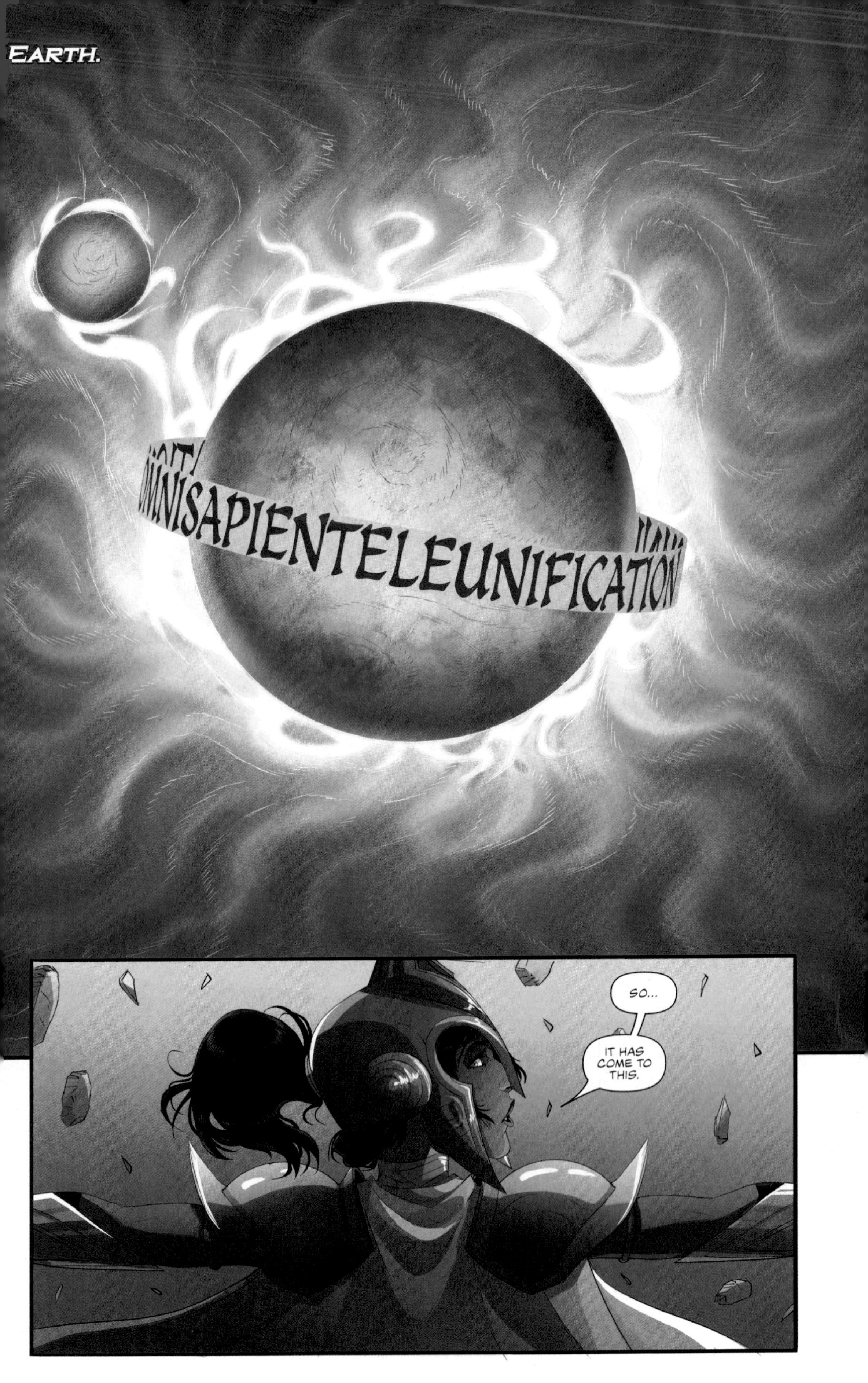
EARTH.
OMNISAPIENTELEUNIFICATION
SO...
IT HAS COME TO THIS.

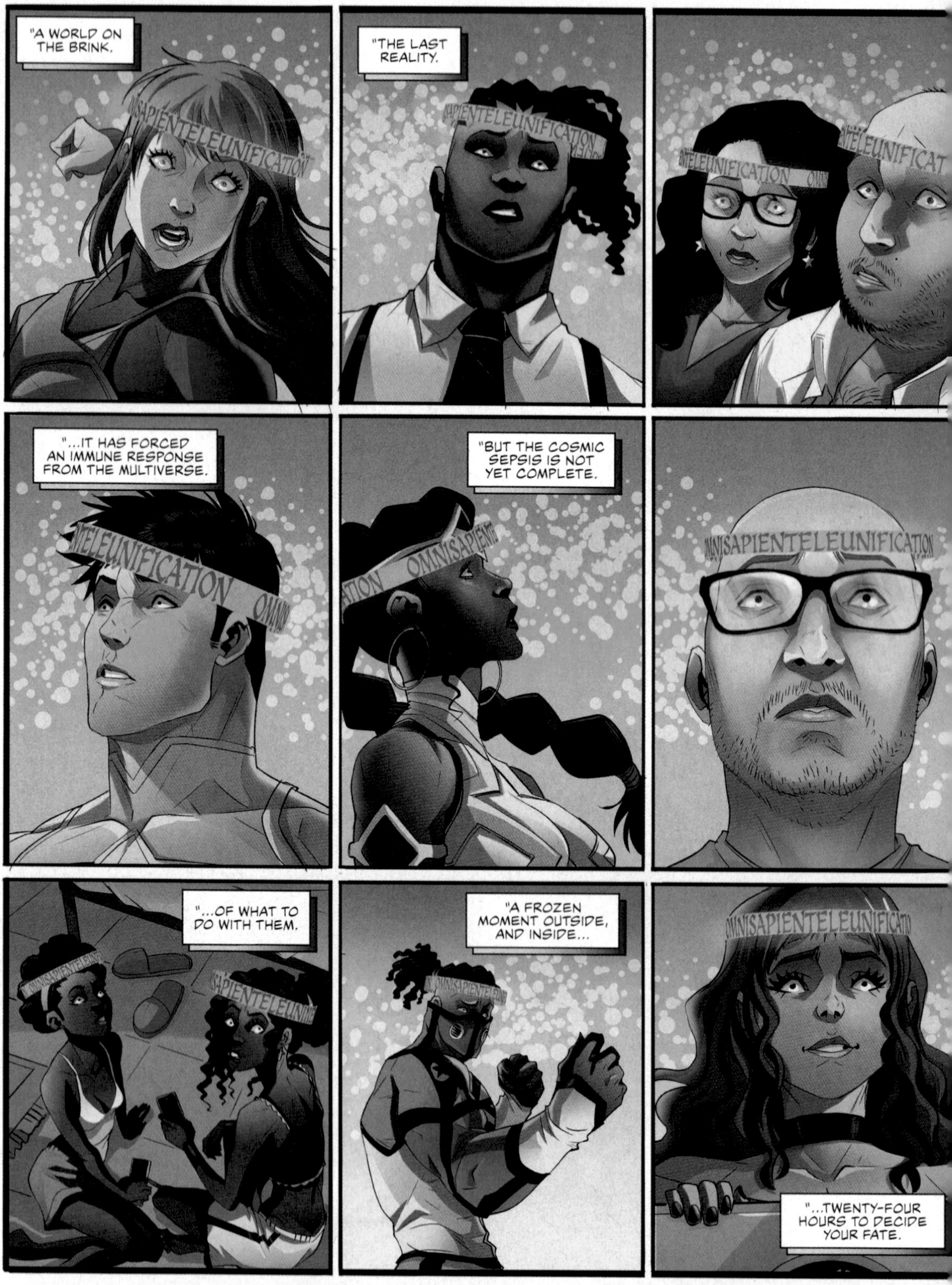
"A WORLD ON THE BRINK.
"THE LAST REALITY.
"...IT HAS FORCED AN IMMUNE RESPONSE FROM THE MULTIVERSE.
"BUT THE COSMIC SEPSIS IS NOT YET COMPLETE.
"...OF WHAT TO DO WITH THEM.
"A FROZEN MOMENT OUTSIDE, AND INSIDE...
"...TWENTY-FOUR HOURS TO DECIDE YOUR FATE.

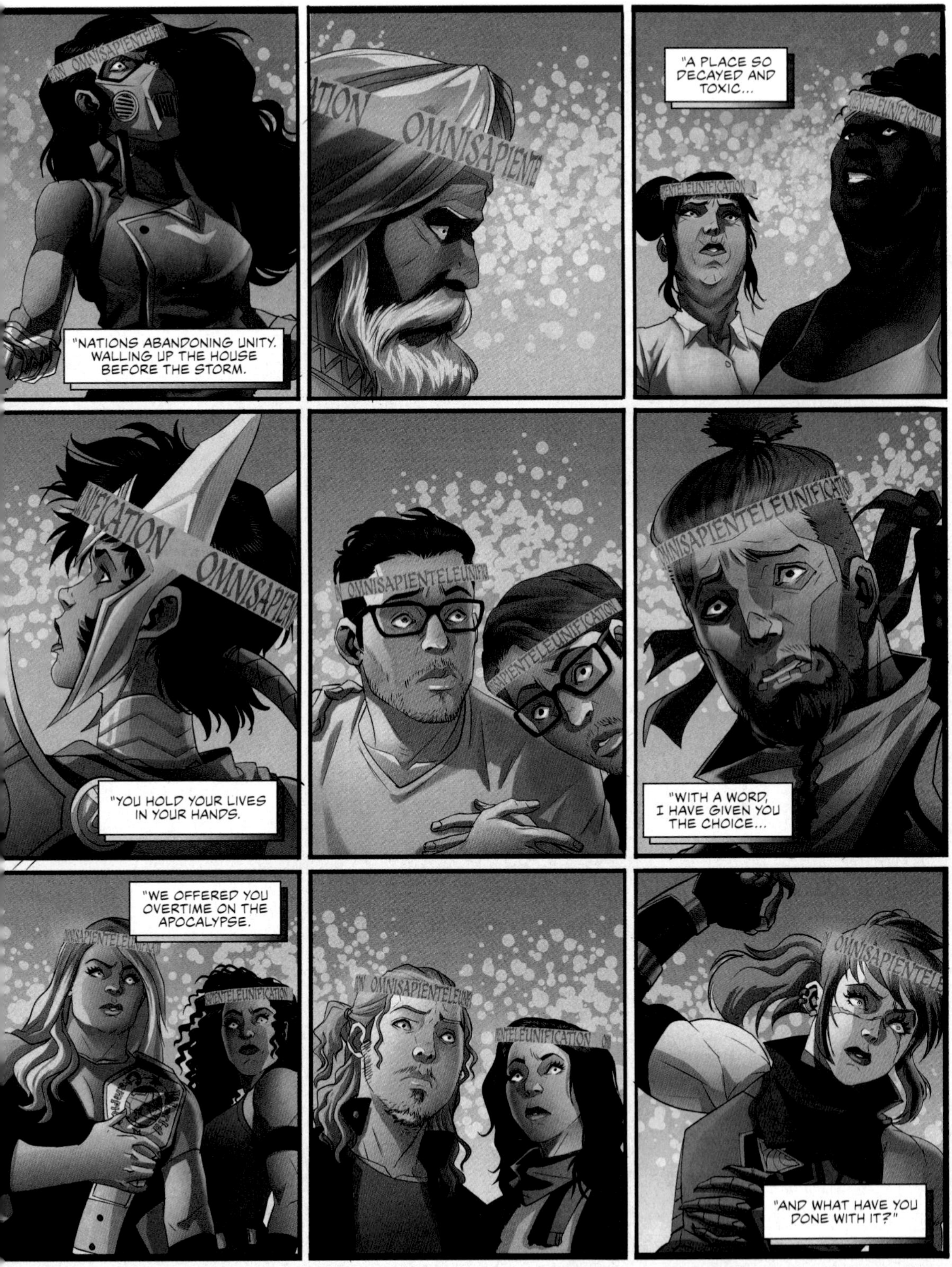
"NATIONS ABANDONING UNITY. WALLING UP THE HOUSE BEFORE THE STORM.
"A PLACE SO DECAYED AND TOXIC...
"YOU HOLD YOUR LIVES IN YOUR HANDS.
"WITH A WORD, I HAVE GIVEN YOU THE CHOICE...
"WE OFFERED YOU OVERTIME ON THE APOCALYPSE.
"AND WHAT HAVE YOU DONE WITH IT?"

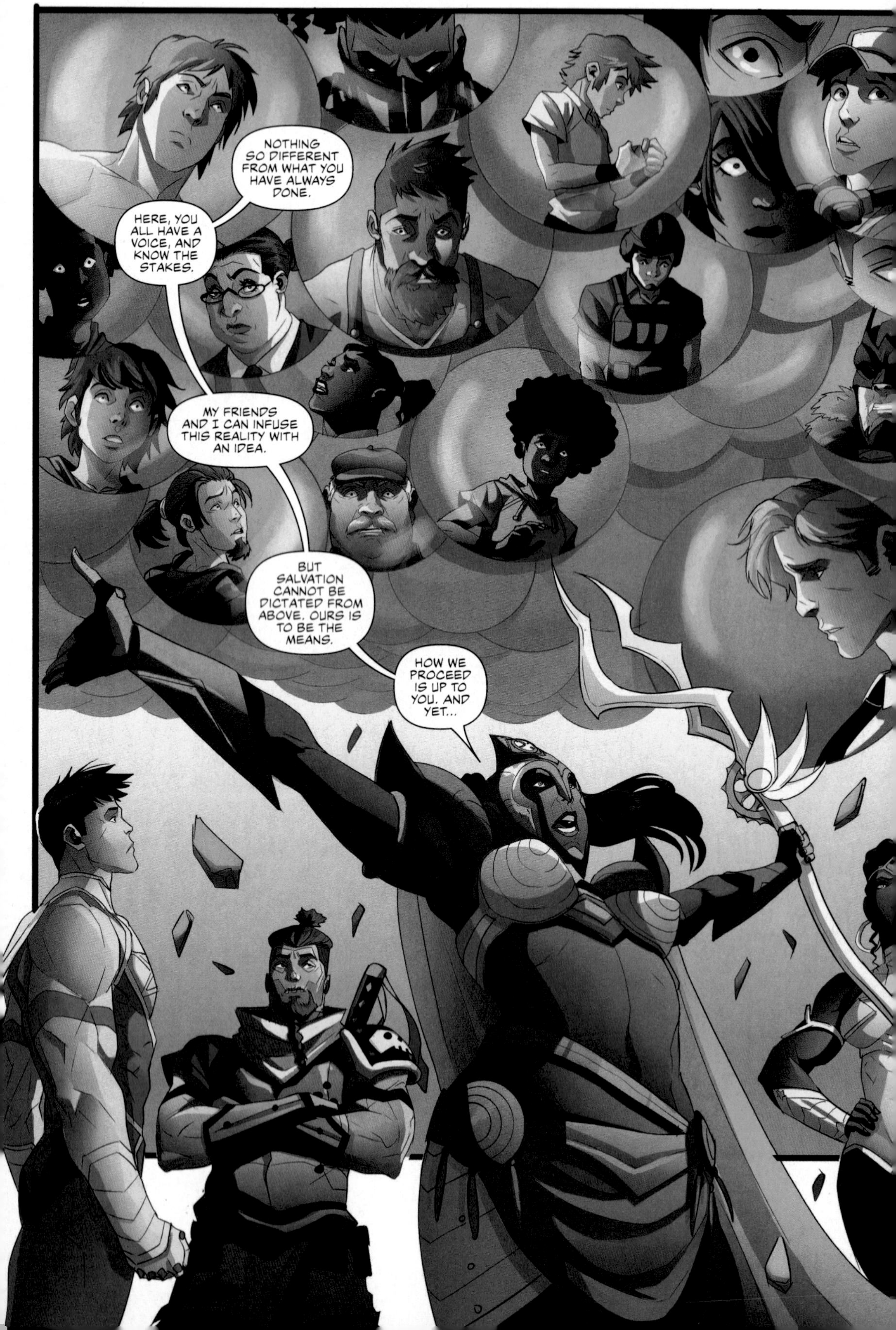
NOTHING SO DIFFERENT FROM WHAT YOU HAVE ALWAYS DONE.
HERE, YOU ALL HAVE A VOICE, AND KNOW THE STAKES.
MY FRIENDS AND I CAN INFUSE THIS REALITY WITH AN IDEA.
BUT SALVATION CANNOT BE DICTATED FROM ABOVE. OURS IS TO BE THE MEANS.
HOW WE PROCEED IS UP TO YOU. AND YET...

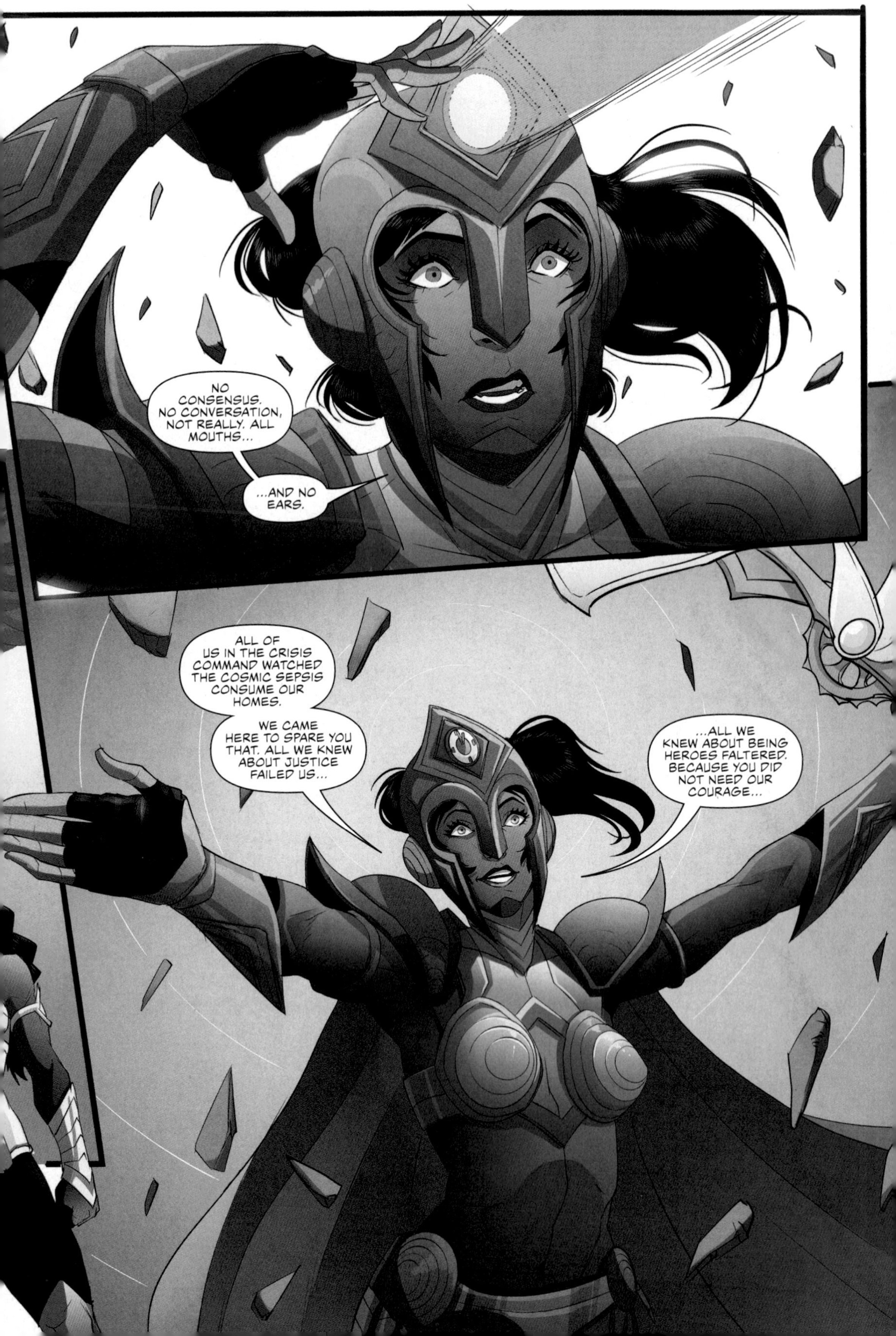
NO CONSENSUS. NO CONVERSATION, NOT REALLY. ALL MOUTHS...
...AND NO EARS.
ALL OF US IN THE CRISIS COMMAND WATCHED THE COSMIC SEPSIS CONSUME OUR HOMES.
WE CAME HERE TO SPARE YOU THAT. ALL WE KNEW ABOUT JUSTICE FAILED US...
...ALL WE KNEW ABOUT BEING HEROES FALTERED. BECAUSE YOU DID NOT NEED OUR COURAGE...

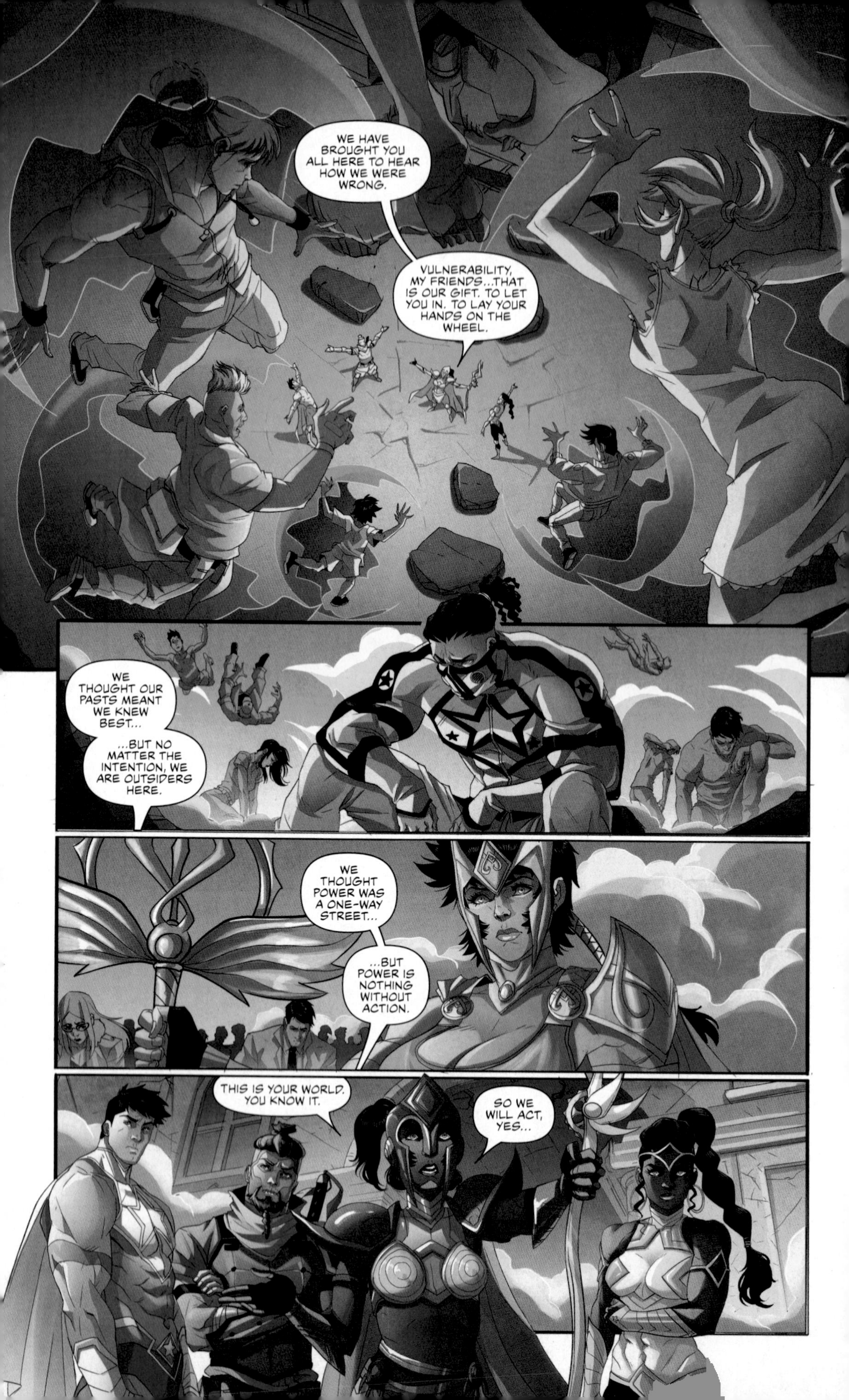
WE HAVE BROUGHT YOU ALL HERE TO HEAR HOW WE WERE WRONG.
VULNERABILITY, MY FRIENDS...THAT IS OUR GIFT. TO LET YOU IN. TO LAY YOUR HANDS ON THE WHEEL.
WE THOUGHT OUR PASTS MEANT WE KNEW BEST...
...BUT NO MATTER THE INTENTION, WE ARE OUTSIDERS HERE.
WE THOUGHT POWER WAS A ONE-WAY STREET...
...BUT POWER IS NOTHING WITHOUT ACTION.
THIS IS YOUR WORLD. YOU KNOW IT.
SO WE WILL ACT, YES...

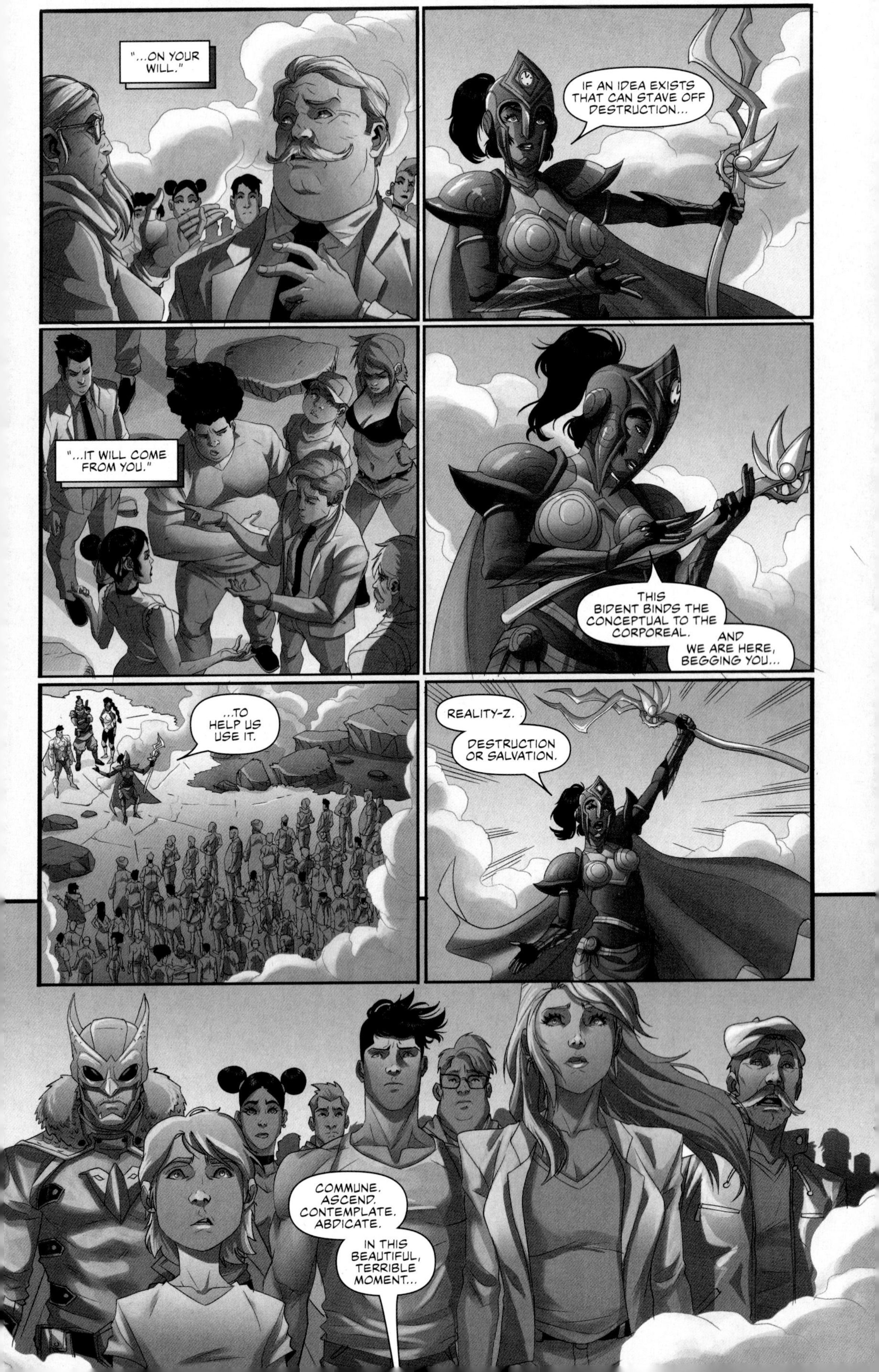
"...ON YOUR WILL."
IF AN IDEA EXISTS THAT CAN STAVE OFF DESTRUCTION...
"...IT WILL COME FROM YOU."
THIS BIDENT BINDS THE CONCEPTUAL TO THE CORPOREAL.
AND WE ARE HERE, BEGGING YOU...
...TO HELP US USE IT.
REALITY-Z.
DESTRUCTION OR SALVATION.
COMMUNE. ASCEND. CONTEMPLATE. ABDICATE.
IN THIS BEAUTIFUL, TERRIBLE MOMENT...

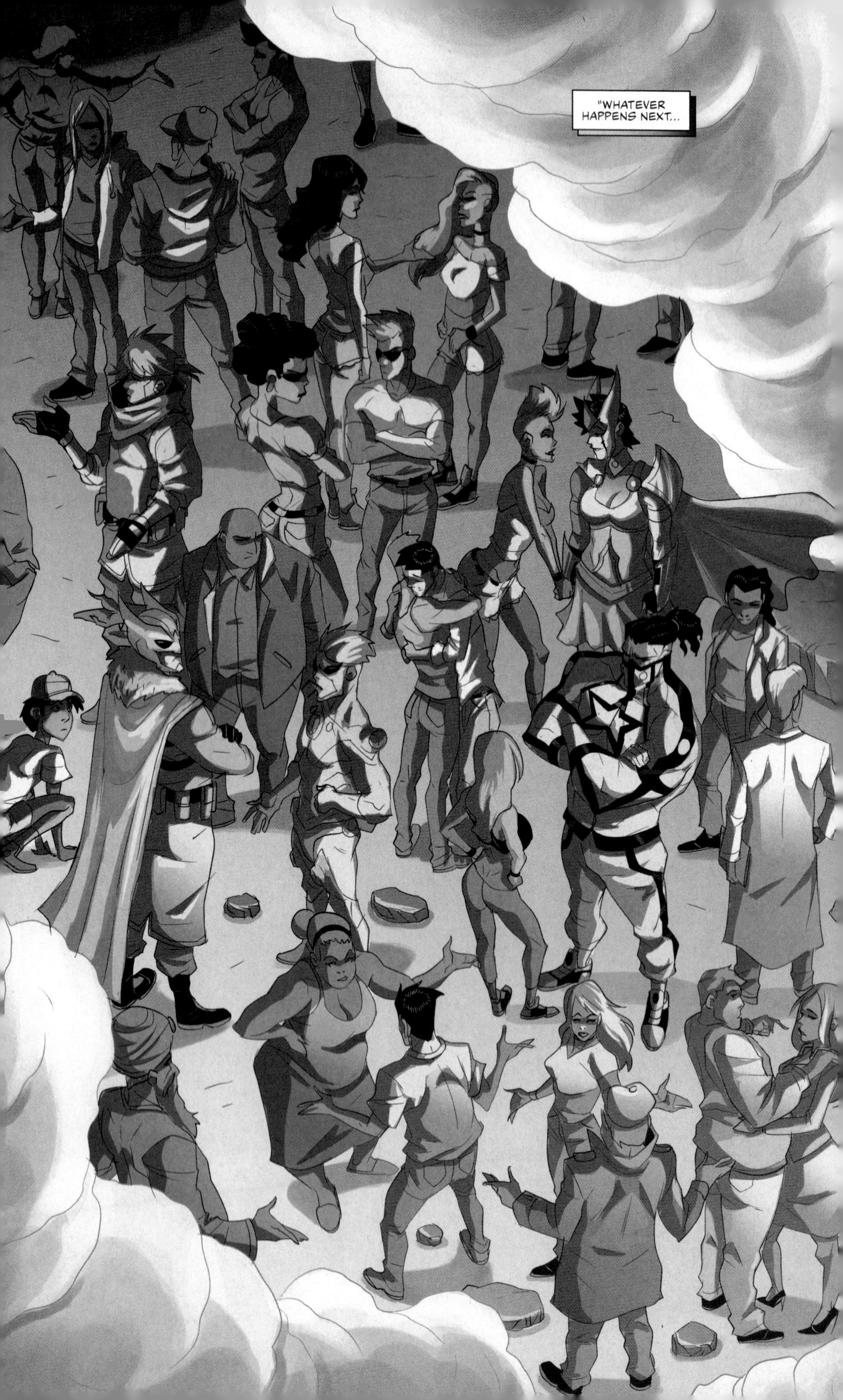
"WHATEVER HAPPENS NEXT...

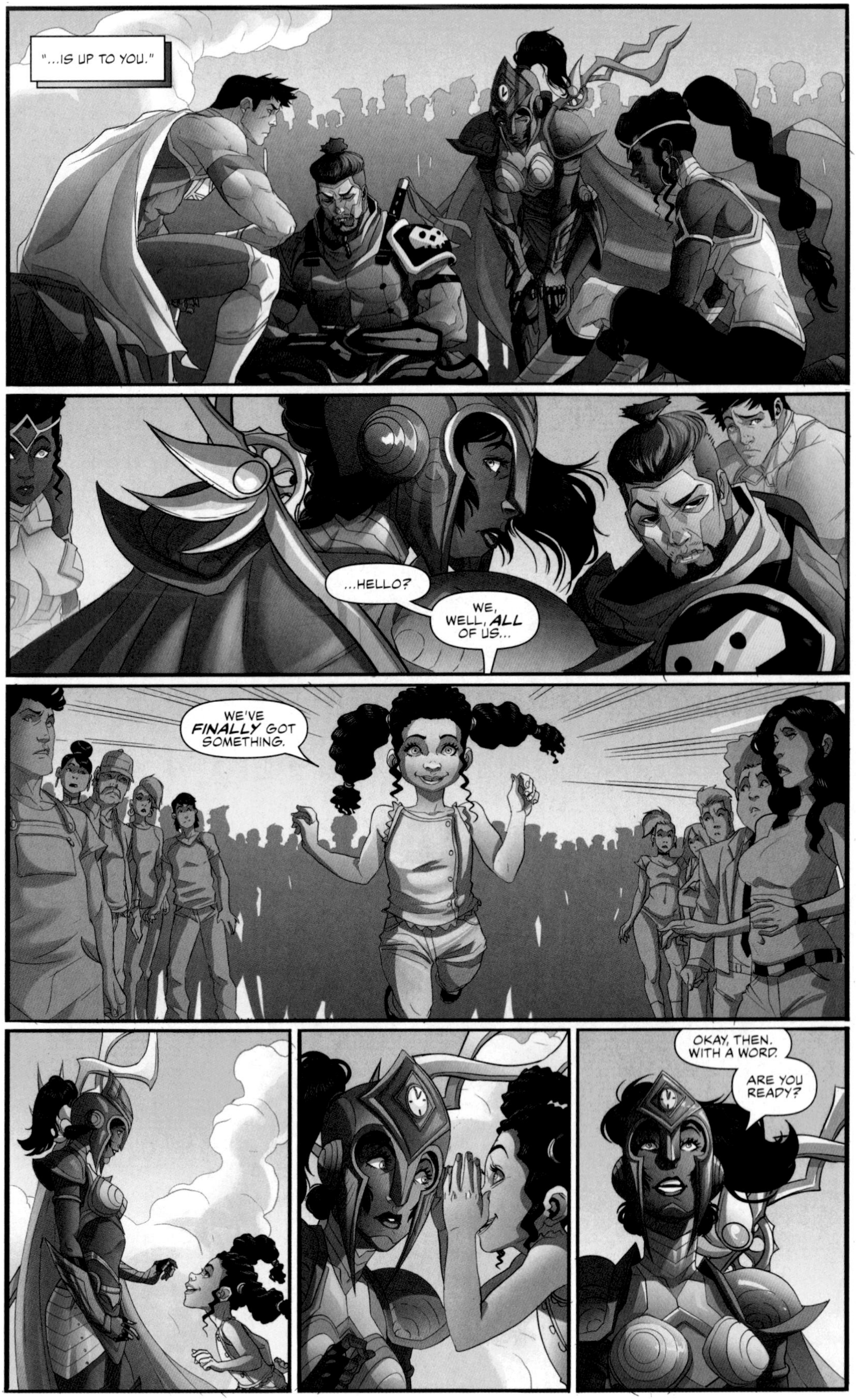
"...IS UP TO YOU."
...HELLO?
WE, WELL, ALL OF US...
WE'VE FINALLY GOT SOMETHING.
OKAY, THEN. WITH A WORD.
ARE YOU READY?

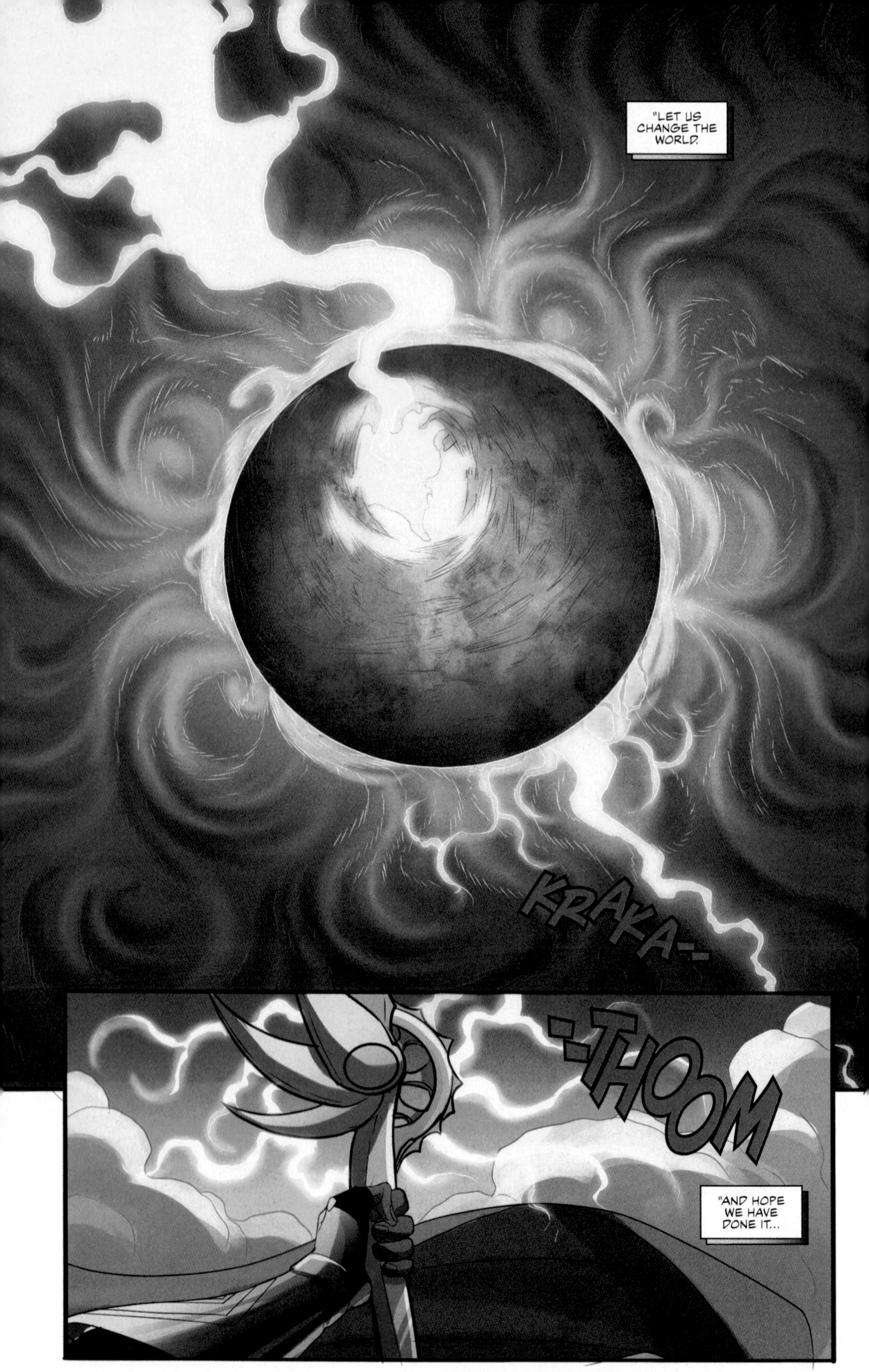
"LET US CHANGE THE WORLD.
KRAKA--
--THOOM
"AND HOPE WE HAVE DONE IT...

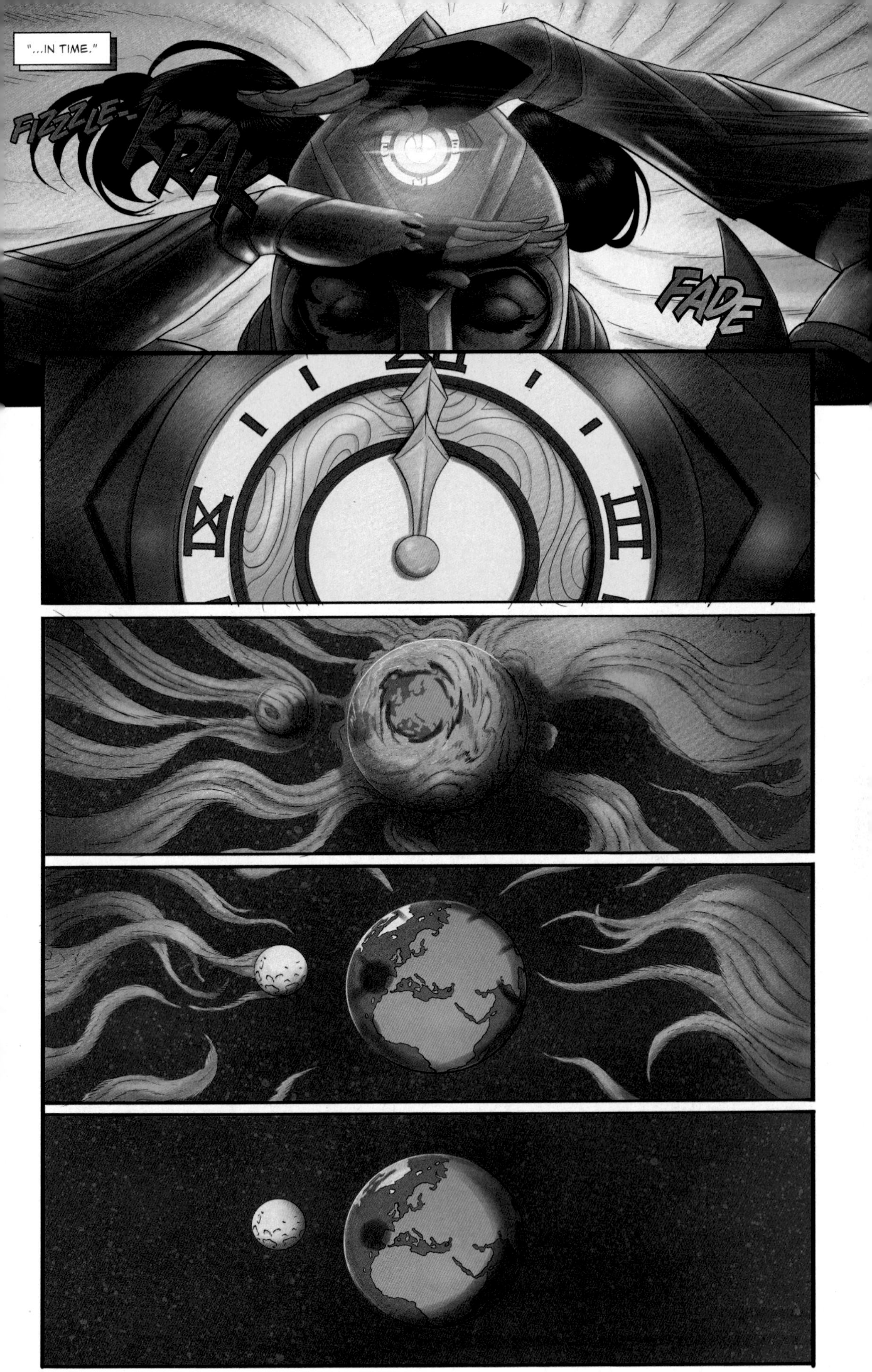
"...IN TIME."
FIZZZLE-
KRAK
FADE

THE BELTWAY.

CHILE.

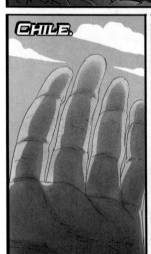

BETWEEN TWO ATOMS.

...FUCK...

WHERE... WERE WE?

WHO CARES? WE'RE STILL ALIVE, EXECUTRIX...

...WHICH MEANS YOU LOST.

FOR *NOW*, FRONTIER. BUT THERE'S STILL *TIME*...

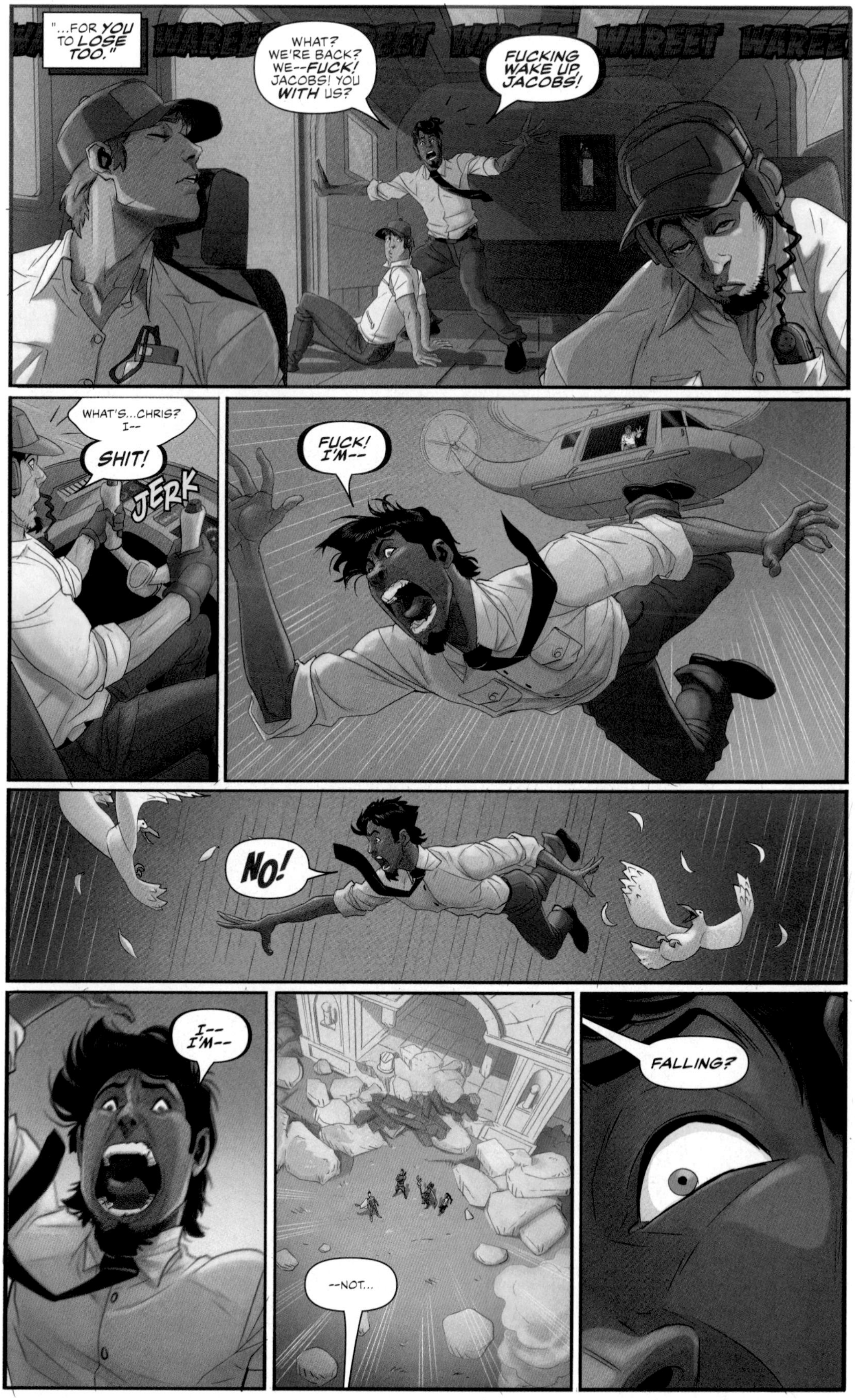
"...FOR YOU TO LOSE TOO."
WHAT? WE'RE BACK? WE--FUCK! JACOBS! YOU WITH US?
FUCKING WAKE UP, JACOBS!
WHAT'S...CHRIS? I--
SHIT!
JERK
FUCK! I'M--
NO!
I-- I'M--
--NOT...
FALLING?

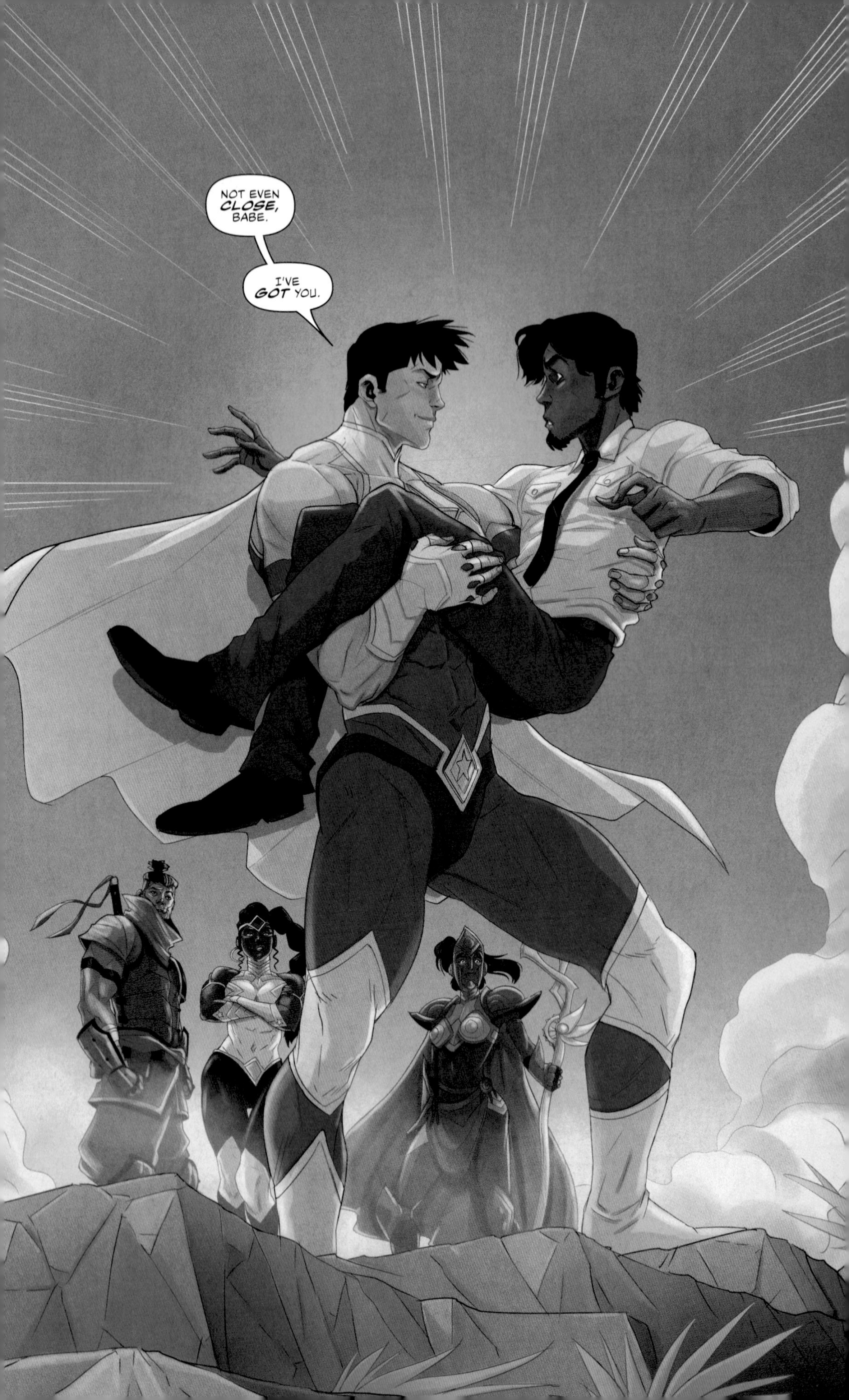
NOT EVEN CLOSE, BABE.
I'VE GOT YOU.

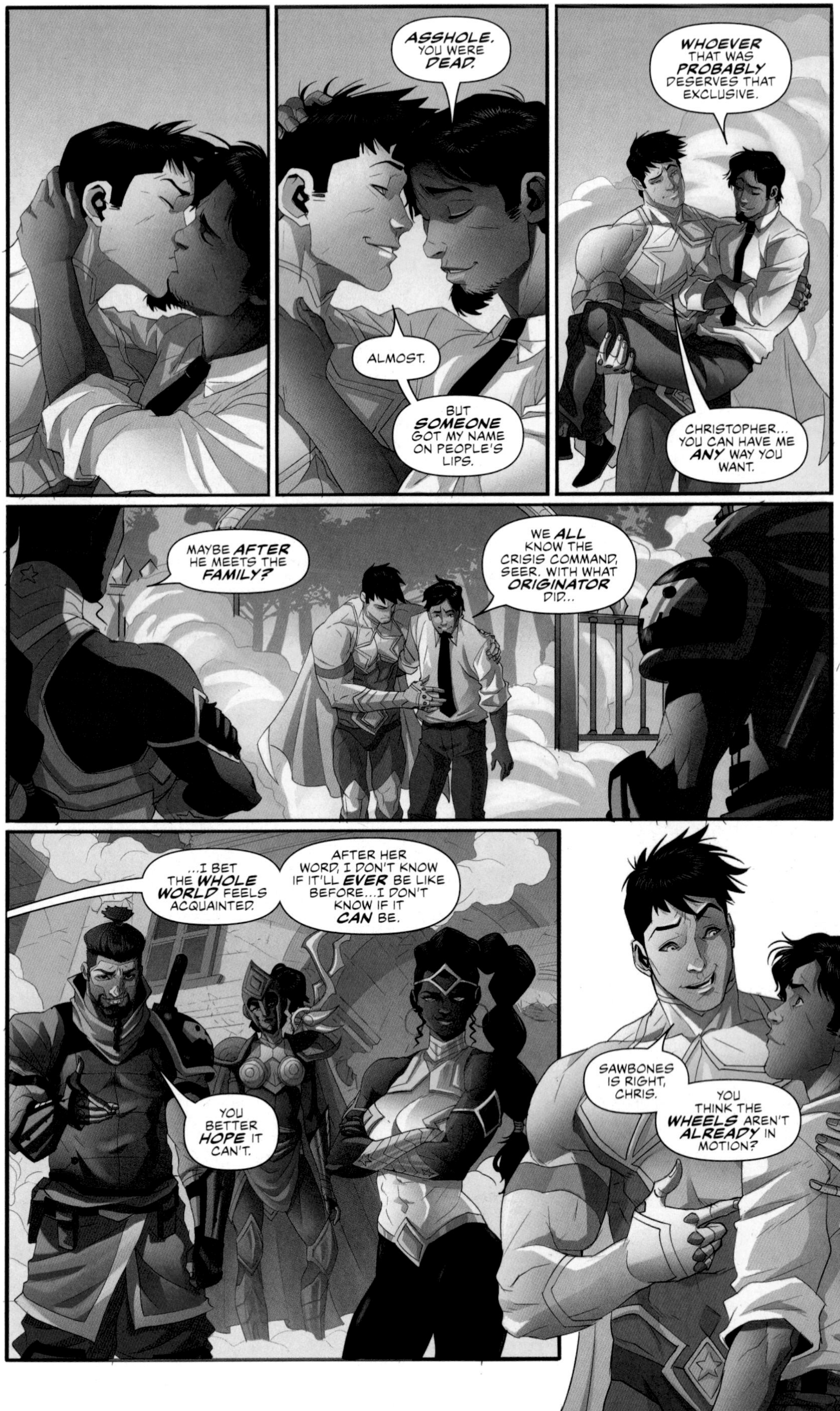
ASSHOLE. YOU WERE DEAD.
ALMOST.
BUT SOMEONE GOT MY NAME ON PEOPLE'S LIPS.
WHOEVER THAT WAS PROBABLY DESERVES THAT EXCLUSIVE.
CHRISTOPHER... YOU CAN HAVE ME ANY WAY YOU WANT.
MAYBE AFTER HE MEETS THE FAMILY?
WE ALL KNOW THE CRISIS COMMAND, SEER. WITH WHAT ORIGINATOR DID...
...I BET THE WHOLE WORLD FEELS ACQUAINTED.
AFTER HER WORD, I DON'T KNOW IF IT'LL EVER BE LIKE BEFORE...I DON'T KNOW IF IT CAN BE.
YOU BETTER HOPE IT CAN'T.
SAWBONES IS RIGHT, CHRIS.
YOU THINK THE WHEELS AREN'T ALREADY IN MOTION?

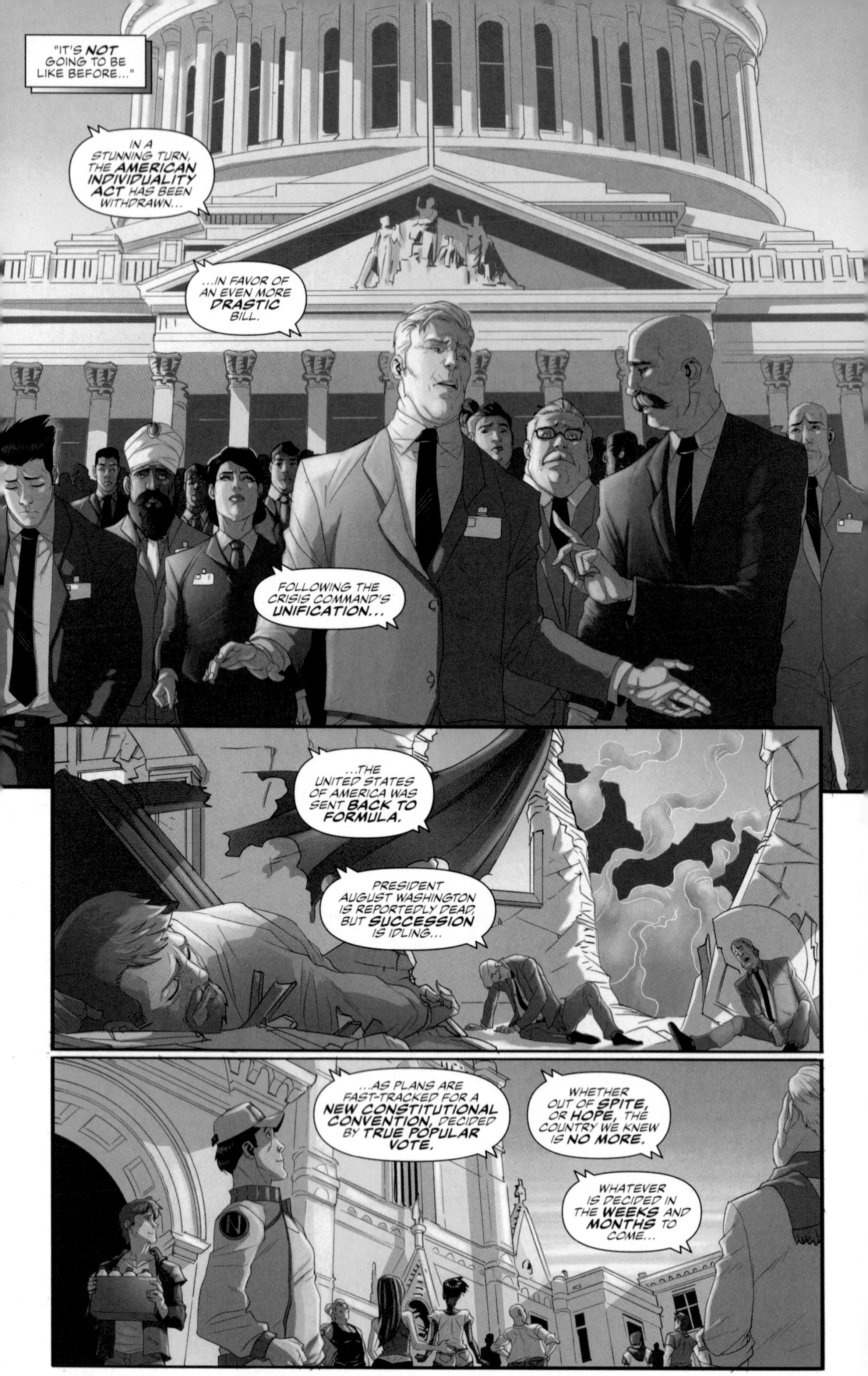
"IT'S NOT GOING TO BE LIKE BEFORE..."
IN A STUNNING TURN, THE AMERICAN INDIVIDUALITY ACT HAS BEEN WITHDRAWN...
...IN FAVOR OF AN EVEN MORE DRASTIC BILL.
FOLLOWING THE CRISIS COMMAND'S UNIFICATION...
...THE UNITED STATES OF AMERICA WAS SENT BACK TO FORMULA.
PRESIDENT AUGUST WASHINGTON IS REPORTEDLY DEAD, BUT SUCCESSION IS IDLING...
...AS PLANS ARE FAST-TRACKED FOR A NEW CONSTITUTIONAL CONVENTION, DECIDED BY TRUE POPULAR VOTE.
WHETHER OUT OF SPITE, OR HOPE, THE COUNTRY WE KNEW IS NO MORE.
WHATEVER IS DECIDED IN THE WEEKS AND MONTHS TO COME...

...EVERYONE WILL HAVE A SAY.

FOR TWENTY-FOUR HOURS...WE WERE **ALL** CONNECTED.

WHAT ARE YOU EVEN **FIGHTING** FOR?

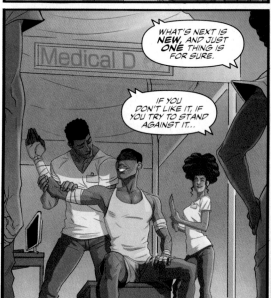

WHAT'S NEXT IS **NEW**, AND JUST **ONE** THING IS FOR SURE.

IF YOU DON'T LIKE IT, IF YOU TRY TO STAND AGAINST IT...

I **TOLD** YOU. **THEY** GET A **TOMORROW**...

...THE **NEW** WILL **RUN YOU OVER**.

...YOU GET OUT OF THE WAY!

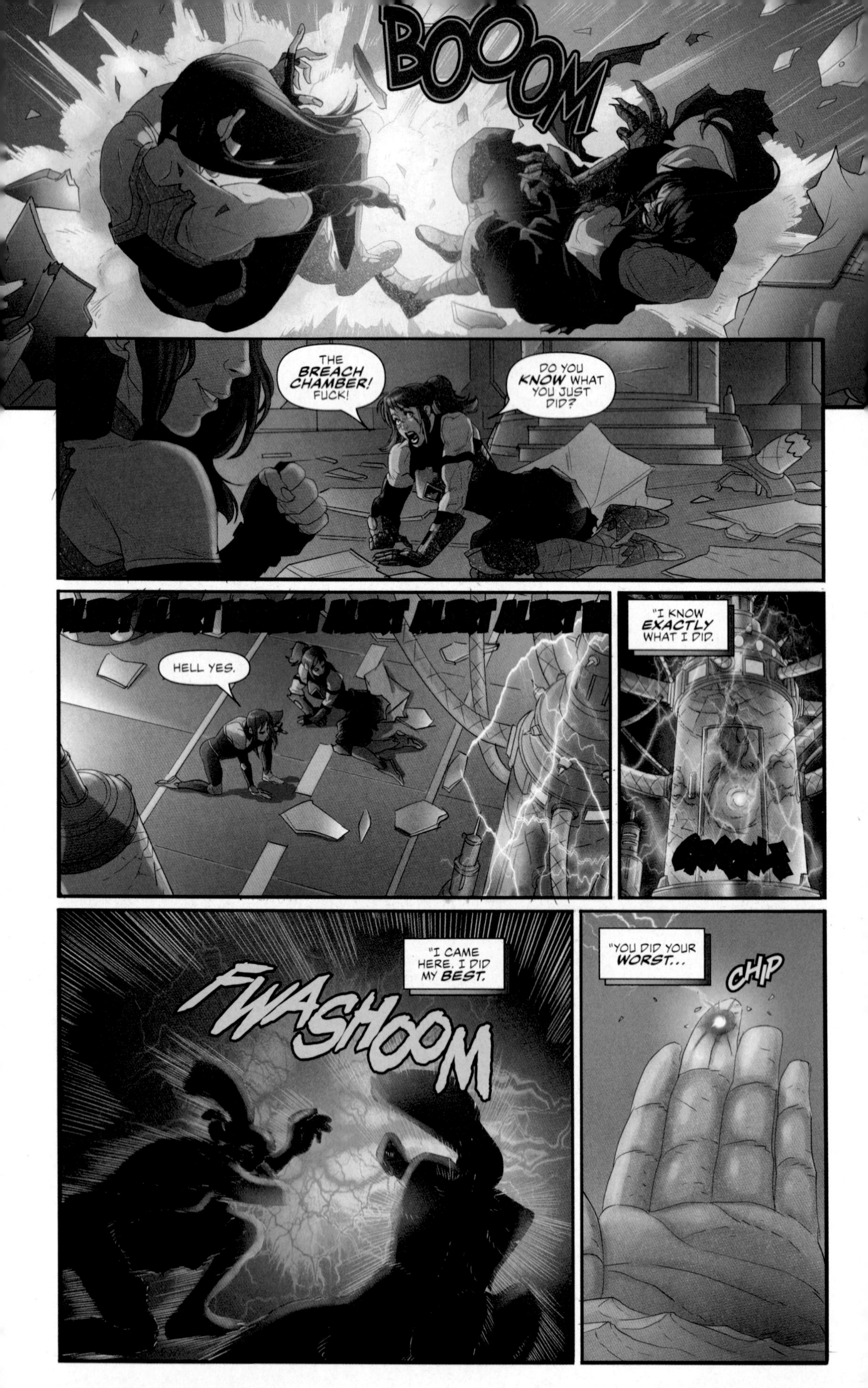
BOOOOM
THE BREACH CHAMBER! FUCK!
DO YOU KNOW WHAT YOU JUST DID?
HELL YES.
"I KNOW EXACTLY WHAT I DID.
"I CAME HERE. I DID MY BEST.
FWASHOOM
"YOU DID YOUR WORST...
CHIP

KRAKOOOM
"...AND WE'VE BOTH DONE ENOUGH."
THUD
sniff sniff
TROT TROT TROT

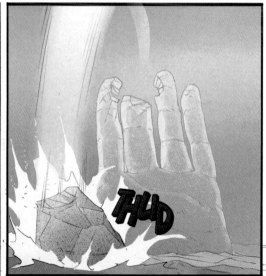

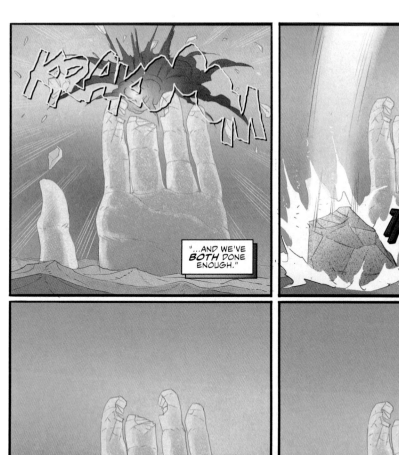

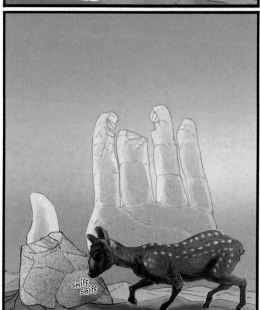

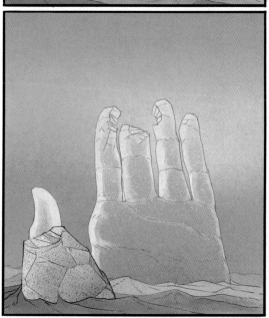

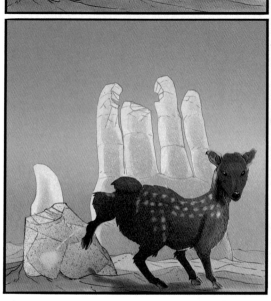

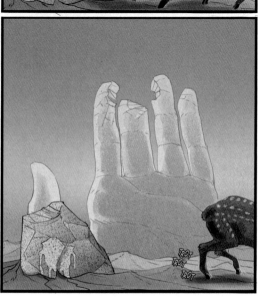

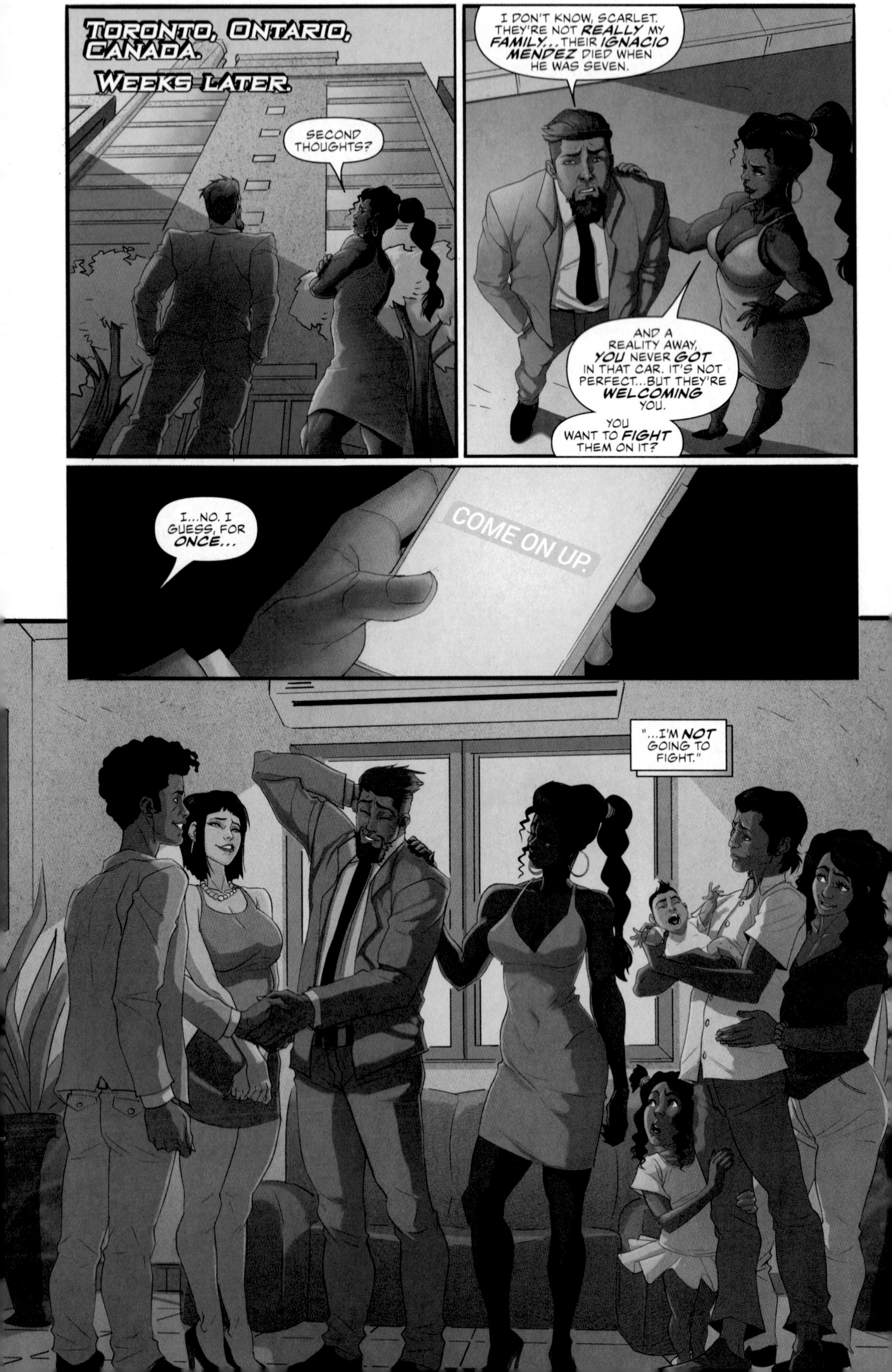
TORONTO, ONTARIO, CANADA.
WEEKS LATER.
SECOND THOUGHTS?
I DON'T KNOW, SCARLET. THEY'RE NOT REALLY MY FAMILY... THEIR IGNACIO MENDEZ DIED WHEN HE WAS SEVEN.
AND A REALITY AWAY, YOU NEVER GOT IN THAT CAR. IT'S NOT PERFECT...BUT THEY'RE WELCOMING YOU.
YOU WANT TO FIGHT THEM ON IT?
I...NO. I GUESS, FOR ONCE...
COME ON UP.
"...I'M NOT GOING TO FIGHT."

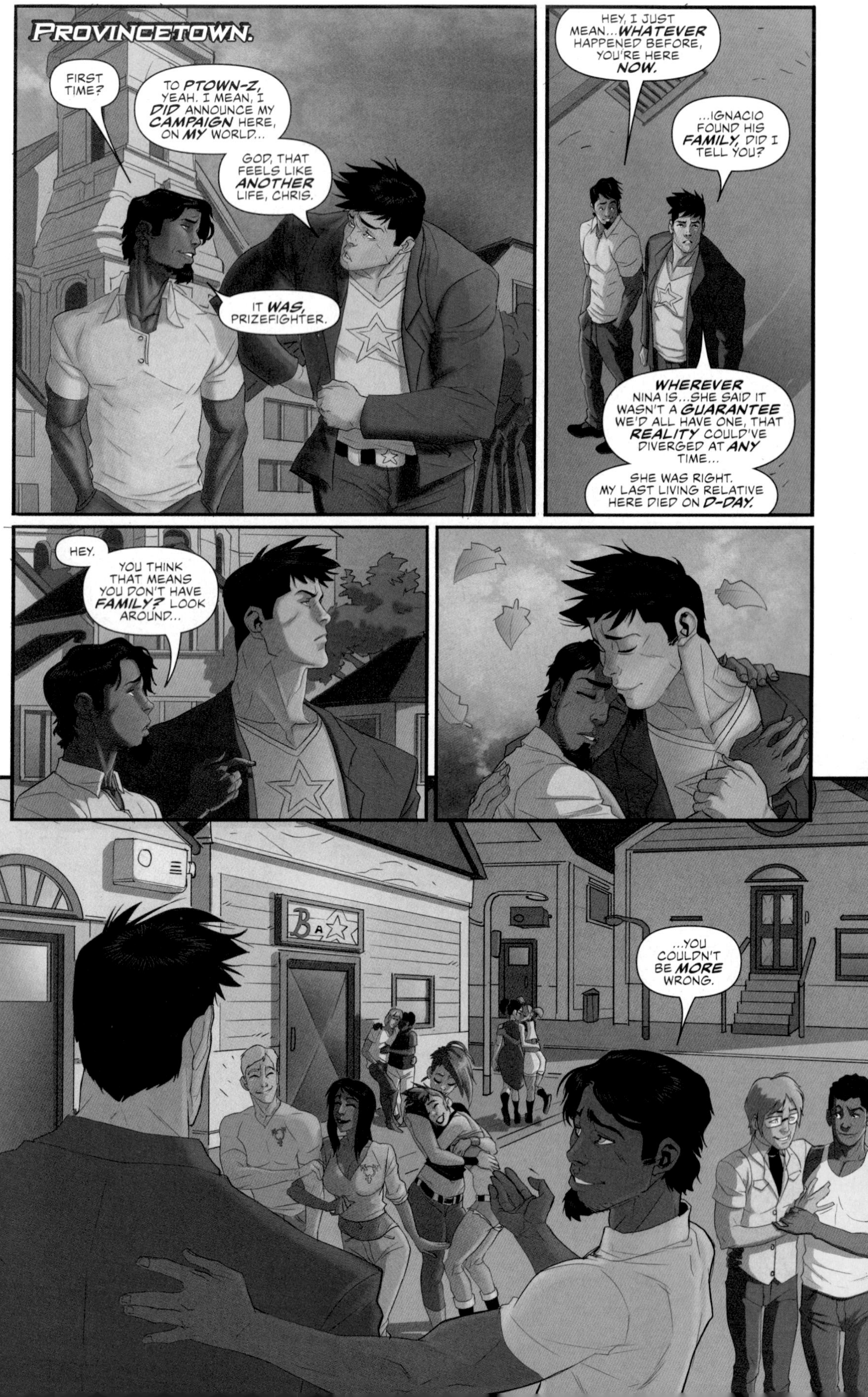
PROVINCETOWN.
FIRST TIME?
TO PTOWN-Z, YEAH. I MEAN, I DID ANNOUNCE MY CAMPAIGN HERE, ON MY WORLD...
GOD, THAT FEELS LIKE ANOTHER LIFE, CHRIS.
IT WAS, PRIZEFIGHTER.
HEY, I JUST MEAN...WHATEVER HAPPENED BEFORE, YOU'RE HERE NOW.
...IGNACIO FOUND HIS FAMILY, DID I TELL YOU?
WHEREVER NINA IS...SHE SAID IT WASN'T A GUARANTEE WE'D ALL HAVE ONE, THAT REALITY COULD'VE DIVERGED AT ANY TIME...
SHE WAS RIGHT. MY LAST LIVING RELATIVE HERE DIED ON D-DAY.
HEY.
YOU THINK THAT MEANS YOU DON'T HAVE FAMILY? LOOK AROUND...
...YOU COULDN'T BE MORE WRONG.

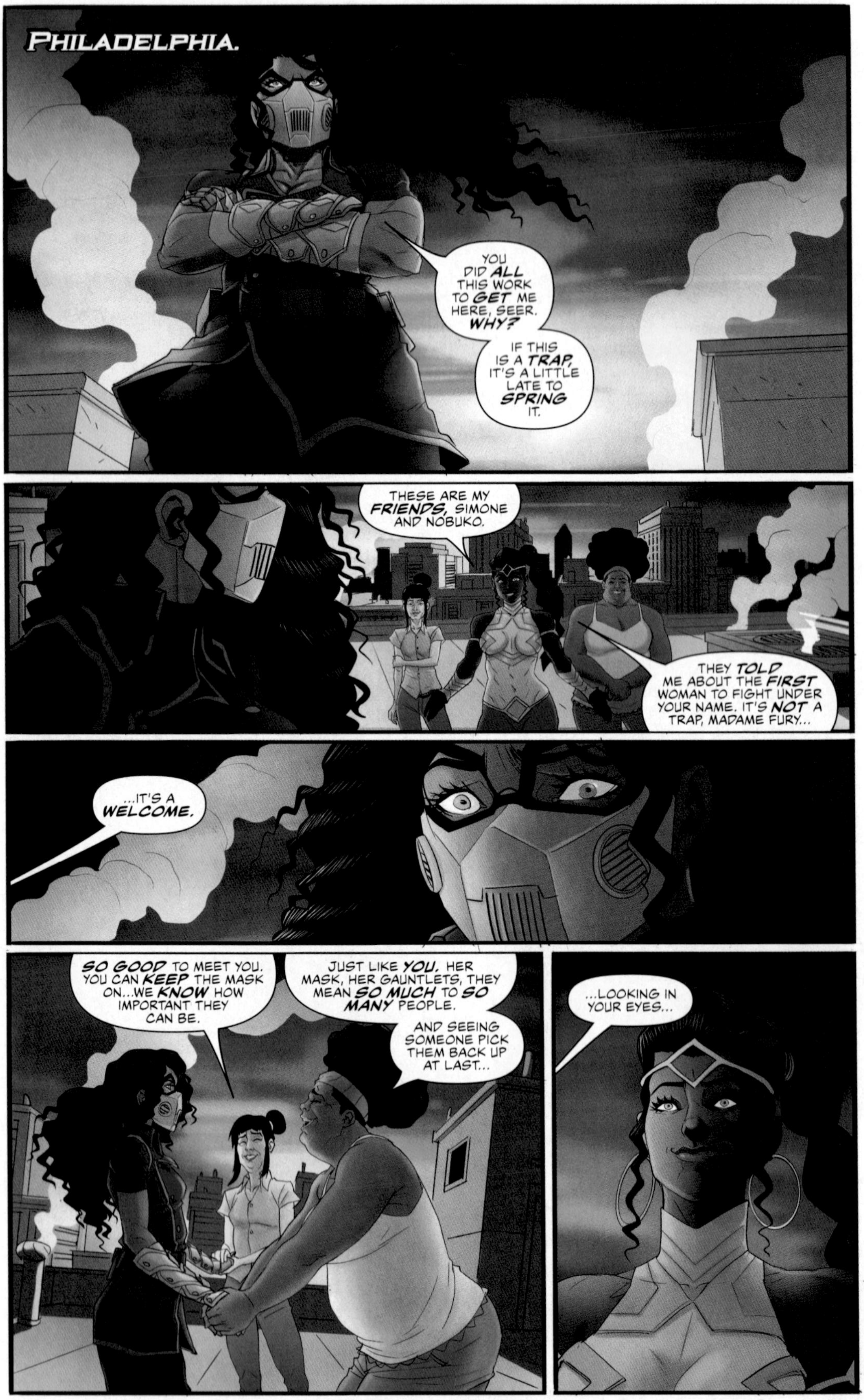
PHILADELPHIA.
YOU DID ALL THIS WORK TO GET ME HERE, SEER. WHY?
IF THIS IS A TRAP, IT'S A LITTLE LATE TO SPRING IT.
THESE ARE MY FRIENDS, SIMONE AND NOBUKO.
THEY TOLD ME ABOUT THE FIRST WOMAN TO FIGHT UNDER YOUR NAME. IT'S NOT A TRAP, MADAME FURY...
...IT'S A WELCOME.
SO GOOD TO MEET YOU. YOU CAN KEEP THE MASK ON...WE KNOW HOW IMPORTANT THEY CAN BE.
JUST LIKE YOU. HER MASK, HER GAUNTLETS, THEY MEAN SO MUCH TO SO MANY PEOPLE.
AND SEEING SOMEONE PICK THEM BACK UP AT LAST...
...LOOKING IN YOUR EYES...

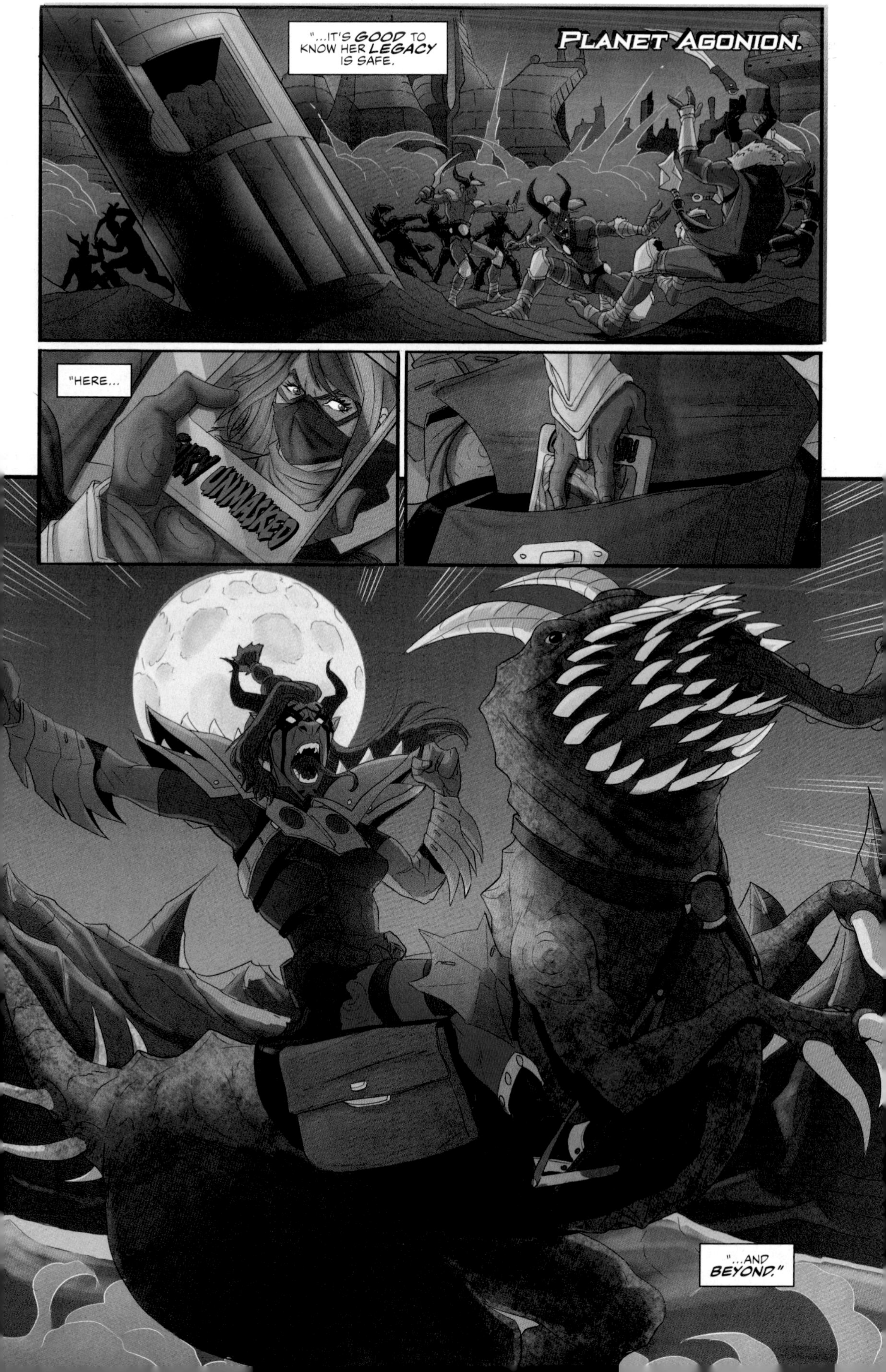
"...IT'S GOOD TO KNOW HER LEGACY IS SAFE.
PLANET AGONION.
"HERE...
UNMASKED
"...AND BEYOND."

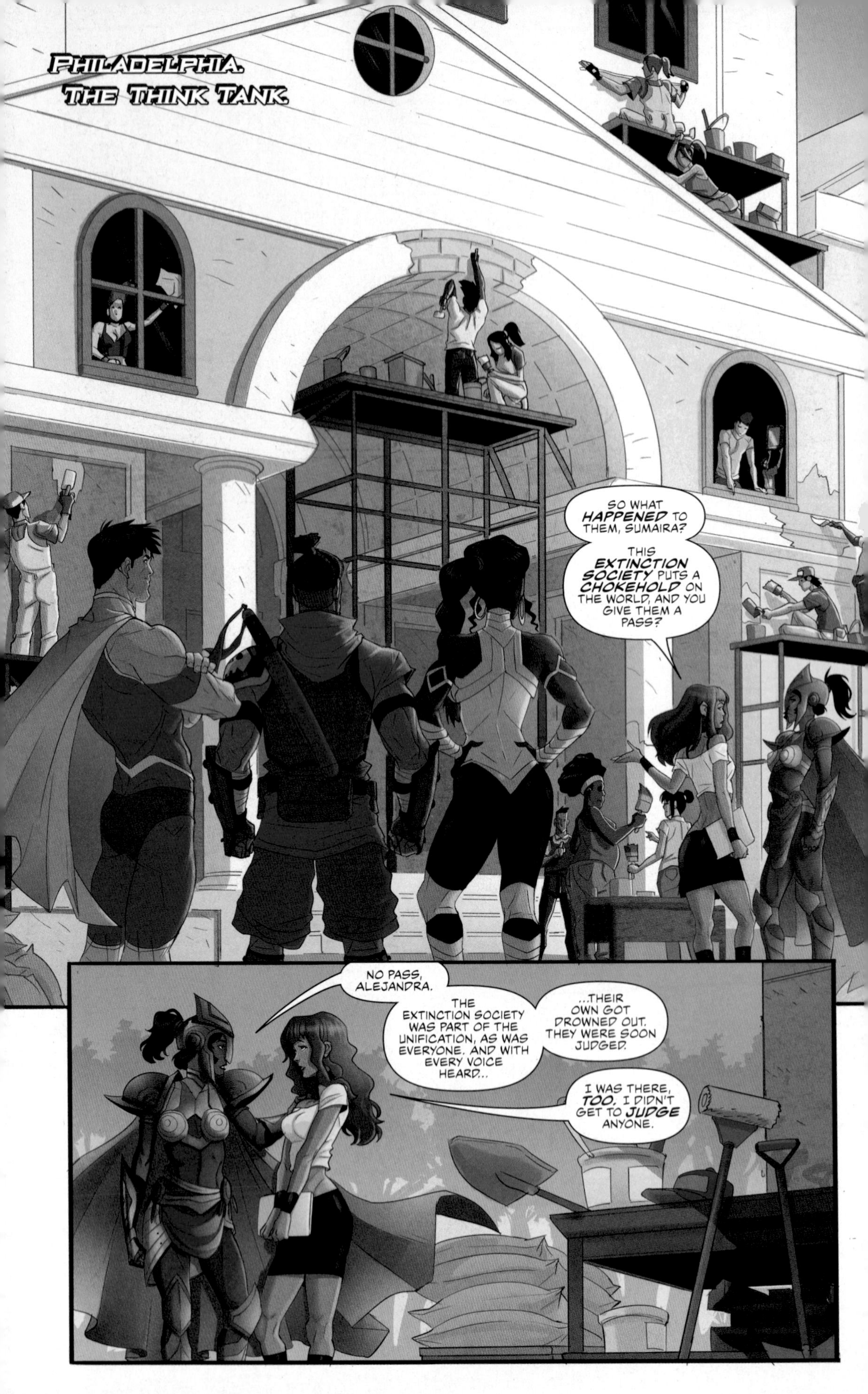
PHILADELPHIA.
THE THINK TANK.
SO WHAT HAPPENED TO THEM, SUMAIRA?
THIS EXTINCTION SOCIETY PUTS A CHOKEHOLD ON THE WORLD, AND YOU GIVE THEM A PASS?
NO PASS, ALEJANDRA.
THE EXTINCTION SOCIETY WAS PART OF THE UNIFICATION, AS WAS EVERYONE. AND WITH EVERY VOICE HEARD...
...THEIR OWN GOT DROWNED OUT. THEY WERE SOON JUDGED.
I WAS THERE, TOO. I DIDN'T GET TO JUDGE ANYONE.

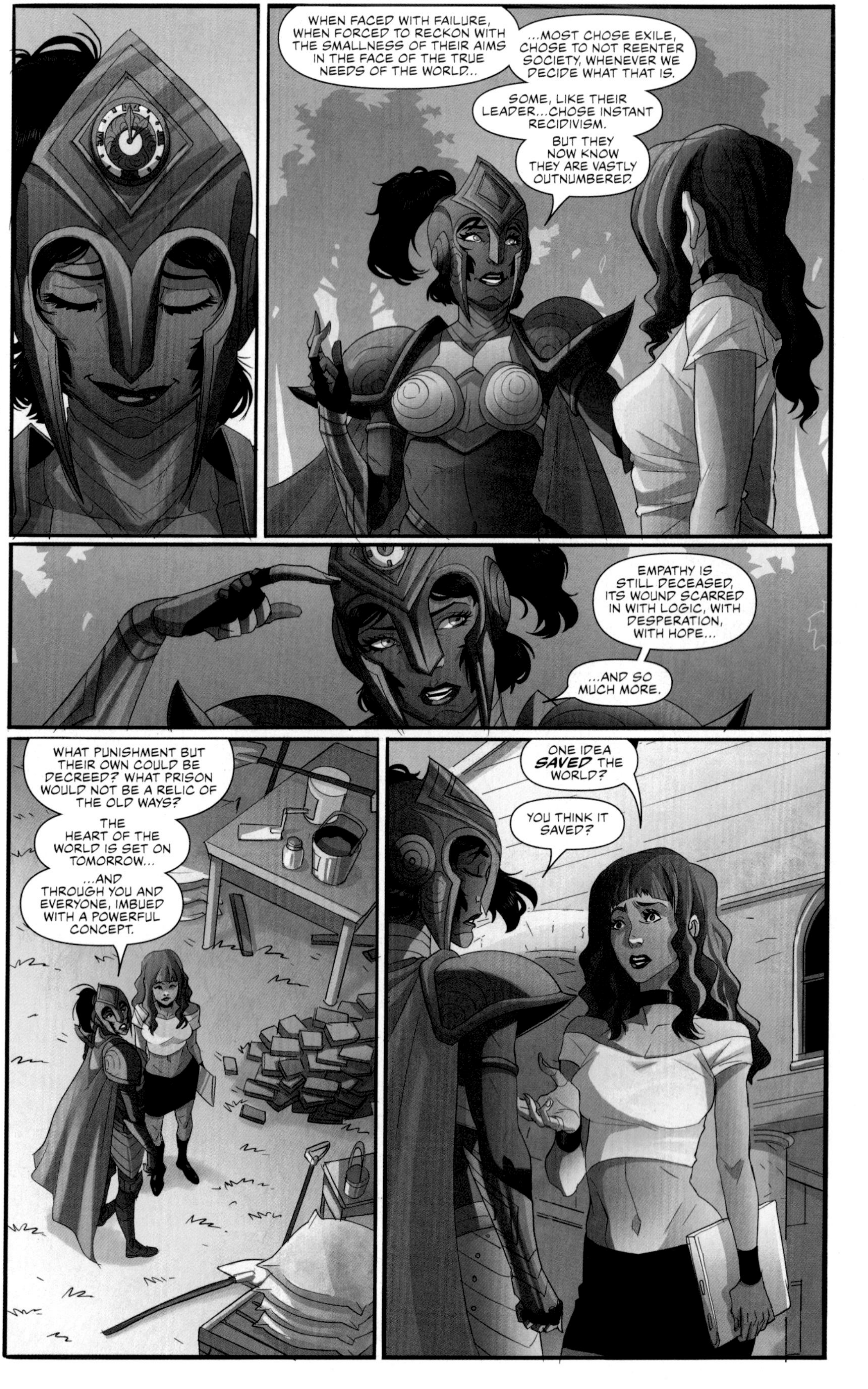

WHEN FACED WITH FAILURE, WHEN FORCED TO RECKON WITH THE SMALLNESS OF THEIR AIMS IN THE FACE OF THE TRUE NEEDS OF THE WORLD...
...MOST CHOSE EXILE, CHOSE TO NOT REENTER SOCIETY, WHENEVER WE DECIDE WHAT THAT IS.
SOME, LIKE THEIR LEADER...CHOSE INSTANT RECIDIVISM.
BUT THEY NOW KNOW THEY ARE VASTLY OUTNUMBERED.
EMPATHY IS STILL DECEASED, ITS WOUND SCARRED IN WITH LOGIC, WITH DESPERATION, WITH HOPE...
...AND SO MUCH MORE.
WHAT PUNISHMENT BUT THEIR OWN COULD BE DECREED? WHAT PRISON WOULD NOT BE A RELIC OF THE OLD WAYS?
THE HEART OF THE WORLD IS SET ON TOMORROW...
...AND THROUGH YOU AND EVERYONE, IMBUED WITH A POWERFUL CONCEPT.
ONE IDEA ***SAVED*** THE WORLD?
YOU THINK IT SAVED?

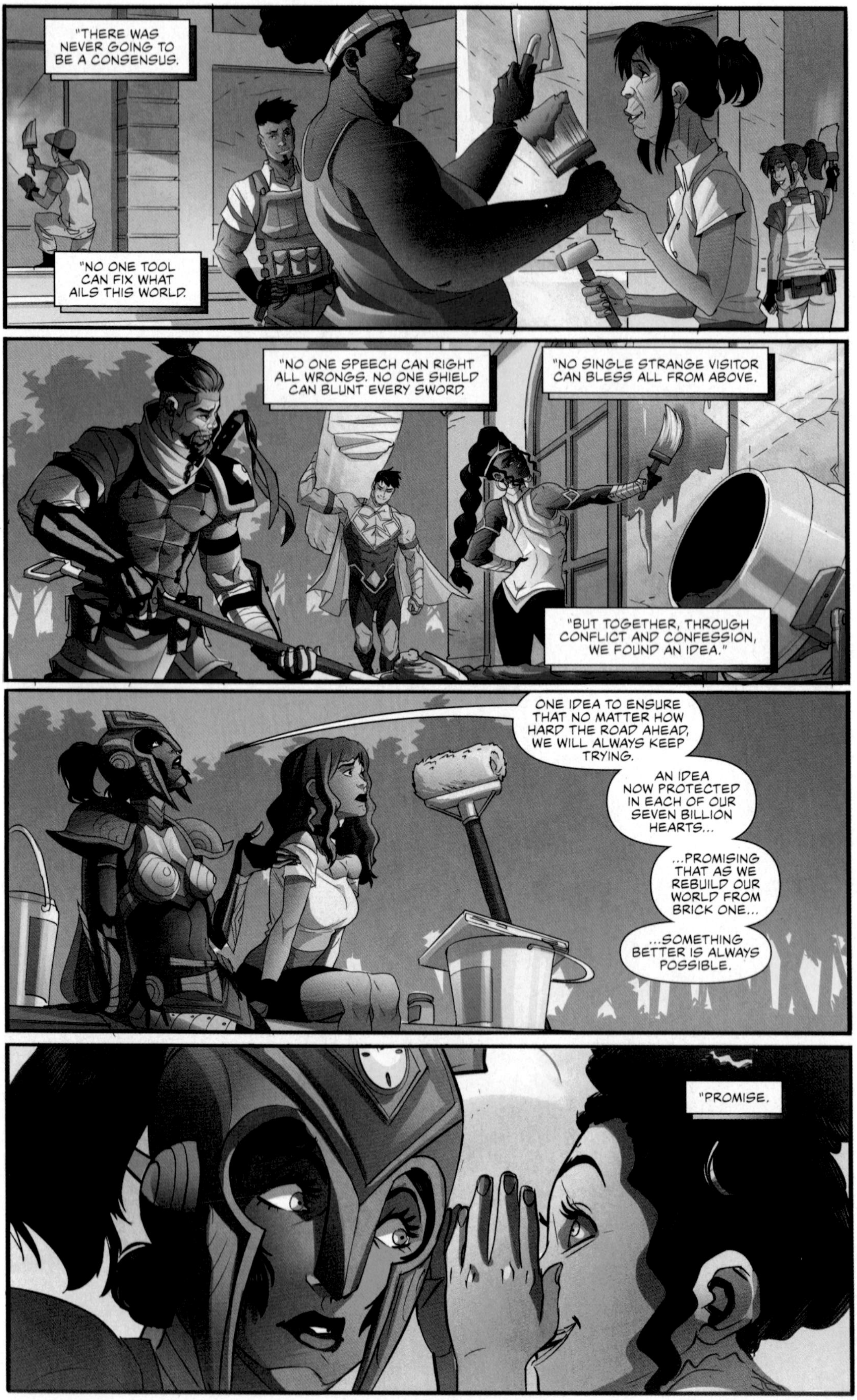
"THERE WAS NEVER GOING TO BE A CONSENSUS.
"NO ONE TOOL CAN FIX WHAT AILS THIS WORLD.
"NO ONE SPEECH CAN RIGHT ALL WRONGS. NO ONE SHIELD CAN BLUNT EVERY SWORD.
"NO SINGLE STRANGE VISITOR CAN BLESS ALL FROM ABOVE.
"BUT TOGETHER, THROUGH CONFLICT AND CONFESSION, WE FOUND AN IDEA."
ONE IDEA TO ENSURE THAT NO MATTER HOW HARD THE ROAD AHEAD, WE WILL ALWAYS KEEP TRYING.
AN IDEA NOW PROTECTED IN EACH OF OUR SEVEN BILLION HEARTS...
...PROMISING THAT AS WE REBUILD OUR WORLD FROM BRICK ONE...
...SOMETHING BETTER IS ALWAYS POSSIBLE.
"PROMISE.

"AS LONG AS EVEN A SINGLE HUMAN BEING LIVES...

"...PROMISE CAN NEVER DIE."

I'M ALIVE?!

BUT THAT... THAT *CAN'T* BE. *IT* CAN'T BE...

THEY'RE *GROWING BACK!*

I...I NEED TO KNOW...

"...I NEED TO *SEE* IT.

"I *HAVE* TO.

"EVEN IF I *NEVER* GET BACK.

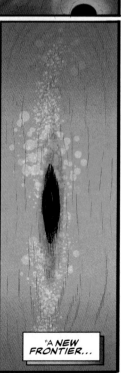

"A *NEW* FRONTIER...

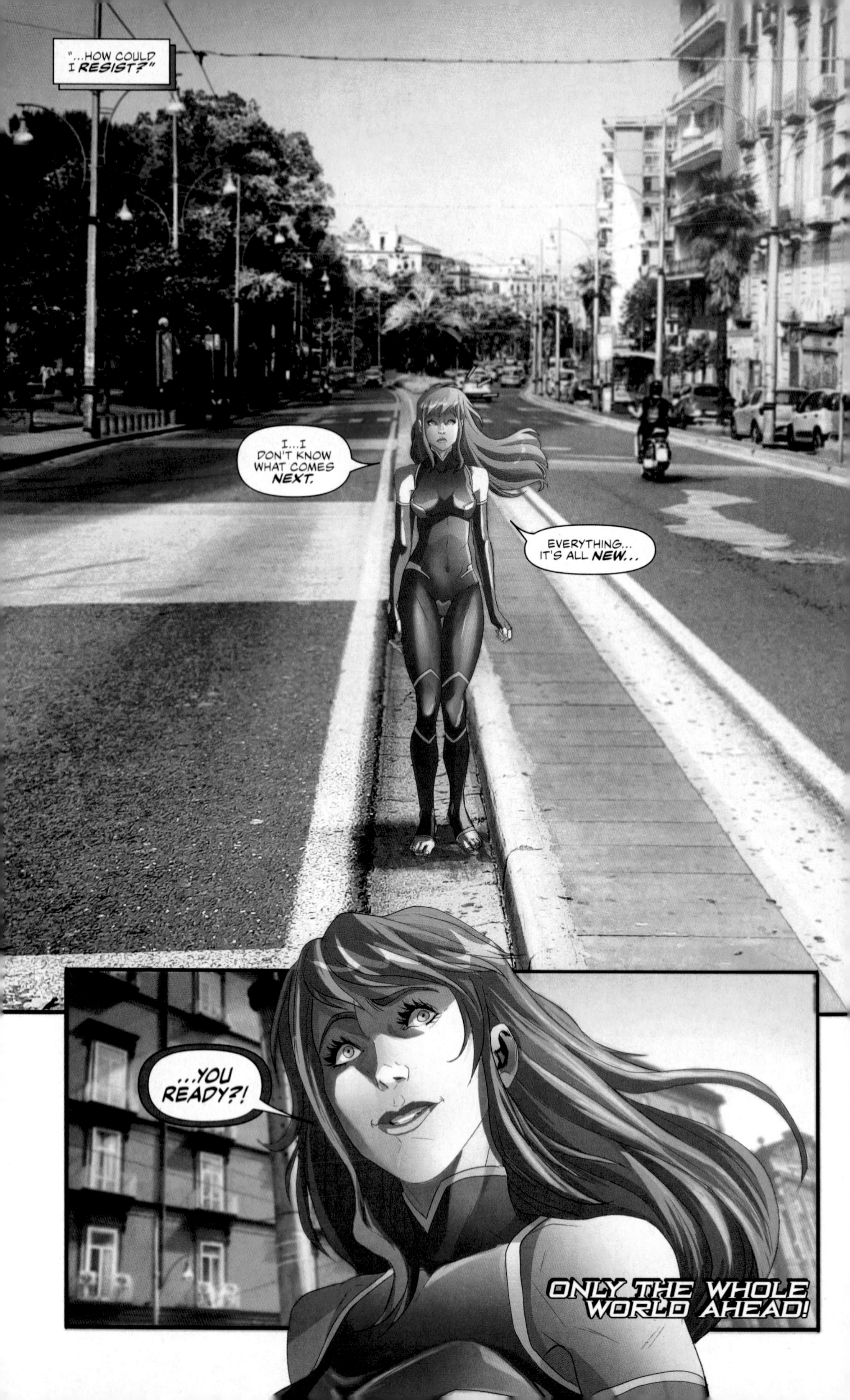
"...HOW COULD I RESIST?"
I...I DON'T KNOW WHAT COMES NEXT.
EVERYTHING... IT'S ALL NEW...
...YOU READY?!
ONLY THE WHOLE WORLD AHEAD!

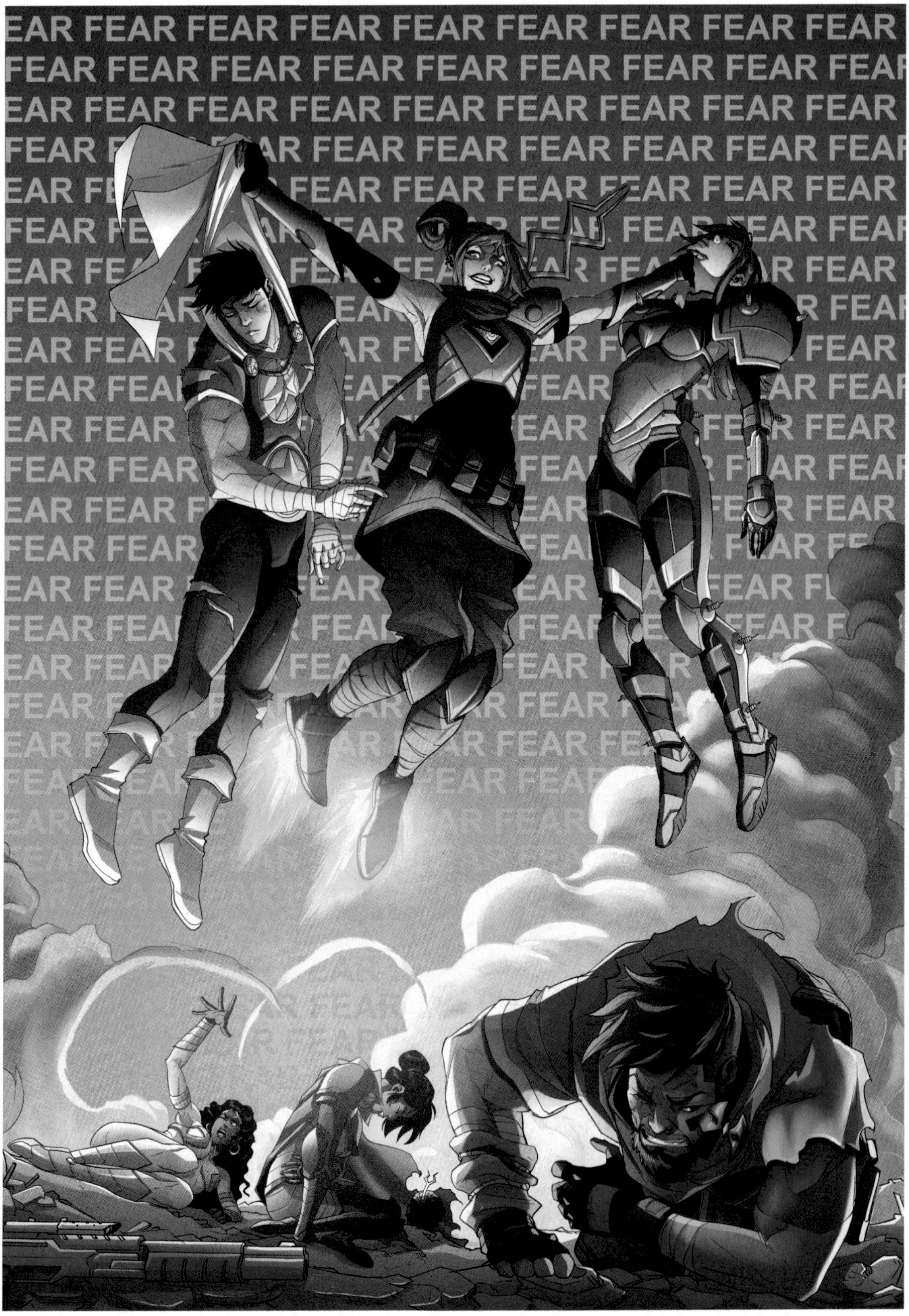
FEAR FEAR FEAR FEAR FEAR FEAR FEAR FEAR

EXCLUSIVE INTERVIEW WITH
IGNACIO MENDEZ · SAWBONES

The following was originally published in the November 18th issue of **The Washington Comet**. It is reproduced below, with the permission of all the parties involved.

The Crisis Command, the world's most mighty, the champions of tomorrow, the super-team of America. Everyday we watch them save our world- a team of diverse individuals who fight off the absurdly abnormal with impossible ideas. They're a busy bunch, and they do difficult work.

But the Crisis Command has graciously agreed to take some time to sit down with us here at The Washington Comet, so that we may all better get to know the people who walk among us with such tremendous talents.
Over the next few months, we'll be covering each and every single member of the team closely. From what they're enjoying on TV to their stance on what they believe their super-team represents, we'll be digging into all the details. Today, we pick up with the most enigmatic of them all. The super-warrior of the Command, the Action Surgeon himself: Sawbones!

It's a chilly night, as we huddle around a fireplace for comfort. The man before me seems untouched by the cold the way me and my team are. He sits with an assured confidence and ease, his hands held together over his knees. His eyes gleam red through his mask, watching us all, seemingly sizing us all up. And yet his face remains calm, offering no hint at all as to whatever it is he's thinking.

One gets the impression this is a man that's never lost a game of Poker.

'Ready?' he asks, with a small grin. Suddenly I am reminded of every sports coach I've ever had.

'Y-Yes,' I manage, lying, as the cold is still too much.

His grin widens. 'Let's get into it' he commands, and I obey.

TWC: I-Thank you for sitting down with us, Mr. Mendez. How are you today?

How do I look? I'm good enough. Both ends of the candle are pretty much burned down between the next crisis, and nights shadowing in the emergency department. Best way to learn about pain, causing it and solving it, is hands-on, and I'm always learning.

TWC: Now, to start us off, I understand you used to play the Violin, yes? Are you much of a music person these days? What does Sawbones like to listen to? What are the Sawbones favorites? What are you into, and what does your musician hall of fame look like?

I miss the violin, I'll tell you that. I miss working with my hands. Before...well, before I was Sawbones, I stood up in protest against abuse of power in my local government. You'll understand I can't really say where I grew up, people to protect. You know the line. But in the violence that followed, I lost the ability to play. It wasn't until I got these powers I found a new way to give something back to the world. Now my obsession with precision and perfection goes into my career in costume, finding out everything there is to know about human bodies...so I can better protect them.

So music was my passion, and I still love it. But sometimes it's hard to go back, and relive that loss. So I try to push forward. Still...give me the right sequence of drinks and we can talk about twentieth century serialism.

TWC: Now, I asked your colleague Noa-I mean, Prizefighter, about this, but I gotta know, how did you put your costume together? From your special lens-mask to everything else, what was the deal?

Talking to Prizefighter you might think we're all in this for a photo-op or a hashtag. But the Sawbones gear is all about function. When I step out into the world, I'm either there to cause pain or heal pain, and in both cases I need to work with precision. My biospectral vision lets me see inside, where everyone hides their secrets. My gear lets me act quickly and efficiently on what I see there – tactical medical devices, goggles with smart displays and targeting software, stab and bullet resistant weaves for when things get messy. When you're an action surgeon, you never leave home

TWC: One thing everyone's dying to know: What was your upbringing like? How did Sawbones come to be?

I grew up surrounded by people. Our community was very tight, and my mom was always cooking for everyone. I forget how old I was when I finally realized our neighbors weren't actually blood, but even so, I never stopped seeing them as family. She loved bringing people together, looking after them. I got my sense of community from her. My hot streak comes from my father - he was the one that taught me to stand up to bullies. He worked at a steel mill, back when that kind of work was plenty for a small family to live comfortably. Tough and, let's say guarded, as he was, though, the violin was all him. Well, not all. He started that fire, and my mom kept it going.

TWC: I understand you're able to see the flaws in all things, is that right? How does that even work? That is, of course, if you're willing to speak on it.

Without getting into the gory details, my biospectral vision lets me see people in more detail than the best medical imaging software. So I can see everything from swollen lymph nodes, old football injuries, cataracts, scar tissue, even an intestinal blockage. I don't know that I'd call them flaws, but everyone's body is a story of their history, the pain they've overcome or are currently dealing with. I can see pressure points, weak points, and if you're someone causing other pains, then I use those to put you down. If you're not, then I can see how fastest to put you at ease. I've found it's best to know when to turn it on or turn it off, learned that the hard way after I got these powers and started trying to date again. Sometimes, a little mystery goes a long way in my private life. But professionally? My eyes are always on.

TWC: That's...how do you even go about everyday life like that? Seeing the weaknesses and messes in all things, as they appear crystal clear. Do you find it hard to do what you do? To believe in people?

I think, growing up like I did, I learned to see when people were hurting, even if they didn't explicitly say what was wrong. Reading people was something I was very used to, even before the powers. So that part of the job is easy. Believing in people can be hard, but all we have is each other. The alternative just leads to

WC: Well then, what do you reckon are the biggest flaws of our current society right now? And does the perspective to see problems display any solutions as well? Do you have any thoughts as to how we might fix things?

think it's easy to get wrapped up in your own problems and think that they're unique. It doesn't take special powers to see that we're all a lot more similar than some folks are willing to admit. A great first step toward a solution would be reminding people of that.

WC: I'm curious then, what are your thoughts on the American Individuality act?

It's a mistake, and it's frustrating to see so many people jumping on this ridiculous bandwagon. Encouraging this kind of divisiveness is irresponsible, at the very least.

WC: What are your thoughts on Madame Fury? Can we expect a team-up soon?

Madame Fury? Well, you wanted the truth...I don't know who that is. Can't say I was so into the costume world before becoming part of it. Probably got some studying to do, as if there's ever downtime.

WC: What is it like being a mortal man with guns and blades next to superhumans like Originator, who can alter reality with a word, and Prizefighter, whose might is limited only by the belief of his audience?

t means always being on, but that's not much different from when I was my own advocate, trying to make it in music. But the reality is those so called superhumans are my friends, and the more powerful you are, the more you need someone to remind you how the powerless might feel. And even with all their abilities, they've still got human bodies, and if it came down to it...I know where they're hiding their secrets.

WC: What is the ultimate goal and purpose of The Crisis Command, for you? Who do you serve, and to what end, in the end?

Every day is a new crisis, but the goal is always the same: keeping people, and hope, alive long enough to see a new day.

WC: Well then, let me ask you this: Have The Crisis Command ever lied or kept vital secrets from us, the people?

can't speak for the others, but look at how I

embarrassed myself above not knowing about Madame Fury. I've answered every question I've been asked since putting on the uniform honestly.

TWC: There are a lot of people of color, particularly men, who are taken by your example. You've grown into quite the symbol. What do you have to say to that?

I've never been comfortable with hero-worship honestly. I'm not just the clips you see on the news I'm a whole person, complete with flaws. If what I do inspires others to strive to be better, that's great, bu every single one of us is a person in progress, including me.

TWC: Do you happen to have any personal heroes? People you look up to?

Well, obvious answer is my parents. They shaped me gave me my work ethic, taught me right from wrong and encouraged me to have empathy for others, like good parents should. One of the biggest impacts on me was this little old guy that ran one of the neighborhood spots. He had two things on the menu, and that was it. Place didn't even have specific hours. He opened at lunch, and closed whenever he sold out for the day Nobody questioned it - well, until me, of course. I asked if he'd ever consider expanding the menu. He stopped what he was doing and sat me down. "Mijo," he said, " can cook just about anything you'd want, but these two dishes are my favorites. So I'll always strive to make the best possible version of them, every day." And tha always stuck with me.

TWC: Do you believe in god then? Are you religious at all?

My whole neighborhood, including my parents, was Catholic, but it wasn't ever something I really bough into. The sense of community was nice, but the Church is so hypocritical - I got disillusioned pretty early on. still believed in some higher power, just not whatever they were peddling. After I got my vision, though, stopped believing all together.

TWC: How do you spend your time off? Who is Ignacio Mendez, truly, beyond the superheroes? What does the 'Action Surgeon' do to relax? How does the man who sees flaws in all things find joy every day? And does that power extend to art as well?

Time off. Now there's a concept. I've always put my all into whatever skill I'm learning, from the violin, to activism, and now, to honing my biospectral vision. I've never been really good at time off. When I'm not "on duty," I'm usually putting time in at hospitals, trying to learn as much as I can about the human body. I'm not averse to blowing off some steam with a colleague, though.

TWC: Now, for the final question that I must ask everyone. Favorite alcoholic drink, go.
The first drink I ever had was a sip of my dad's Paloma. Since then, it's always been my go-to on the off chance I allow myself time to unwind.

And that was Ignacio Mendez, Sawbones! Join us next month, as we speak to the most approachable of the Command, Seer!

[Interview by: **Ritesh Babu**. Answers by: **Jarrett Melendez**, with **Steve Orlando.**]

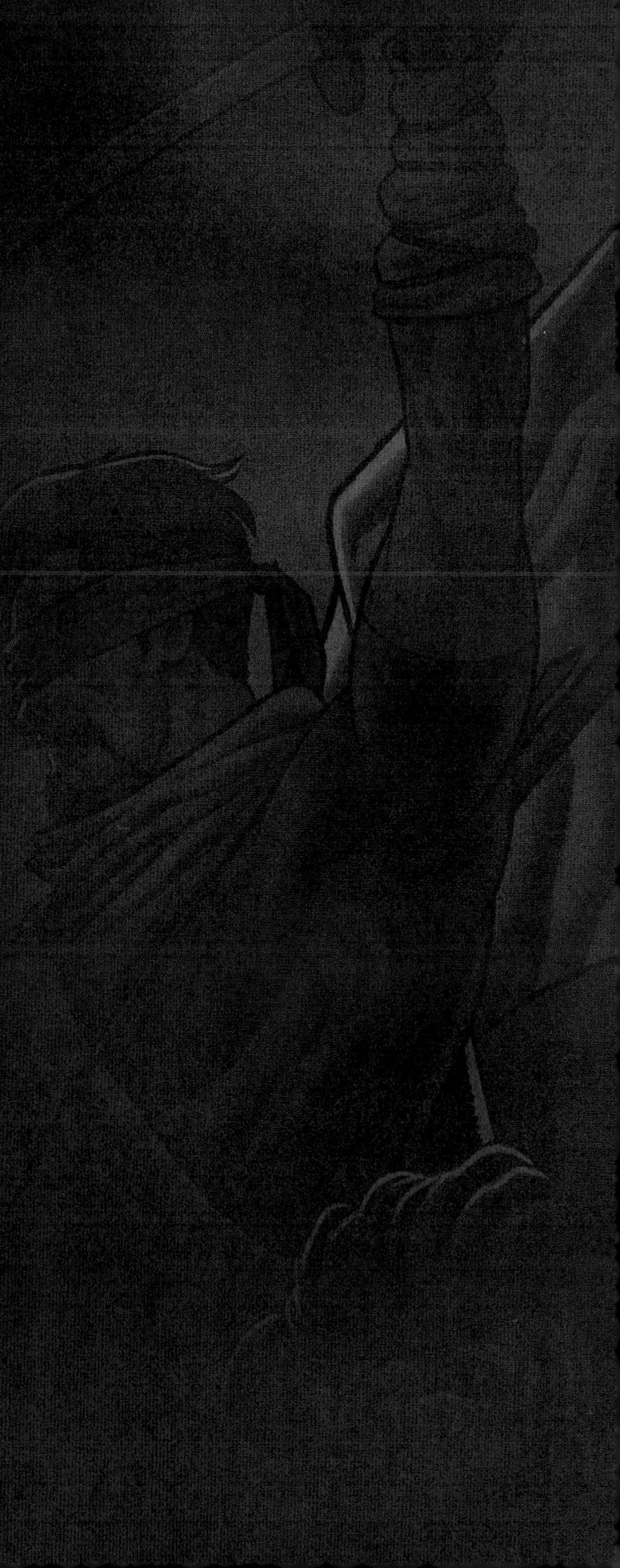

EXCLUSIVE INTERVIEW WITH
SCARLET DAVIS · SEER

The following was originally published in the February 10th issue of **The Washington Comet**. It is reproduced below, with the permission of all the parties involved.

The Crisis Command, the world's most mighty, the champions of tomorrow, the super-team of America. Everyday we watch them save our world- a team of diverse individuals who fight off the absurdly abnormal with impossible ideas. They're a busy bunch, and they do difficult work.

But the Crisis Command has graciously agreed to take some time to sit down with us here at The Washington Comet, so that we may all better get to know the people who walk among us with such tremendous talents.

Over the next few months, we'll be covering each and every single member of the team closely. From what they're enjoying on their off-time to their stance on what they believe their super-team represents, we'll be digging into all the details. And who better to start with than the wisest of them all? The oracle of the Crisis Command, The All-Seeing One, Seer!

It starts pouring when I least expect it. Just moments earlier, the skies had been perfectly clear. Nothing could've ever possibly suggested that it'd be a day like this.

I look once more to the woman standing before me, waiting. I now understand. Only moments before, I had found her attire on this particularly sunny day quite peculiar. She was dressed in a seemingly heavy raincoat, holding up an umbrella. 'What's up with that?! Do all superheroes walk about like this?' I'd wondered, sheepishly. But looking over to her now, I understood that she'd known this was going to happen. She was, afterall, the almighty Seer. She always knew what lay ahead.

'Are you alright?' she asks, holding her umbrella over me. Her eyes gleam gold, and her concern is sincere. I nod, and she grins, 'I'm glad. Let's get inside and begin. I have a feeling this rain will last for a bit.'

TWC: Thank you so much for sitting down with us, Scarlet.

Of course, Gray. Thank you so much for taking the time out of your busy schedule.

TWC: Now, I understand you're something of a Quantum God? They say you have The God's Eye. Could you walk us through that? Is that like Thunder Woman? Or one of their gods?

[shakes her head] I experience something called a "quantum moment." It allows me to see and feel the ways in which all things are linked with one another--past, present, and future. I'm not a god. I'm just a witness.

TWC: It must be quite a burden, being able to peer into the future like that. What does that do to you, day-to-day? How do you cope with looking into what's coming, with the world as it is? How do you shoulder the responsibility of such a power?

Experiencing a quantum moment is incredibly fatiguing, so I only do it when it's absolutely necessary. On a day-to-day basis, I live the same way as everyone else, experiencing events one at a time. I shoulder it the same way I imagine you do. I signal when I change lanes; I look both ways before I cross the street. I treat my actions as though they're connected to the lives of others. I put my life in the hands of others too. My ability gives me a glimpse into those connections, when it's absolutely critical, but my power? My power is equal to yours.

TWC: You reckon we all still have a shot, amidst all this American Individuality Act mess?

I think there's always "a shot," as you say. There's always hope. It is my hope that the Senate will make the right decision in this matter.

TWC: If you're so willing, given we're all curious about it, how did you even come by such power? Were you born with it, or was there some manner of incident that did it? What is the secret origin of Seer, if you're comfortable sharing?

[smiles pleasantly] I'm glad you asked. The truth is, my ability was born when I was four years old. I didn't really understand it and so I would get sick a lot and have to go to the hospital. But really, if you want my origin story. Once, my mother's car got stuck in the snow on the way to the hospital and a stranger, a teenager--I guess, who someone else might have called a delinquent--helped dig our car out and made sure we got to the hospital safely. I don't think we ever learned her name. I think that was when I decided that I would do whatever I could to help people.

TWC: Some might believe that was an act of god. What do you believe? Are you religious in any capacity? You reckon there's really somebody all the way up there, beyond all the super-gods that seem to pop up everyday?

I'm not sure if a god is what I believe in or that there is or isn't someone up there, but the quantum moment makes me certain that there are things at work that are greater than all of us. It's like I said before: I'm a witness. Whether what I witness is God's work, or something else, I don't know--but I am witnessing something. That connection is there. It's hard not to believe when I can see and feel it.

TWC: And how about the costume? It's constantly discussed as being a favorite both online and in fashion circles. We all love it. What's the story behind that? Did you design it? If not, who's the talented designer we need to credit?

The costume helps me get the most out of my powers. It keeps me grounded so I can experience the moment for as long as possible before needing rest. You can sort of think of it as a super-science version of those copper bracelets people wear to enhance their health.

TWC: I spoke to you peer, Prizefighter, and he described you as the vision of the team. What do you have to say to that? And what's your relationship with your fellow members of the Command? How would you describe them yourself?

[laughs] Prizefighter is very clever. I like him quite a bit. I like all of my colleagues. I suppose I would describe Sawbones as, hm, "rough around the edges but with a very good heart." The Originator is a person who is very careful with her words, but always means what she says. And Frontier...well, Frontier always does what she thinks is best.

TWC: What is the end-goal of The Crisis Command at least for you? Why are you really here?

We're here to help in whatever way we can. That's al

any of us can really do, whatever our ability.

TWC: There are so many stories of you helping out local communities with your power. So many look up to you and admire you. Many feel represented by you, your very presence and power. Is it tough to carry that? That expectation and weight, that all-seeing eye, the hopes and dreams of people, alongside the ability to look ahead?
Honestly? I try not to think about it too much. Part of doing what I do means putting the right thing before everything. It makes me extremely happy to think that my work makes people feel seen. I imagine part of that is because I don't think about the expectations; I just think about what's right and how I can help, which is no different to anyone else.

TWC: Can't be easy, what with the right-wing press printing blatantly monstrous lies and scrutinizing every action you take, as White Supremacists tend to do. How do you relax and unwind from all that? What does Scarlet Davis do, when she's not being a Quantum God? Are you into meditation? Poetry? Film? Do you even have time for any hobbies at all?
Sure, I have time! I really like hot yoga. And I've been trying to get into taking care of plants, though I'm not very good at it. I've been trying to grow mushrooms too--not the really fun kind, though. I'm working on some golden oyster mushrooms. They're beautiful, and generally, I like how mushrooms exist. They're not alive; they're not dead. They create life through death. They connect with each other in all of these interesting ways.

TWC: Any notable heroes for you growing up? You've joined a long line of Black icons now, so who are yours?
Is it tacky to say Beyoncé? Beyoncé. But also Audre Lorde. Angela Davis. Warsan Shire. Diana Ross for everything, but especially in The Wiz. Phylicia Rashad. Missy. Rihanna. Serena Williams.

TWC: Now, for one final question. Favorite alcoholic drink, go.
A grasshopper. Love the color and love the taste.

And that was Scarlet Davis, Seer! Join us next month, as we speak to the most mystical of the Command, Originator!

[Interview by: **Ritesh Babu**. Answers by: **J.A. Micheline**, with **Steve Orlando**.]

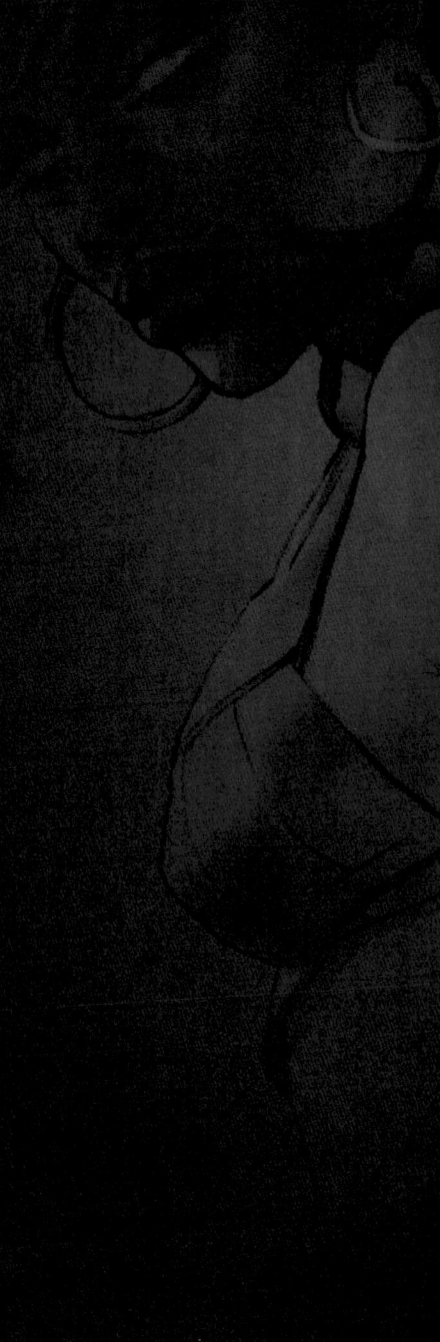

EXCLUSIVE INTERVIEW WITH

SUMAIRA SHAMSIE · ORIGINATOR

The following was originally published in the March 10th issue of **The Washington Comet**. It is reproduced below, with the permission of all the parties involved.

The Crisis Command, the world's most mighty, the champions of tomorrow, the super-team of America. Everyday we watch them save our world- a team of diverse individuals who fight off the absurdly abnormal with impossible ideas. They're a busy bunch, and they do difficult work.

But the Crisis Command has graciously agreed to take some time to sit down with us here at The Washington Comet, so that we may all better get to know the people who walk among us with such tremendous talents.
Over the next few months, we'll be covering each and every single member of the team closely. From what they're enjoying on their off-time to their stance on what they believe their super-team represents, we'll be digging into all the details. And who better to start with than the most mighty of them all? The wondrous wordsmith of the Crisis Command, The Mystic Marvel herself, Originator!

A lady sits comfortably, surrounded by a mountain of books. The library in Fishtown, Philly, is her regular hangout spot. She's been known to spend most of her off-time here. So it's certainly not a surprising sight for me as I get there. But the sheer number of works she's seemingly going through, and their wide variety, that blows me away. Clearly, she's a passionate reader. But then again, I suppose one has to be, to do what she does.
She notes my presence and nods, beckoning me to take a seat. She then whispers a word, which I only manage to catch the end of.

'...encosilence'
A rush of energy moves through me. I blink, unsure of what's just happened. The lady smiles, speaking properly at last. 'I've just made it so that anyone in this specific zone of the library can speak freely, without being heard by anyone beyond it for the next 24 hours.'
I tilt my head, still taking it all in. It's a response she seems to be familiar with, as her smile deepens. "Well

TWC: How would you prefer to be addressed? Sumaira or your official title?

I am perfectly happy to be called Sumaira, or Sumaira Shamsie.

TWC: Alright! Sumaira it is! Now, I have to ask. How did you even find out you had this power? I imagine it must've been one hell of a surprise.

Every word we use can have enormous potency. Take, for example, the word series. It can mean a sequence, a distribution or an arrangement, as well as a half a dozen different meanings. It originates from Latin, Serere, to join. Now it is a word we use to interconnect. That is the case for all of language. I interconnect words into physical manifestation, but directly.

My mother and father were well versed in language and instilled it in me at an early age. They studied Magical Linguistics before I was born. I was very fortunate to be versed in such trainings as a child. When I began to invoke my unique skills I already had that baseline. The way we speak shapes reality, always, so I learned to be even more deliberate.

TWC: No kidding. How do you even manage after that? Knowing any set of words you smash together, even as a joke, could maybe launch something out into the world. Picking and choosing what you say more carefully than ever. How has that been for you?

You understand what it means to be polite and how, when to be measured with phrases. I must always carry with me consideration. There's so much potential in language to carry hurt. There are so many phrases we use that can foster misunderstanding. For me, a misunderstanding can be even worse. I act so that, hopefully, others don't bear the burdens of my mistakes.

TWC: So why superheroics? Why not something else? I imagine that power of yours has a lot more applications in numerous other enterprises.

I must once again thank my parents. Let us go back to the word, "series." Another meaning of series is a total or sum. When words are crafted, we are always adding to what has come before and reforming reality anew. This is true whether you are commenting on the weather or explaining something new. It is imperative that in a changing world we have language to deal with the new. We live in imperfect systems, a word that changes finance will spread to every market. Can we do

that for what we define morally as good and evil? This is what I try to do.

TWC: I have to ask, that pocket watch you keep on your costume at all times, family heirloom? I've never seen you without it when you're out there doing this stuff. I assume it's of personal significance in some way? Or is it one of Frontier's much spoken about super-gadgets?

It is a gift from Frontier. Watches were premier technology in their time and have had a part in what is possible now. It is the same as words, the past being built upon in service to the future. I do have a sentimentality to it.

TWC: Does the tuning fork have some symbolic meaning? I'm sorry, but I'm really fascinated by your lovely costume. How'd you put it together? I know a great number of readers are dying to hear about it.

The tuning fork is focus. Vibrations are resonance of the heart. This world is as much a living being as it is a place. When I put on the tuning fork, I am reminded of why I am so careful with words. Words are useless if there is no thought behind them.

TWC: On top of the tricky powers, you're out in the open, under the spotlight, as a brown woman. And as someone who understands the impact of words, you know what they largely say and write about our people, the assumptions they make about us, which they never would with white folks. How has it been managing all that, navigating what you do, while seeing things like The American Individuality Act be even considered?

I am reminded of the Hippocratic Oath, these two tenets in particular:

1. I solemnly pledge myself to consecrate my life to the service of humanity.

2. I will not permit considerations of religion, nationality, race, party politics or social standing to intervene between my duty and my patient.

I would not stand here in this world without my own dedication to humanity. Without it I cannot imagine any purpose. The first tenet is the standard I seek to embody with my powers. We are all imperfect in unique ways. But our own inequality cannot be solved with inequity. The American Individuality Act is a pathway that ignores that we, all people, and we as a country, have a deeper commitment to one another. It is a direct refutation of the second named tenet.

Our way through strife is never going to be to cordon ourselves off. Neither is it to ceaselessly compromise. In unity is where we must progress, and I must use my own voice first. My hope is that by leading with my voice others will also learn to use their own voices to serve in their own unique ways.

TWC: Clearly, you're a big reader, so do go on, what are some of your favorites? Any creators you always find yourself coming back to? Who're the voices that you most admire?

I find one reading leads me to my next. Recently, I've recently been revisiting Socrates and Plato, which sent me to Diotima of Mantinea, then to Iris Murdoch. That was stirred by a recent reading of Mulla Sadra and Rumi. "Morphology of a Folklore" by Vladimir Propp was the narrative examination that allowed me to enjoy fiction, literary or not, and I believe it is time I revisit it also. It is how I learned of Hilary Mantel, and I am 100 pages from completing her Cromwell Trilogy.

TWC: Beyond the reading, who is Sumaira Shamsie when she's not Originator? How do you spend your time and catch a breath?

I am not particularly artistic, but I do know how to play the piano. The arrangements of other people contain a wealth of imagination that I love to tap into. At libraries and cafés I enjoy people watching. There are countless conversations and interactions. I hope that is not too strange. I will put in noise cancelling headphones and play white noise whilst doing yoga, or I will visit a museum.

Disengaging has been how I re-engage and work best in a superhuman-filled world. There is seldom time for that, but I always want to sit and read and learn so I am best prepared. I always want to be ready for the next series, be it a summation or a development.

TWC: Now, for one final question. Favorite drink, go.

As you may imagine, I do not drink: I cannot even imagine what would happen if I were to slur my words or say something that changed the nature of gravity.

And that was Sumaira Shamsie, Originator! Join us next month, as we speak to the most powerful of the Command, Frontier!

[Interview by: **Ritesh Babu**. Answers by: **L.A. Thornill**, with **Steve Orlando**.]

EXCLUSIVE INTERVIEW WITH
NINA NEXT · FRONTIER

The following was originally published in the February 10th issue of **The Washington Comet**. It is reproduced below, with the permission of all the parties involved.

The Crisis Command, the world's most mighty, the champions of tomorrow, the super-team of America. Everyday we watch them save our world- a team of diverse individuals who fight off the absurdly abnormal with impossible ideas. They're a busy bunch, and they do difficult work.

But the Crisis Command has graciously agreed to take some time to sit down with us here at The Washington Comet, so that we may all better get to know the people who walk among us with such tremendous talents.

Over the next few months, we'll be covering each and every single member of the team closely. From what they're enjoying on their off-time to their stance on what they believe their super-team represents, we'll be digging into all the details. And who better to start with than the leader of them all? The commander of the Crisis Command, The Terrific Technomancer herself, Frontier!

It's a strange little space, the lab. I'd been to many in my time, in speaking to various scientists. And while this had a lot in common with those, it was also unlike any of them. Strange metals gleamed in corners, contorted into shapes that seemed implausible. Mad machinery lined the walls, seeming far too large to fit in the room, and yet somehow managing. There was a strange smell in the air that I just could not place. It felt...alien. It was unlike anything else.

I hear a knocking on the other end and turn to look. And there she is, Frontier, in a clean lab-coat.

'We good?' she asks. I nod. 'Yes. Yes.'

She nods, walking over. 'Let's get started. I suspect we both have a busy day ahead.'

TWC: So, I guess, to start off, why the Crisis Command? And why now? What made Nina Next transform into Frontier?

I've always been interested in science and tech. I remember, my parents got me a chemistry set for Christmas when I was a kid, and it was love at first sight.

I studied as many different kinds of science as I could as I grew up, but it wasn't until college--I went a few years early--that I understood I could combine my love of the natural sciences and technology. The natural order of the world is so poetic--beautiful--and to me, technology is an extension of that.

Along with encouraging my love of learning, my parents also instilled a strong sense of responsibility in me. They believed very strongly in service to others; I grew up volunteering at soup kitchens and nursing homes. Logically, as I started to develop new technologies, I had an eye towards how it could be used to help others. I wanted to be more active in helping others. Crisis Command is an extension of that, for all of us.

As for why now, I say just look around you. People are in pain, in crisis, more than ever. And we can help them. So we do what we can with our gifts and strengths.

TWC: Do you feel you and the team lived up to that goal? That mission? Where do you see The Crisis Command at this moment?

On the bad days, the work feels Sisyphean. The goal is to help people, and there will always be people to help. But on the good days, it feels a little like building a house from the ground up--you have to work hard to get a good foundation, to build a solid frame, but it's god work.

Each time we go out there, we are building a house, and each time we do, we get better at it. The team is always learning, so we can do better.

TWC: How would you describe your fellow team-mates?

Like family, complete with complicated dynamics.

We have the tough guy with the heart of gold who is guarding his wounded heart [Sawbones].

There's the one who some might say has her head in the clouds, but really just sees the forest instead of the trees [Seer]. We have the confident golden child, who is learning to see beyond his own shine [Prizefighter]. And of course, we have the voice of reason [Originator].

TWC: Any thoughts on Thunder Woman or Madame Fury?

Thunder Woman has been an inspiration for me since I was a kid! Her strength, both physical and mental, is something I come back to and use as north stars for myself. Truly incredible, iconic!

It's such a shame that the first masked hero's legacy is tainted by unscrupulous tabloids. Madame Fury did so much good--helped so many people--but rumors about her being intimate with her driver are what people always bring up.

TWC: You and the Command have certainly made a number of enemies over time. Any ones in particular that stand out to you, across all that time?

I don't want to give them any press, which might encourage more incidents, but I will say that it is incredibly frustrating that we have not been able to catch the Social Callers. I think there's more to them than causing mayhem, as radiosapiens they may not understand fully what an impact they are having, but they are dangerous and need to be stopped.

TWC: What do you do when you clock out? Both as a team, and just for yourself, personally. Do you all watch TV, go camping? Do you just read some Dostoyevsky alone? Where does the hero life end and the civilian life begin?

Honestly, I live for the lab! I'm energized by seeing results of long running experiments, and starting new projects. It's almost a bonus that it all ends up being helpful in my work with the Crisis Command, but I get as much out of doing science as most people do a night on the town!

TWC: What's the one thing people don't know about you, that they would be surprised to learn?

They say cooking is an art, and baking is a science. Well, baking is the only science I don't excel in! Something about it confuses my understanding of physics, and I can't ever avoid a "soggy bottom" or "stodgy loaf."

TWC: Do you have a particular favorite invention or gadget of yours?

I'm working on a portable way to deploy instantaneous

gene therapy. I haven't quite cracked it yet, but I think this could have really big implications for field medicine!

TWC: Now, for one final question. Favorite alcoholic drink, go.

Call me old fashioned, but working with highly complicated science all day makes me appreciate simplicity. And there is something about whiskey, bitters, and sugar that will never go out of style.

And that was Nina Next, Frontier! That concludes things for now, folks! Make sure you keep an eye out for further issues of The Washington Comet for more exciting new things!

[Interview by: **Ritesh Babu**. Answers by: **Vita Ayala**, with **Steve Orlando**.]

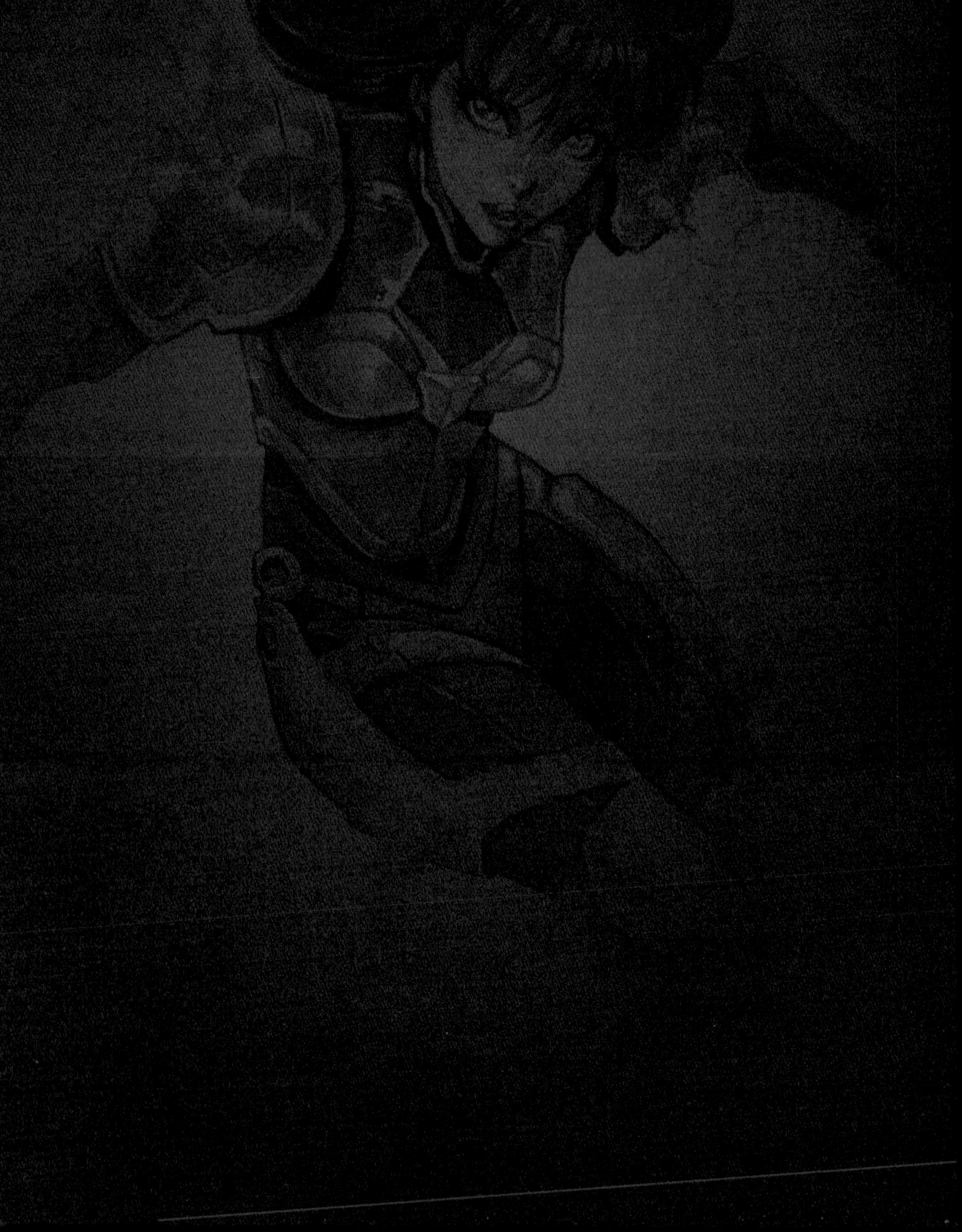

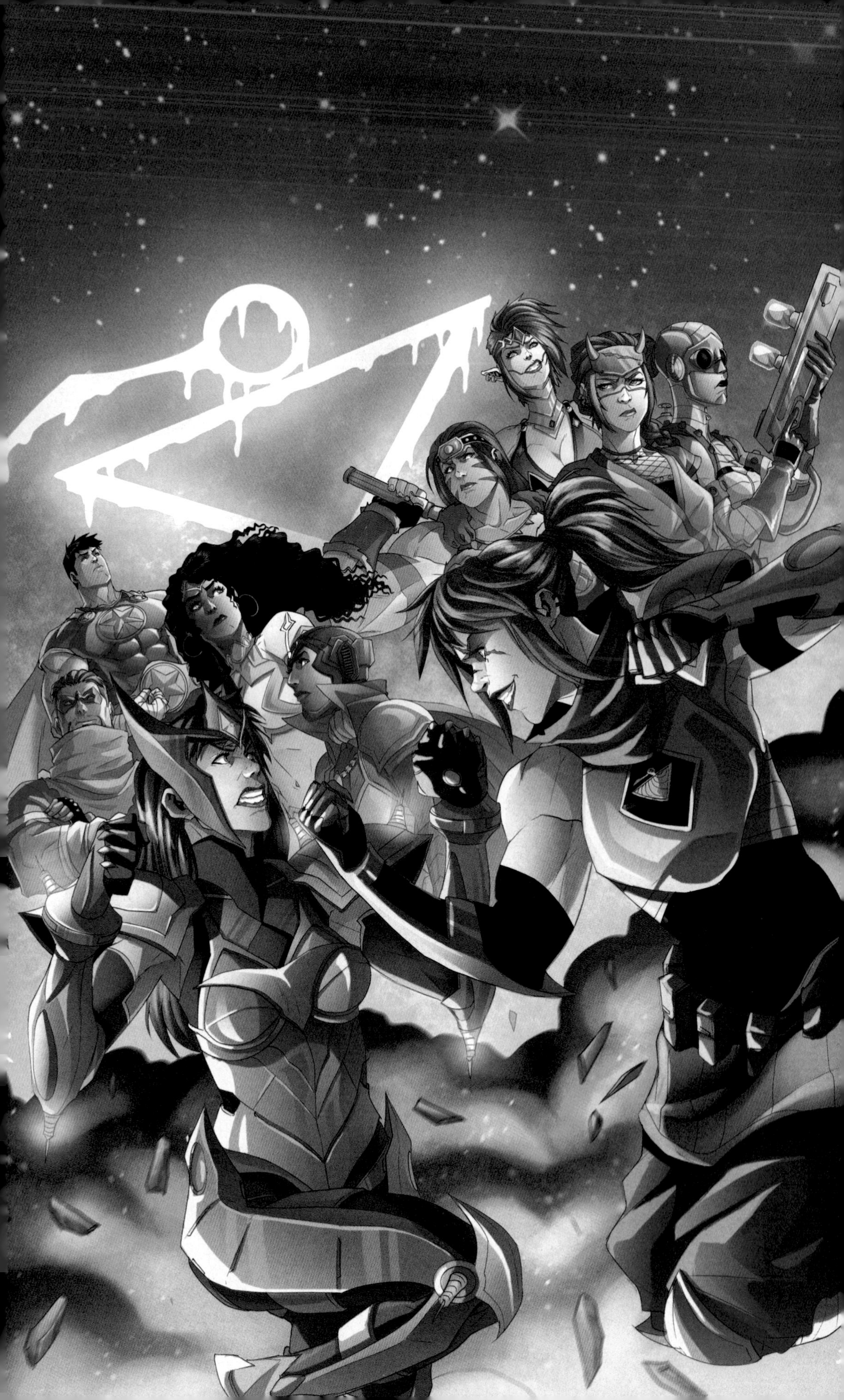

COMMANDERS AND COCKTAILS

Welcome to COMMANDERS AND COCKTAILS! Some folks know that before I was able to work full time in comics, I worked in a variety of jobs in the wine and spirits field. And the final one of those was for my good friend Nicolas Palazzi's PM Spirits.

Just *COMMANDER IN CRISIS*, PM works its ass off to be unique, to create trends rather than follow them, and offer craftsmanship and creativity in a field that has, at times, been known to stagnate. I wouldn't be where I am, writing this, without the support of friends and employers like Nicolas.

So, I thought it would be fun to turn the tables and feature him and his crew below, offering some in-universe cocktail recipes to honor the heroes of the Crisis Command. In the paraphrased words of a greater power, when I left PM I was but the learner.

Now, I am the master (well, or closer to it)! And either way, I'm happy to return the support with a feature here, and invite creatives from other fields into the world of the Crisis Command.

STEVE ORLANDO

PRIZEFIGHTER

2oz Navazos Palazzi Malt or Corn Whisky
0.75oz La Quintinye Rouge Vermouth
0.5oz cherry liqueur
2 dashes Angostura Bitters
Barspoon Absinthe

Instructions:
Build in rocks glass over ice and stir briefly. Garnish with burnt blood orange peel.

SEER

2.5oz Neta Espadin Destilado de Agave
0.5oz La Quintinye Dry
Barspoon of olive brine
Pinch of salt

Instructions:
Build in mixing glass over ice and stir until cold. Strain into chilled cocktail glass and garnish with 3 green olives on a pick.

SAWBONES

2oz Père Labat Rhum Blanc 59%abv
4 dashes Peychaud's Bitters
Sparkling mineral water

Instructions:
Pour Rhum into highball glass over ice. Stir briefly to chill. Top with sparkling water and bitters. Stir once again to combine. Serve without garnish.
or
Neat pour of Jacky Navarre Cravache d'Or Cognac

ORIGINATOR

1oz Nouaison Gin by G'Vine
0.75oz lemon juice
0.5oz Laurent Cazottes Folle Noire
0.5oz simple syrup
2oz sparkling wine

Instructions:
Build all ingredients except sparkling wine in a shaker and shake lightly to combine. Add sparkling wine to the shaker and strain into chilled cocktail glass. Garnish with a spring of fresh lavender.

FRONTIER

2oz Père Labat Rhum Blanc 40% or 59% abv - Choose your strength
0.5oz Laurent Cazottes 72 Tomatoes

Instructions:
Build in mixing glass over ice and stir until cold. Strain into chilled cocktail glass and garnish with freshly ground black pepper.

COCKTAIL CREDITS:
David Yi-Hsian Dong and Nicolas Palazzi of PM Spirits.

JOURNEY THROUGH LITERATURE #37

PRIZEFIGHTER

In this bi-monthly series, critic Sean Dillon interviews various weird and interesting people and talks to them about books, new and old, and how they relate to the people who read them. This month, Sean follows up his interview with director Mike Flanagan with a talk with the people's champion, Prizefighter! As per Flanagan's suggestion, they are reading If The Devil Didn't Exist... by Steven Moffat.

Wikipedia Summary (italics added for clarification): 008 (Rebecca Swanson) has stolen a dossier of ongoing operations. From Operation Moonraker to Project Spectre, these projects have been key to MI6's global operations for policing the world for decades. With the recent leakage of The Belgium Affair, MI6 has tasked it's number one agent, James Bond, to hunt down and eliminate this rogue operative. There's just one problem: they were once lovers. Many years ago, 007 and 008 were tasked with infiltrating a suspected Spectre cell in America. Their budding romance is on the verge of collapse and Bond doesn't even realize it. With the world on the brink of devastation, will Bond be able to prevent his lover turned enemy from making things worse? And what secrets does Swanson hold of her own.

I was told that traveling via Atom Rider was a bit like being a washing machine. This is what I was told. The actual experience of traveling this way is perhaps more akin to holding onto a bear for dear life while lightning strikes next to you every five seconds. To say I was frazzled when I found myself in Berlin would be an understatement. Later when I was asked if I wanted to go home the way I came, I instead asked for plane tickets and spent the night with a friend of mine who lives in the city of stones with their husband.

We meet in a place I am led to believe was once a speakeasy for various queer people to meet and hook up. It's still a bar and it's still extremely queer, but it's a bit more legal now. Prizefighter sits in a booth a few feet away from the stage. No one's performing right now, and it's a real shame they aren't. Prizefighter sits coolly in the booth, arms outstretched and resting on the shoulders of the booth. I sit on the opposite side of the table, placing my phone down, ready to hit record. He pulls out a copy of the book we are about to discuss. The cover is the American version used to promote the movie that was out at the time, so it's rather bland design wise, with Daniel Craig posing like he's Sean Connery. My copy, which I also pull out, is the more traditional international version of the cover. The logo was designed by Rian Hughes, and the art is that of a man cut up like in a Saul Bass cover while falling from a great height.

Prizefighter smiles at me the way one always imagined it'd be like to have Santa Clause in your kitchen. There's a sense of warmth to the smile that contradicts the seemingly superficial nature of a man who needs the people to love him in order to save them. He is genuine even in the moments when he's being disingenuous. I briefly lose composure

How are you doing?

How could someone like me not be doing great? That doesn't mean there's not work to do. There's always more work to do, people to save, hashtags to create, trends to set. I need to keep my strength up, after all. The second people get bored by Prizefighter, I start to get weaker. Who knows? I could even end up not being bulletproof anymore, and who wants that? So I'm always good, always working, always on brand. Am I ever really not, behind the costume? I'll never tell. That's the price of being an icon.

What's your familiarity with Bond prior to reading this book? Equally, have you seen any of Moffat's work before reading this one?

For sure I knew more about the Bond stuff. I wasn't what you'd call...a nerd? Before the powers, I was a pretty typical captain of the football team type. I'm still trying to learn and listen my way out of that. Not easy! So I steered clear of Science-Fiction stuff which to me was what you'd get with Moffat. Maybe I was wrong? Assumptions and all, you know? But Bond? I could take a girl to Bond when I was still in the closet and no one would know where were both checking out Daniel Craig. You'd be surprised how vindicating just a quick, even passing joke about Bond having been with a guy in SKYFALL was for me. Then when I was finally out, I could say the secret part out loud. I figured I'd end up the gay James Bond, but hell, even Bond can't stop bullets. I DID sort of end up dating him though, but that -- that didn't end...well. It didn't end well.

The way he looks when talking about his ex isn't quite the reaction one would expect from him. It's not that Prizefighter is openly weeping per-say or even appearing to be outwardly miserable. In fact, at first glance, it doesn't look like he's changed emotion in the least. It's the eyes though that show everything. There's a profound melancholy to them, the kind often held when the sky is grey and you can't cry for your dead grandfather. His smile is slightly weaker than it was before, less toothy and more wry. He's still relaxed, like even this moment of sorrow can't

I suppose no relationship with James Bond could end well. Then again, Roger Moore was very daddy. Do you have any thoughts on any of the other Bond films? Equally, have you read any of Fleming's books?

If I've got thoughts they're probably not high-minded ones, or at least they weren't back then. But now, I am trying to look at things more critically and understand what's around me, instead of floating through. Probably comes as no surprise then that I wasn't ever really a "read the book" type of guy when there was a movie right there, begging for less commitment. Back then, I thought Bond was an idol, but I was stuck in my own bubble. I still admire his focus and drive, but the way he treats people as disposable for the most part, just an utter lack of empathy, acting like the blunt object people assume he is, it's not something I aspire too. In some ways, that attitude is everything we're out here fighting in the Crisis Command. No one, not a single person's disposable. I saw that pretty quickly when I started thinking above the belt.

What did you think of If the Devil Didn't Exist?

Man...that ending! Honestly, just like Bardem and Craig in SKYFALL, I won't say I wasn't excited to see even some passive gay moments like Leiter's husband who died on the job. Would I like it better if we didn't have to have dead husbands in movies? Sure. But that's what I'm here for. When they make my movie, we live to the end. Hell yes. I thought seeing how 008 saw the romance versus how Bond saw it was awesome, it'll probably help me think about how to hone my own persona in the future. Who needs to think more about how their actions are perceived than I do? And if you think I didn't relate to the fact Bond seemed to be playing the character of James Bond, rather than being himself, whatever that is, then you haven't really thought about what it's like to have the way your body works linked to public perception. I said I wanted to be Bond when I was just coming out, and sort of, if you squint, this Bond was like me. Which again make the ending a pretty big punch in the crotch.

Well, I thought it was relatable. And not just to me, to a lot of people. Or it should be. Yeah, I lose a lot more obvious things if my persona starts to falter and people start to doubt. But is that any different than anyone whose career involves being in the public eye? Social media especially means people expect you to be "on" all the time, in every public setting. There's no such thing as not having everything you say be analyzed super deeply, maybe taken out of context, maybe used against you. When you're in the public eye, like an actor, or any type of creative person that might need things like social to make a living, you're always playing the version of yourself that's good for business. And man, that can be tiring for anyone, even if you're not a super spy or a super hero.

Given the political climate we're living in, it seems nationalistic heroes like Bond are growing to be a bit more... dangerous. Given how much you see yourself within Bond, and your powers relate to the perception people have of you, how do see yourself in relation to the image that you are an American hero, if not seen as such?

Well, like I said above, I saw myself in Bond. And I still do want to be as relentless as him once I set myself to doing something. But there's other things about him, these days, I think I more learn from in opposition. I certainly consider more than ever how I treat people when I put on this uniform, and I think I would even if my powers didn't depend on it. Maybe that's wishful thinking? I don't think so. As for being an American hero, I think that journey is a lot like a big version of my own. When I was a kid, before the powers, I just think I took things at face value. But now, I try to be critical of everything so I can better serve the people than need me. I wouldn't say I'm an American hero specifically, since we answer to those in danger, not to a flag. That's one of Frontier's best lines, hell, it became a meme. But if I were to be one, I'd say that means it's on me more than ever to analyze my actions and question what I do and why I do it. The needs of the endangered has to be my northstar, not one nation or creed. It's need, and our ability to help those with it if we can.

That's absolutely fair. But at the same time, we

can't necessarily control how people see us. We can absolutely say we're not an arm of the US military, but that won't stop people from saying that a team complied of Americans-- a diverse group of Americans, but Americans nevertheless-- are an American team of superheroes. As someone whose powers lie in perception and whose aesthetic invokes a man who stands for "Truth Justice, and the American Way," how does one go about pushing against such a perception beyond merely saying you're not?

See, you're right. We definitely can't control how people see us, so the best we can do is keep acting as we say we will, not as others might expect us to due to their own perceptions. There's always going to be pundits on TV, or people on social media, putting their own assumptions on us. But we don't answer to them any more than we answer to a government or a corporation. They can think or suppose what they want, you know? Who am I to say that life hasn't showed them not to trust us? Or that other people like us haven't delivered? That's their right to think how they want. But we answer to the people in danger. And we keep doing that. Actions are how you push against a perception, following up what we say with what we do. If people want to keep looking at an apple and seeing an orange, they can. If they're ever in danger, we'll still be on their side whether they want to believe it or not. And if they're the ones causing the danger, we won't be.

The title of the book, If the Devil Didn't Exist... is quite evocative. A play on the Voltaire quote "If God didn't exist, it would be necessary to invent him." But with the Devil, there's a sense of the creation of the enemy. Fitting considering the information 008 leaks to the world. That Spectre and all the other evil organizations Bond has fought are nothing more than shell organizations to justify English Imperialism rather than, say, unite the world against a common foe. What's you take on this notion?

I think fear sells, and it always has. Look at the question you asked earlier - people with power have given people without it plenty of reason to distrust. And it's often justified. Fear, urgency, scapegoating.

It's all a nice way to keep people distracted, keep those with power safe where they sit, and make sure folks don't see they're being manipulated. A big, simple, enemy is how businesses and governments have kept their citizens from looking too closely at what they're really doing for decades. And I think that's real, I am sure I've -- no doubt I've been a part of it in the past, no matter my intent. So like above, all I can do is go forward and show people in action that they don't have to be afraid. I can go forward dealing with threats that do matter and aren't fabricated, and hopefully help people in turn to figure out who is really working in their best interests.

You've been alluding to some rather toxic aspects of your younger self (apt, given we're talking about a Moffat work). Bond has frequently been critiqued as a "sexist, misogynistic dinosaur." Is this the angle of your toxicity or, if you feel comfortable talking about it, something that rhymes with it?

No I think I definitely had room to grow, and I'm happy to admit I wasn't perfect. I took me longer than it should have to give up old, stupid ideas about "what makes a man" and what is and isn't masculine. Or even honestly, who cares if something is or isn't masculine at all? I was programmed, like we all are, to think one way by my parents and people around me. And I had it relatively easy, so I didn't get on myself to do the work I needed to to break that programming until later than I should have. I certainly thought being a "masculine" guy was superior to being a "feminine" one. But that was a young idiot's point of view. When I got out into the world, and got these powers, and got to listening, I realized that was bullshit. And it's important people hear me say I was wrong, and I had learning to do. Strength is strength, there's no one way it looks, or one definition. I wish I'd known that sooner, and I'm still learning. But I'm working.

Do you feel Bond deserved the death he got? For that matter, do you feel Moffat made the ending work considering the grandeur of the Bond icon?

Well, sure. I mean, I don't know if I think anyone really "deserves" death in real life, but this isn't real

us do things we can't do, or explore stuff we maybe wish we could, but know we can't for one reason or another. I think someone like Bond finally meeting his end at a woman he was incapable of seeing wasn't under his spell is pretty fitting. And pretty ironic! Some poetic justice for a guy who got plenty of women killed. My ex...he would've been laughing, this was his kind of book.

Let's talk a little about Rebecca Swanson, 008, the woman who gave Bond a Rebecca Swanson ending. How do you feel about her in comparison to other Bond girls with more outlandish names like Pussy Galore, Holly Goodhead, and Oodles O'Quim?

I mean, as much as I love Pussy Galore, and I do! Early gay icon right there, and someone who I really thought met Bond on his own terms. I heard it's even more that way in the novels but like I said, me and reading weren't tight back in the day. But as much as I love her, I think all that stuff needs to be left in the past. Turning these women into sex puns, to me, it already starts dehumanizing them from the get-go. But they're not objects, Bond shouldn't treat them like they are, and we shouldn't just laugh on with it. So I think like I said, it's fitting to watch the way Bond stuff depicts women evolve and evolve, until I guess what it was always going to be: Bond's sexist bullshit catching up with him and making him pay the price. It feels maybe too smart for the schlocky eras maybe? But it makes sense. I'm there for it.

And finally, as is tradition with this series, what book do you want our next guest to read?

FURY UNMASKED, it's got to be. There's a documentary streaming now, one of the Command, Seer, she tried to get me to watch it. But I told you, I'm trying to get into source materials, get into reading and actually absorbing stuff, so I got the original diaries they published before the docuseries. It's wild stuff, the secret diaries of Madame Fury and Hack, the first ever masked vigilantes on this world - I mean the world, on "the" world. Their secret...whoa, I'll say this. Things would've been a whole lot different here if they hadn't waited so long to tell their real story.

CRISIS COMMAND F.A.Q. BY STEVE ORLANDO & DAVID MANN

I believe I'm in danger right now. How do I get you to come?

Don't wait. Our contact form on this site is linked directly to our Crisis Alert. You'll be connected to our main server, or to the emergency service of your choosing. You'll also be given the option to download our pre-programmed, emergency-use Atom Rider app, which can instantly deliver you to the closest viable hospital from any location on the planet.

Who are you? You appeared out of nowhere, working together with little seemingly in common beyond planet-shaking power. In spite of sharing your names, most word on your background comes from guessed-at commonalities or connections with past heroes and what's known of their own origins, or flavors of conspiracy theories.

First and foremost, we're here to help. Some of us, like Frontier, keep few secrets about their lives. Others like Prizefighter live 100% of the time in their public persona. For the rest of us, the answer is somewhere in between. The secrets we keep, we keep to protect ourselves, and also to protect you. We know you'd like to know more, and we'd like to tell you. Hopefully, it'll be safe to do so eventually. But in the meantime, we hope our actions speak loudest as to who we are: people who want to help.

What exactly do you do? You're on the news dealing with mind-muggers and the Social Callers to save civilization, but what about 'smaller' crimes? Are you only there for the big stuff? Is getting cats out of trees not a crisis worth your time?

You're all worth our time. You're all important. What we do, above all, is help those in danger. However, the unfortunate fact about this world, our world, is that there is nearly always a crisis with more life at risk than something as platonic and pure as a cat in a tree. That doesn't mean it's unimportant. But five people, even with our abilities, can't be everywhere at once. Dealing with danger on a global scale almost always means making triage decisions, which is why we've learned to trust those we protect to stand for themselves, knowing we have their back if they get in too deep over their head.

Whose side are you on? You're called "the super-team of America," but you operate outside the country, you don't make any secrets of your politics (like old superheroes/unlike old superheroes), and you've been taped arguing with law enforcement in Portland. What makes you say you stand for us?

Well, we've never called ourselves that. What we've always said is that we're on the side of those in danger. We don't answer to any flag, we answer to people in harm's way, and the need to pull them out of it. Sadly, we're not naïve. We knew from the start that those actions would be politicized, since it's an unfortunate fact that safety and comfort for some is sometimes seen as an affront to others. We've made no secret of putting the well-being of people, and the world, above all. It's those who stand in the way of that that inject politics. There's no ceremony we'll stand on if it means someone in pain longer than we can help, and that's what was seen in Portland. We were best suited to save the lives of people with emergency medical issues and acted.

What's your stance on use of lethal force? Frontier carries a gun, and Sawbones is covered in deadly weapons.

If the Crisis Command answers to those in pain, those in danger, then violence always needs to be a last resort. That doesn't mean it doesn't occur, and it unfortunately doesn't mean that saving the lives of many may mean ending a life. But that's something to be avoided at all costs. Even with the public attack of the Mind-Muggers, the attackers were contained and delivered to the World Court for trial. Frontier carries a gun of her own design, with functionality often used to deliver lifesaving medicine or scientific remedies

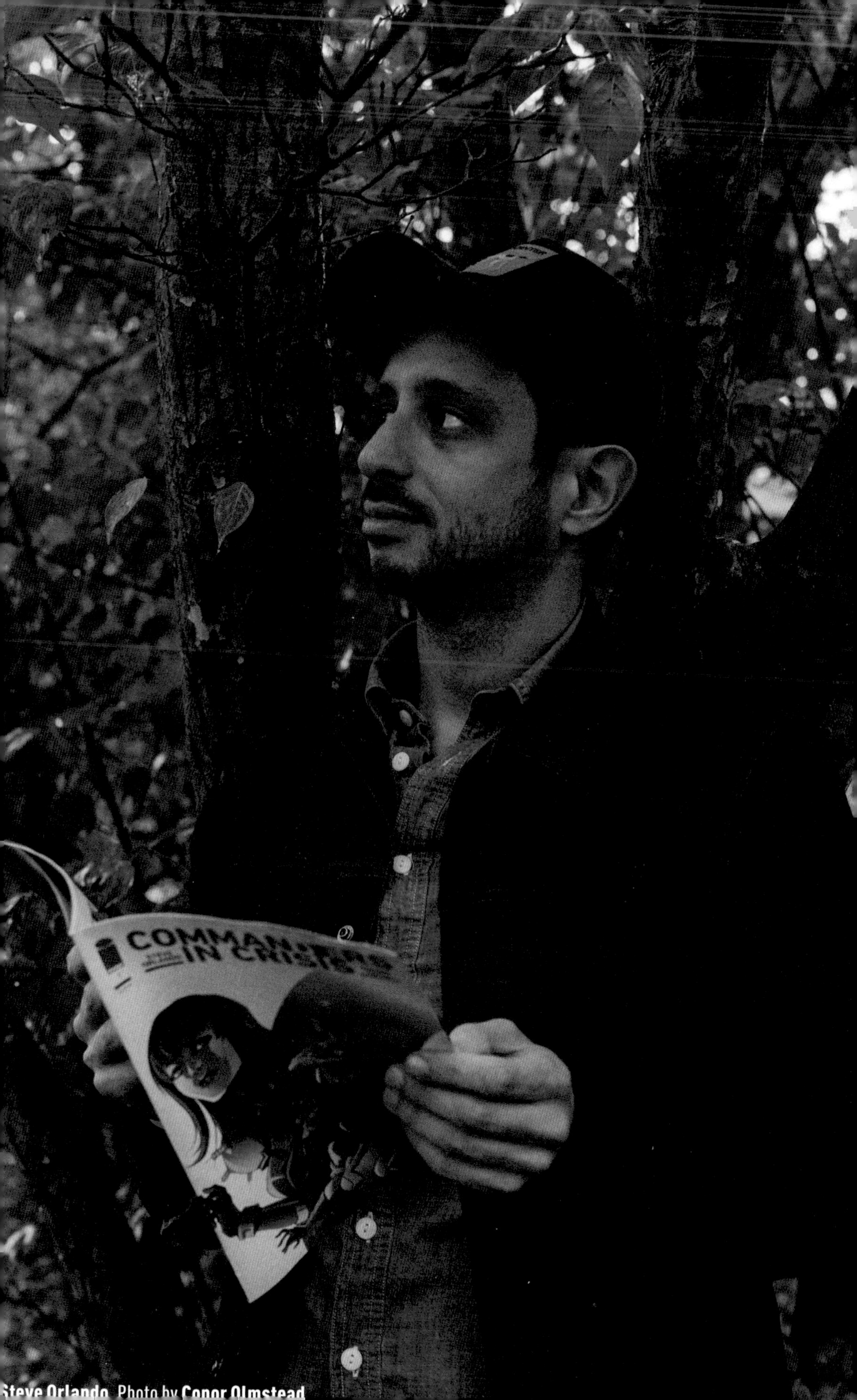
COMMAN
IN CRISIS

Steve Orlando. Photo by Conor Olmstead.

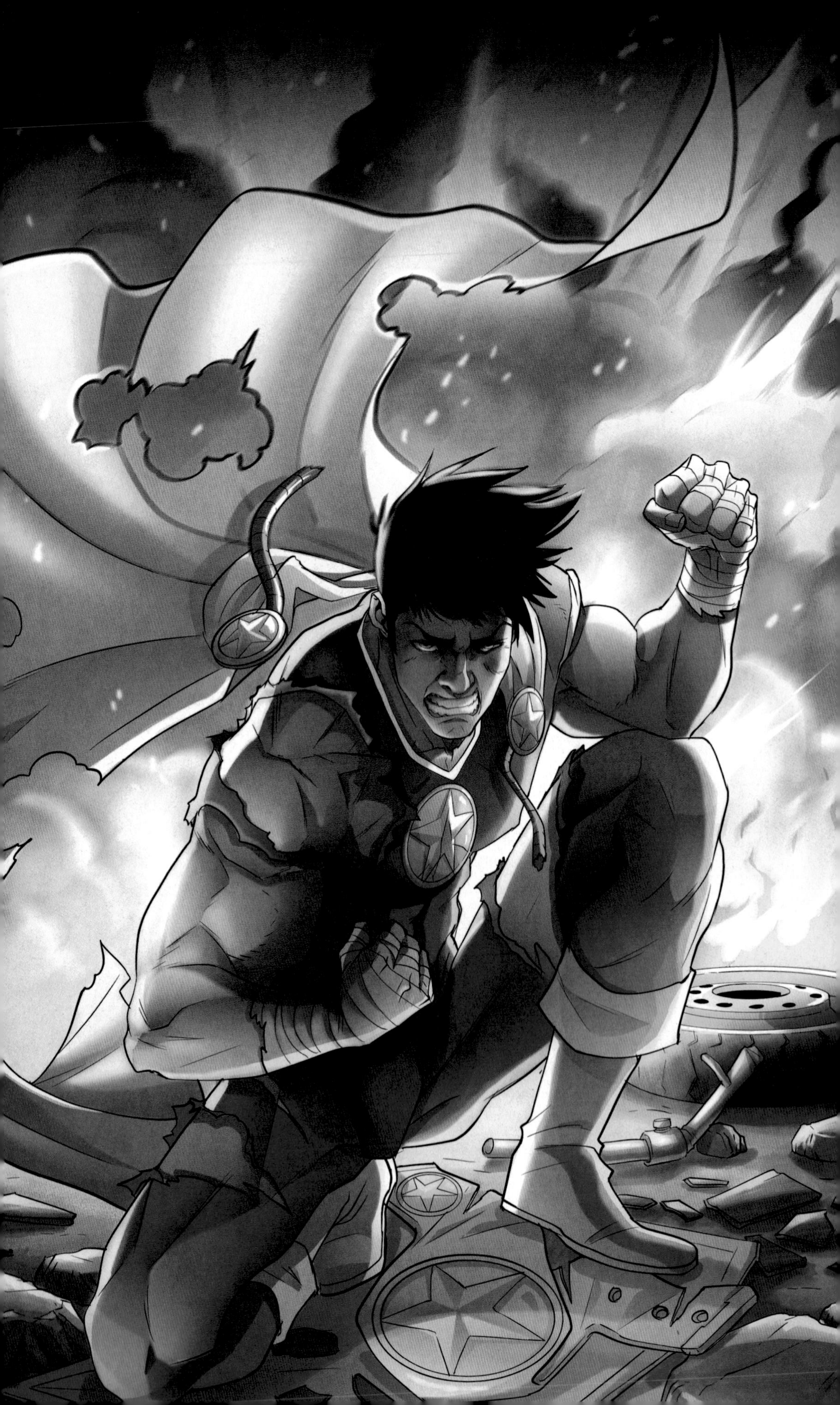

Sawbones carries many deadly weapons, but part of his wielding them with the precision of a surgeon is ensuring there are no surprises. By being precise and decisive, he has no need to use deadly force.

On a related note, what do you say to rumors Sawbones spends his time away from the team going to hospitals to stab patients?

This seems like a misrepresentation. Sawbones does spend time away from the team in a variety of hospitals, learning all he can about medicine and lifesaving procedures. However he is not a doctor, and limits himself to the use of his Bio-Spectral vision when in a hospital setting, aiding those qualified to administer emergency medicine by seeing what they can't. What Sawbones learns as an observer, he applies in the field until first responders arrive at the scene.

What are the Command referring to when you say you're clocking in or out? Are you on a set workweek/rotation? Do you have to abide by mandatory minimums or maximums? Do you take vacations from saving us?

We'll take a vacation as soon as danger, or catastrophe, decides to sit one out. At the same time, we're still limited by our bodies. We can't go without sleep, we do get worn down. Even the strongest among us, Seer, gets worn down the fastest when using her amazing godlike abilities. We have no mandates, and also no vacations. But we do rotate through who is on the job watching the Crisis Alert, so that the others can recharge and be ready to deploy in the cases of a problem that requires we all activate. To better protect you when we're on, we all need time off.

Who else do you work with? The world only sees the five of you, but between maintaining the Think Tank, funding your equipment, and any legal challenges you face, surely you receive some kind of support, with their own roles – and agendas? – we'd want to know about.

The Crisis Command regularly works alongside the world's other heroes, whether it's Thunder Woman or

Brick Bat, or anyone else who can do the work and aid everyday folks. While we appreciate questions about our funding, as we've said above there are secrets we keep in order to better protect this world. That said, funding for the Crisis Command does come from within our five team members.

I believe I or someone I know may have been affected by the Originator's warping of reality, in a way that cannot be brushed aside for the duration of the effect.

Please use the contact form above, download the Emergency Atom Rider app for treatment.

For anything else you have to say: how can we trust you to be honest with us, especially when the powers of one of your team members literally depends on us liking you?

We'll start with the obvious – trust in of itself is always a risk. All we can provide is the evidence of our actions, just like anyone else on this world. We can say whatever we want, we can even tell you whatever you want to hear, but actions are what matter. And we hope that as our backlog of aid continues to grow, trust will come. And more to the point, someone like Prizefighter is all the more reason to feel your agency. If you started to doubt him, for whatever reason, his powers would begin to wither. His needing your belief puts the power in your hands, not his.

Is there anything I can do to help?

You can do your best, just as we always try to do. We're here to make life easier than it is, not harder. We hope you don't have to think about us, or anyone else in the superhuman community, on a daily basis. Show compassion, listen to those around you, and remember you're not an island but one of billions just trying to get by. That's how you help. Don't worry about helping us, help those in your community. Radical compassion might just mean, in time, that there's less and less for us to do. And we wouldn't mind that at all.

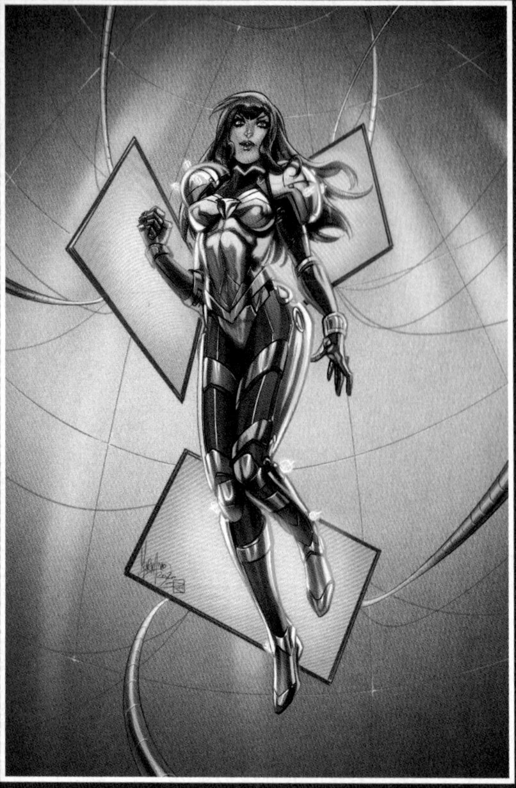

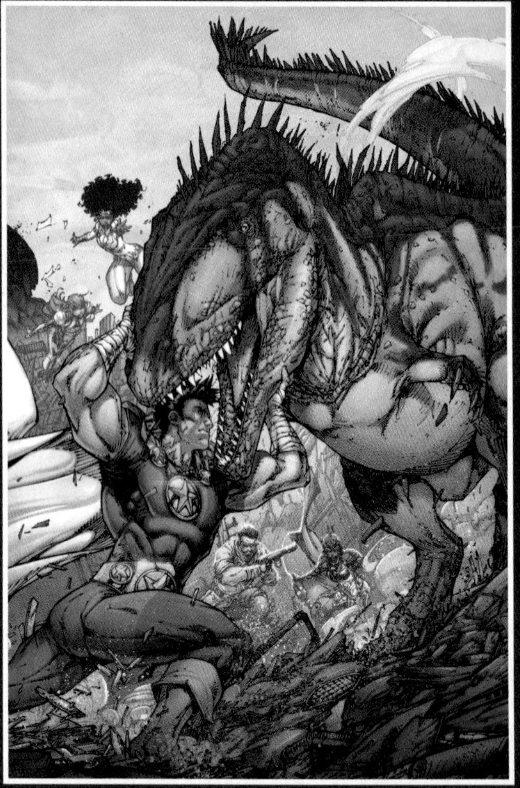

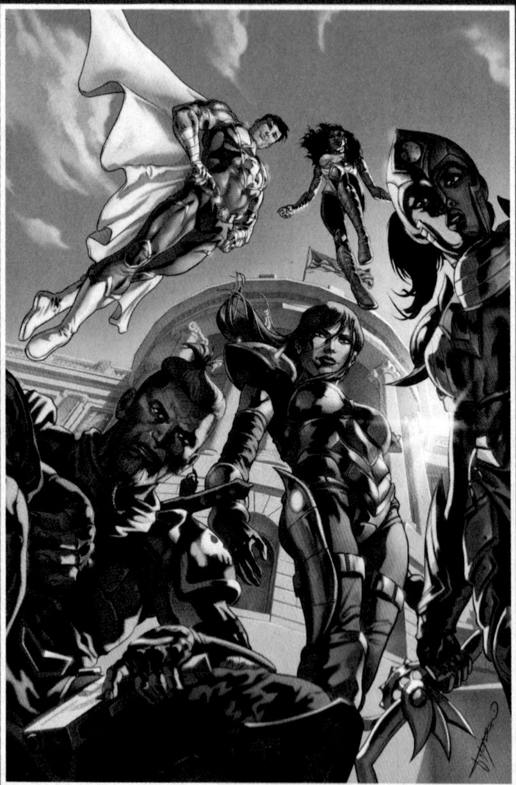

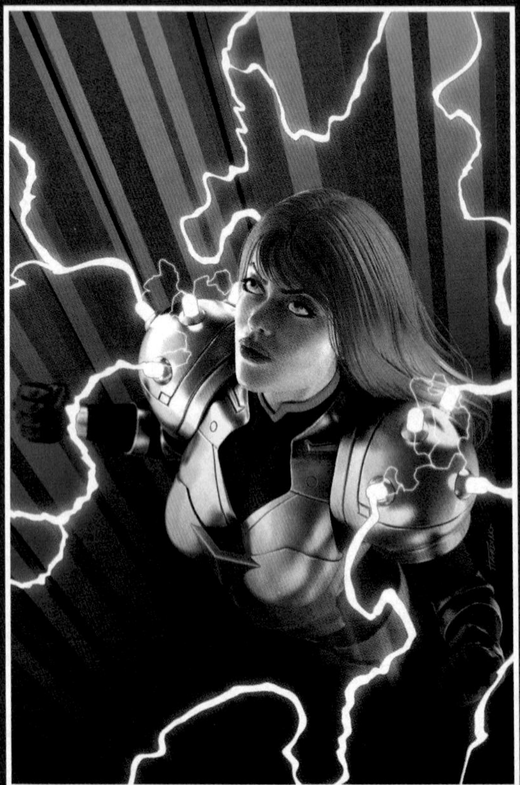

MIRKA ANDOLFO, PEACH MOMOKO,
GIOVANNI TIMPANO, PAUL HARDING.

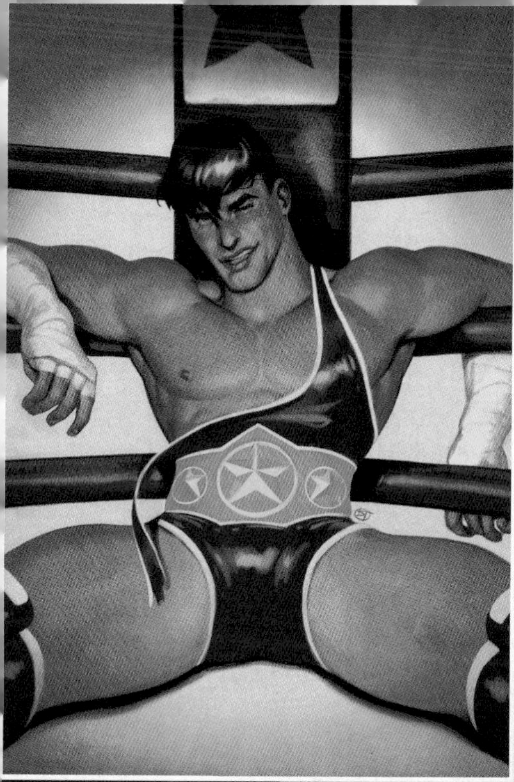

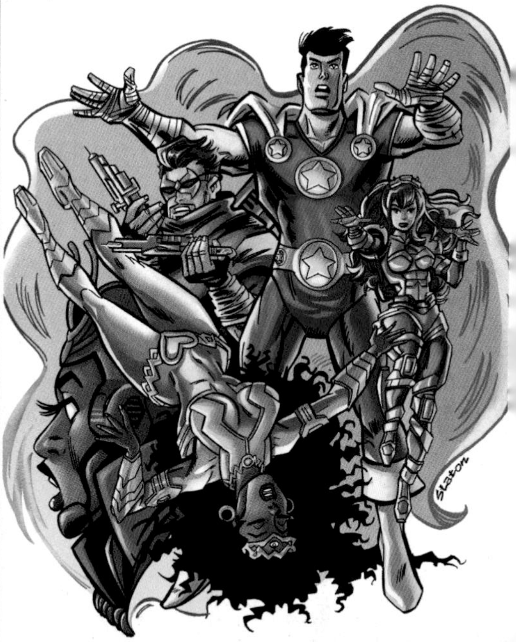
Staton

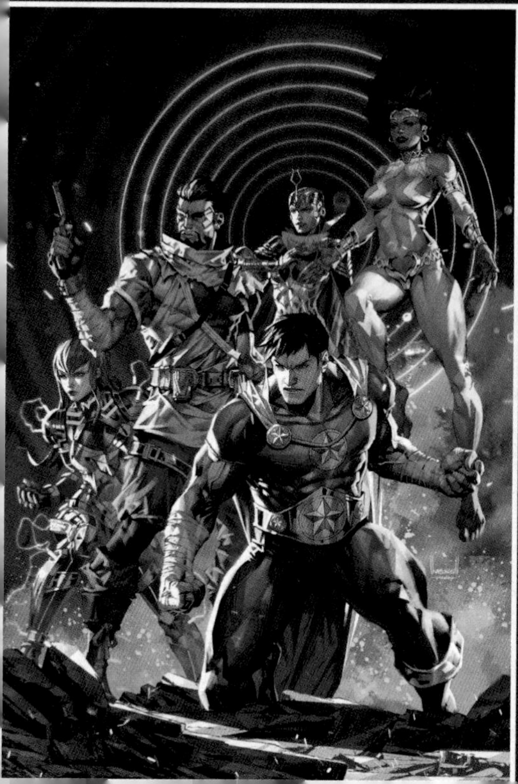

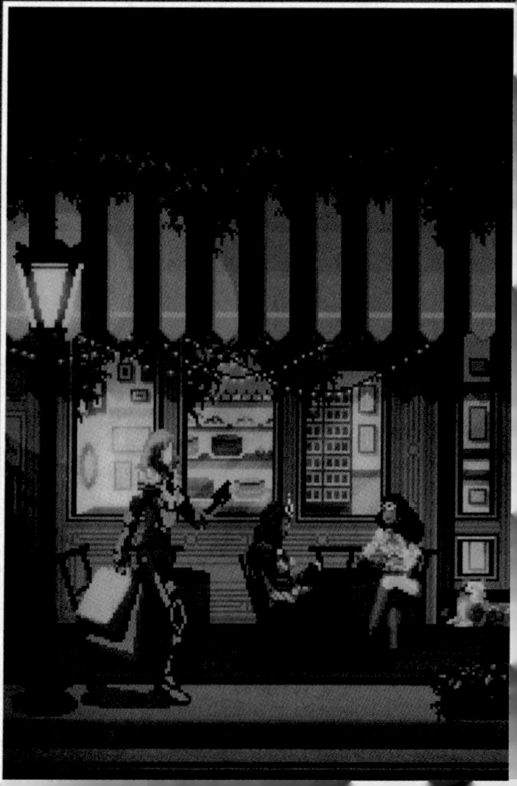

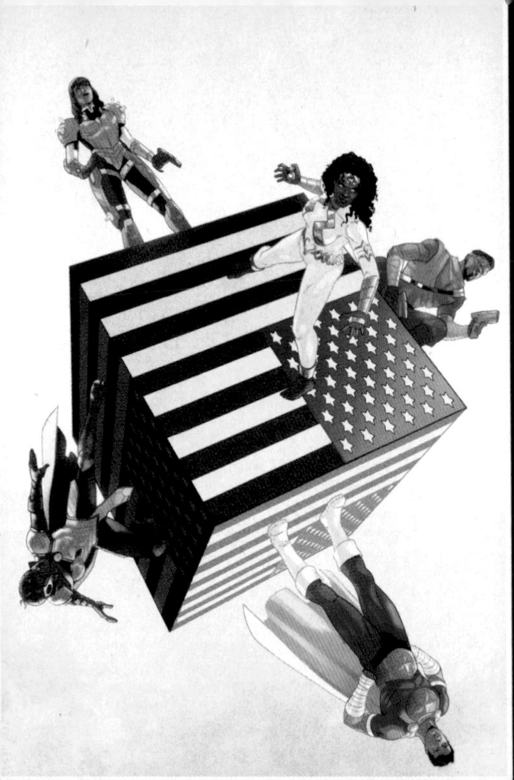
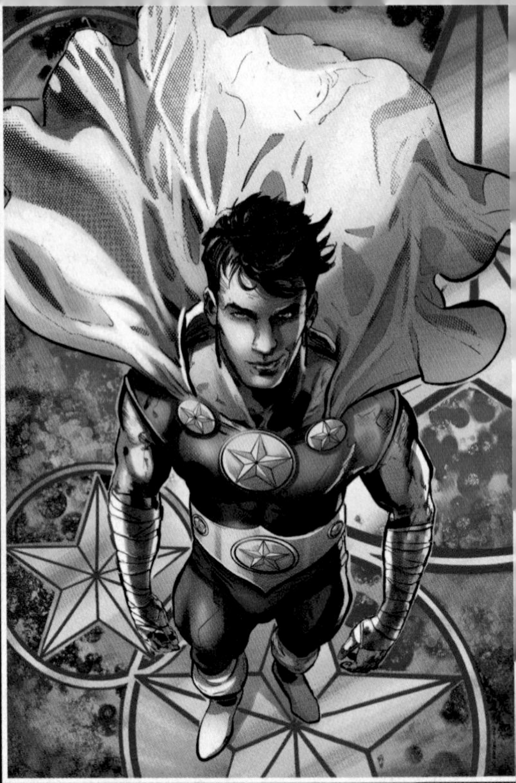
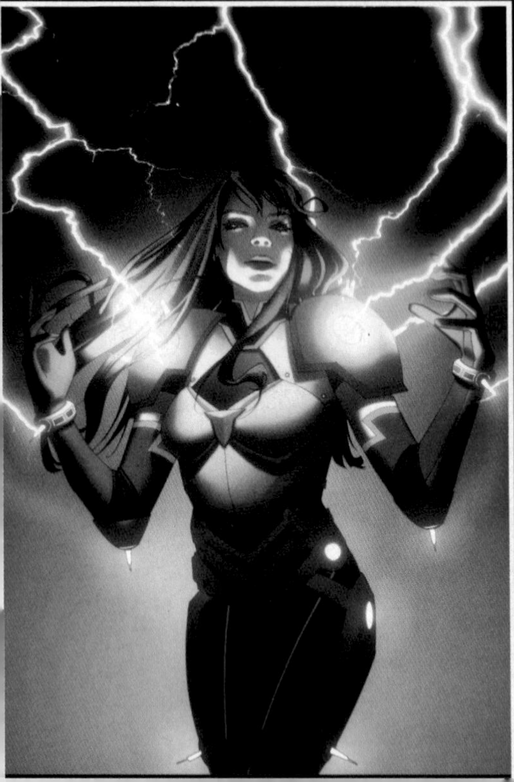
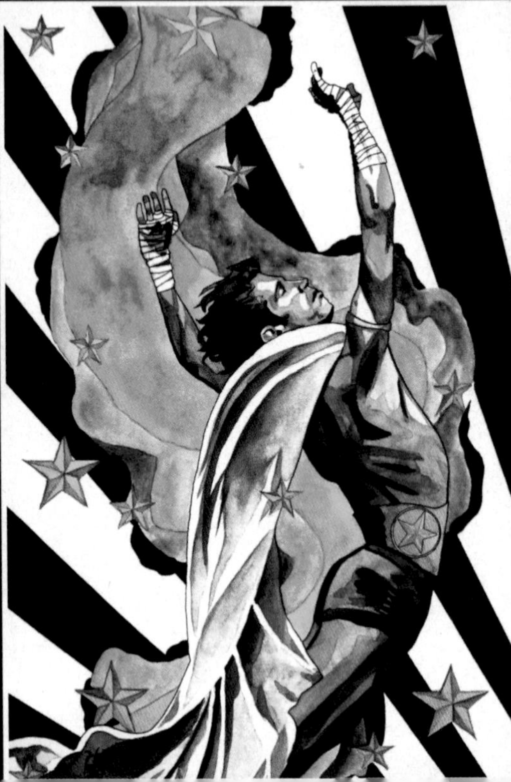

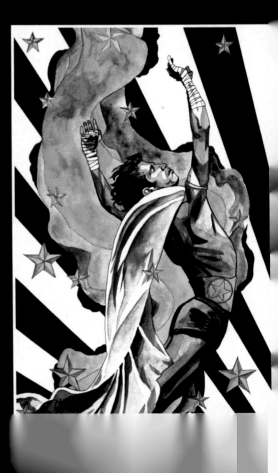

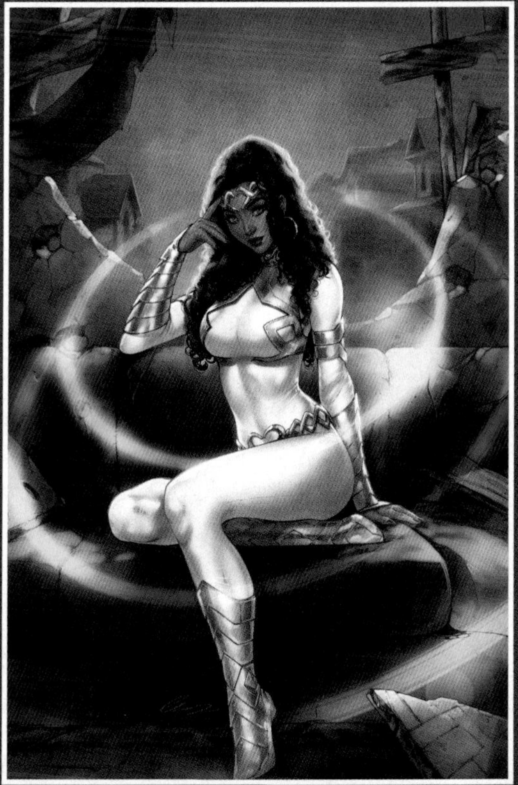

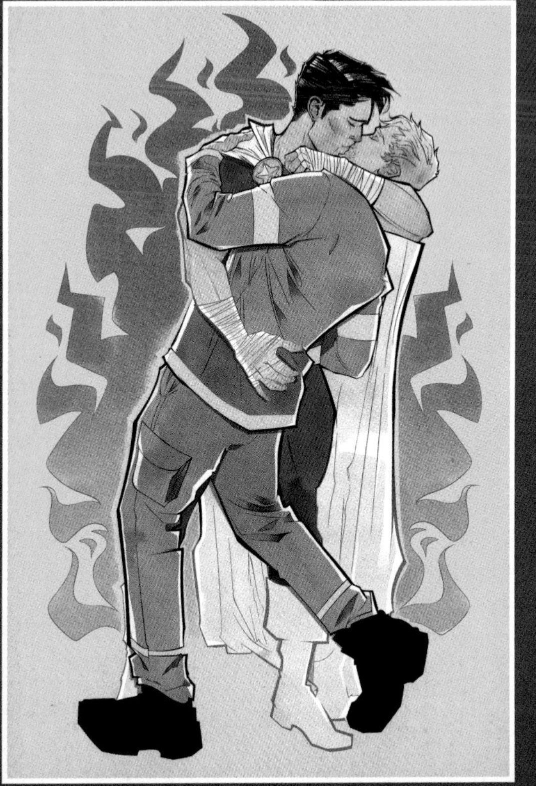

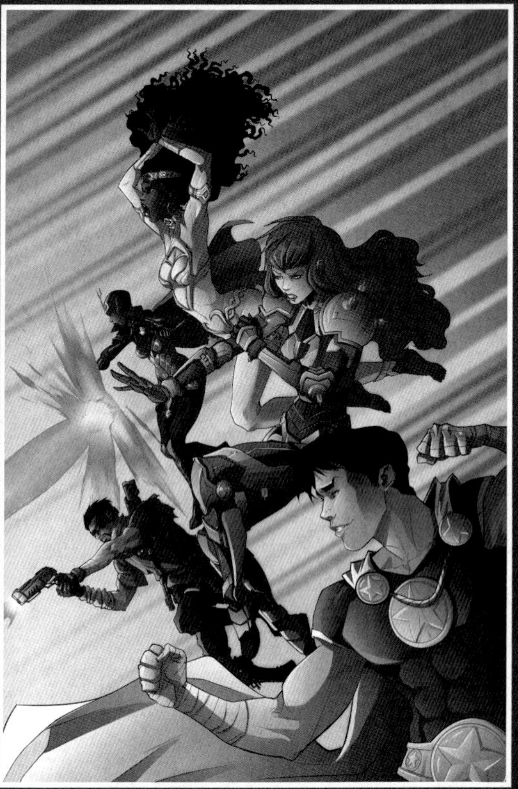

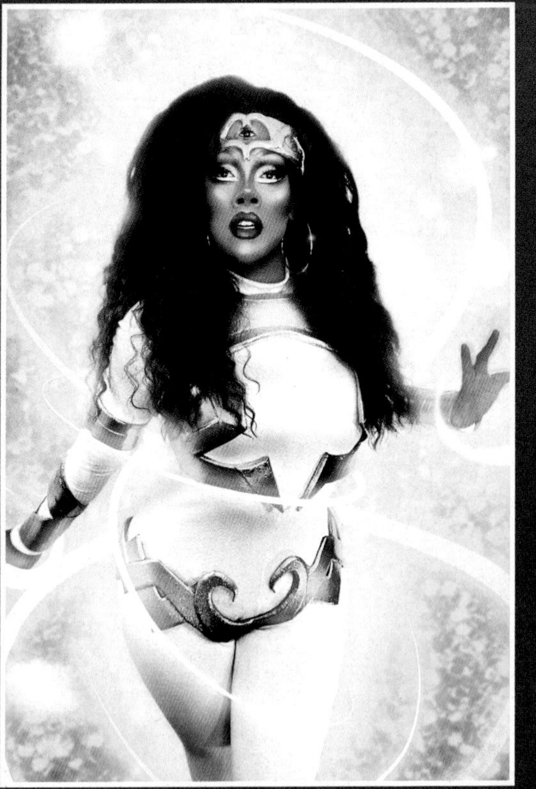

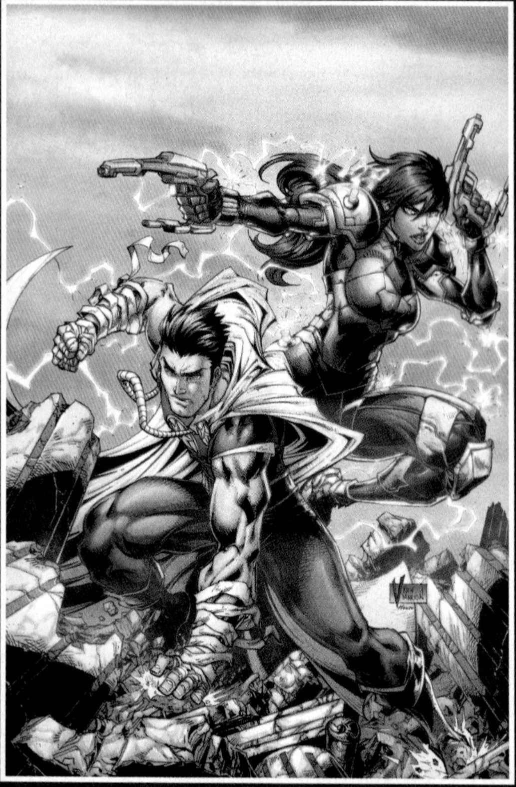

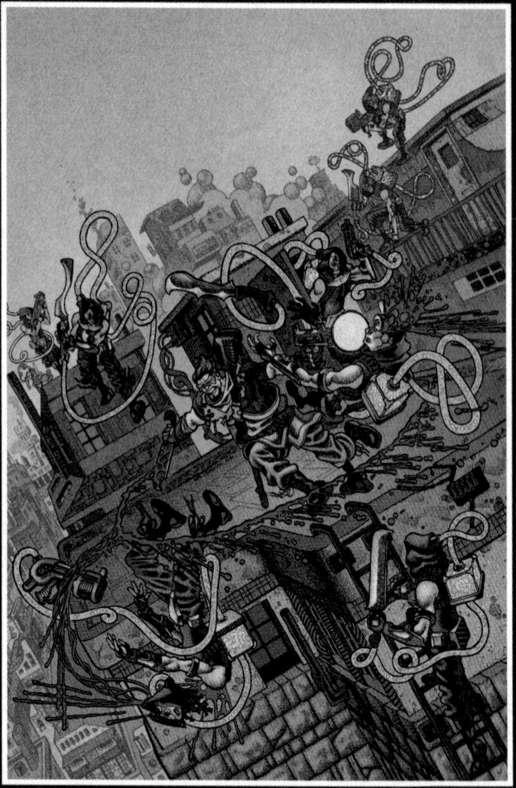

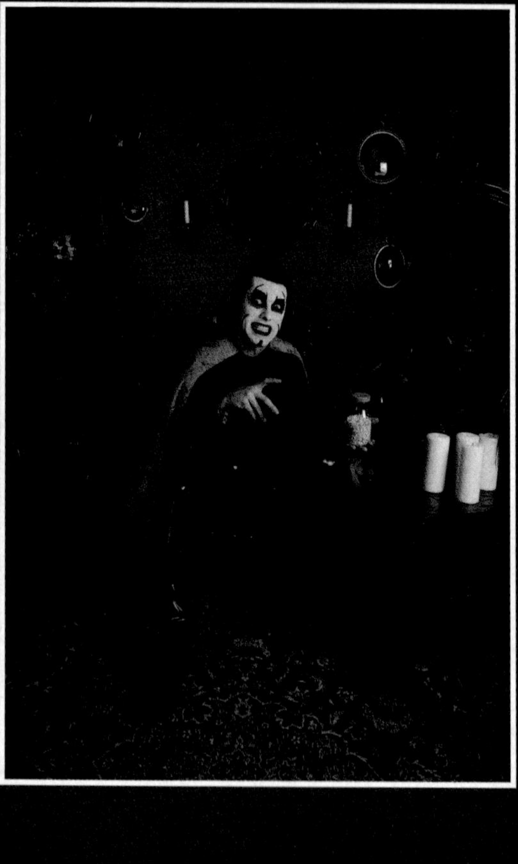

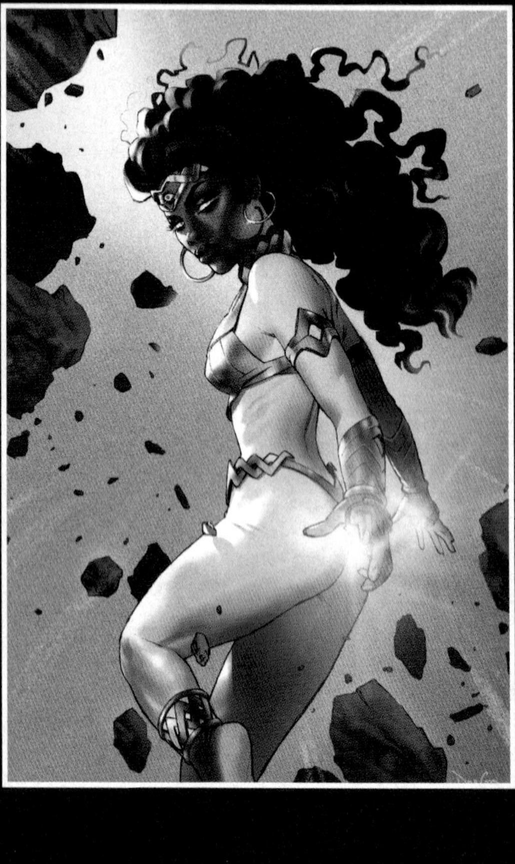

V KEN MARION [1], MATT LESNIEWSKI [2],
DANHAUSEN [3], DAVI GO [4].

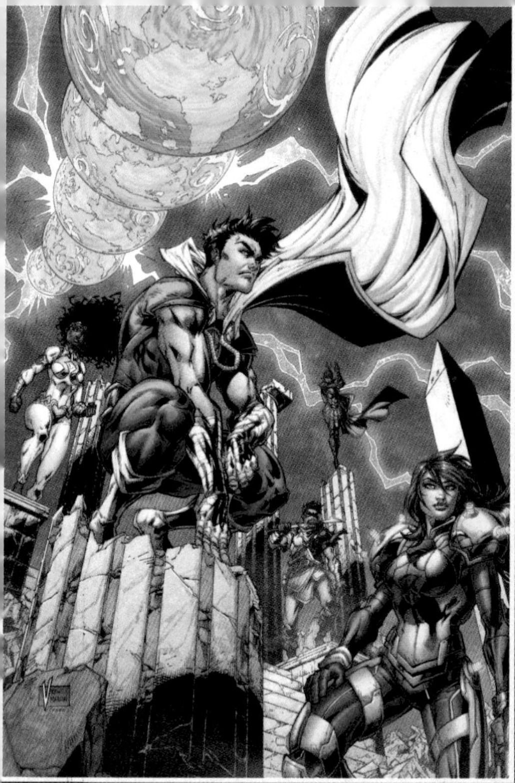
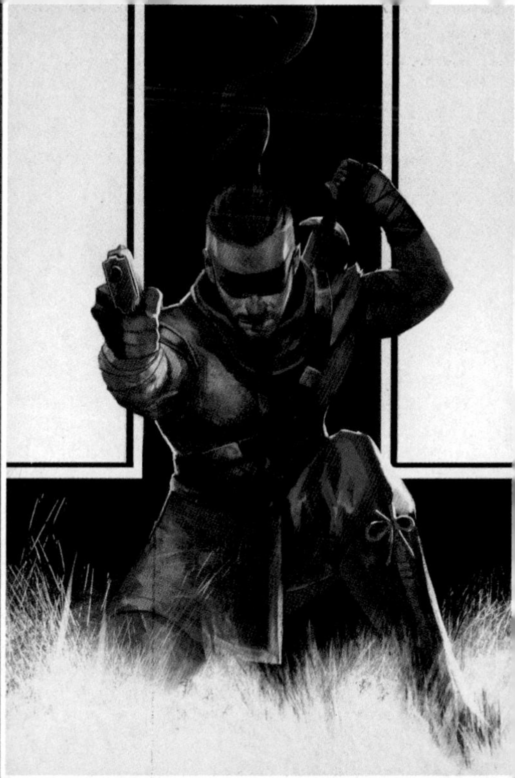
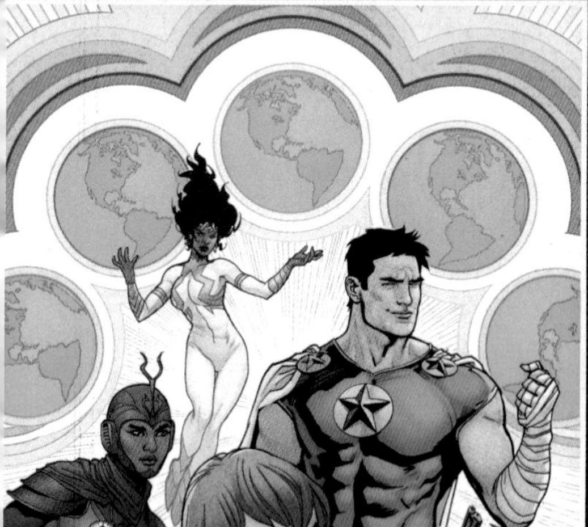
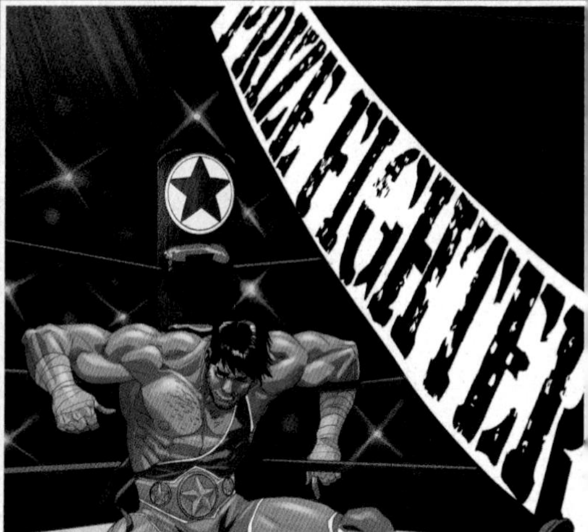
PRIZE FIGHTER

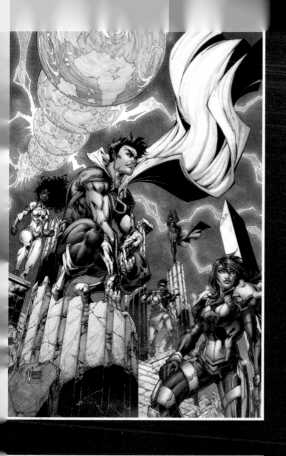

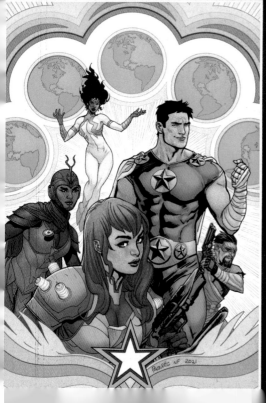

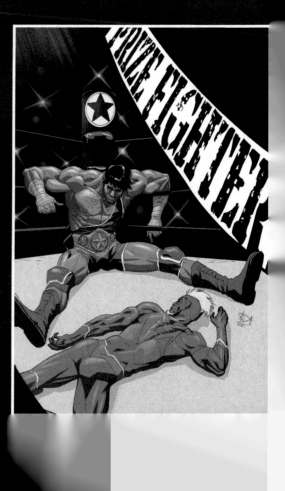

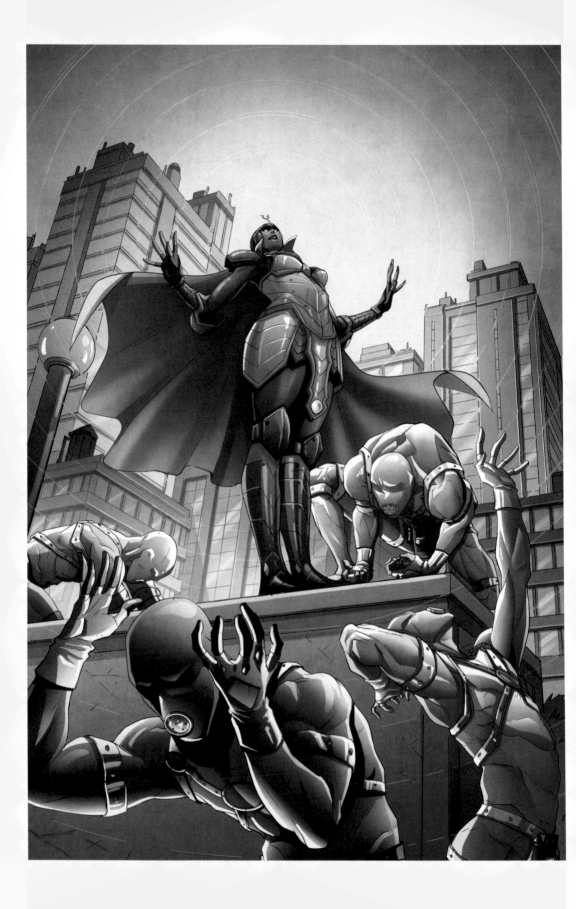

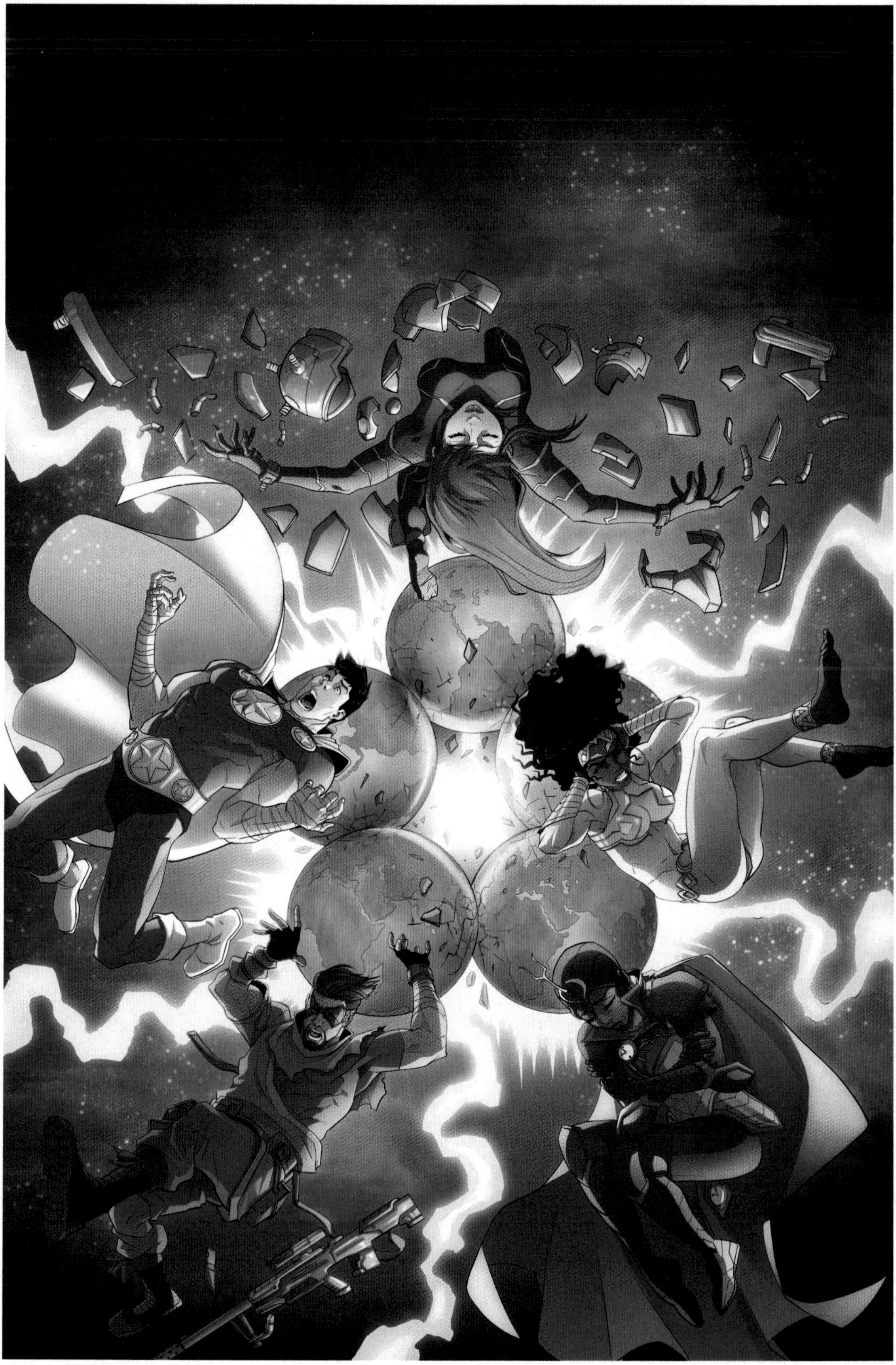

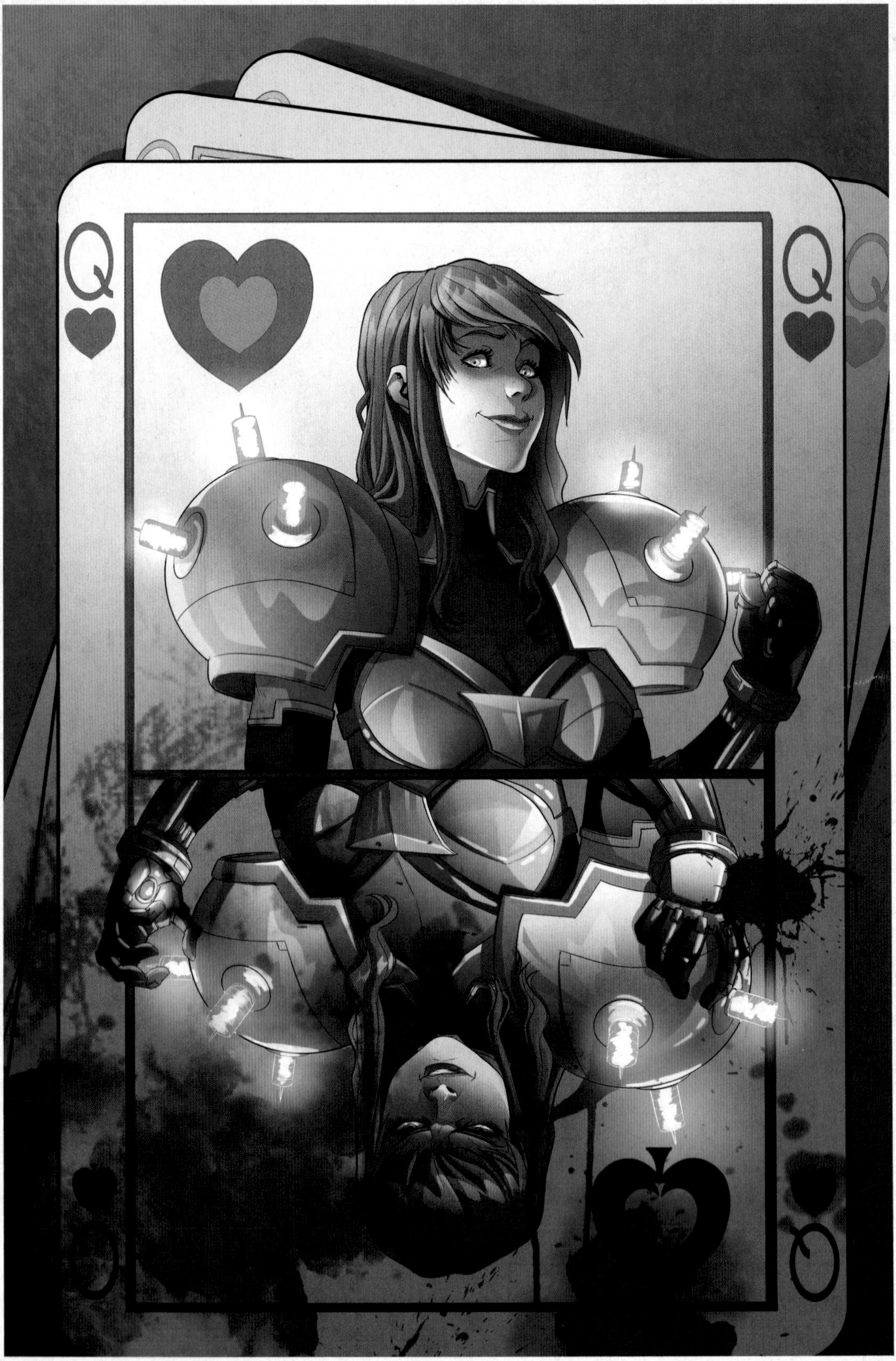

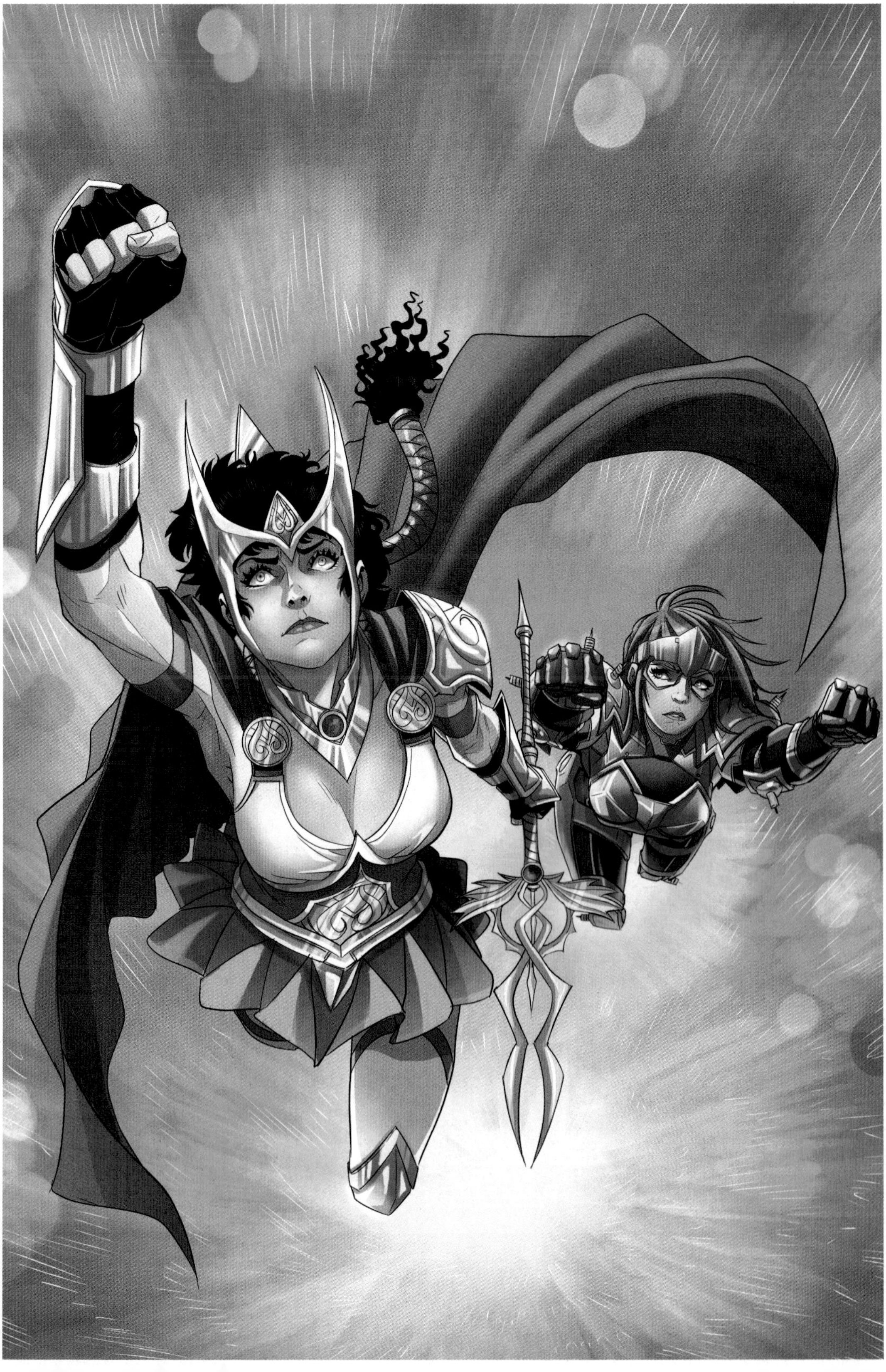

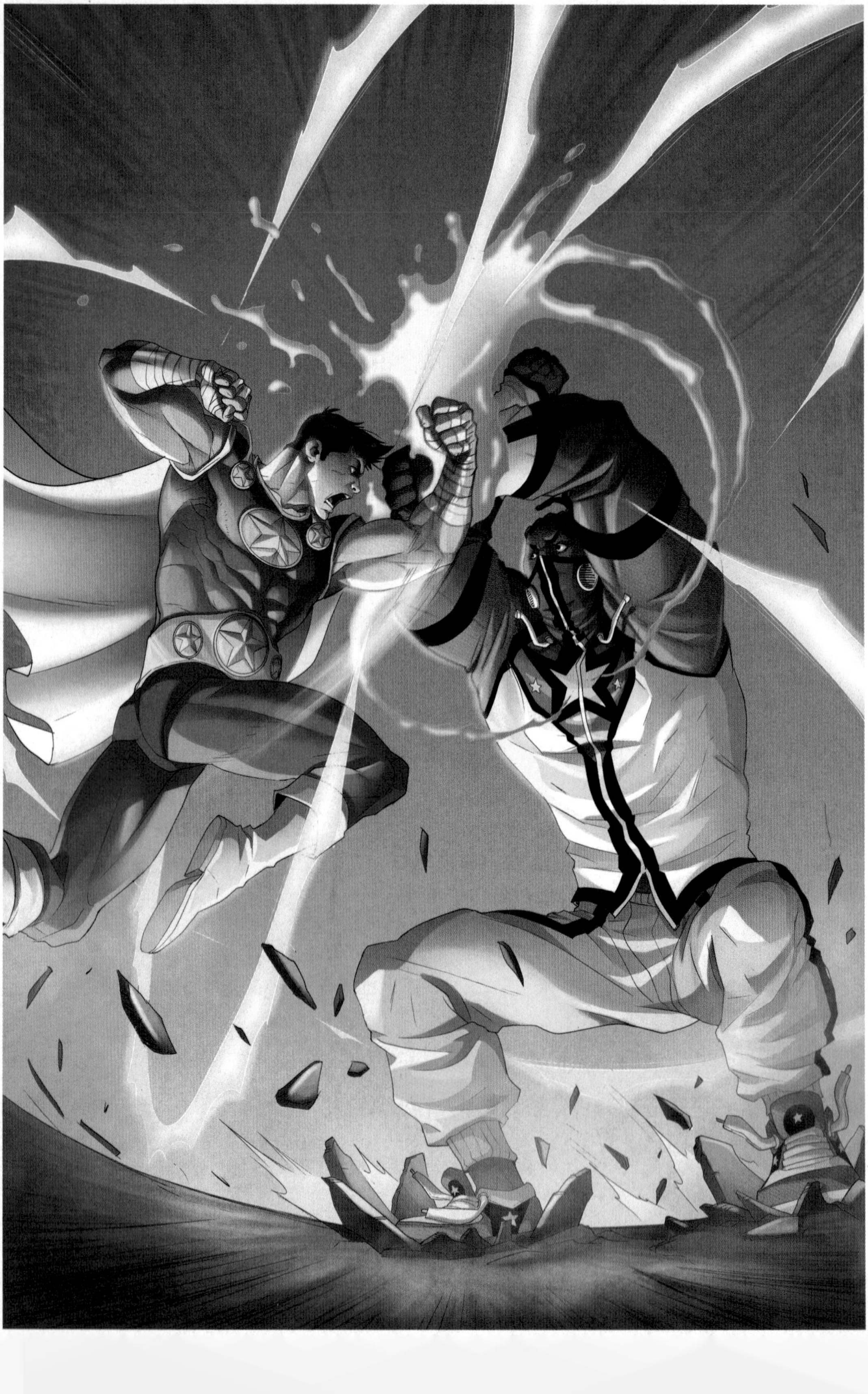

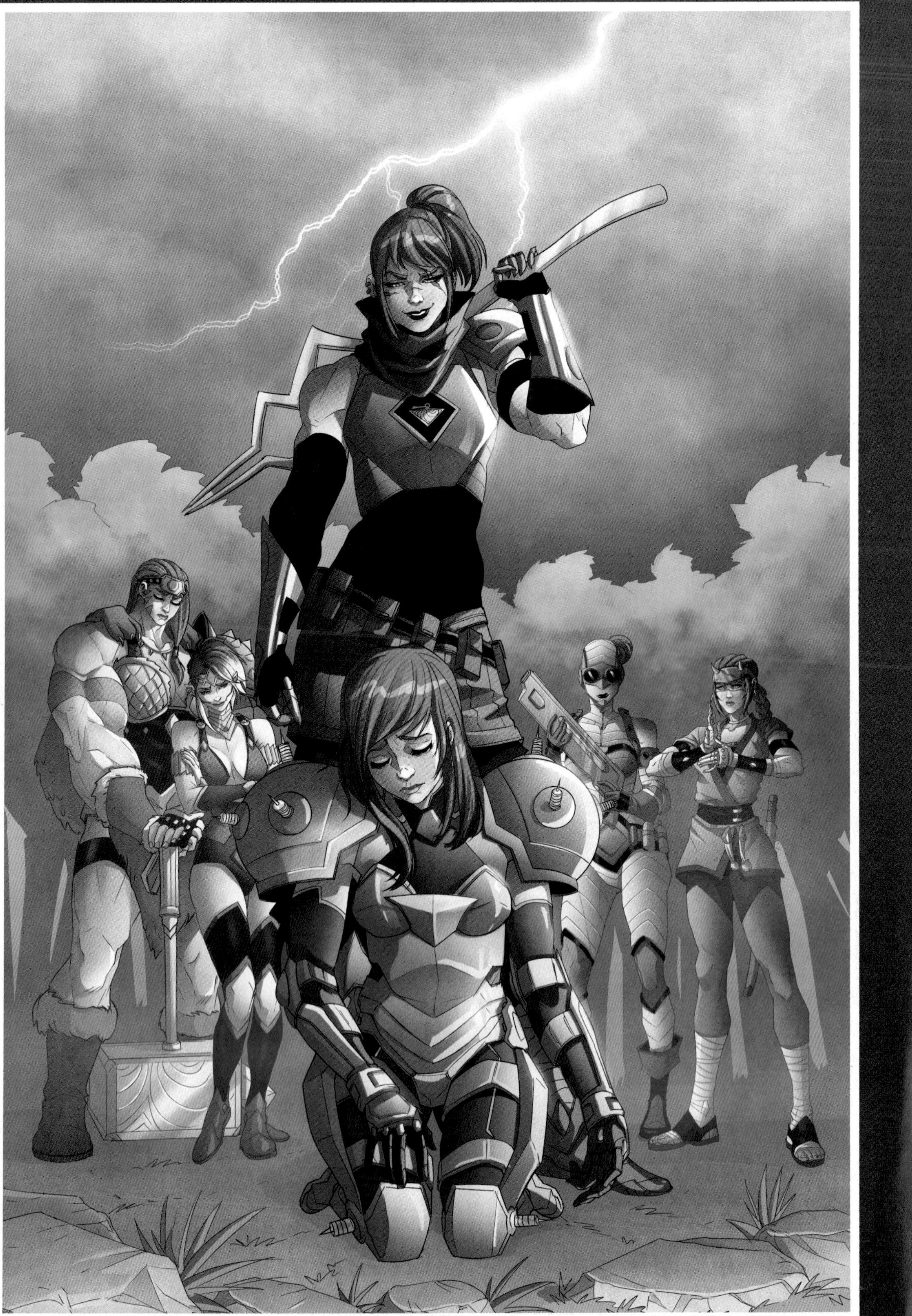

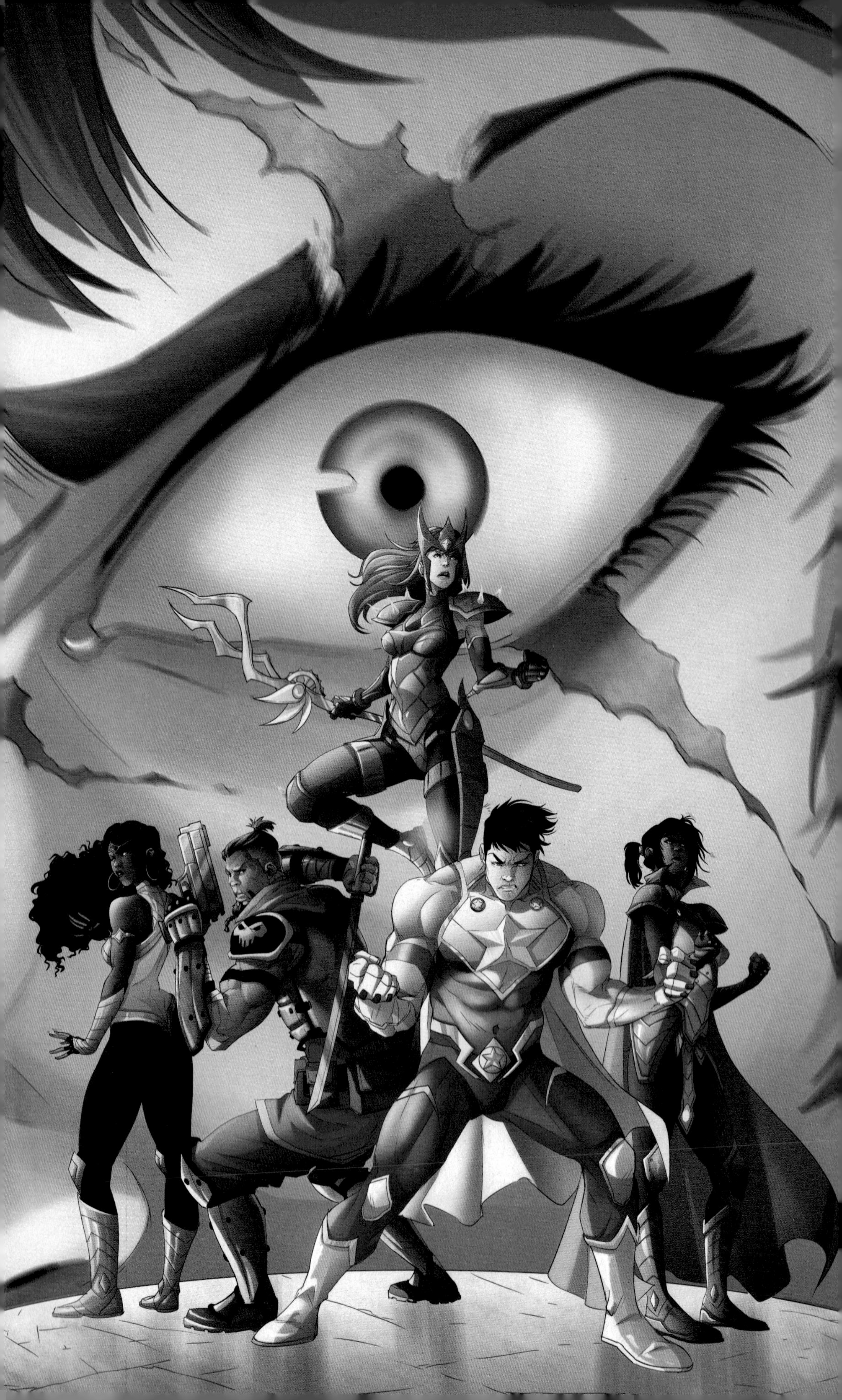

COMMANDERS IN CRISIS

STEVE ORLANDO

DAVIDE TINTO

BOOK 2

THE REACTION

STEVE ORLANDO
CREATOR, WRITER

DAVIDE TINTO
CREATOR, ARTIST

AMERICAN DREAMER CREATED BY L.A. THORNHILL & STEVE ORLANDO

L.A. THORNHILL
WRITER (issue #8)

FRANCESCA CAROTENUTO
COLORIST

FRANCESCA VIVALDI
COLORIST (issue #12)

FABIO AMELIA
LETTERER

DAVIDE G.G. CACI
EDITOR

ANTONIO SOLINAS
ASSOCIATE EDITOR

FABRIZIO VERROCCHI
DESIGN

COMMANDERS IN CRISIS: THE REACTION, VOL. 2. First printing. December 2021. Published by Image Comics, Inc. Office of publication: PO BOX 14457, Portland, OR 97293. "Commanders in Crisis," created by Steve Orlando and Davide Tinto. Copyright © 2021 Orlando, Arancia Studio s.n.c. All rights reserved. Contains material originally published in single magazine form as COMMANDERS IN CRISIS #7-12. "Commanders in Crisis," its logos, and the likenesses of all characters herein are trademarks of Steve Orlando, Arancia Studio s.n.c., unless otherwise noted. "Image" and the Image Comics logos are registered trademarks of Image Comics, Inc. No part of this publication may be reproduced or transmitted, in any form or by any means (except for short excerpts for journalistic or review purposes), without the express written permission of Steve Orlando, Arancia Studio s.n.c. or Image Comics, Inc. All names, characters, events, and locales in this publication are entirely fictional. Any resemblance to actual persons (living or dead), events, or places, without satirical intent, is coincidental. Printed in the USA. For international rights, contact: licensing@aranciastudio.com. ISBN: 978-1-5343-1927-1.

IMAGE COMICS, INC. • Todd McFarlane: President • Jim Valentino: Vice President • Marc Silvestri: Chief Executive Officer • Erik Larsen: Chief Financial Officer • Robert Kirkman: Chief Operating Officer • Eric Stephenson: Publisher / Chief Creative Officer • Nicole Lapalme: Controller • Leanna Caunter: Accounting Analyst • Sue Korpela: Accounting & HR Manager • Marla Eizik: Talent Liaison • Jeff Boison: Director of Sales & Publishing Planning • Dirk Wood: Director of International Sales & Licensing • Alex Cox: Director of Direct Market Sales • Chloe Ramos: Book Market & Library Sales Manager • Emilio Bautista: Digital Sales Coordinator • Jon Schlaffman: Specialty Sales Coordinator • Kat Salazar: Director of PR & Marketing • Drew Fitzgerald: Marketing Content Associate • Heather Doornink: Production Director • Drew Gill: Art Director • Hilary DiLoreto: Print Manager • Tricia Ramos: Traffic Manager • Melissa Gifford: Content Manager • Erika Schnatz: Senior Production Artist • Ryan Brewer: Production Artist • Deanna Phelps: Production Artist
imagecomics.com

COMMANDERS IN CRISIS is proudly produced at Arancia Studio, Torino, Italy • #weArancia
ARANCIA STUDIO S.N.C. • Davide G.G. Caci: Chief Executive Officer • Andrea Meloni: Chief Creative Officer • Mirka Andolfo: Art Director • Fabrizio Verrocchi: Marketing, Design, and Communication Guru • Fabio Amelia: Editorial Production Manager • Antonio Solinas: Talent Relations Manager • Luca Blengino: Senior Editor • Damiano Tessarolo: Junior Editor • Elena Fontana: Talent Relations, Editorial Assistant • Giulia Dell'Accio: Executive Assistant • Cecilia Raneri: Junior Associate Agent • Fulvio

INTRODUCTION

One of the things comics fans seem to truly love is a good crossover. One of those mega-events featuring every character in known creation teaming up to stop a super-villain threatening every version of earth in all realities. You know the mantra, "Worlds Live, Worlds Die, and nothing will ever be the same."

As a reader, an event book is something to enjoy, a chance to see all your favorites interact in one giant tale. As a writer, the event series is a daunting task where you're balancing all the characters and giving each of them a chance to shine in a very limited space. It's a hard thing to do when you're working with characters people already know.

Imagine how difficult it would be to do that same style epic storytelling, but with characters you've never heard of. Not only do you have to introduce every character, but you also need to make the fans care about them too, all while you're telling a massive story. Sounds like a crisis to me.

Now, Steve Orlando loves comics. I mean he REALLY loves comics. As a kid he had his mother take him to conventions and over time he developed an encyclopedic knowledge of characters and stories that could rival the combined might of the DC editorial department. So naturally, it only makes sense that he would take on the incredibly daunting task of creating COMMANDERS IN CRISIS, a universe-encompassing event with all-new characters, as his latest original project.

With COMMANDERS IN CRISIS, Steve tackles the familiar tropes of comic storytelling with characters that have a familiar ring, but in a style all his own. Earth-shattering, mind-bending adventures have become Steve's stock in trade and this series is no exception.

Enter the world, meet the heroes, and you're off to the races.

At a time when we are all locked away in our homes, it's great to find a tale that takes us outside of the confines of our lives and imaginations. One thing is for sure, once you read this series, nothing will ever be the same.

DAN DIDIO · 2020

Dan DiDio has been a DC mainstay since 2002 in various creative/editorial roles such as writer, editor, executive editor, and publisher. He was the co-publisher of DC from